P9-EER-210

BLACKS IN THE NEW WORLD
August Meier, Series Editor

*A list of books in the series appears at the end of this book.*

# Black Milwaukee

161653

# Black Milwaukee

The Making of an
Industrial Proletariat,
1915–45

Joe William Trotter, Jr.

977.595
T858

University of Illinois Press    *Urbana and Chicago*

Alverno College
Library Media Center
Milwaukee, Wisconsin

Publication of this book was supported in part by
a grant from the Andrew W. Mellon Foundation.

©1985 by the Board of Trustees of the University of Illinois
Manufactured in the United States of America

*This book is printed on acid-free paper.*

Library of Congress Cataloging in Publication Data

Trotter, Joe William, 1945–
  Black Milwaukee.

  Bibliography: p.
  Includes index.
  1. Afro-Americans—Employment—Wisconsin—Milwaukee—
History. 2. Discrimination in employment—Wisconsin—
Milwaukee—History. 3. Race discrimination—Wisconsin—
Milwaukee—History. 4. Afro-Americans—Wisconsin—
Milwaukee—Social conditions—To 1964. I. Title.
  HD8081.A65T76    1984        331.6'3'96073077595        84–83
  ISBN 0-252-01124-4 (alk. paper)

For H. LaRue, my wife,
and Mrs. Thelma O. Trotter, my mother

# Contents

# Preface

Historical and sociological studies of blacks in northern cities have increased tremendously over the past two decades. Emphasizing housing segregation as the chief expression of northern race relations, the ghetto theoretical model has emerged at the center of this research. Black urban institutions, economic status, race relations, and politics have received treatment mainly in relation to the rise of the ghetto as few recent scholars have departed from the prevailing ghetto synthesis. But urban blacks were not only ghetto dwellers; they were also workers, who moved increasingly out of agricultural, domestic, and personal service jobs into urban-industrial pursuits. The proletarianization framework used in this study of Milwaukee blacks, as discussed in detail in Appendix 7, suggests a different but complementary way of looking at the black urban experience.

Focusing on Milwaukee between 1915 and 1945, this study examines the Afro-American experience as an instance of proletarianization. Defined as the process by which blacks became urban-industrial workers, the proletarianization of Milwaukee blacks entailed complex interactions of racial and class consciousness and behavior. The persistence of racial discrimination in the socioeconomic and political life of the city frustrated the efforts of middle- and working-class blacks to create class unity across racial lines. Thus, a continuous (though tenuous) intraracial unity developed between the black bourgeoisie and the Afro-American industrial proletariat, and both groups expressed their class interests in explicitly racial terms.

The notion of a process of proletarianization attempts to focus our attention not merely upon the "making of a ghetto" but also upon the "making of an Afro-American industrial working class." Unlike conventional Marxist notions of proletarianization, however, the proletarianization of Milwaukee blacks did not involve a fundamental prior loss of autonomy over land or skilled crafts; rather, the making of Milwaukee's Afro-American industrial working class was almost exclusively a shift upward into factory jobs, from a depressed status as southern rural sharecroppers on the one hand and from low-paid, northern, nonfactory common laborers, domestics, and personal service workers on the other. If the proletarianization of blacks appeared progressive or benign beside their prior economic experience, it was, nevertheless, an intensely harsh and precarious process compared to prevailing conditions in Milwaukee industries. Industrialists and labor leaders nearly uniformly made room for blacks only at the floor of the urban economy: in low-paying, dirty, difficult, unpleasant, and dangerous tasks that whites often refused to perform. Afro-Americans, however, were by no means passive in their shift to an urban-industrial foundation. Black workers and the small black middle class forged both distinctive and highly unified responses to their industrial experience.

Milwaukee's Afro-American population and the period 1915 to 1945 have been selected for several reasons. First, Milwaukee provides an area where black dependence on factory employment was more intense than elsewhere. Of several prominent northern and western cities, the percentage of Milwaukee blacks engaged in manufacturing and mechanical pursuits was exceeded only by Detroit and Cleveland between World War I and the onset of the Depression. Second, Milwaukee also offers a unique opportunity to view the Afro-American experience in a city of strong Socialist influence. Since Milwaukee functioned with a Socialist mayor between 1916 and 1940, that experience allows us to ask to what extent the egalitarian emphasis of socialism made a difference in the socioeconomic and political experience of blacks. Third, since most of our knowledge of black life in northern cities is drawn from larger centers of black population, a focus on Milwaukee, with one of the smallest black populations among major United States cities, will help to sharpen our generalizations about the black experience in the urban North.

Finally, the chronological period represents the most dynamic decades of Afro-American incorporation into the industrial work force. The production demands of two world wars, the curtailment of European immigration, and the Depression provide an opportunity to assess black working-class experience under conditions that range from rapid expansion to severe contraction. Moreover, few studies of black life in northern cities treat the Depression and World War II. A focus on the proletarianization of Milwaukee blacks during the period 1915 to 1945 helps to rectify that chronological deficiency while seeking to transcend conceptual limitations of the ghetto synthesis.

The study is divided into three parts. Part One, the introduction, analyzes the socioeconomic and political experiences of blacks in pre–World War I Milwaukee. Here the emphasis is placed on the nearly complete relegation of Afro-Americans to the domestic and personal service sector of the industrializing city. The process of proletarianization is the subject of Part Two. Chapter 2 presents in detail the migration of southern blacks into the city, their movement into the industrial work force, and their struggle for better housing conditions. This chapter also identifies factors contributing to the transformation of Afro-Americans into an industrial proletariat. Particular note is made of the response of industrialists, labor unions, and the established local black community to the expanding black working class. Equal attention is given the active role played by black workers in their shift to an urban-industrial economic foundation. Here also is an attempt to uncover the complex relationship between proletarianization and ghettoization. The chapter ends with a discussion of the tenuous nature of black proletarianization as Afro-Americans lost much of their industrial footing by 1932.

Chapter 3 focuses on the full emergence of the tiny black business and professional elite that had gradually expanded by World War I. Emphasis is placed upon its new viability grounded in a larger demographic base, increasing spatial segregation, and the expanding economic resources provided by factory wages. The question of race relations and consciousness is dealt with in Chapter 4. An intensifying pattern of white racial hostility against blacks, aggravated by the increasing movement of Afro-Americans into the industrial work place, is traced through a wide range of urban institutions. Chapter 4 also documents an expanding working-class consciousness. These different modes of thought and behavior, often reflecting intraracial class divisions between black workers and the expanding Afro-American middle class, are charted through an examination of race relations, politics, and institutional life.

Part Three, comprised of three chapters, examines the highly tenuous position of black industrial workers between 1933 and 1945. Chapter 5 documents the eruption of racial violence in Milwaukee's labor market, the growing CIO-black alliance, and the persistence of black unemployment until World War II production stimulated their belated return, after all white workers, to industrial jobs by 1943. The issues of fair employment practices in war industries with government contracts and the gradually expanding ghetto are given particular attention as a labor shortage, coupled with continuing restrictions on foreign immigration, restimulated black migration to the city.

Chapter 6 traces the persistent interaction of racial and proletarian interests through a focus on black institutions, politics, and race relations during the Depression and World War II. The organizing efforts of the CIO precipitated a dramatic expansion of black working-class consciousness and activities. Even the black middle class made a decided, but extremely cautious, shift toward a prolabor stance. But the persistence of racial discrimination by industrialists and labor unions coalesced with the vested economic, political, and social interests of the black business and professional elite and blunted the forthright articulation of working-class goals. Thus, black proletarian aims would continue to find expression through cooperation with the highly race-conscious agenda of the Afro-American bourgeosie.

While each section incorporates a comparative dimension, the study concludes with a more focused discussion of the comparative experience of blacks in Milwaukee. Chapter 7, using Milwaukee as a special case, argues for the utility of the concept of proletarianization both as an alternative to the concept of ghetto formation in research on black life in northern cities and as a vehicle for fresh comparative research on Afro-American urban history. This is approached by contrasting the making of Milwaukee's black industrial working class with the emergence of a white proletariat and with Afro-Americans in northern and southern cities. While the scope of this study precludes a transnational comparison of black proletarianization, I believe the theoretical model offers rich prospects for the comparative study of Afro-American, African, and perhaps even European urban-industrial working class formation.

# Acknowledgments

Inspiration and assistance from numerous people have made this book possible: mentors, colleagues, friends, relatives, secretaries, archivists, librarians, students, and funding agencies. I wish to extend collective thanks to all of these people. Special thanks are extended to John Modell and Clarke A. Chambers, University of Minnesota, who guided this study through the dissertation phase. Their rigorous, but gentle and always helpful, suggestions have been deeply appreciated. I am also indebted to Allan Spear, Lansiné Kaba, and Allen Isaacman for stimulating many ideas that have gained fruition in this study. Rollie Poppino, David Brody, Jim Shideler, Bill Smith, Roland Marchand, Manfred Fleischer, Norma Landau, Luis Arroyo, Jacquelyn Mitchel, Antonia Castañeda, and other colleagues at the University of California–Davis have provided invaluable encouragement and support. For their typing, xeroxing, and other services in connection with this book, I extend my sincere thanks to the entire administrative and secretarial staff of the UCD department of history: Charlotte Honeywell, Bill Antaramian, Evelyn Echevarria, Diane Dean, Carole Hinkle, and Yolanda Starr.

Several libraries and their staff members immensely facilitated my research and I appreciate their kind assistance: the city of Milwaukee, Legislative Reference Bureau; Milwaukee County Historical Society; Milwaukee Public Library; University of Wisconsin–Milwaukee, Area Research Center; State Historical Society of Wisconsin–Madison; Library of Congress, Manuscript Division; National Archives, Industrial and Social Branch; and Inter-Library Loan and Government Publications Divisions, University of Minnesota and University of California–Davis. Among librarians and archivists, I especially want to thank Ralph Otto, Legislative Reference Bureau; Stanley Mallach, University of Wisconsin–Milwaukee, Area Research Center; Paul Woehrmann, Milwaukee Public Library; Jerry Hess, National Archives; and Paul Heffron, Library of Congress.

I wish to thank each of the nineteen persons who kindly granted me interviews during the summer of 1979. Special gratitude is extended to Mrs. Ardie Halyard and Rev. Ernest Bland, who gave generously of their time in several follow-up interviews. In this connection, I also owe a particular debt to Reuben Harpole, University of Wisconsin–Milwaukee Extension, whose broad knowledge of black Milwaukee's history and personalities helped to establish my oral interview agenda. I also wish to thank Bernard and Christina Hill and my friends Floyd and Josephine Mosley for providing essential contacts and company during nearly two months of interviews in Milwaukee. For the maps and illustrations, provided by Sargina Tamimi, UCD Reprographics Department, Bibi Hazel, UCD design student, and Sarah Ann Ford, Director of the Milwaukee Black Heritage Project, I am deeply appreciative.

Financial assistance from diverse sources has made this research possible. I particularly thank the Office of Research, University of California–Davis for several grants to complete research for enlargement and revision of this study for publication. Gratitude is also extended to the Bush Foundation, the National Fellowships Fund–Ford Foundation, the Danforth Foundation, and the University of Minnesota for providing invaluable assistance during the dissertation phase of this research.

I owe my greatest debt to my wife, LaRue, who has provided indispensable love, encouragement, and support from the beginning of this endeavor. Through her ideas and willingness to engage me in debate, LaRue has also contributed to the intellectual development of this book. I also owe an immeasurable debt to my mother for encouraging me to persevere at an early age despite tremendous hardships. To my wife and mother this book is appreciatively dedicated. Other relatives (sisters and brothers, Melvin and Velma Anderson, Robert and Voncille Hines) and dear friends (Quintard and Carol Taylor, Albert and Mary Broussard, Samuel and Joyce Wilson, and

Rachier Mbeche) have also given invaluable inspiration and support. Former and current graduate students at the University of Minnesota have enhanced this study through their friendship, good conversation, and ideas: Arthur C. Hill, John Edgar Tidwell, Paul Barrows, Saundra Lynn Coulter, Earl Lewis, Joaõ Reis, Malik Simba, and David Taylor, to name only a few. Undergraduate and high school students in several institutions (University of California–Davis, University of Minnesota, and Tremper Senior High School, Kenosha, Wisconsin) have likewise generated enthusiasm for many of the ideas in the study.

For providing forums for the presentation and discussion of my ideas, I am grateful to several professional organizations: the American Historical Association, Pacific Coast Branch; the Association for the Study of Afro-American Life and History; and the Southern Historical Association. Temple University's conference on the social impact of industrialization and Southern Methodist University's symposium on black urban history also offered valuable opportunities to discuss Milwaukee blacks. Finally, I wish to thank Thomas R. Buchanan, whose exceedingly detailed master's thesis provides the substance for most of my analysis in Chapter 1, and Richard Walter Thomas, whose Ph.D. dissertation on blacks in Detroit confirmed my interest in proletarianization as a conceptual framework.

# PART ONE

## Introduction

# 1

## Common Laborers and Domestic and Personal Service Workers in an Industrializing Economy, 1870–1914

The pre–World War I experience of black common laborers, domestic, and personal service workers provided the urban backdrop to the industrial proletarianization of Milwaukee's Afro-American population. Milwaukee's black population grew as the city shifted from a commercial to an urban-industrial economy between 1870 and 1914. Several scholars have described this period as the "formative years of the black ghetto in the United States."[1] This was a period of gradual black migration to northern cities from upper South and border states. Such cities as New York, Chicago, Philadelphia, and others had sharp increases in black populations. As Afro-Americans increased their numbers within northern cities, they became increasingly segregated within the spatial, economic, social, and political structure of the cities. Racial barriers blocked their access to a diverse range of urban institutions, socioeconomic necessities, and opportunities: labor unions, manufacturing jobs, housing facilities, churches, and public accommodations of various sorts.[2]

White racial hostility, it should be noted, and its spatial expression in the ghetto were not entirely irrational psychic responses. These developments had roots in tangible issues such as competition for better-paying jobs, scarce housing resources, and the struggle for control over the city's government and other urban institutions. Afro-Americans, though, were by no means passive in the competitive struggle for economic, social, and political survival and development within the urban environment. In fundamental ways, they actively shaped and directed their own existence. The black experience in Milwaukee exhibited both parallels to and divergences from general trends in black life in northern cities. Many of the differences pivoted around three basic factors: the small size of Milwaukee's black population, its relatively more depressed position within the urban economy, and the greater economic and social attractions of nearby Chicago. Black Milwaukeeans also reflected similarities and contrasts with diverse white ethnic groups within the city. Before we can understand the Afro-American experience in pre–World War I Milwaukee, however, it is first necessary to survey briefly the urban context.

As did other northern American cities, Milwaukee witnessed a dynamic transition from commercial to industrial capitalism during the late nineteenth and early twentieth centuries. Although better rail connections to the west and the Erie Canal route to the east enabled Chicago to emerge as the major urban center in the region, by the 1870s such industries as flour milling, slaughtering and meat packing (especially of pork), tanning, and brewing became firmly entrenched in Milwaukee, yet the long-range trend in the city, as in other Great Lakes cities, was toward iron and steel rather than toward agricultural processing. By 1901, the city's major iron and steel firm, the Bay View Works, had been reorganized as the Illinois Steel Corporation and consolidated as part of the giant United States Steel Corporation.[3]

Industrial expansion created economic opportunities that increased the city's population from 71,616 in 1870 to 373,857 in 1910, thereby raising Milwaukee's rank among American cities from nineteenth in 1870 to twelfth in 1910. Immigrants made up a high, though declining, percentage of the population during the entire period: 1870 (47.1) and 1910 (29.8) (see Table 1.1). While Germans and Irish predominated among the foreign born during most of the period, by 1910 new immigrants from southern and eastern Europe (especially Poles and Russian Jews) became increasingly important.[4]

Economic and social changes of the late nineteenth century transformed the spatial structure of Milwaukee, as in most large northern cities, from the "walking city" of the mid-nineteenth century into a more dispersed and highly specialized form. The replacement of horsecar service with electric street railways in the 1890s pushed the city limits into surrounding suburbs[5] (see Map 1.1). Shifts in the city's geographic pattern reflected a deepening trend toward urban eco-

Table 1.1. Population of Milwaukee by Racial and Ethnic Group, 1870–1910

| | Year | | | | | | | |
|---|---|---|---|---|---|---|---|---|
| | 1870 | Percent | 1880 | Percent | 1890 | Percent | 1900 | Percent |
| Total Population* | 71,616 | 100.0 | 115,587 | 100.0 | 204,468 | 100.0 | 285,315 | 100.0 |
| Blacks | 176 | 0.2 | 304 | 0.2 | 449 | 0.2 | 862 | 0.3 |
| Foreign-born whites | 33,773 | 47.1 | 46,073 | 39.9 | 79,540 | 38.9 | 88,948 | 31.2 |
| American-born whites | | | | | | | | |
| Foreign-born/mixed parentage | N/A | N/A | N/A | N/A | 97,224 | 47.6 | 146,885 | 51.5 |
| American-born parentage | 37,667 | 52.5 | 69,210 | 59.8 | 27,237 | 13.3 | 48,598 | 17.0 |

| | 1910 | Percent | Percentage Increase | | | |
|---|---|---|---|---|---|---|
| | | | 1870–80 | 1880–90 | 1890–1900 | 1900–1910 |
| Total Population | 373,857 | 100.0 | 61.3 | 76.9 | 39.5 | 31.0 |
| Blacks | 980 | 0.2 | 73.7 | 47.7 | 92.0 | 13.7 |
| Foreign-born whites | 111,456 | 29.8 | 36.4 | 72.7 | 11.8 | 25.3 |
| American-born whites | | | | | | |
| Foreign-born/mixed parentage | 182,530 | 48.8 | N/A | N/A | 51.1 | 24.3 |
| American-born parentage | 78,823 | 21.1 | N/A | N/A | 78.4 | 62.2 |

*Includes a small number of other nonwhite ethnic groups.

Source: U.S. Census Office, *Compendium of the Ninth Census: 1870* (Washington: Government Printing Office, 1872), p. 368; *Ninth Census, Population of the U.S.*, *vol. 1* (Washington: Government Printing Office, 1872), p. 292; U.S. Census Office, *Compendium of the Eleventh Census: 1890, pt. 1, Population* (Washington: Government Printing Office, 1892), pp. 744–45; U.S. Census Office, *Twelfth Census of the U.S.*, *vol. 1, Population, pt. 1, 1900* (Washington: Government Printing Office, 1901), p. 684; Bureau of the Census, *Thirteenth Census of the U.S.*, *vol. 1: Population, 1910* (Washington: Government Printing Office, 1913), p. 210; *Thirteenth Census of the U.S.*, *vol. 3: Population, 1910*, p. 1101.

nomic and ethnic segregation. American-born whites of English stock, heavily concentrated in business and professional occupations, resided on the far West and upper East Side. Higher-paid German factory operatives and skilled tradesmen occupied the northwest portion of the city. Poles settled south of the Menomonee River, although a few lived on the North Side near major tanneries, flour mills, and other pursuits requiring many unskilled laborers. Smaller new immigrant groups, Italians and Jews among others, located around the edges of the central business district (CBD). They subsequently moved to space formerly occupied by German immigrants of the 1860s and 1870s. The Jewish area would figure prominently in the Afro-American experience, for it was in this area that blacks settled in increasing numbers before World War I.

Paralleling the development of spatial, ethnic, demographic, and economic change was the emergence of an increasingly articulate urban-industrial working class. By 1910, the Social Democrats, a trade union-oriented Socialist party, mobilized sufficient strength among workers and middle-class reformers to win the mayoralty and a majority of city council seats. On the other hand, countervailing trends in the labor movement undermined the social, economic, and political significance of Socialists in the city. In Milwaukee, as in other cities, the militant Knights of Labor had sought to unite both skilled and unskilled workers into a common union. After 1886, however, the skilled craft-oriented Milwaukee Federated Trades Council (FTC), an American Federation of Labor (AFL) affiliate, displaced the Knights. Although Socialists gained control of the executive board of the FTC in 1899, the FTC virtually ignored unorganized and largely unskilled laborers.[6]

Strong currents of ethnic conflict characterized political, social, and labor relations. Democrats, for example, generally gained the support of Irish and Polish voters, especially Catholics. Republicans appealed to what Bayrd Still has called the "increasingly acclimated and hence increasingly conservative German-American element in the voting population." German workers, for their part, primarily supported the Socialists. The FTC, one scholar of the Milwaukee labor movement has noted, was largely an association of organized German workers, which barred other ethnic groups and unskilled laborers because "craft unions were also social clubs." Neither Democrats, Republicans, nor Socialists completely dominated city politics during the period.[7]

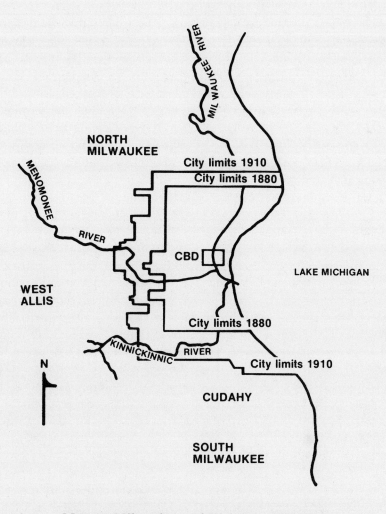

NORTH
MILWAUKEE

MILWAUKEE RIVER

MENOMONEE

RIVER

City limits 1910

City limits 1880

CBD

LAKE MICHIGAN

WEST
ALLIS

City limits 1880

KINNICKINNIC RIVER

N

City limits 1910

CUDAHY

SOUTH
MILWAUKEE

**Map 1.1 Milwaukee and Vicinity, 1880–1910**

Source: Adapted from Roger D. Simon, "The Expansion of an Industrial City: Milwaukee, 1880–1910" (Ph.D. dissertation, University of Wisconsin, 1971), p. 127.

Milwaukee's Afro-American population developed within the foregoing context. The black population increased from 176 in 1870 to 980 in 1910. During the first decade of the twentieth century, the Afro-American population rose by a mere 13.7 percent, compared to a 92.0 percent increase between 1890 and 1900. This slow rate of black population growth represented the negative impact of the new immigration on the small black community. The foreign-born population increased by 25.3 percent between 1900 and 1910. With the exception of 1900, when blacks constituted 0.3 percent of the total, Afro-Americans made up only 0.2 percent of the city's population for the entire period. While most northern cities had small black populations, rarely exceeding 5 percent of the total, Milwaukee's black community ranked among the smallest[8] (see Table 1.1).

Despite small numbers, the sources and characteristics of the black migration to Milwaukee were similar to those of other northern cities. Upper South, border, and midwestern states contributed the bulk of newcomers to the city. In 1870, migrants from the upper South and border states of Virginia, Tennessee, and Kentucky, collectively, made up 34.7 percent of the city's black population. In 1910, blacks from Kentucky, Missouri, Tennessee, and Virginia provided the largest single percentage (18.1) of newcomers to the city. The second most important contributing states were Illinois, Ohio, Indiana, and Michigan with 15.6 percent of the total. Only one deep South state, Georgia, significantly contributed to Wisconsin's black population and that was a mere 3 percent. Expansion of the black population during the late 1880s and early 1890s responded to a labor market that attracted more men than women. The sex ratio became severely unbalanced by 1890 when there were 148 men to every 100 women; this resembled the pattern for Chicago, Detroit, and Cleveland. From the 1890s to World War I, however, the pattern of employment turned in favor of black female domestic and personal service employees, a trend with parallels among New York and Philadelphia blacks. By 1910, black women accounted for 51.2 percent of Milwaukee's enumerated black population, a percentage which was probably slightly inflated since census takers usually undercount black men. The prewar migration likewise exhibited an unbalanced age structure: 69.3 percent of Milwaukee blacks were between the ages of 15 and 44 in 1910, compared to 53.5 percent in the total population.[9] The majority of black migrants to Milwaukee between 1870 and 1910 probably came via Chicago where extensive rail and river transport systems enabled that city to absorb most of the migration to the Midwest. Many Afro-American newcomers to Chicago later migrated outward to nearby cities like Milwaukee.[10] A disproportionate number of educated mulattoes characterized these migrants. In 1906, William T. Green, a black attorney, estimated that some 200 blacks passed for white in Milwaukee each day. The 1910, United States Census identified 37.8 percent (or 377) of the city's 980 blacks as mulattoes. Because some of these people, especially in larger centers of black population, had been prominent southern politicians, business people, and professionals, Carter G. Woodson called the prewar population movement the "migration of the talented tenth." But, as Gilbert Osofsky noted, these were not "the typical" urban black migrants.[11]

Most black newcomers to the city belonged to what some students of the period have called the "laboring class." These people entered the city primarily to improve their economic position. In upper South and border states, as in cities throughout the United States, Afro-Americans were being excluded as artisans from skilled crafts during the late nineteenth and early twentieth centuries. Particularly in southern cities, displacement accompanied exclusion since a long tradition of black skilled craftsmen had developed under slavery. Moreover, the exploitative sharecropping and contract labor system spread throughout the lower South, where blacks increasingly lost out to white farmers in the struggle for adequate farm lands. Thus, the number of blacks coming from such deep South states as Alabama, Mississippi, Georgia, and others gradually increased, but lower South states would not dominate the black migration to Milwaukee and other northern cities until World War I.

Although Milwaukee emerged as one of the top industrial centers in the nation by World War I and ranked twelfth in size, Afro-Americans were almost totally excluded from this dynamic industrial expansion. Blacks, almost exclusively, entered the city's expanding domestic, personal service, and common laborer positions. Five occupations (porters, waiters, servants, cooks, and common laborers) made up 67.9 percent of all black jobs in 1880. The percentage remained largely the same in 1900, when 68 percent of the men and 73.0 percent of black women worked in domestic and personal service pursuits[12] (see Table 1.2 and appendixes 1 and 2).

Black men worked as laborers on the various construction projects within the expanding industrial metropolis. Contractors hired Afro-Americans in these positions, as elsewhere, in accord with the racial

Table 1.2. Occupational Structure of Milwaukee by Racial and Ethnic Group, 1900

Males: Total Labor Force = 85,157*

Occupational Category

|  | Skilled | | Professional | | Proprietary | | Clerical | |
|---|---|---|---|---|---|---|---|---|
|  | Number | Percent | Number | Percent | Number | Percent | Number | Percent |
| Blacks | 7 | 1.8 | 35 | 9.3 | 19 | 5.0 | 6 | 1.5 |
| Foreign-born whites | 10,586 | 26.0 | 1,184 | 2.9 | 4,336 | 10.6 | 2,399 | 5.9 |
| American-born whites Foreign-born/mixed parentage | 8,204 | 23.7 | 1,696 | 4.9 | 3,561 | 10.2 | 6,304 | 18.2 |
| American-born whites American-born parentage | 1,626 | 16.9 | 1,022 | 10.6 | 1,050 | 10.9 | 2,519 | 26.3 |
| All workers | 20,423 | 23.9 | 3,937 | 4.6 | 8,966 | 10.5 | 11,228 | 13.1 |

|  | Semiskilled | | Unskilled | | Domestic | |
|---|---|---|---|---|---|---|
|  | Number | Percent | Number | Percent | Number | Percent |
| Blacks | 2 | 0.5 | 32 | 8.5 | 256 | 68.0 |
| Foreign-born whites | 9,829 | 24.2 | 1,790 | 4.4 | 8,272 | 20.3 |
| American-born whites Foreign-born/mixed parentage | 7,436 | 21.5 | 1,890 | 5.4 | 3,567 | 10.3 |
| American-born whites American-born parentage | 1,597 | 16.6 | 396 | 4.1 | 918 | 9.5 |
| All workers | 18,864 | 22.1 | 4,108 | 4.8 | 13,013 | 15.2 |

*This figure is slightly higher than the number of occupations that the census actually specified.

Occupational Category

Females: Total Labor Force = 26,399*

| | Skilled | | Professional | | Proprietary | | Clerical | |
|---|---|---|---|---|---|---|---|---|
| | Number | Percent | Number | Percent | Number | Percent | Number | Percent |
| Blacks | – | – | 7 | 7.0 | 4 | 4.0 | 2 | 2.0 |
| Foreign-born whites | 156 | 2.2 | 199 | 2.8 | 336 | 4.8 | 404 | 5.8 |
| American-born whites Foreign-born/mixed parentage | 519 | 3.2 | 900 | 5.6 | 284 | 1.7 | 2,572 | 16.1 |
| American-born whites American-born parentage | 69 | 1.6 | 407 | 11.7 | 107 | 3.0 | 870 | 25.0 |
| All workers | 744 | 2.8 | 1,513 | 5.7 | 731 | 2.7 | 3,848 | 14.5 |

| | Semiskilled | | Unskilled | | Domestic | |
|---|---|---|---|---|---|---|
| | Number | Percent | Number | Percent | Number | Percent |
| Blacks | 12 | 12.0 | – | – | 73 | 73.0 |
| Foreign-born whites | 2,441 | 35.3 | 43 | 0.6 | 2,826 | 41.0 |
| American-born whites Foreign-born/mixed parentage | 6,065 | 37.9 | 13 | 0.0 | 4,676 | 29.4 |
| American-born whites American-born parentage | 828 | 23.4 | – | – | 961 | 27.6 |
| All workers | 9,346 | 35.4 | 56 | 0.2 | 8,536 | 32.3 |

*This figure is slightly higher than the number of occupations that the census actually specified.

Source: U.S. Census Office, *Twelfth Census, 1900: Special Reports, Occupations* (Washington: Government Printing Office, 1904), pp. 608–12.

myth that "their superior ability to endure heat" gave them "an advantage over the white laborers."[13] Thus, wherever the work was hot,
dirty, low-paying, and heavy, black men could usually be found.
More often blacks found employment in the city's hotels, in various
exclusive resorts and recreation spots, in the homes of wealthy white
families, on major rail lines serving the city, and in other areas of
domestic and personal service. While some blacks worked as porters
and dining car attendants on the Chicago and Northwestern Railroad, the chief employers of blacks in these capacities were the large
hotels: the Plankinton, Davidson, Pfister, Globe, Windsor, Avon,
and the Kirby House among others.

The Plankinton House was the largest and oldest of these employers of black labor. Afro-Americans worked there and in other similar
establishments as bellboys, cloakroom and washroom attendants,
cooks, maids, porters, waiters, and so on. Only the waiters in these
hotels seemed to transcend somewhat "the stigma of servility" attached
to this type of work and gained modest opportunities for advancement. They could look to promotion as "third, second, and finally
headwaiter, a lucrative position of considerable prestige" in the small
Afro-American community. In only a few exceptional cases were
blacks employed in large downtown department stores.[14]

Wages ranked lowest in domestic and personal service employment. Workers in these capacities almost uniformly received less pay
than skilled, semiskilled, and even unskilled workers in the industrial,
trade, and transportation sectors. Advertisements in Milwaukee's
black weeklies announced wages of $4 to $6 per week for black women
as domestic workers. Although available evidence for Milwaukee provides information only on the wages for women domestic and personal
service employees, black men in service occupations worked different
jobs and probably fared slightly better. In his study of blacks in Philadelphia at the turn of the century, W. E. B. Du Bois noted that a black
man, skilled in the stonecutter's trade, made $21.00 a week until he
lost his job and entered domestic service at $6.25 a week.[15]

Demand increased markedly for black female domestic and personal service workers for private homes during the 1890s and early
1900s. The black press consistently advertised for black female
domestics. Beginning in 1892, the *Wisconsin Afro-American* carried an
ad directed "To Our Southern Readers": "Any one desiring to obtain
work as a domestic, no matter where your home is, write to us, at this
office, we will make for you all arrangements." Similarly, the editor of

the *Wisconsin Weekly Advocate* advertised for black women to serve as domestics: "We are in a position to place from twenty to thirty good respectable colored girls in first-class Wisconsin families at wages ranging from $4 to $6 per week." In 1898, the *Advocate* also established an employment bureau called the Colored Helping Hand Intelligence Office in order to facilitate domestic employment. Calls for black female workers continued unabated as the twentieth century got underway. In 1907, the *Advocate* even lamented the lack of applicants for available positions: "We have constantly calls for general house-work, paying good wages, and cannot find sufficient help to place in these positions. There is no cause to be idle."[16]

Despite the apparent demand for black female help in private homes, Afro-Americans in the city experienced increasing economic difficulties at the turn of the twentieth century because of competition from new immigrants. Unlike in larger cities where an older tradition of blacks in skilled and semiskilled trades such as barbering, masonry, and others still existed, blacks in Milwaukee mainly lost jobs as waiters and porters. The Plankinton House, which hired blacks from the 1860s on, replaced its Afro-American help with Greeks and other foreign-born employees by 1906. Likewise, at the turn of the century, Gimbels Department Store, heretofore an exception in its policy of hiring blacks, replaced its entire Afro-American labor force with whites, the rationale being that blacks "did not tend to business."

Few Afro-Americans entered the industrial work force. Only 10.8 percent of the black male labor force found employment as skilled, un-skilled, and semiskilled workers in 1900, and only 2.3 percent of these worked in skilled and semiskilled positions. Black women were equal-ly barred from the city's industries with only 12.0 percent of their numbers in factory jobs (see Table 1.2). None of these women worked in skilled jobs. Blacks entered the factory only as a result of excep-tional personal contacts with influential whites or as strikebreakers. John J. Miles, the Plankinton waiter, used his connections with key whites to secure industrial jobs for a few blacks by the turn of the cen-tury. The minor skilled and semiskilled jobs in factories, transporta-tion, and trade were generally monopolized by "light-skinned and well-educated blacks" with strong ties to the white community.[17]

The largest number of blacks to enter pre–World War I industries did so as strikebreakers. The use of blacks as strikebreakers in Mil-waukee, however, was not practiced on the scale evident in other large cities such as Philadelphia, Chicago, and New York, where violence often erupted. Nevertheless, strikebreaking offered an avenue of entry for some blacks into the city's industrial work force. As in other cities, however, Milwaukee industrialists largely turned blacks out once their strikebreaking function was served. When white workers struck the Illinois Steel Company over reduction of wages in 1898, the leading black newspaper, the *Advocate,* sought to recruit black strikebreakers through its columns. The *Advocate* advertised for "250 colored men to work in the rolling mills of Bay View." Black and white strikebreakers were brought in from Ohio and Pennsylvania. The strikebreaking efforts of the company apparently succeeded, for black furnace hands continued to work, according to Thomas Buchanan, as "part of a heterogeneous labor force, whose diverse elements the union would find difficult to unite" and hard to rely upon in subsequent labor disputes. Nevertheless, the Afro-American labor force gradually disappeared in favor of white workers by 1904. In 1910, blacks could not be found in any of the city's blast furnaces and rolling mills.[18]

Among Milwaukee's many ethnic groups, none were more thoroughly relegated to the cellar of the urban economy than blacks. In 1900, when 68.0 percent of black men and 73.0 percent of black women worked as domestic and personal servants, only 15.2 percent of all male workers and 32.3 percent of all women filled such jobs. Foreign-born men had 20.3 percent of their numbers so employed; immigrant women, though the gap was somewhat less, likewise had far fewer of their numbers (41.0 percent) in such jobs than black women. American-born whites of American parentage were least likely as men or women to work in domestic and service jobs. This pattern of economic inequality between blacks and whites and among whites persisted to World War I and after (see Tables 1.2 and 1.3).

Blacks in Milwaukee also experienced greater confinement to domestic and personal service than blacks in other northern cities of various sizes. About 8 percent of Chicago's black male population worked in manufacturing and mechanical pursuits in 1900, as contrasted to the 2.6 percent for black men in Milwaukee. Black women in the two cities, however, equally occupied domestic and personal service work with 81 percent of their numbers so employed. Milwaukee's 1.8 percent of black men in skilled occupations in 1900 contrasted even more sharply with a city like Cleveland, which had an unusually high though declining 15.3 percent of black men in skilled positions in 1890 and 11.1 percent in 1910.

In varying degrees, Afro-Americans throughout the urban North experienced occupational decline during the late nineteenth and early twentieth centuries. Kenneth Kusmer has suggested that the rate of decline varied from city to city in relation to three factors: a continuing tradition of racial liberalism; a small population size and slow rate of industrial expansion; and a small immigrant population. He maintains that such cities as Cleveland and New Haven, with high percentages of skilled male workers in 1890 (15.3 percent and 16.6 percent, respectively), underwent slower occupational decline because of a persisting liberal racial atmosphere. In most cities, however, it was the second and third factors or a combination of the two that were more important.[19] In Milwaukee, neither a continuing tradition of liberalism, nor slower industrialization, nor a smaller immigrant population saved Afro-Americans from the plunge into the worst common laborer and domestic service occupations. A tradition of racial liberalism persisted, but it was extremely weak; industrialization was not slow but rapid; and the percentage of immigrant population was among the largest in the country. In fact, Milwaukee, with New York, led the nation in the percentage (78.6) of population of foreign stock (foreign-born and American-born of foreign parentage) in 1910.

Afro-Americans, then, occupied the bottom of Milwaukee's urban economy for two interrelated reasons. First, a tremendous influx of foreign-born labor filled the unskilled labor demands of the expanding urban-industrial system. Second, the racist attitudes and practices of both industrialists and labor unions blocked black entrance into industrial jobs. Milwaukee employers, like other northern industrialists, articulated the myth that blacks were inherently "inadaptable" to the intellectual and physical requirements of the machine. Thus, employers considered blacks peculiarly suited only for arduous common laborer jobs as well as for menial domestic and personal service tasks. Even so, these myths broke down during the exigencies of strikes by all-white work forces; the availability of black labor was ever held ready to break the backs of white unions as it did in the Illinois Steel Company strike of 1898.

The myth of Afro-Americans as the most fit servants was also breached (especially in the hotels) when an expanding white immigrant population demanded such jobs. Employers then evaluated blacks as unable to "serve efficiently." Afro-Americans were not the only victims of such racial or ethnic stereotypes and discriminatory practices. Milwaukee industrialists relegated Poles, Italians, Greeks,

Table 1.3. Occupational Structure of Milwaukee by Racial and Ethnic Group, 1910 Selected Occupations

Males: Total Labor Force = 125,678*

| | Occupational Category | | | | | |
| | Professional | | Proprietary | | Clerical | |
| | Number | Percent | Number | Percent | Number | Percent |
|---|---|---|---|---|---|---|
| Blacks | 22 | 5.0 | 26 | 5.9 | 10 | 2.2 |
| Foreign-born whites | 485 | 0.8 | 5,601 | 10.0 | 2,720 | 4.9 |
| American-born whites | | | | | | |
| Foreign-born/mixed parentage | 944 | 1.8 | 5,007 | 9.6 | 9,051 | 17.5 |
| American-born whites | | | | | | |
| American-born parentage | 601 | 3.3 | 1,393 | 7.6 | 4,387 | 24.2 |
| All workers | 2,052 | 1.6 | 12,027 | 9.5 | 16,168 | 12.8 |

| | Skilled | | Semiskilled | | Unskilled | | Domestic | |
| | Number | Percent | Number | Percent | Number | Percent | Number | Percent |
|---|---|---|---|---|---|---|---|---|
| Blacks | 35 | 8.0 | 22 | 5.0 | 71 | 16.2 | 61 | 13.9 |
| Foreign-born whites | 13,753 | 24.8 | 4,440 | 8.0 | 12,592 | 22.6 | 896 | 1.6 |
| American-born whites | | | | | | | | |
| Foreign-born/mixed parentage | 13,858 | 26.9 | 3,850 | 7.4 | 4,290 | 8.3 | 1,286 | 2.4 |
| American-born whites | | | | | | | | |
| American-born parentage | 4,334 | 24.0 | 1,048 | 5.7 | 1,506 | 8.3 | 429 | 2.3 |
| All workers | 31,980 | 25.4 | 9,360 | 7.4 | 18,459 | 14.6 | 2,672 | 2.1 |

*This figure is slightly higher than the number of occupations that the census actually specified.

Occupational Category

Females: Total Labor Force = 39,425*

| | Professional | | Proprietary | | Clerical | |
|---|---|---|---|---|---|---|
| | Number | Percent | Number | Percent | Number | Percent |
| Blacks | 4 | 2.1 | 14 | 7.5 | 4 | 2.1 |
| Foreign-born whites | 334 | 4.2 | 553 | 7.0 | 668 | 8.5 |
| American-born whites | | | | | | |
| Foreign-born/mixed parentage | 1,490 | 6.2 | 651 | 2.6 | 5,576 | 23.3 |
| American-born whites | | | | | | |
| American-born parentage | 825 | 10.8 | 233 | 3.0 | 2,705 | 35.5 |
| All workers | 2,653 | 6.7 | 1,451 | 3.6 | 8,953 | 22.7 |

| | Skilled | | Semiskilled | | Unskilled | | Domestic | |
|---|---|---|---|---|---|---|---|---|
| | Number | Percent | Number | Percent | Number | Percent | Number | Percent |
| Blacks | – | – | 28 | 15.1 | – | – | 118 | 63.7 |
| Foreign-born whites | 173 | 2.3 | 1,950 | 25.0 | – | – | 2,898 | 37.2 |
| American-born whites | | | | | | | | |
| Foreign-born/mixed parentage | 398 | 1.7 | 7,883 | 33.0 | – | – | 4,427 | 18.5 |
| American-born whites | | | | | | | | |
| American-born parentage | 43 | 0.5 | 1,590 | 20.9 | – | – | 1,380 | 18.1 |
| All workers | 614 | 1.5 | 11,451 | 29.0 | – | – | 8,823 | 22.3 |

*This figure is slightly higher than the number of occupations that the census actually specified.

Source: U.S. Bureau of the Census, Thirteenth Census of the United States, vol. 4: Population, 1910, Occupation Statistics (Washington: Government Printing Office, 1913), pp. 565–66.

and other new immigrants to the bottom, though not to the level of blacks, as "ignorant newcomers . . . less stable than the Germans, and, in times of unemployment, given to quarreling and pilfering." Finally, the exclusion of blacks by labor unions limited Afro-American movement into the city's industries. Even when blacks organized a general strike of their own during the labor struggles of the 1870s and 1880s, no effort was made to organize black laborers for many years. Ranking among the least skilled laborers in the city, black workers also suffered, as did unorganized and unskilled white workers, from the FTC's organization along narrow craft lines.[20]

Afro-American domestic, personal service, and common laborers were not passive in the face of stiff socioeconomic competition and racial discrimination. They responded to their urban experience through both class and racial unity, though mainly through the latter. Some bootblacks organized a Shoe Artists Association in 1897. Protesting the practice of some stores of giving free shines to purchasers of shoes, these men sought to protect and secure their position in the shoeshine trade. Bootblacks, they maintained, had to "live as well as the shoe dealers." The most forceful response of the black working class to its plight occurred during the vigorous struggle between capital and labor during the 1870s and 1880s. In 1877, blacks employed in rebuilding structures destroyed by fire on Market Street struck in protest against the treatment they received both as blacks and as workers. They marched to the corner of Strand and Twenty-Fourth streets and succeeded in getting another group of blacks to quit. Before long, Afro-Americans working at Levine's Picklery, Stump's planing mill, the freight depot, flour mills, and other establishments joined the demonstration. A large force of policemen was sent to control the strikers and the movement was suppressed.[21]

This was indeed a dramatic show of unity among working-class blacks, yet black workers proved unable to move this working-class movement beyond its racial limits; the strike only garnered its support from black workers in diverse establishments. Although there is no evidence of direct white involvement, the strike took place within the context of growing solidarity among white workers. Blacks were certainly conscious of these broader trends. In reality, then, the working-class consciousness of blacks intersected with a strong racial consciousness. The two were intertwined and inseparable within the larger socioeconomic, political, and cultural context in which blacks had to operate. Blacks in pre–World War I Milwaukee were able ultimately to organize most vigorously, consistently, and effectively around the integrationist and protest goals of the old elite on the one hand and the goals of racial solidarity, unity, and self-help of the emerging new elite on the other.

Despite their small demographic base and the predominance of low-wage domestic, personal service, and common laborer employment, Afro-Americans succeeded in establishing themselves in several small businesses and in some professions. The majority of blacks in business functioned as barbers, saloonkeepers, rooming house operators, dressmakers or seamstresses, and the like. In 1900, the United States Census of Occupations listed nineteen black men and four women as proprietors of small businesses; in 1910, a selected census of black occupations revealed that twenty-six men and fourteen women were so engaged. Black business investments increased from an estimated $60,000 in 1895 to $200,000 by 1908. Some black businesses proceeded in secret, under the names of white men, "on account of the prejudice against which they would have to contend."[22] Blacks found it increasingly difficult to secure property for the conduct of business enterprises. When Harry Williams sought facilities for his barber shop in the expanding suburb of West Allis, his efforts were resisted at every turn. He finally persuaded someone to rent a place, but pressure from local whites forced the landlord to rescind the bargain.

As in other northern cities of the late nineteenth and early twentieth centuries, these Milwaukee establishments represented a gradual shift from businesses serving a white clientele to those with predominantly black customers. Businesses operated by light-skinned blacks and serving a largely white clientele, however, retained a strong influence among blacks in pre–World War I Milwaukee. Some of these establishments, notably Rufus Nobles's East Side restaurant, even excluded blacks from their services. An 1898 "Colored Men's Business Directory" listed four barbers and four steam bath operators with predominantly white clientele. Nevertheless, the most successful black business in pre–World War I Milwaukee, John L. Slaughter's Turf Hotel, served an integrated clientele, in legal and apparently shady activities as well.

Originally from Lynchburg, Virginia, Slaughter came to Milwaukee in 1890. After working for a while as a porter, he began a gambling career that eventually enabled him to open his own establishment in 1893. By 1902, Slaughter joined with a white partner and opened a

$50,000 gambling house, the New Turf European Hotel and Restaurant. Slaughter's downfall came after 1908 when the reform district attorney, Winfred Zabel, and the new Socialist mayor sought to "clean up the 'bad lands,' " the city's major vice district on the edges of the CBD. Slaughter then turned toward a nearly all-black clientele. He left the city for Chicago in 1914, not to return until the 1920s.[23]

Most black businessmen, whether their clientele was black, white, or mixed, found it difficult to sustain their enterprises. The lack of capital and business experience combined with racial animosity, foreign-born competitors, and expanding, highly capitalized commercial institutions to undermine black business in the city. Various new immigrant groups increasingly supplied the small personal service business functions for whites. Black businesses, like many white businesses, were small and increasingly undermined by the consolidated chain grocery, department, and five-and-ten-cent stores. Corporate enterprises took advantage of bulk buying, extensive advertising campaigns, and a variety of other tactics to undersell and drive their smaller competitors out of business. Thus, black businesses were undercut on all sides, and those that survived usually relied on several sources of income or pooled the resources of several individuals.[24]

Black professionals constituted the other wing of the city's black elite. These professionals catered primarily to whites, while often serving the small black community as well. The editor of the *Advocate* argued that if black professional people relied entirely on blacks, they "would starve." Afro-Americans practiced only a limited number of professions; the 1910 United States Census listed fourteen black musicians and teachers of music, four lawyers, and four physicians among black men. Black women in the professions were even more restricted with only two musicians and teachers of music, one nurse, and one teacher. The fastest growing segment of white-collar employment, clerical occupations, had the lowest black participation, but 2 percent of black men and women were so employed in 1910 (see Table 1.3 and Appendix 3).

Only one black lawyer, William T. Green, one dentist, Dr. Clifton A. Johnson, and one physician, Dr. Allen L. Herron, catering primarily to white clients, consistently stood out during the period. All of these men attracted a substantial white clientele, while serving blacks as well. In addition, Milwaukee had a separate black newspaper for most of the prewar period. Although catering primarily to a black readership, the black press, similar to other black professional and business pursuits, relied heavily on white support through initial capital, advertisements, and outright contributions. The first black newspaper to be published in the city was a weekly, the *Wisconsin Afro-American,* under editors George A. Brown and Thomas H. Jones. The paper began publication in April 1892. After suffering severe financial hardships, changing its name to *Northwestern Recorder* and converting to a monthly, the paper folded by March 1893. A second black news-paper, the *Wisconsin Weekly Defender,* began publication in 1906 and continued through 1916. This organ was developed by J. D. Cooke, a coal dealer, and H. B. Alexander, an itinerant minister. The most successful black weekly to develop during the period, Richard B. Montgomery's *Wisconsin Weekly Advocate,* began publication in 1898 and persisted through 1916, when the paper was moved to Minnea-polis and published as the *National Advocate.* [25]

The struggle between blacks and whites for jobs, business, and pro-fessional opportunities extended to the city's scarce housing supply. As blacks lost out in the competitive bid for better jobs, they were forced deeper and deeper into the most dilapidated sections of the urban housing market. Here a growing pattern of white racism in the socioeconomic and political life of the city often kept even those who had the material means from moving out. By 1870, the black popula-tion had expanded westward from its historic location east of the Mil-waukee River. Only a few blacks remained on the East Side as Afro-Americans shifted increasingly west of the Milwaukee River, where 76 percent of the black population resided in the Second and Fourth wards. Growing antagonism on the East Side between blacks and Irish and Italians, both of whom competed with blacks for jobs and housing, undergirded this population shift.[26] (see Map 1.2).

The number of wards in the city increased from ten in 1870 to twenty-three in 1910, yet five wards (1st, 2nd, 4th, 6th, and 7th) housed 84 percent of the Afro-American population in 1910. A single black area, covering nearly thirty-five blocks, gradually took shape in parts of the Second, Sixth, and Fourth wards. This district was roughly bounded by Kilbourn (Cedar) Street on the south, Walnut on the north, Third Street on the east, and Eighth Street on the west.[27] The index of dissimilarity, a statistical device for measuring the relative spatial segregation of different social groups on a scale of 0–100, for Milwaukee between 1870 and 1910 reveals the segregation of blacks in one area of the city as thorough as in other northern cities

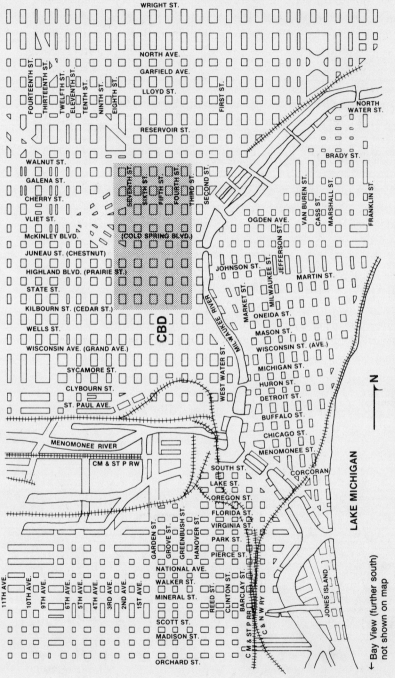

**Map 1.2. Milwaukee's Black District, 1915**

Source: Wright Directory Company, *Wright's Map of Milwaukee* (Milwaukee: Wright Directory Company, 1918); Milwaukee City Engineers Department, *Map of Milwaukee Ward Boundaries, 1931* (City of Milwaukee, 1931); Paula Lynagh, "Milwaukee's Negro Community" (Milwaukee: Citizen's Government Research Bureau, 1946), p. 2.

at the time. Based on ward-level data, the index between blacks and American-born whites increased, although slowly, from 59.6 in 1870 to 66.7 in 1910. The 1910 index between blacks and all American-born whites was about the same as that for Chicago and significantly higher than several other cities[28] (see Table 1.4). Milwaukee's segregation index between blacks and the foreign born decreased slightly from 70.2 to 68.7 between 1870 and 1910. This shift represented the increasing spatial proximity of blacks to certain new immigrant groups, mainly Italians, Greeks, and Jews, for the Poles settled almost exclusively on the South Side as blacks moved further north and west of the CBD. On the eve of World War I, the black community occupied an area that could expand in only two directions: north and west. The CBD, which itself pushed northward, restricted southward expansion. Moreover, by 1910, light manufacturing and commercial establishments began forcing blacks out of an area between Wisconsin Avenue and State Street. Afro-American expansion to the East Side was blocked by the Milwaukee River and Third Street shopping district (see Map 1.2).

Table 1.4. Index of Dissimilarity: Segregation of Milwaukee Blacks from American-born Whites and the Foreign-born, 1870–1910

| Year | American-born | Foreign-born |
| --- | --- | --- |
| 1870 | 59.6 | 70.2 |
| 1880 | N/A | N/A |
| 1890 | 46.6 | 69.5 |
| 1900 | 71.3 | 74.6 |
| 1910 | 66.7 | 68.7 |

Source: See Table 1.1.

Despite these facts, a classic black ghetto that has been documented for larger northern cities[29] did not emerge in Milwaukee. Blacks remained significantly spread out among whites within the various wards. As late as 1910, in the Second and Fourth wards, areas of highest black concentration, Afro-Americans made up only 2.9 and 2.4 percent, respectively, of the total population. These areas were far from exclusively black. Even within the Fourth Ward, "old prominent residents," who worked as pullman porters or railway clerks, lived outside the central black neighborhood. A small settlement of these so-called high society blacks lived between Eighth and Tenth streets near St. Paul Avenue. On the South Side, about twenty black families settled around the Bay View Works of the Illinois Steel Company until the enclave gradually collapsed after 1904, following the dismissal of blacks from the plant. A number of black families (15 percent of the black population) also lived north of North Avenue in the Seventh Ward.

Milwaukee's black community, as in other large cities of the period, abutted the "vice district." During the 1890s, River Street on the East Side emerged as the "red light district." This area also extended west of the Milwaukee River into a zone called the "Bad Lands," bounded by Third, Sixth, Grand (West Wisconsin), and Cedar (Kilbourn Street). A local journalist later described the locale as "full of saloons, dives, tenements, gambling houses, cheap cabarets and a few cutrate whorehouses that couldn't make the grade on River Street." Although the district had been the locale of fashionable German neighborhoods in the 1880s and 1890s, by 1900 Germans moved farther north and Russian Jews and Greeks began to occupy the area. Just before World War I, the Jews also began to make their exit northward to better neighborhoods. An influx of blacks increasingly occupied the large and aging structures. Housing conditions in the district rated among the lowest in the city. Descriptions of the housing revealed several old and dilapidated buildings, many basement dwellings, and inadequate and unsanitary housing and yard conditions in general. The area also contained some of the worst health conditions. The Milwaukee health commissioner conducted a study of health conditions for the period 1911–15, which revealed that 26.5 percent of deaths from acute diseases of childhood, tuberculosis, and typhoid occurred in the poorest residential areas, where only 12 percent of the population resided.[30]

Blacks largely rented rather than owned their homes during the entire period. Many black families took in lodgers in order to meet the rental costs of dwellings usually too large for single individuals or married people with few children. The Wisconsin state census for 1905 enumerated about 30 percent of blacks as lodgers, boarders, or roomers, excluding the large numbers living in their places of employment, hotels and private homes of the city.[31]

Besides having to live in the poorest sections of the city because of low incomes and competition with the lowest socioeconomic strata of foreign-born workers, an expanding color line made it increasingly difficult for blacks of economic means to find housing suitable for their income levels. The editor of the *Advocate* often complained of the expanding color bar in housing. "Men will not rent to decent, respectable Negroes a house," Montgomery wrote, "even though the latter are in a position to pay with equal regularity as much rental as any other class of whites." The increasing pattern of housing discrimination was also evident in the city's hotels and rooming houses. Out-of-town black guests and newcomers, almost without exception, had to find lodging at rooming houses or with private families within the black community.[32]

Transcending the competitive struggle for jobs and housing, racial discrimination also affected black-white contacts in Milwaukee's institutional life and politics. Despite its weak demographic and economic foundation, the black professional and business elite became the most forceful voice protesting such racial discrimination against blacks in the pre–World War I era. The old elite, as in other cities, reflected the persistence of abolitionist sentiment among influential whites. This elite sought to end all vestiges of racial discrimination and segregation in the city's economic, political, and social life. Its role was dramatically highlighted in the Afro-American response to the shifting pattern of race relations of the late nineteenth and early twentieth centuries.

Unfortunately, though, the competition for jobs and housing intersected with a growing climate of racial prejudice in the city, which in turn reflected an expanding national and international racism as America turned toward the colonization of foreign populations in Latin America and the Pacific. America increasingly adopted the racist outlook of the South as part of the national ideology regarding black people. A growing pattern of racial hostility was evident in the increasing difficulties of Milwaukee blacks in matters of public amusements (theaters, hotels, and restaurants), interracial social relations (particularly marriage), and a variety of other instances. In the spring of 1906, the Davidson Theater staged Thomas Dixon's racist drama, *The Klansman.* As early as 1889, the Bijou Theater ushered Owen Howell, a railway porter, to segregated balcony seats and simply refused to admit Daniel T. Coates, operator of a massage parlor. The theater's proprietor, Jacob Litt, owner of several theaters in Chicago, Minneapolis, and St. Paul, claimed that he bore no ill will toward blacks but simply followed the most economic arrangement since white customers objected to the presence of blacks. Litt's actions unleashed a spate of activities that led to the Wisconsin Civil Rights Act of 1895. The old elite and their white allies, especially the *Daily*

*Journal* and the *Sentinel,* reacted vigorously against efforts to segregate blacks. About seventy-five blacks held an "indignation meeting" and formed a committee to take Litt to court. By mid-October, the committee formed a permanent organization, the Wisconsin Union League, to prosecute the Litt case and develop plans for a state civil rights bill. The Wisconsin circuit court heard the Litt case in May 1890 and ruled that a person could not be excluded from equal access to places of public amusement upon the grounds of race, color, or previous condition of servitude.[33]

Despite the favorable ruling in the Litt case, Afro-Americans persisted in their efforts to obtain a civil rights bill. In 1890, Milwaukee blacks established a branch of T. Thomas Fortune's Afro-American League, a national black civil rights organization. Attorney William T. Green and Shadrick B. Bell, a bath-house proprietor, served as delegates to the 1890 Chicago convention of the organization. Upon their return, Green drafted a comprehensive civil rights bill for the state. The bill specified that places of accommodation and amusement be open to all regardless of race. Violators would be charged with a misdemeanor and fined from $25 to $500 and/or imprisoned for up to one year.

The measure, introduced into the Democratic-controlled state legislature in January 1891, failed to pass until a Republican administration returned to power three years later. Radical modifications, however, were made before passage. The new measure reduced penalties to fines of $5 to $100 and/or six months in jail. Judges usually imposed such lenient penalties, the lowest allowed by law, that the color line in public accommodations and amusements continued. The new Schlitz Palm Garden refused service to John J. Miles, the well-known waiter and grocery store owner. Miles brought suit and won a legal award of only $5, the minimum permitted by the new law.

Growing animosity against interracial marriages and couples constituted one of the clearest signs of an expanding color line in Milwaukee. Police harassment became more common and some state legislators attempted, though unsuccessfully, to enact laws prohibiting interracial marriage in the state. These bills, introduced by both Republicans (1901 and 1903) and Democrats (1913), were defeated by an aroused black community, particularly the old elite, and their white allies in the legislature.[34]

Blacks in northern cities such as Harlem and Chicago developed a tradition of black, mainly Republican, elected and especially appointive officials between 1870 and the turn of the century. By then, black involvement with Republican politics lessened under growing racial restrictions. Blacks found it increasingly difficult to get elected to state or even county offices by depending on white support. Thus, as Spear has noted for Chicago, between 1906 and 1915, "a core of professional politicians" emerged in order to secure the election of blacks to local and state offices based primarily on black votes.[35]

Though in weaker form, blacks in Milwaukee exhibited elements of a similar tradition in Republican politics. Lucien H. Palmer, from Huntsville, Alabama, came to Milwaukee in 1878 and spent most of his life working in the hotel and catering business. He also operated a real estate and insurance company. Palmer's support of the Republican party brought him several appointive positions including United States weigher of mails, commissioner for negro exhibits at the New Orleans Exposition, census enumerator, checking clerk in the United States marshal's office, and messenger of the United States District Court.

Palmer also became the first black to be elected to the Wisconsin state legislature in 1906. He was elected on the Republican ticket from the district covering Milwaukee's Third, Fourth and Seventh wards. Palmer served his term partly because of mistaken identity; many voters apparently mistook him for a prominent white resident of the same name, which helps to explain why a black man entered the state legislature at a time when Afro-Americans found it increasingly difficult to garner white support on a variety of issues. While a tradition of white liberalism continued to some extent, it was not sufficient to support the election of a black to such an important position in 1906.[36] As blacks turned to ward-level politics in other cities, the small demographic base and meager economic resources prevented Milwaukee blacks from doing the same. Only the migration of World War I and movement of blacks into the city's industrial workplace would establish such ward-level resources among blacks in Milwaukee.

The interplay of racial hostility, economic competition, housing segregation, and black resistance succeeded in forging a greater sense of community among Afro-Americans in Milwaukee. Blacks intensified their efforts toward building self-sufficient, indigenous social, economic, political, and religious institutions. These activities, however, were not conducted without deep internal conflicts among blacks themselves. Friction slowly developed between an old elite dependent on white patronage and an emerging new elite based upon black support. The old elite, for example, viewed black institutions as only temporary expedients along the road to full integration. The emerging new elite, for its part, did not fully appreciate the need to persistently combat racial discrimination in the city's socioeconomic and political life. Moreover, an expanding working-class population with origins primarily in upper South, border, and several midwestern states (but augmented by deep South blacks) increasingly influenced Afro-American socioeconomic, political, and institutional life.

An understanding of black institutional life requires a fuller perspective on the black class structure. The narrow demographic and economic base of blacks before World War I attenuated internal stratification. Compared to class divisions within the larger urban political economy, increasingly dominated by powerful manufacturers, bankers, and railroad magnates, social stratification among blacks in most northern cities before 1915 was indeed severely restricted. From the perspective of changes within the Afro-American community, however, class divisions within northern black urban communities became more pronounced by World War I. Milwaukee's black class structure, though, remained less developed than elsewhere. In Chicago, for example, a new bourgeois elite, with roots in an expanding black clientele, gradually supplanted a small, educated business and professional elite tied to white patronage, and largely to white ancestry as well. In the middle stood a somewhat larger, though extremely small, middle class of artisans or urban craftsmen, public service employees, clerical workers, and better-paid domestic and personal service employees (e.g., headwaiters and a few porters). Finally, there was a broad-based working class of common laborers and domestic and service workers. The low wages received from such employment left little room for the development of a black professional and business elite linked primarily to black clients; nevertheless, sharp population increases and accelerated white refusal to serve black clients in restaurants, barber and beauty shops, funeral establishments, and other businesses enabled a "New Middle Class" to emerge in Chicago between 1900 and 1910.[37]

By comparison, a middle stratum, particularly of skilled craftsmen, was almost nonexistent in Milwaukee. Moreover, because the black population remained so small, Milwaukee's new middle class failed to develop as fully as did those in other northern cities. The old elite remained firmly anchored in the economic, political, and social life of

Milwaukee's black community until World War I. Thus, the social class distinctions that emerged so clearly elsewhere were modified in Milwaukee. Attenuated stratification notwithstanding, however, institutional life and modes of resistance to increasing racial proscription reflected social class divisions among Milwaukee blacks.[38]

In Milwaukee, as in other cities, Afro-Americans responded to the socioeconomic, political, and racial restrictions by intensifying their efforts to build a separate black institutional life. An emerging new elite looked toward the Booker T. Washington-inspired ideology of self-help, race pride, and solidarity as a model for such an undertaking. Even the old elite modified its stand in the face of the increasingly hostile racial climate. As early as the 1890s, the Milwaukee Afro-American League explicitly enunciated the philosophy of self-help and racial unity. The idea, however, gained its fullest expression in the black press and the proliferation of black clubs, fraternal organizations, mutual benefit societies, social welfare organizations, and churches.[39]

Washington's ideology received its greatest prewar articulation from the pen of Richard B. Montgomery, editor of the *Wisconsin Weekly Advocate*. Montgomery, born a slave in Mississippi, migrated to Knoxville, Philadelphia, New York, and Chicago before moving to Milwaukee in 1897. Although Montgomery entered the city as a "traveling missionary" with the intent of starting a church, he opened a newsstand instead. He sold several white and black papers and became a city correspondent for the black weekly *Indianapolis Freeman*. After soliciting the aid of wealthy whites, Montgomery issued the first edition of the *Advocate* on 7 May 1898.

Montgomery adopted the motto, "The Negro must work out his own problem." He consistently praised Washington's industrial education program and attacked his detractors, well-known black weeklies such as the *Chicago Broad Ax,* the *Boston Guardian,* and the *Washington Bee.* Montgomery almost religiously supported black businesses and racial institutions. In his zeal to promote black self-help, however, Montgomery often underplayed and excused the existence of racial discrimination. When the General Federation of Women's Clubs, meeting in Milwaukee in 1900, refused to seat black women, the editor rationalized the actions of the white organization, stating that black women had their own association and should "be content to remain by themselves and toil for the uplift of their race."

Montgomery's apparent growing accommodation to racial proscription, in part, fueled the resistance of the old elite to the increasing emphasis on racial solidarity and a separate Afro-American institutional life. Members of Milwaukee's prewar old elite were, as Buchanan has noted, like that in other cities, "usually light-skinned and well educated. . . . [T]hey usually worked in the service trades and professions and had strong ties with prominent whites, which they depended on for patronage, favors, and protection." Some were even somewhat culturally closer to whites than to fellow blacks, especially the newer arrivals from the deep South. Members of the old elite included such men as John J. Miles, headwaiter at the Plankinton House; Lucien H. Palmer, one-time state assemblyman; Samuel R. Banks, an aid to the governor; Clifton A. Johnson, a dentist; Allen L. Herron, a physician; and others. Like their counterparts in other cities, these blacks vigorously protested various manifestations of racial discrimination in the city's social and political life.

The old elite took sharp issue with editor Montgomery's ideology and several of his actions. When the General Federation of Women's Clubs refused to acknowledge black women, Milwaukee's old elite "engineered a 'great indignation meeting' " that denounced the actions of the federation and the *Advocate*'s editor as well. In another instance, the old elite defeated Montgomery's plans for an industrial school for blacks in northern Wisconsin. This group further expressed its displeasure with the ideology of racial self-help and accommodation by boycotting a 1902 speech given by Booker T. Washington in the city. For his part, Montgomery consistently attacked the elite source of his opposition, referring to them as the "cod fish aristocracy," which lacked race pride and "clogged the wheels of progress."

Division between the new middle class and working-class blacks also became more apparent in the prewar period. Along with his attacks on the old elite, Montgomery directed sharp criticisms toward the poor or "lower element" in the community. He criticized them for failing to display proper race pride and particularly for lacking "thrift and industry." The behavior of these blacks in the city's saloons and on streetcorners was even more vehemently attacked. Montgomery delivered scathing editorials against what he called "a floating, shiftless and depraved element," which had come from the South and whose "misdeeds," he believed, were falsely "credited to the resident population." He carried this position to an extreme when he blamed the transient element for why "colored people have been barred from all halls in Milwaukee." In some cases, Montgomery took an antimigration stand: "We do not . . . decry the Northern migration . . . but we would impress upon our Southern brethren and sisters to locate in the smaller towns and villages where they will not be subjected to the same temptations" as in the big cities.

The foregoing ideological and class divisions found expression in an expanding network of black institutions between 1890 and 1914. Similar to the pattern in other black urban communities, the church was the oldest and most stable black institution in pre–World War I Milwaukee. Although Milwaukee's first black church began in 1869, black religious activities intensified after 1900. By 1915, three major black churches and a number of storefront missions had emerged. As in other cities, black churches became more numerous as the population increased and white congregations increasingly closed their doors to black members. When black Baptists sought financial support for a black church from the Wisconsin Baptist Association at the turn of the century, the white body refused their request and advised them to join St. Mark, a black Methodist congregation, or a white church. Both suggestions proved unsatisfactory, and in the case of white churches virtually impossible to execute, for black Baptists continued to meet as a separate body. Similarly, white Catholics exhibited increasing hostility toward Afro-American parishioners. The Irish St. Gall's Catholic Church in Milwaukee had over one hundred black members in 1895; the number had dropped to less than five by 1911.[40]

In 1869, black Methodists founded St. Mark African Methodist Episcopal Church, the oldest, largest, and most stable black church in the city. St. Mark had a membership of over one hundred in 1914. Drawing its membership from both the old elite and better-off portions of the working class, the church appealed to "middle class respectability by conducting decorous, dignified services." Shouting, for example, was condemned early as "ignorant" behavior. The church usually secured seminary-trained ministers who set the format of restrained, sophisticated, and so-called progressive services. Calvary Baptist, the second most important prewar black church, took its base from the increasing migration of blacks to the city at the turn of the century. Marked by constant feuding and schisms, Calvary failed to achieve firm cohesion until the eve of World War I. The third religious institution serving blacks, St. Benedict the Moor Mission and School of the Capuchin order, developed as a separate parish in 1909.

Next to the churches, lodges and fraternal organizations were the most significant prewar black institutions. Formed in 1891 with

Lucien Palmer as its chief officer, the oldest of these was the Prince Hall Masonic Widows Son Lodge, Number 25. Blacks organized a Knights of Pythias in 1892 and an Afro-American branch of the United Order of Odd Fellows in 1903. The number of black secret organizations reached a prewar peak of eight in 1905. The old elite invariably dominated these pre–World War I fraternal organizations. William T. Green and John J. Miles, for example, held offices in as many as four or more of these organizations by 1900. Fraternal organizations played a particularly useful role in providing members sickness, disability, and burial benefits as well as social, cultural, and entertainment activities.

Several social and service clubs, literary societies, self-improvement associations, and women's clubs rounded out the institutional life of prewar blacks. Some of the women's clubs survived through various parts of the migration, the Depression, and World War II. These included the Silver Leaf Charity Club (1890s), the Woman's Improvement Club (1908), and the Phyllis Wheatley Club (1912). Like the churches, lodges, and fraternal organizations, these social and service clubs also reflected increasing class stratification among blacks. The Cream City Social and Literary Society, founded in the 1880s, was made up primarily of wives of Milwaukee's oldest black residents. On the other hand, the Woman's Improvement Club, and others formed just before World War I, represented the distinct influence of an emerging new middle class. These clubs sponsored fundraising socials, balls, picnics, and entertainments of various types. The proceeds were then donated to charitable work among blacks.

While the expansion of Afro-American institutional life reflected racial unity in response to white hostility in the larger urban social, political, and economic life of the city, internal social class differentiation splintered these structures. Despite racial proscription, blacks did not entirely drop their class biases in favor of full racial unity. As newcomers from the South increased, established black residents exhibited a decided resolve to maintain their social status, which entailed close relations with influential whites. St. Mark, Widows Son, and other elite institutions mirrored their aspirations. This elite, however, viewed separate black institutions as temporary way stations on the path toward full integration into the larger society.

Montgomery's *Advocate,* Calvary Baptist, and the growing number of black women's clubs symbolized the slow emergence of a "new" middle class on the one hand and a gradually expanding working class of common laborers and domestic and service workers on the other. The new middle class, unlike the old elite, affirmed the inherent utility of race-based institutions as a means of Afro-American socioeconomic development and survival in the city. Although drawing their support from the delivery of business and professional services mainly to the black community, the nascent new middle class also exhibited its own elite bias against working-class blacks and further fragmented racial unity. Despite these divisions within the black community, deepening racial hostility evidenced in jobs, housing, and various public accommodations fostered greater intraracial unity during the entire period.

By 1915, an unofficial but decided separation of blacks from whites in the city's economic, political, and social life had intensified. Except briefly as strikebreakers, stiff competition with American- and foreign-born white workers blocked Afro-American access to factory jobs. The discriminatory practices of employers and labor unions gave white workers distinct advantages over their black counterparts. The same forces increasingly relegated blacks to a segregated housing market as well. Despite the small size of the black population and the weak economic foundation provided by common laborer, domestic, and personal service jobs, however, Afro-Americans waged a consistent struggle against racial barriers. It was against this background that Milwaukee blacks faced the socioeconomic and political conditions of World War I. The war would unleash unprecedented forces that would transform the majority of Afro-Americans into an urban-industrial working class. This process would, in turn, have profound consequences for the patterns of both intra- and interrace relations.

## NOTES

1. Allan H. Spear, *Black Chicago: The Making of a Negro Ghetto, 1890–1930* (Chicago: University of Chicago Press, 1967); Gilbert Osofsky, *Harlem: The Making of a Ghetto, 1890–1930,* 2nd. ed. (1963; rev. ed. New York: Harper Torchbooks, 1971); Kenneth L. Kusmer, *A Ghetto Takes Shape: Black Cleveland, 1870–1930* (Urbana: University of Illinois Press, 1976).
2. See n. 1 and David Katzman, *Before the Ghetto: Black Detroit in the Nineteenth Century* (Urbana: University of Illinois Press, 1973); W. E. B. Du Bois, *The Philadelphia Negro: A Social Study* (1899; rept. New York: Schocken Books, 1967); Robert A. Warner, *New Haven Negroes: A Social*

*History* (1940; rept. New York: Arno Press, 1969).

3. Bayrd Still, *Milwaukee: The History of a City* (1948; rept. Madison: State Historical Society of Wisconsin, 1965), pp. 321–55.

4. Ray Hughes Whitbeck, *The Geography and Economic Development of Southeastern Wisconsin* (Madison: State of Wisconsin, 1921), pp. 41–120; Roger D. Simon, "The Expansion of an Industrial City: Milwaukee, 1880–1910" (Ph.D. diss., University of Wisconsin, 1971), pp. 20–90; Still, *Milwaukee,* pp. 52–69, 168–99, 257–78, 321–55; Justin B. Galford, "The Foreign Born and Urban Growth in the Great Lakes, 1850–1950: A Study of Chicago, Cleveland, Detroit, and Milwaukee" (Ph.D. diss., New York University, 1957), pp. 267–86.

5. This data on spatial differentiation and ethnic composition of Milwaukee is based on John R. Ottensman, *The Changing Spatial Structure of American Cities* (Lexington: D. C. Heath, 1975), pp. 27–41, and Simon, "The Expansion of an Industrial City," pp. 35–47, 59–90.

6. Thomas W. Gavett, *Development of the Labor Movement in Milwaukee* (Madison: University of Wisconsin Press, 1965), pp. 35–125; Still, *Milwaukee,* pp. 279–320.

7. Gavett, *Development of the Labor Movement in Milwaukee,* pp. 77–85; Still, *Milwaukee,* pp. 279–80; Gerd Korman, *Industrialization, Immigrants, Americanizers: The View from Milwaukee, 1866–1921* (Madison: The State Historical Society of Wisconsin, 1967), pp. 42–53.

8. Thomas R. Buchanan, "Black Milwaukee, 1890–1915" (master's thesis, University of Wisconsin–Milwaukee, 1973), p. 17; Bureau of the Census, *Negro Population, 1790–1915* (1918; rept. New York: Arno Press, 1968), p. 93.

9. Osofsky, *Harlem,* pp. 17–34; Spear, *Black Chicago,* pp. 11–15; Kusmer, *A Ghetto Takes Shape,* pp. 35–52; Buchanan, "Black Milwaukee," pp. 4–5. For perspectives on pre–World War I conditions in southern areas see Howard Rabinowitz, *Race Relations in the Urban South, 1865–1890* (New York: Oxford University Press, 1978), pp. 18–30, 61–76, and Lorenzo Greene and Carter G. Woodson, *The Negro Wage Earner* (New York: Russell and Russell, 1930), pp. 48–74. For full references to the demographic characteristics of Milwaukee's prewar black population, see Joe William Trotter, Jr., "The Making of an Industrial Proletariat: Black Milwaukee, 1915–1945" (Ph.D. diss., University of Minnesota, 1980), tables 2.2 through 2.7.

10. Buchanan, "Black Milwaukee," pp. 3–5. This treatment of the pre–World War I black experience is indebted to Buchanan's master's thesis on blacks in the city between 1890 and 1915.

11. Carter G. Woodson, *A Century of Negro Migration* (1918; rept. New York: AMS Press, 1970), pp. 147–66; Osofsky, *Harlem,* pp. 20–21.

12. Buchanan, "Black Milwaukee," p. 142.

13. Ibid., pp. 41–42.
14. Ibid., pp. 42–46, 50–51.
15. Ibid., p. 47; Du Bois, *The Philadelphia Negro,* pp. 97–146; Greene and Woodson, *The Negro Wage Earner,* pp. 159–60.
16. "Notice to Our Southern Readers," *Wisconsin Afro-American,* 22 Oct. 1892; Buchanan, "Black Milwaukee," pp. 47–48; Thomas R. Buchanan, "Blacks in Milwaukee's Labor Force," *Historical Messenger* 28, no. 4 (1972): 131–40.
17. Buchanan, "Black Milwaukee," pp. 17–18, 49–51.
18. Sterling D. Spero and Abram L. Harris, *The Black Worker: The Negro and the Labor Movement* (1931; rept. New York: Atheneum, 1968), especially pp. 250–55, 264–68, 198–99; Spear, *Black Chicago,* pp. 36–40; William M. Tuttle, Jr., "Labor Conflict and Racial Violence: The Black Worker in Chicago, 1894–1919," *Labor History* 10, no. 3 (Summer 1969): 408–32; Osofsky, *Harlem,* pp. 35–52; Thaddeus Radzialowski, "The Competition for Jobs and Racial Stereotypes: Poles and Blacks in Chicago," *Polish American Studies* 33, no. 2 (Autumn 1976); Buchanan, "Black Milwaukee," pp. 18–21.
19. Spear, *Black Chicago,* pp. 30–31; Kusmer, *A Ghetto Takes Shape,* pp. 71–72, 74–75, n. 10.
20. Buchanan, "Black Milwaukee," p. 17; Gavett, *Development of the Labor Movement,* pp. 25–36, 72–87; Korman, *Industrialization, Immigrants, Americanizers,* pp. 42–53.
21. Buchanan, "Black Milwaukee," p. 45; Gavett, *Development of the Labor Movement,* pp. 25–26.
22. Buchanan, "Black Milwaukee," p. 21; *Souvenir: Journal and Directory of the Colored People* (Milwaukee: n.p., Aug. 1891); "Milwaukee and Her Progressive Citizens," *Wisconsin Enterprise Blade,* 4 Jan. 1917; William T. Green, "Negroes in Milwaukee," in Milwaukee County Historical Society, ed., *The Negro in Milwaukee: A Historical Survey* (Milwaukee: Milwaukee County Historical Society, 1968), pp. 5–11.
23. Buchanan, "Black Milwaukee," pp. 22–29; Robert W. Wells, *This is Milwaukee* (Garden City, N.Y.: Doubleday, 1970), pp. 136–42.
24. Buchanan, "Black Milwaukee," p. 24; Still, *Milwaukee,* pp. 399–400, 448.
25. Buchanan, "Black Milwaukee," pp. 100, 21–40; Green, "Introductory Note" by Harry Anderson, in Milwaukee County Historical Society, ed., *The Negro in Milwaukee,* pp. 5–6; Armstead Scott Pride, "A Register of Negro Newspapers in the United States" (Ph.D. diss., Northwestern University, 1950), pp. 166–67, 391–92.
26. William J. Vollmar, "The Negro in a Midwest Frontier City, Milwaukee, 1835–1870" (master's thesis, Marquette University, 1968), p. 87.
27. Buchanan placed the 1915 southern boundary of the black community at

State Street. This was slightly too far north. Kilbourn Avenue, located south of State Street, constituted the northern boundary of the Fourth Ward, with the Menominee River marking its southern limit. The Fourth Ward contained the CBD and 26.5 percent of the city's black population. See Buchanan, "Black Milwaukee," pp. 7–8.

28. Karl E. and Alma F. Taeuber, *Negroes in Cities: Residential Segregation and Neighborhood Change* (Chicago: Aldine, 1965), p. 54. For a fuller discussion of the question of ethnic segregation, see Stanley Lieberson, *Ethnic Patterns in American Cities* (Glencoe: Free Press, 1963).

29. Osofsky, *Harlem,* pp. 105–49; Spear, *Black Chicago,* pp. 11–27; Kusmer, *A Ghetto Takes Shape,* pp. 35–52.

30. Vollmar, "The Negro in a Midwest Frontier City," pp. 65–73; Still, *Milwaukee,* pp. 276–77; Wells, *This is Milwaukee,* pp. 136–42.

31. Buchanan, "Black Milwaukee," p. 10; Louis Swichkow and Lloyd P. Gartner, *The History of Jews in Milwaukee* (Philadelphia: The Jewish Publication Society of America, 1963), pp. 89–90, 166–68; *WPA Real Property Inventory, 1939: City of Milwaukee* (Milwaukee Public Library); Edith Elmer Wood, *Slums and Blighted Areas in the United States* (Washington: Federal Administration of Public Works, Housing Bulletin No. 1, 1935); Buchanan, "Black Milwaukee," p. 13.

32. Buchanan, "Black Milwaukee," pp. 14, 78–80.

33. Ibid., p. 54; Harry H. Anderson, "Landmark Civil Rights Decision in Wisconsin," in Milwaukee County Historical Society, ed., *The Negro in Milwaukee,* pp. 22–29.

34. Buchanan, "Black Milwaukee," pp. 54–94.

35. Spear, *Black Chicago,* pp. 118–26; Osofsky, *Harlem,* pp. 59–68.

36. "Milwaukee Negroes Elected to Public Office," in The Milwaukee County Historical Society, ed., *The Negro in Milwaukee,* p. 31.

37. Spear, *Black Chicago,* pp. 51–89.

38. For discussions of black class structure in other cities see Kusmer, *A Ghetto Takes Shape,* pp. 90–112; Katzman, *Before the Ghetto,* pp. 135–74; Du Bois, *The Philadelphia Negro,* pp. 309–21; Rabinowitz, *Race Relations in the Urban South,* pp. 226–27; August Meier, *Negro Thought in America, 1880-1915* (Ann Arbor: University of Michigan Press, 1963), particularly Chapter 9.

39. Buchanan, "Black Milwaukee," pp. 97–100. The remainder of this section on intraracial class conflict is based upon Buchanan, "Black Milwaukee," pp. 36–37, 100–14.

40. The institutional analysis that follows is drawn from data presented in Buchanan, "Black Milwaukee," pp. 114–34.

# PART TWO

# Process and Significance of Proletarianization, 1915–32

# 2

## Migration, Industrial Jobs, and Housing, 1915–32

Changes in both the economy and political system coincided with a shifting pattern of race relations as the chief catalysts in the emergence of Milwaukee's Afro-American, urban-industrial working class between 1915 and 1932. The outbreak of World War I in Europe produced demands for almost all types of manufactured goods throughout the industrial North. The war also diminished the supply of cheap immigrant labor and precipitated a search for local and national sources of industrial workers. Federal immigration restriction legislation during the 1920s sustained the limited supply of European immigrants. Under the impact of wartime labor shortages, the American labor movement greatly augmented its power, but a strong postwar counteroffensive by employers caused a precipitous decline in labor's influence by the mid-1920s.[1]

Although less vigorously than elsewhere, Milwaukee industrialists called upon blacks along with American-born rural whites to fill the labor needs of the city's wartime economic expansion. For the first time in Milwaukee's history, Afro-Americans, especially black men, moved decisively out of the domestic and personal service sector into factory jobs. But the proletarianization of Milwaukee blacks was not a smooth process. Obstacles erected by the racist attitudes and hiring practices of industrialists and restrictions on black membership in labor unions impeded the transformation. The vagaries of the business cycle reinforced such racial restrictions and ensured that

Afro-Americans would gain only a tenuous footing in the industrial work force. Even so, Milwaukee blacks achieved and maintained a basic footing in the industrial system. Black workers themselves played an active role in the process, for they were indeed agents in their own transition to an urban-industrial working class.[2] This process of proletarianization, though partially thwarted, conditioned the struggle for housing and several other facets of the black urban experience.

As in the pre–World War I era, changes in the larger economy shaped the economic experience of Milwaukee blacks. Milwaukee's economy expanded tremendously on the basis of war contracts for manufactured goods. The value of manufactured products increased by over 200 percent between 1914 and 1920. Although the end of World War I brought a reduction of war orders, industry continued to receive stimulation from the inflated demands and extremely high prices of the postwar period. Between 1921 and 1922, however, market collapses in steel, silk, hides, wool, cotton, and other raw materials produced an economic depression. By the close of 1922, though, the economy had revived and expanded, especially in the automotive, iron, and steel-related industries. The value of manufactured products expanded from an estimated $790 million in 1922 to over $1 billion in 1928. Even the Depression reached Milwaukee later than elsewhere, but the tide turned in 1932–33, as economic depression penetrated Milwaukee more deeply than most other metropolitan areas. The number of wage earners in 1933 (66,010) had declined by 43.8 percent from its 1929 level (117,658).[3] Lack of purchasing power among farmers, the railroads, and general consumers sent the city's chief industries, the iron, steel, and heavy machinery aspects of the metal trades, into steep decline.

The accelerated industrial expansion of the city had broadened its geographic and demographic base. Annexation of adjacent areas increased Milwaukee's physical size from 25.3 to 41.1 square miles between 1920 and 1930. The population increased by 22.3 percent from 373,857 to 457,147 between 1910 and 1920. During the next decade, the population expanded to 578,249, a 26.4 percent increase, the largest absolute decennial increase in the city's history (see Table 2.1), yet the proximity of Chicago and Detroit undercut the potential industrial expansion of Milwaukee. During the decades 1910–20 and 1920–30, respectively, Detroit's population increased by 113.3 and 57.9 percent. Growing from 2,185,283 in 1910 to 3,376,438 in 1930,

Table 2.1. Population of Milwaukee by Racial and Ethnic Group, 1910–1930

| | Year | | | | | | | Percent Increase | |
| --- | --- | --- | --- | --- | --- | --- | --- | --- | --- |
| | 1910 | Percent | 1920 | Percent | 1930 | Percent | | 1910–20 | 1920–30 |
| Total Population* | 373,857 | 100.0 | 457,147 | 100.0 | 578,249 | 100.0 | | 22.3 | 26.4 |
| Blacks | 980 | 0.2 | 2,229 | 0.4 | 7,501 | 1.2 | | 127.4 | 236.5 |
| Foreign-born whites | 111,456 | 29.8 | 110,068 | 24.1 | 109,383 | 18.9 | | -1.2 | -0.6 |
| American-born whites | | | | | | | | | |
| Foreign-born/mixed parentage | 182,530 | 48.8 | 213,911 | 46.8 | 241,695 | 41.7 | | 42.0 | 12.9 |
| American-born whites | | | | | | | | | |
| American-born parentage | 78,823 | 21.1 | 130,845 | 28.6 | 217,729 | 37.6 | | 66.0 | 66.4 |

*Includes a small number of other nonwhite ethnic groups.

Source: Thirteenth Census of U.S., vol. 1: Population, 1910 (Washington: Government Printing Office, 1913), p. 210; Fourteenth Census of U.S., vol. 3: Population, 1920 (Washington: Government Printing Office, 1922), p. 1131; Fifteenth Census of U.S., vol. 3, pt. 2, 1930 (Washington: Government Printing Office, 1932), p. 1368.

Chicago similarly outdistanced Milwaukee in its rate of population growth.

Immigration declined to a mere trickle during and following World War I. The number of immigrants coming to the city dropped from 22,508 (1900–1910) to 1,369 in the decade before 1920. During the 1920s, the foreign born increased by only 451 persons. Although the period between 1915 and 1932 would witness the increasing homogenization of the white population as foreign immigration subsided, ethnic lines retained strength. Germans continued to live in the northwest portion of the city (Fifteenth, Twentieth, Twenty-second and Twenty-fifth wards), and American-born whites of Old English ancestry predominated in the Nineteenth and part of the Eighteenth wards, which they shared with Germans. Irish and Austro-Hungarians shared the Sixteenth, Scotch and Scandinavians lived in the Seventeenth and Twenty-third, and a settlement of Slavs occupied parts of the Second Ward. Bohemians and Hollanders shared the Ninth Ward, while Jews occupied the Sixth and Tenth wards with blacks increasing in numbers. Although some Poles lived on the North Side, the South Side, below the Menomonee River, remained the chief settlement of Polish residents. Most of the newest arrivals — Mexicans, Italians, Greeks, and Afro-Americans — lived in the low-cost areas near the central business district (CBD), namely portions of the Third, Fourth, and Sixth wards. These groups, finding it difficult to achieve an economic footing, moved only slowly to outlying sections of the city[4] (see Map 2.1).

The struggle between labor unions and industrialists continued during World War I and its aftermath. The trade union movement in the city had tapered off in the decade preceding World War I, but in 1916 a revival of activities took place, as labor unions achieved representation in diverse war-related governmental agencies: the National Council of Defense, the Emergency Construction Board, and the War Industries Board among others. These war-related developments strengthened the trade union movement in Milwaukee and split the Federated Trades Council of Milwaukee (FTC) from its historic prewar alliance with the Socialists. As the crisis deepened, the FTC, initially opposed to war, turned against the antiwar position of the Socialists, bought war bonds, and participated in preparedness rallies. The end of World War I brought a resurgence of labor union militancy. The FTC even launched a drive to organize unorganized workers — meat cutters, butchers, flat janitors, tannery workers, and

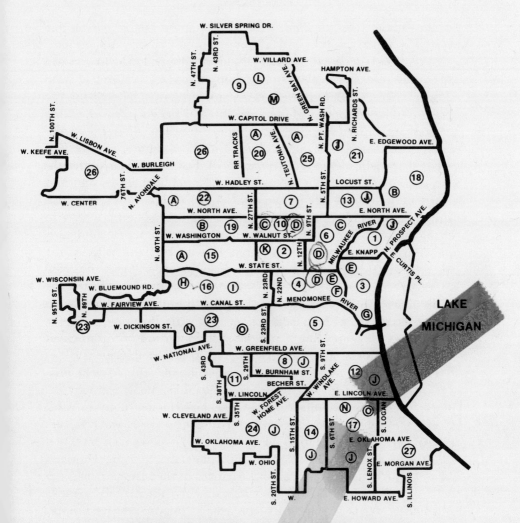

## Map 2.1. Spatial Distribution of Milwaukee's Population by Ethnic Group and Wards, 1931

| | | |
|---|---|---|
| A  German | F  Mexicans | K  Slavs |
| B  American-Born Whites (particularly of English stock) | G  Italians | L  Bohemians |
| | H  Irish | M  Hollanders |
| C  Jews | I  Austro-Hungarians | N  Scotch |
| D  Blacks | J  Poles | O  Scandinavians |
| E  Greeks | | |

Note: Since ethnic neighborhoods were not mutually exclusive, this map simply highlights some of the salient ethnic features of Milwaukee's landscape.
Source: Adapted from Bayrd Still, *Milwaukee: The History of a City* (1948; rept. Madison: State Historical Society of Wisconsin, 1965), pp. 598, 453–75.

others—under the Labor Forward Movement in 1918. These efforts collapsed by 1921 as the postwar depression hit the city and employers, organized in the Milwaukee Employers Council, waged a powerful counteroffensive against union shops.[5]

Local politics reflected the relative influence of capital and labor. Organized labor continued, as in the prewar period, to have an impact on municipal government. Labor expressed its influence by consistently supporting Socialist Mayor Daniel W. Hoan, who headed city government between 1916 and 1940, but the prewar pattern of cooperation between Democrats and Republicans continued in efforts to undermine the influence of Socialists in municipal affairs. Although the ethnic component in municipal politics declined from its strong prewar pattern, ethnic interests continued to play a significant role. Hoan, for example, had to rely upon a coalition with several otherwise anti-Socialist Polish aldermen in order to institute his municipal reforms, the low-cost Garden Homes Project, a municipal stone quarry, and a city-owned street lighting system. This alliance was necessary since Hoan lacked a Socialist majority on the city council, and his measures often met the stiff opposition of the so-called nonpartisan (Republican and Democrat) or fusion alderman.[6]

These changes within the larger socioeconomic and political life of the city helped to radically transform Milwaukee's black population. Black migration to Milwaukee, while less intense than to other northern cities, increased dramatically during World War I and the 1920s. The black population increased by 127.4 percent, from 980 to 2,229, between 1910 and 1920. During the war years, the *Milwaukee Journal,* one of several leading newspapers in the city, noted the increasing influx: "One who knew Milwaukee a half dozen years ago, and who knows it today will be surprised if he stops to note the number of colored people he meets on the streets now as compared with preceding years. So silently have they slipped into the city that few of us have noted their coming."[7] An even larger increase came during the 1920s. By 1930, the Afro-American population reached 7,501, an increase of 236.5 percent over 1920, yet blacks comprised only 1.2 percent of Milwaukee's total population, compared to 6.9, 4.7, and 11.3 percent, respectively, in Chicago, New York, and Philadelphia (see Table 2.1).

The curtailment of European immigration, destructive conditions in southern agriculture such as the boll weevil and devastating floods, industrial recruitment campaigns, the lure of higher wages in northern industries, and favorable press comment (especially during the war) from both blacks and whites encouraged the flow. During the war years, Afro-American journalists and their white counterparts printed positive commentary on the migration. The *Milwaukee Journal* editorialized its belief that "the newcomers" would "make good" with the support and encouragement of white citizens. Locally circulated black newspapers were even more articulate in supporting the influx of black migrants. The Madison-(later Milwaukee) based *Wisconsin Enterprise Blade* enthusiastically editorialized: "Let the Exodus Continue. Let them come, and let their brethren and kindred welcome them, and see that they are not exploited while becoming accustomed to their surrounding."[8]

Black migration to Milwaukee appears to have come, as it did to Detroit and several other northern cities, during what a student of Detroit's black community has called two migratory peaks: 1916–17 and 1924–25. The increasing wartime demand for labor and the impact of immigration restriction measures, respectively, underlay the two waves of migration. The sources of migrants now drastically shifted from upper South, border, and midwestern states to lower South states.[9] In 1920, blacks born in three deep South states (Mississippi, 13.4; Georgia, 8.0; and Alabama, 3.8) comprised the largest percentages of Wisconsin's black population. Together, the two largest upper South and border states, Tennessee and Kentucky, added 11.5 percent. Illinois, Ohio, and other midwestern states accounted for the bulk of the remainder; except that migrants from Georgia came to greatly outnumber those from Mississippi, Arkansas, Alabama, and other deep South states, this pattern persisted until 1930.

Intensive migration severely unbalanced the age and sex ratios of Afro-Americans. Children under five made up only 5.5 and 7.4 percent of males and females in 1920, contrasted to a city average of 10.0 percent for such ages; a similar pattern prevailed in 1930. While the migration was largely selective of young men and women, it favored men over women. Just before World War I, black women outnumbered men with 105 females to every 100 males. In 1920, there were nearly 124 men to every 100 women. During the same period, 60.1 percent of males and 58.9 percent of females were concentrated in the ages 20–44. The sex ratio of the black population closely paralleled that of the foreign-born, but immigrants had a much smaller percentage of children than blacks.

On the one hand, the proximity of Chicago and Detroit limited Milwaukee's potential as a destination point for black migrants. Detroit's black population increased from 5,741 in 1910 to 120,066 in 1930. Chicago's Afro-American population expanded even more dramatically, from 44,103 to 233,903 during the same period. Chicago was especially well known among southern blacks for several reasons: it was the northern terminus of the Illinois Central Railroad, home of nationally known mail-order houses like Sears and Roebuck and Company, and headquarters of the militant black weekly, the *Chicago Defender*. Knowledge of the exceptional racial policies of Detroit's Ford Motor Company also circulated widely among southern blacks. Conversely, little was known of Milwaukee in the South and most of what was known was related to its breweries. Potential black migrants often asked whether or not Milwaukee was a wet or dry town, since many southern states had prohibited the sale of alcoholic beverages. Facing difficulty attracting black migrants, the larger Milwaukee plants launched recruitment drives that brought in some 1,200 southern blacks between 1917 and 1918. The labor agent, especially during the war years, became a pivotal link in the growth of Milwaukee's small black population. These agents, according to one contemporary observer, "snapped up" those "who were able to move on shortest notice, those with few responsibilities and few interests at home."[10]

On the other hand, the proximity of Chicago augmented Milwaukee's small black population. The largest influx of black migrants (those arriving during the 1920s) resulted chiefly from the huge migration to Chicago and environs. All of the newcomers to Chicago did not remain there, as Emmett Scott noted: "They were only temporary guests awaiting the opportunity to proceed further and settle in surrounding cities and towns. . . . A great many of the migrants who came to Chicago found employment in these satellite places. . . . Milwaukee was one of the ready recipients of negro migrants from other points in the North."[11] Post–World War I economic retrenchment in Chicago and other surrounding areas (particularly Beloit, Wisconsin) increased the number of blacks seeking work in Milwaukee.

The labor needs of Milwaukee industries and the increasing migration of blacks to the city radically transformed the Afro-American occupational structure. As indicated in Chapter 1, black men and women were almost totally confined to common laborer, domestic, and personal service work in the pre–World War I era. In the wake of the great migration, the percentage of black men employed in skilled, semiskilled, and unskilled work (chiefly in manufacturing and mechanical jobs) increased from 19.2 percent in 1910, to 71.0 percent in 1920, and to 79.6 percent as the Depression got underway. The percentage of black women in factory jobs also increased. In 1920, 38.4 percent of black females worked in manufacturing occupations. Black women, however, continued to work mainly in domestic and personal service, 61.5 percent in 1930 (see Tables 2.2 and 2.3).

Compared to southern conditions, Afro-Americans improved their economic position in Milwaukee. Most of them entered industrial jobs where wages ranged from 30.5 cents to 64 cents an hour and from $3.67 to $4.79 per day. This contrasted sharply with conditions in the South where, even in urban industrial centers such as Birmingham, unskilled workers earned a maximum of $2.50 for a nine-hour day. Southern farm hands made even less, usually 75 cents to $1.00 per day.[12] This significant improvement over southern conditions gave a progressive character to black proletarianization, but, from the vantage point of Milwaukee, Afro-Americans were undoubtedly the most exploited element of the labor force.

Although black men entered manufacturing jobs in increasing numbers, they were relegated to the bottom. Most black men found employment in difficult, low-paying, and generally disagreeable jobs in four major industrial groups: iron and steel; slaughtering and meat-packing; tanneries; and building and construction. Charles S. Johnson's industrial survey showed that only about 11 of the city's more than 2,000 manufacturing establishments hired black workers during the World War I migration, and 6 of these companies hired a little more than 75 percent of all black workers: Plankinton Packing, Albert Trostel Leather, Pfister-Vogel Tannery, Allis Chalmers (mining, milling, and manufacturing equipment company), Faulk Manufactory (an iron foundry), and the Milwaukee Coke and Gas Company. Other companies hiring blacks included Illinois Steel, A. J. Lindeman-Hoverson, National Malleable Iron, and Solvay Steel[13] (see Table 2.4 and appendixes 4 and 5).

The oral testimonies of black men who worked in Milwaukee industries during the 1920s illustrate the types of jobs open to blacks during the period. John Williams worked for a short time at the Illinois Steel Company. Black men, he said, "were limited, they only did the dirty work. . .jobs that even Poles didn't want." Afro-Americans

Table 2.2. Occupational Structure of Milwaukee by Racial and Ethnic Group, 1920

**Males: Total Labor Force = 153,419***

| | Occupational Category | | | | | |
| --- | --- | --- | --- | --- | --- | --- |
| | Professional | | Proprietary | | Clerical | |
| | Number | Percent | Number | Percent | Number | Percent |
| Blacks | 41 | 4.1 | 36 | 3.6 | 17 | 1.7 |
| Foreign-born whites | 1,081 | 1.9 | 5,397 | 9.8 | 3,012 | 5.5 |
| American-born whites | | | | | | |
| Foreign-born/mixed parentage | 2,533 | 3.8 | 5,874 | 8.9 | 11,726 | 17.9 |
| American-born whites | | | | | | |
| American-born parentage | 2,184 | 6.7 | 3,233 | 9.8 | 7,909 | 24.2 |
| All workers | 5,839 | 3.8 | 14,540 | 9.4 | 22,664 | 14.7 |

| | Skilled | | Semiskilled | | Unskilled | | Domestic | |
| --- | --- | --- | --- | --- | --- | --- | --- | --- |
| | Number | Percent | Number | Percent | Number | Percent | Number | Percent |
| Blacks | 90 | 9.1 | 125 | 12.6 | 488 | 49.3 | 186 | 18.8 |
| Foreign-born whites | 16,363 | 30.2 | 10,430 | 19.2 | 15,456 | 28.4 | 2,091 | 3.8 |
| American-born whites | | | | | | | | |
| Foreign-born/mixed parentage | 20,561 | 31.3 | 13,874 | 21.1 | 8,485 | 12.9 | 2,161 | 3.2 |
| American-born whites | | | | | | | | |
| American-born parentage | 8,952 | 27.5 | 5,662 | 17.3 | 3,379 | 10.3 | 1,243 | 3.8 |
| All workers | 45,966 | 29.9 | 30,091 | 19.6 | 27,808 | 18.1 | 5,681 | 3.7 |

*This figure is slightly higher than the number of occupations that the census actually specified.

Occupational Category

Females: Total Labor Force = 51,344*

| | Professional | | Proprietary | | Clerical | |
|---|---|---|---|---|---|---|
| | Number | Percent | Number | Percent | Number | Percent |
| Blacks | 4 | 1.3 | 19 | 6.4 | 14 | 4.8 |
| Foreign-born whites | 407 | 5.1 | 537 | 6.7 | 1,179 | 14.8 |
| American-born whites Foreign-born/mixed parentage | 2,074 | 7.2 | 791 | 2.4 | 9,515 | 33.2 |
| American-born whites American-born parentage | 1,594 | 10.9 | 317 | 2.1 | 6,847 | 47.1 |
| All workers | 4,079 | 7.9 | 1,664 | 3.2 | 17,555 | 34.1 |

| | Skilled | | Semiskilled | | Unskilled | | Domestic | |
|---|---|---|---|---|---|---|---|---|
| | Number | Percent | Number | Percent | Number | Percent | Number | Percent |
| Blacks | 3 | 1.1 | 113 | 39.1 | 12 | 4.1 | 114 | 39.4 |
| Foreign-born whites | 162 | 2.0 | 2,917 | 36.6 | 344 | 4.3 | 1,473 | 29.5 |
| American-born whites Foreign-born/mixed parentage | 527 | 1.8 | 10,603 | 37.1 | 659 | 2.3 | 3,597 | 12.5 |
| American-born whites American-born parentage | 249 | 1.7 | 3,599 | 24.7 | 166 | 1.1 | 1,741 | 11.5 |
| All workers | 941 | 1.8 | 17,215 | 33.5 | 1,181 | 2.3 | 6,925 | 13.4 |

*This figure is slightly higher than the number of occupations that the census actually specified.

Source: U.S. Census Bureau, *Fourteenth Census of the U.S., vol. 4: Population, 1920, Occupations* (Washington: Government Printing Office, 1923), pp. 1141–44.

Table 2.3. Occupational Structure of Milwaukee by Racial and Ethnic Group, 1930

Males: Total Labor Force = 191,005*

| | Occupational Category | | | | | |
| --- | --- | --- | --- | --- | --- | --- |
| | Professional | | Proprietary | | Clerical | |
| | Number | Percent | Number | Percent | Number | Percent |
| Blacks | 97 | 3.4 | 67 | 2.3 | 19 | 0.6 |
| Foreign-born whites | 1,311 | 2.5 | 5,822 | 11.0 | 3,603 | 6.8 |
| American-born whites | | | | | | |
| Foreign-born/mixed parentage | 5,940 | 4.4 | 12,821 | 9.4 | 28,043 | 20.7 |
| All workers | 7,348 | 3.8 | 18,710 | 9.7 | 31,665 | 16.5 |

| | Skilled | | Semiskilled | | Unskilled | | Domestic | |
| --- | --- | --- | --- | --- | --- | --- | --- | --- |
| | Number | Percent | Number | Percent | Number | Percent | Number | Percent |
| Blacks | 161 | 5.8 | 530 | 18.9 | 1,557 | 55.6 | 366 | 13.0 |
| Foreign-born whites | 14,473 | 27.7 | 10,448 | 19.9 | 12,914 | 24.6 | 2,925 | 5.5 |
| American-born whites | | | | | | | | |
| Foreign-born/mixed parentage | 35,735 | 26.5 | 27,413 | 20.3 | 15,372 | 11.3 | 8,532 | 6.3 |
| All workers | 50,369 | 26.3 | 38,391 | 20.0 | 29,843 | 15.6 | 11,823 | 6.1 |

*This figure is slightly higher than the number of occupations that the census actually specified.

Occupational Category

Females: Total Labor Force = 63,332*

| | Professional | | Proprietary | | Clerical | |
|---|---|---|---|---|---|---|
| | Number | Percent | Number | Percent | Number | Percent |
| Blacks | 29 | 3.4 | 62 | 7.3 | 27 | 3.2 |
| Foreign-born whites | 436 | 5.4 | 632 | 7.8 | 1,503 | 18.8 |
| American-born whites | | | | | | |
| Foreign-born/mixed parentage | 5,729 | 10.5 | 2,094 | 3.7 | 23,525 | 43.2 |
| All workers | 6,194 | 9.7 | 2,788 | 4.4 | 25,055 | 39.5 |

| | Skilled | | Semiskilled | | Unskilled | | Domestic | |
|---|---|---|---|---|---|---|---|---|
| | Number | Percent | Number | Percent | Number | Percent | Number | Percent |
| Blacks | 6 | 0.7 | 152 | 18.0 | 32 | 3.8 | 518 | 61.5 |
| Foreign-born whites | 136 | 1.7 | 2,621 | 32.8 | 144 | 1.8 | 2,517 | 31.5 |
| American-born whites | | | | | | | | |
| Foreign-born/mixed parentage | 464 | 0.9 | 15,020 | 27.9 | 538 | 0.9 | 7,055 | 12.9 |
| All workers | 606 | 0.9 | 17,793 | 28.0 | 714 | 0.9 | 10,090 | 15.9 |

*This figure is slightly higher than the number of occupations that the census actually specified.

Source: U.S. Census Bureau, *Fifteenth Census of the U.S.: 1930. Population, vol. 4: Occupations* (Washington: Government Printing Office, 1933), pp. 1767–71.

Table 2.4. Top Four Industries Hiring Black Labor by Skill Levels, 1920 and 1930

| Industrial Category | 1920 | | | | | | 1930 | | | | | |
|---|---|---|---|---|---|---|---|---|---|---|---|---|
| | Unskilled | | Semiskilled | | Skilled | | Unskilled | | Semiskilled | | Skilled | |
| | Number | Percent | Number | Percent | Number | Percent | Number | Percent | Number | Percent | Number | Percent |
| Iron and steel | 155 | 15.6 | 18 | 1.8 | 18 | 1.8 | 588 | 21.0 | 72 | 2.5 | 58 | 2.0 |
| Food/meat packing | 66 | 6.6 | 35 | 3.5 | — | — | 87 | 3.1 | 54 | 1.9 | — | — |
| Tannery | 68 | 6.8 | 16 | 1.6 | — | — | 39 | 1.3 | 15 | 0.5 | — | — |
| Building/ construction | 42 | 4.2 | — | — | — | — | 167 | 5.9 | — | — | — | — |
| Total black male labor force | 331 | 33.5 | 69 | 6.9 | 18 | 1.8 | 881 | 31.4 | 141 | 5.0 | 58 | 2.0 |

Source: See appendixes 4 and 5.

worked in the hottest areas of the plant. They fed the blast furnaces and performed the most tedious operations in rolling mills that made rails for the railroads.

Black tannery employees worked primarily in the beam house, where dry hides were placed into pits filled with lime in order to remove the hair. According to Lawrence Miller, a black tannery worker, this operation required rubber boots, rubber aprons, rubber gloves, "everything rubber because that lime would eat you up." Moreover, nearly intolerable fumes characterized the process. Although some blacks worked as stretchers and buffers — cleaner and more-skilled tanning jobs — whites dominated these positions.

Packinghouses also relegated Afro-Americans to the worst occupations. Few blacks worked in the butcher category, a skilled job requiring use of the knife; they were usually employed as muckers or slaughterers. These men unloaded trucks, slaughtered the animals, transported intestines, and generally cleaned the plant. Although white workers monopolized the cleaner and higher-paying jobs in each industry, blacks invariably shared the most disagreeable jobs with large numbers of foreign-born white workers such as Poles and Hungarians, yet the percentages of immigrants in these jobs fell significantly below that of blacks. Black males had 49.3 percent of their numbers in unskilled jobs in 1920 and 55.6 percent in such positions in 1930; this compared to 18.1 and 15.6 percent for all men in 1920 and 1930, respectively[14] (see tables 2.2 and 2.3).

Working conditions, degree of exertion, and wages for unskilled laborers contrasted sharply with those of skilled workers. The wages for unskilled manual laborers ranged from a low of 30 cents per hour ($19.80 weekly for an eleven-hour day) for a female packinghouse worker to a high of 43 cents per hour ($28.38 weekly for an eleven-hour day) for male packinghouse employees. Weekly wages for porters and janitors, on the other hand, averaged $15–$18. A Milwaukee Urban League (MUL) and Council of Social Agencies survey revealed that 1928 wages in the black district averaged $22.50 per week for unskilled men and $10.00 per week for domestics. Skilled molders, among the lowest-paid skilled workers, by contrast, made from 35–47 cents per hour and butchers made from 55–64 cents per hour. The wage contrast was even greater between unskilled laborers and electricians, machinists, and other more skilled trades. Sparce evidence suggests that some blacks in Milwaukee received less pay than whites for performing the same work. "A moulder," the MUL reported, "said

he had been a moulder on one job four years. . . . Some moulding jobs
pay whites more than Negroes on the same pattern."[15] Blacks probably earned less than whites principally because they were disproportionately concentrated in both low-paying jobs and low-paying firms.

Afro-Americans constantly complained about the lack of opportunities for skilled work. Despite the labor demands of World War I,
only three blacks found acceptance as apprentices in all the skilled
crafts; by 1930, there were none. Southern blacks who arrived in
Milwaukee with a trade, whether shoemaking, tailoring, or others,
were usually forced "to learn over again" what they thought they "had
mastered, or abandon" their trades altogether and enter unskilled
work. The few blacks who entered skilled and semiskilled jobs invariably worked as molders in foundries and butchers in packinghouses. They were nearly completely barred from several skilled
trades (as blacksmiths, boilermakers, millwrights, and electricians)
and from semiskilled lines of work in the liquor and brewing industries, butter, cheese and condensed milk plants, and electrical supply
factories (see tables 2.2 and 2.3; appendixes 4 and 5).

For blacks who entered the city with skills, the transition to an industrial labor force stood in marked contrast to the majority of blacks.
The movement of skilled blacks into the factory represented a downward thrust into unskilled labor. Were it not for the fierce erosion of
the southern and northern black craftsman's economic position on the
eve of World War I (particularly their displacement by white workers), we might conclude unreservedly that skilled blacks, like their
white counterparts, suffered not only a loss of skills but also a loss of
autonomy and income as well. But the tremendous debasement of
black skilled workers before World War I probably meant that they
(even if relatively less than their unskilled brothers) also often improved their economic position by entering unskilled work in
Milwaukee industries.[16]

Several barriers obstructed black access to better industrial jobs.
Racist attitudes and practices of employers and labor unions coincided with up- and downturns in the urban economy to create a fragile
foundation for the emerging black industrial working class. Charles
S. Johnson's wartime survey of the racial attitudes of Milwaukee
manufacturers revealed a mixture of satisfaction with and stereotypes
about black workers. On the one hand, industrialists praised blacks
for delivering satisfactory service during the war emergency. On the
other hand, employers perceived Afro-Americans as unsteady and in-

capable of adapting to the requirements of factory employment: "The principal fault of negro workmen is, they are slow and very hard to please. Not good on rapid moving machinery, have not had mechanical training; slow; not stable. Inclined to be irregular in attendance to work. Very unsteady. Leave in summertime for road work." As we will see, there was an obverse side to this behavior that reflected ways in which blacks helped shape their own industrial experience, but these verbalizations clearly articulated commonly held employer stereotypes of black character and work habits. Even the merits accorded black employees entailed vivid racial stereotypes: "They are superior to foreign labor because they readily understand what you try to tell them. Loyalty, willingness, cheerfulness. . . . Quicker, huskier, and can stand more heat than other workmen."[17]

White workers shared the racism of employers, and, for their own reasons, sought to erect barriers to black industrial opportunities. From the outset, labor unions feared the possibilities of accelerated dependence on low-wage black labor. Frank Weber, organizer of the AFL-affiliated Milwaukee Federated Trades Council, concluded from a study of labor conditions during the migration that there was no industry in the city that had a "shortage of common or any other labor, providing that Big Business will pay what labor needs and earns." "IN SHORT," Weber concluded in bold print, "THE SHORTAGE OF LABOR CRY IS, A PROPAGANDA FOR LOW WAGES."[18]

Milwaukee labor leaders desired to keep Milwaukee white and free of low-wage black labor. For example, the well-known Milwaukee Socialist, Victor Berger, believed that blacks constituted a "lower race," and, as in other cities, labor unions discriminated against blacks through exclusionary clauses, rituals, or by separate all-black locals. Socialist Mayor Daniel W. Hoan recognized the hostility of white workers when he took a stand in favor of separate locals: "I do want to urge work among Negroes. . . . I don't like segregation in theory but colored locals are better than no locals among colored people and may be a step on the road to united locals." Yet, compared to other northern cities, a careful student of labor conditions in the city concluded, the "attitude of white and black workmen toward one another in none of the plants visited presented anything like a serious situation."[19] The low level of overt friction between black and white workers generally persisted through the early 1930s.

Afro-Americans also experienced the vagaries of the business cycle

as they sought to retain a foothold in the urban economy. In addition
to the onslaught of the Depression in the late 1920s, Afro-Americans
faced the brief, but destructive, postwar depression of the early 1920s.
The experience of Afro-Americans on Jones Island, located on the
city's southeast side, highlighted increasing unemployment among
blacks in the immediate postwar era (see Map 2.2). During the war,
the Illinois Steel Company recruited 175–200 black men to work at its
Jones Island facility. Postwar depression reduced the black work force
on the island to about 12 men in 1922.[20]

The most revealing evidence of economic difficulties confronting
blacks in the early 1920s was the increasing shift toward an anti-black
migration attitude within the city. When white workers struck the
Milwaukee Road in protest against wage cuts in 1922, this trend came
into sharp focus. White unions traditionally feared the use of blacks as
strikebreakers and had even opposed their regular recruitment during
the labor shortages of World War I. Now this opposition took on a new
militancy. Labor unions also had a sympathetic mayor in D. W.
Hoan. As early as 1919, in the Illinois Steel Company strike, Hoan
supported labor's stand against the use of black strikebreakers. In a
sharply worded letter to Richard Charlton, superintendent of the Illinois Steel Company, Hoan emphasized the racial violence occuring in
other cities and stated his resolve to prevent such in Milwaukee. Industrialists apparently heeded his request: "We beg to advise that it is
not true. . .that we intend to import several hundred negroes into
Milwaukee for the purpose of taking the place of certain white
laborers."[21]

In 1922, when the railroads brought in about thirty-five blacks from
Chicago to take the place of striking workers, Eugene Cooney, president of the striking Local System Federation of Northwestern Railroad, requested Hoan's assistance. "It is the sincere desire of the
striking railroad workers to conduct our strike in a peaceable and
lawful manner," Cooney wrote, "and knowing that in times of strikes
often acts performed by outsiders are imputed to the strikers. We view
with serious apprehension the continued importation of negro strike
breakers into Milwaukee. . . . We therefore. . .request that you do
everything in your power as mayor of the city, to stop this practice of
the roads." Mayor Hoan informed the owners that he would not
tolerate the use of black strikebreakers and permit racial strife to
disrupt what he called "the most peaceful city in the entire world."
Upon receiving Hoan's letter, William H. Finley, president of the

Chicago, Milwaukee, and St. Paul Railway, assured Hoan that he had "issued instructions that no more colored labor be sent to Milwaukee."[22]

While the Local System Federation failed in its bid to prevent wage cuts, white workers had blocked the widespread use of blacks as strike-breakers. Failure to use black strikebreakers in greater numbers was also related to the desires and demands of local blacks. Conscious of their small numbers during a period of rising unemployment, Milwaukee blacks hoped to avoid the plight of black workers in East St. Louis, Chicago, and other northern cities, where violence against black workers often spread into general attacks on all blacks. A broad cross section of local blacks requested measures to curtail the use of blacks as strikebreakers. The local branch of the National Association for the Advancement of Colored People (NAACP), the Milwaukee Urban League, and the City Federation of Colored Women's Clubs, endorsed a resolution (drawn up by the local Garvey organization) which stated in part: "The Negro citizens of Milwaukee . . . are opposed to any railroad importing Negro labor to take the places of strikers. . . . [A]ll Negro organizations in Milwaukee are using every means and effort to prevent the employment of Negroes for such purposes and ask cooperation of city officials and citizens."[23] The *Blade* also changed its earlier tone and editorialized against the use of black strikebreakers and against the continued influx of blacks generally: "Observation is that, generally speaking, it is not well for members of colored race to adopt migratory tactics. Any considerable movement from one place to another is the invitation for an outbreak of resentment usually merging into violence."[24]

Public officials linked efforts to curtail black migration with a concerted campaign against local blacks, especially the most recent arrivals. In 1923, three squads of detectives entered the black community and arrested thirty-nine men for vagrancy. Twelve proved that they had jobs and money; the others were brought before the Milwaukee District Court. According to a local journalist, Judge Michael Bienski told the men that Milwaukee had no use for "their kind" and that he would give them "a chance to work for the county for 90 days." At the end of that period, the judge warned the men, "You will have 90 minutes to get out of town." He also suggested that those arrested write South and advise their relatives not to venture North, particularly to Milwaukee. As the reporter concluded, "Most Milwaukeeans seem to have agreed with Bienski's attitude."[25] Only the upturn in the economy after 1923 would mitigate such attacks on local blacks.

Economic recovery and industrial expansion took place anew between 1923 and 1928. Black migration to the city again accelerated. In 1923, J. Harvey Kerns, director of the Milwaukee Urban League, estimated Milwaukee's black population at 5,000. By 1930, there were 7,501 Afro-Americans in the city. Kerns also observed the changed character of the migration: "Negroes who have been coming to Milwaukee recently . . . are bringing their families with them and have money." This migration augmented Milwaukee's black business and professional elite. Such people as Wilbur and Ardie Halyard, founders of the Columbia Building and Loan Association (CBLA); Clarence and Cleopatra Johnson, proprietors of a well-known tailoring establishment; Dr. L. T. Gilmer, a successful physician; and several others entered the city during this period.[26]

Although the number of families increased, the majority of migrants continued to be single young men and women between the ages of twenty and forty-four. These newcomers entered the city's industrial work force primarily as unskilled laborers. Industrial employment opportunities for blacks indeed expanded between 1923 and 1928. The steel foundries began recalling black employees who had been laid off in the postwar retrenchment. The MUL cited International Harvester Corporation, manufacturer of farm equipment, for having the most encouraging record of reemploying blacks. The firm asked the league's employment bureau to provide as many men as possible with foundry experience. Common laborer jobs with the firm paid $4.50 a day and men on piecework made as much as $6 and $7 per day. Although not as high as wages for Detroit auto workers, these wages compared favorably with those of blacks in other industrial cities, but they were nevertheless the lowest wages in Milwaukee's industrial workplace. The MUL especially lauded International Harvester for its policy of hiring only those workers with the league's "stamp of approval." In addition to places in the iron foundries, blacks increasingly found employment as common laborers in the building trades.[27]

Despite the expansion of industrial activity by the mid-1920s, the position of black industrial workers remained tenuous. The Illinois Steel Company moved to Gary, Indiana, in 1928 and dismissed the entire force of black workers on Jones Island. James A. Fields, whose father was a labor recruiter for the firm, has related how his family lost their personal savings in efforts to support the unemployed men.

Work at the plant became progressively more irregular; sometimes the firm operated for only two or three days per week, before closing altogether.[28]

Compared to other northern metropolises, the Depression hit Milwaukee later than elsewhere. According to the city's chief historian, Milwaukee was indeed the envy of other American cities until 1932, but Milwaukee's small black population went under much earlier than did the city at large. More than a year before the great stock market crash of 1929 and nearly three years before Milwaukee succumbed to the Depression, Milwaukee blacks faced a deepening economic crisis. The MUL conducted twelve interviews with local employers in March 1928 and found a decided shift from the otherwise optimistic outlook of the mid-1920s. Two plants employing sizeable proportions of Afro-Americans reported extensive layoffs. The Milwaukee Coke and Gas Company closed twenty-five furnaces, affecting fifty black workers for an indefinite period. The MUL report for December 1927 and January 1928 showed that several blacks, some having worked as long as six years, were being laid off. Expanding unemployment affected the skilled and unskilled alike.[29]

Unemployment intensified near the end of 1928; by December 1929, the MUL reported that the industrial depression had "assumed alarming proportions among people served by the Urban League." The 1930 United States unemployment census for Milwaukee revealed a 9.6 percent unemployment rate for blacks compared to 2.6 percent for the city. Black men had 14.5 percent of their numbers out of work in contrast to 4.6 percent for all men. Afro-American women, though the gap was less, also had more of their numbers out of work than white women (see Table 2.5). Probably more than any other indicator, the increasing numbers of black women seeking employment

Table 2.5. Unemployment in Milwaukee by Race and Ethnicity, 1930*

|  | Total | Percent | Male | Percent | Female | Percent |
|---|---|---|---|---|---|---|
| Whites/all | 15,103 | 2.6 | 13,317 | 4.6 | 1,786 | 0.6 |
| Blacks | 722 | 9.6 | 588 | 14.5 | 134 | 3.8 |
| Foreign-born whites | 4,397 | 3.9 | 4,192 | 6.9 | 205 | 0.4 |
| American-born whites | 10,706 | 2.3 | 9,125 | 4.0 | 1,581 | 0.6 |

*Class A: Persons out of a job, able to work, and looking for a job.

Source: Bureau of the Census, *Fifteenth Census of U.S.: 1930. Unemployment, vol. 1* (Washington: Government Printing Office, 1931), p. 1092.

exposed the destructive impact of the Depression on the black community. The 30.8 percent of Milwaukee's black families (23.0 percent
for the city) with two or more gainfully employed members in 1930
reflected the importance of women workers in the Afro-American
community. The highest number of black women applying for work
with the MUL in 1928, according to available statistics, was 82 in the
month of June; in 1930, the highest number of such applicants
reached 346 in October. This pattern persisted until the end of 1932,
when the MUL shifted to operate almost entirely as an employment
agency providing black female domestic and personal service help.
Wage cuts, longer periods of unemployment, and a growing transient
population combined with the foregoing factors in heightening the
difficulties confronting the local black population.[30]

By the early 1930s, concrete signs of economic depression had
spread throughout the black community. Street begging, drunken-
ness, and idle men loafing in pool halls and on street corners became
common sights. The depths to which the Depression had plunged the
small black population gained its sharpest expression in the increasing
benefits of public relief, though barely at subsistence level, over low-
paying private employment. "The slogan of the Urban League movement; 'Not alms but opportunity,' " the February 1931 report stated,
"becomes more significant each day as many individuals who at one
time called at the Urban League in search of a job now seem to give
work but little thought. They come now to be referred for the second,
third or fourth time to some relief agency." "Timidity and embarrass-
ment," the report continued, "are rapidly giving way to bold begging
and in a few instances abusive demands."[31]

Milwaukee's black population, with its greater dependence on factory work, was hit relatively harder by the Depression than were Afro-
Americans in several other northern cities. Out of a selected sample of
cities of various sizes and regions, only Detroit (70.1 percent) and
Cleveland (63.2 percent) exceeded Milwaukee in the percentage of
their male work force in manufacturing and mechanical pursuits in
1920. By 1930, only Detroit outdistanced Milwaukee in this respect.

The different levels of dependence on industrial employment made
a difference in the degree to which sporadic change in the urban-
industrial economy affected blacks in the various cities. For example,
as the economic downturn deepened at the end of the 1920s, higher
unemployment levels emerged in cities with heavy reliance on manufacturing. The unemployment rate for blacks in such cities as St. Paul

(3.6), Minneapolis (3.6), Chicago (6.6), and even New York (5.0) was significantly below that of Milwaukee, Detroit, and other similar cities (see Table 2.6). The process of black industrial proletarianization, which had proceeded further in Milwaukee, Detroit, and a few other cities than elsewhere, made them highly vulnerable to the falling demand for manufactured products ushered in by the Depression. Conversely, blacks in cities with greater economic links to domestic and personal service occupations experienced the effects of high unemployment later than did their manufacturing counterparts.[32]

Table 2.6. Unemployment by Race and Ethnicity: Selected
Northern Cities, 1930

| | Percent Unemployed | | | | | |
|---|---|---|---|---|---|---|
| | Black | | White | | Black | White |
| | Male | Female | Male | Female | Total | |
| Northern Cities | | | | | | |
| Chicago | 9.6 | 3.6 | 7.0 | 1.2 | 6.6 | 4.1 |
| New York | 7.3 | 2.8 | 5.3 | 1.0 | 5.0 | 3.2 |
| Detroit | 15.7 | 3.8 | 7.4 | 0.9 | 10.1 | 4.3 |
| Cleveland | 14.5 | 3.3 | 7.2 | 0.9 | 8.1 | 4.1 |
| Milwaukee | 14.5 | 3.8 | 4.6 | 0.6 | 9.6 | 2.6 |

Source: Computed from *Fifteenth Census of U.S.: 1930. Unemployment, vol. 1.*

Although Afro-Americans in Milwaukee faced stiff socioeconomic constraints on their advancement in the industrial labor force, they were not passive. Through their own activities, Afro-American workers played an active role in their transition to factory employment. They actively shaped their own industrial experience in both subtle and highly organized ways. Their responses reflected strategies designed to combat the discriminatory practices of both employers and labor unions, as well as the vagaries of the business cycle.

Afro-Americans in Milwaukee, as noted earlier, faced a labor market in which labor unions and employers practiced racial discrimination. Employers, in particular, characterized blacks as slow, unsteady, and unable to manage rapidly moving machinery. To be sure, as indicated by their high turnover rate in some industries, there was an element of truth in employer allegations that Afro-Americans exhibited instability and irregular work habits. As working class historians Herbert Gutman and David Montgomery have suggested in another context, however, much of this activity reflected subtle Afro-American resistance to the most restrictive and oppressive aspects of the proletarianization process.[33]

Such resistance derived both from an objective assessment of exploitative working conditions (defined as low wages for the most exacting — in health and other terms — physical labor) and from traditional values about work. For example, the turnover rate of black labor, indeed all labor, was most acute in the tanning industry. The Pfister-Vogel Company hired 300 blacks during the war years but had only 75 black employees at any one time. Simple "unsteadiness," as industrialists perceived it, was certainly not the chief cause of black labor turnover in the industry. A more telling explanation involved the conditions of work in the plant. The only employment permitted blacks "was wet and very disagreeable beam work, and at wages not in excess of those paid by neighboring plants with a different grade of work." As one tannery worker related, and he spoke for many, "I worked there one night and I quit."[34]

Afro-Americans presented even more intimate and personal reasons for changing jobs: dissatisfaction with their treatment by petty white bosses, the need for ready money for the care of their families, and the distance of the plants from the district in which they lived. Such personal reasons often clearly indicated what Gutman has called the persistence of "pre-modern work habits . . . and the cultural sanctions sustaining them" in the transition of rural people to an urban-industrial work force. For example, there were no amusements for the men living on Clinton Street and employed at the Pfister-Vogel Company. Since the streetcars stopped running at a relatively early hour, if the workers visited the main black community (located some eight miles away), they had to take an expensive taxicab back or remain overnight and wait for the next train. Many chose not to report; others reported late; but few, it appears, chose to give up their social life for a record of stability and regularity at the Pfister-Vogel Company.[35]

In addition to the more subtle behavioral responses to the industrial process, Afro-Americans promoted their interests through formal labor organizations. From the beginning, blacks established organizations that reflected an expanding working-class consciousness. This worker consciousness was overlaid with a strong emphasis on racial unity and solidarity. Afro-Americans organized the Colored Workingmen's Liberty Club during the war years. Comprised mainly of newly arrived southern black factory employees, the club sought essentially social, fraternal, and mutual benefit goals. The Workingmen's Club's approach persisted with the formation of the Working Men's League in 1926. With their burial funds and social welfare committees, though usually inadequate to the pressing needs, these clubs helped to cushion black families against unexpected deaths, as well as against destructive downturns in the business cycle.[36]

On the other hand, rising black membership in predominantly white labor unions and the emergence of separate all-black locals reflected a deepening trade union awareness, which focused on issues of higher wages and better working conditions. By 1918, three unions (carpenters, hod carriers, and butchers) had black members. The largest number (120) belonged to the 200-member butcher's union, an AFL local in which blacks, too numerous to exclude totally, were increasingly segregated. Only about four blacks had membership in the carpenters' and hod carriers' locals. The growing hostility toward black labor in the postwar era, engendered by economic depression and the powerful employer counteroffensive against labor unions, undermined the participation of blacks in Milwaukee's labor movement. The butchers' union declined to near insignificance by the mid-1920s, and by 1930 blacks belonged to only four unions: Asphalt Workers Local 88; Musicians Local 587; a carpenters' local; and a common labor local. Two of the unions (asphalt and musicians) were all-black separate locals; the common labor union was 50 percent black; and only two blacks belonged to the carpenters' union.[37]

By the mid-1920s, while Afro-Americans continued to share trade union aims of higher wages and better working conditions, which entailed demands on employers, they also increasingly used separate locals to articulate demands for better treatment of black workers by organized white labor. In June 1925, for example, the Asphalt Workers' local met and passed a resolution petitioning the Milwaukee FTC, the Wisconsin State Federation of Labor, and Milwaukee trade unions generally "to use all possible influence toward lifting the ban on colored workers said to exist in some of the organized trades." "The prevailing attitude toward the Negro worker on the part of organized labor," the resolution concluded, "is a potent weapon for the capitalist . . . and a tremendous drawback to the successful achievements of the workers in general."[38]

Organized labor conceded the importance of black labor in the city's economy when the Milwaukee FTC endorsed a molders' union petition calling for active support of the Communist-spearheaded American Negro Labor Congress (ANLC). Organized in Chicago in 1925, the ANLC aimed to "unify the efforts. . .of all organizations composed of both Negro workers and farmers as well as organizations composed of Negro and white workers and farmers. . .for the abolition of all discrimination, persecution and exploitation of the Negro race and working people generally."[39]

A Milwaukee chapter of the ANLC, the Progressive Labor League, was soon established and became one of the most potent examples of black labor militancy during the 1920s. The Milwaukee branch of the organization immediately turned its attention to political action with the formation of the Milwaukee Labor Council for United Political Action. The council, organized in 1927, consisted of black and white labor organizations. It aimed chiefly to elect a black alderman from the city's Sixth Ward, where blacks concentrated. The council argued that "a colored worker" who worked "in a packing plant" was "just as capable to represent the interest of workers as anybody else, and because of his understanding of the objective conditions" even more so. Although the council failed to elect a black alderman, it dramatized the growing consolidation of a black urban proletariat and its dynamic role in helping to shape its own experience.[40]

Separate all-black locals and the ANLC revealed the convergence of race and class among blacks in Milwaukee. They sought to organize first and foremost as blacks in order to break down racial barriers in the socioeconomic and political life of the city. Thus, there developed a coalescence of both worker and race consciousness and interests. This intersection of race and class was fostered by the continuation of racial discrimination and hostility toward blacks by organized labor and organized capital. Moreover, a link was at the same time being forged between the black industrial working class and the expanding, though extremely weak, black bourgeoisie. The activities of Rev. Jesse S. Woods, pastor of St. Mark AME church, graphically demonstrated the connection. Receiving the support of local industrialists, Woods resigned his ministerial post and established in September 1917 the Booker T. Washington Social and Industrial Center (BTWSIC), Milwaukee's earliest avowedly secular program of assistance to black migrants. Woods, from Hannibal, Missouri, and graduate of both Beloit College in Wisconsin and the Northwestern University theological department in Evanston, Illinois, became the chief warden and J. Walter Minor, born in Brunswick, Georgia, served as secretary. The Booker T. Washington Center, a three-story, forty-eight room boarding, lodging, and recreational facility, received billing in the black local weekly as the only "industrial League Club for men...of its kind in the middle northwest for our people." The BTWSIC remained active until the mid-1920s, when it was ultimately supplanted by the Milwaukee Urban League which proved more effective as a social welfare agency among blacks.[41]

When black elite institutions and leaders began a cautious but decided shift toward a prolabor stance by the mid-1920s, the connection between black workers and the black bourgeoisie gained even more articulation. In its early years, the *Blade* had condemned the exclusion of blacks from labor unions and subtly placed its weight behind black strikebreaking activities, but from the railroad strike of 1922 onward, the *Blade* condemned strikebreaking by blacks and encouraged closer cooperation between blacks and organized labor. The *Blade,* for example, supported the ANLC's efforts to organize black workers and link them more directly to the predominantly white labor movement.[42] A similar shift characterized the Milwaukee Urban League.

The Milwaukee Urban League's program, like that of the parent organization, was interracial, conciliatory, and condemnatory toward blacks for their socioeconomic difficulties. For example, J. Harvey Kerns, the league's executive secretary between 1923 and 1927, concurred with industrialists that the black worker lost jobs in foundries and steel mills "due largely to his irregular habits and instability." Yet, partly through the urging of national headquarters, the MUL adopted a more prolabor stance by the mid-1920s. The National Urban League (NUL) permitted local affiliates to develop their own labor policies, including strikebreaking against unions that barred blacks, while, where possible, simultaneously encouraging cooperation with AFL unions. The national office actively encouraged the Milwaukee local to link blacks to the labor movement.[43]

The MUL directed its greatest energy toward obtaining industrial jobs for blacks and preventing their mistreatment in the workplace. Such activities helped to cement a closer bond between black workers and the Afro-American middle class. When the city refused black workers common laborer jobs on a public building project, the league met with the mayor in an effort to assure their employment. The MUL was particularly vigilant in its attempts to prevent the extreme exploitation of black women. In several cases, it intervened for better working conditions and higher wages.

In one case brought before the Wisconsin Industrial Commission, a state employment regulatory agency, the MUL obtained a 40 percent wage increase for twenty-three black women in one firm. In another case placed before the commission, the league was "able to persuade one company employing white and Negro girls that the posting of signs designating separate toilets for the two races was a bit out of line." The MUL was not entirely successful in this case. "Although the signs have been removed," the league reported, "another system has been instituted which is perhaps less flagrant."[44] Black women apparently continued to use the segregated facilities, but without the signs. Failure to eliminate such abuses reflected the limitations of the league's conciliatory approach.

A heavy schedule of personal interviews, designed to secure industrial positions for black men and women, represented the most consistent Urban League effort in the struggle for jobs. The MUL sometimes gained concrete commitments that were later honored. The International Harvester Corporation, as noted earlier, agreed to hire only blacks referred by the league and upheld the commitment. Other firms such as the Milwaukee Electric Light and Railway Company gave "definite promises. . .as to their intentions of employing some colored persons," but these companies failed to follow through by hiring Afro-Americans. Under the onslaught of the Depression, the league turned its attention just as vigorously toward securing material relief and domestic service employment for Afro-Americans, especially women.[45]

The black community, then, was active and not passive in its shift to an urban-industrial footing. Afro-American workers and the middle class fashioned both distinctive and unified responses to the transformation of blacks into primarily a wage-earning, urban-industrial proletariat. Both subtle and highly organized forms of activities characterized their responses to the proletarianization process.

Closely intertwined with the proletarianization of Milwaukee blacks was their increasing ghettoization. Indeed, within the context of Milwaukee, the emergence of the black proletariat intensified black ghetto formation. The tenuous economic and political power base of Afro-Americans placed them at a distinct disadvantage in the competitive housing conflict with entrenched white ethnic and working-class communities. Landlords aggravated the struggle by exploiting housing shortages through consistent rent increases. Afro-Americans fought a largely, but not entirely, losing battle for better housing as they concentrated in the poorest neighborhood with increasing symptoms of ghetto formation. Better housing for some, however, became a slowly increasing reality as the black community itself became more sharply stratified along class lines.

From the migration of World War I to 1930, the geographical core of Milwaukee's black community expanded dramatically northward to North Avenue and westward to Twelfth Street. The CBD pushed the southern boundary of the black community northward to State Street, with Third Street continuing to mark its eastern limit. Two lesser contingents of blacks still lived around Water and Market streets on the East Side and Clinton Street on the South Side. In 1920, two wards (Second, 44.3 percent and Sixth, 35.2 percent) contained 79.5 percent of the black population. By 1930, blacks in the Sixth (56.5 percent) and Second (26.2 percent) wards accounted for 82.7 percent of all Milwaukee blacks. Four wards (Sixth, Second, Ninth, and Tenth) comprised 93.7 percent of the city's 7,501 blacks[46] (see Map 2.2).

The growing segregation of blacks is indicated by the index of dissimilarity (based on ward-level data) and available census tract data for 1920 and 1930. The index of dissimilarity shows that by 1920 Afro-Americans in Milwaukee (78.1) were no less segregated from American-born whites than blacks in Chicago (75.7), Cleveland (70.1), Buffalo (71.5), and several other cities. Afro-Americans in Milwaukee became more segregated from all white ethnic groups except Italians and Jews between World War I and 1930. While gaining access to areas being vacated by Jews and Italians, blacks became more segregated from American-born whites and other foreign-born residents, namely Poles and Germans (see Table 2.7). Census tract statistics show the rapid movement of whites out of areas of dramatic black population growth. Located exclusively within the Sixth and Tenth wards, census tracts 19, 20, 21, 29, and 30 had the sharpest white population declines between 1920 and 1930 (see Table 2.8).

Although Milwaukee blacks experienced increasing spatial separation from whites, the characteristic large-scale black ghetto had not developed. In their highest areas of concentration, the Second and Sixth wards, Afro-Americans made up only 22.2 and 13.0 percent of the total population in 1930. Black residential areas continued to be significantly interspersed with white residential areas. Moreover, although Milwaukee realtors exhibited their determination to confine

**Map 2.2. Milwaukee's Black District, 1932**

Source: Wright Directory Company, *Wright's Map of Milwaukee* (Milwaukee: Wright Directory Company, 1918); Milwaukee City Engineers Department, *Map of Milwaukee Ward Boundaries, 1931* (City of Milwaukee, 1931); Paula Lynagh, "Milwaukee's Negro Community" (Milwaukee: Citizen's Government Research Bureau, 1946), p. 2.

Table 2.7. Index of Dissimilarity: Segregation of Milwaukee Blacks from American-born and Foreign-born Whites, 1910–1930

| Year | American-born | Foreign-born | Selected Foreign-born only, 1910–20 | 1910 | 1920 |
|------|---------------|--------------|-------------------------------------|------|------|
| 1910 | 66.7 | 68.7 | German | 73.5 | 82.1 |
| 1920 | 78.1 | 73.6 | Irish | 62.2 | 69.6 |
| 1930 | 85.1 | 78.7 | Italian | 92.4 | 79.8 |
| | | | Russian Jews | 74.4 | 56.0 |
| | | | Poles | N/A | 89.3 |
| | | | English | 63.6 | 73.7 |

Source: See Table 2.1.

Table 2.8. Total Population by Census Tracts: Milwaukee's Near Downtown Area, 1920 and 1930

| Census Tracts | 1920 | 1920 | Percent Change 1920–30 |
|---------------|------|------|------------------------|
| 20 | 3,686 | 2,656 | – 27.9 |
| 21 | 4,784 | 3,300 | – 31.0 |
| 29 | 5,196 | 4,947 | – 4.8 |
| 30 | 3,984 | 3,922 | – 1.6 |
| Total | 17,650 | 14,825 | – 16.0 |
| 19 | 5,352 | 3,795 | – 29.1 |
| 35 | 4,547 | 4,862 | + 6.9 |
| 36 | 7,271 | 6,802 | – 6.5 |
| Total: All tracts | 34,820 | 30,284 | – 13.0 |

Source: Paula Lynagh, "Milwaukee's Negro Community" (Milwaukee: Citizens' Governmental Research Bureau, 1946), p. 34.

blacks to a black belt, there was no organized and violent citizen opposition to black housing that paralleled Chicago's Hyde Park Improvement Corporation; such hostile reactions to black housing needs would not erupt in Milwaukee until the 1940s,[47] yet the geographical boundaries of what would later become Milwaukee's predominantly black ghetto were clearly established by 1930.

The pattern of segregation reflected increasing deterioration in black housing. An acute contemporary observer noted the impact of the newcomers on the quality of housing in Milwaukee: "The neighborhoods in which negroes live have long showed evidence of physical and moral deterioration. The addition of 1400 negroes from the South . . . hastened the deterioration and gave rise to problems where only tendencies existed before." By the mid-1920s, the *Blade* expressed

growing disappointment with the quality of black housing in the city
and sometimes compared it to black residential conditions in southern
towns.[48]

A 1926 MUL study pinpointed housing as one of the "greatest problems confronting the Negro in Milwaukee." The MUL based its conclusion on a study of 275 homes, the majority of which were found inadequate for "average comfort." Homes surveyed disclosed a series of
debilitating features: no gas or bath; dampness on account of water
standing in the basement; roofing in bad order; dark rooms in need of
plastering; and so on. Rats, a health hazard for all but especially
dangerous for small children, infested several of the homes. Over-
crowding, not yet a serious problem, gradually increased; there were
cases where six persons occupied one room and where fourteen people
lived in three rooms. As elsewhere, a high incidence of disease, declining births, and rising death rates accompanied poor housing conditions among Milwaukee blacks.[49]

Whites, landlords in particular, consistently expressed the belief
that blacks resided in poor housing because they "were quite careless
and in many instances very destructive and made no effort to beautify
the homes in which they lived."[50] The problem was much deeper than
simply pride in surroundings. Inadequate housing for Afro-Americans fundamentally resulted from their precarious industrial foundation, but the economic basis of poor housing was reinforced and intensified by an interlocking combination of factors: stiff competition with
working-class and poor whites, lack of necessary power resources, and
growing internal pressure from blacks themselves for a separate institutional, economic, cultural, and social existence.

Afro-Americans lacked the means to finance significantly better
housing in the community. The 1928 MUL housing survey reported
less than ten homes owned and occupied by Afro-Americans; 99 percent of blacks rented their homes. According to the 1930 United States
Census of Families, 42.3 percent of all Milwaukee families owned
their homes. While blacks paid the lowest rents in the city (an average
of $27.69 per month compared to $34.08 and $40.88, respectively, for
foreign- and American-born whites), given the poor quality of
housing available to them, they actually paid comparatively more for
housing than other groups. The 1926 MUL survey of housing, for example, reported rent increases of 30 to 200 percent after blacks moved
into a neighborhood. Moreover, like blacks in larger northern cities,
most Afro-Americans found the housing structures too large for the

needs of single newcomers or young married people with few children. Families were thus often "compelled to take in lodgers to help pay the rent."[51]

Lack of political influence in municipal affairs and strong competition from poor and working-class whites aggravated the economic constraints on black housing. This combination of factors gained sharp focus when the city financed the Garden Homes Project between 1921 and 1923. Garden Homes, the first low-income housing project of its kind in the United States, was built by the Garden Homes Corporation. The corporation constructed and sold one hundred homes to working-class families, and owners saved about $1,500 by building under the cooperative system. Blacks were not allowed to participate in this "progressive" housing experiment.[52]

Discriminatory real estate policies and zoning legislation also impeded Afro-American access to adequate housing. Realtors evidenced a decided resolve to contain blacks within a circumscribed area of the city. "Milwaukee will have a 'black belt,' " reported the *Milwaukee Journal* in 1924, "if the Real Estate Board can find ways and means to make it practicable." The basic devise for restricting blacks in Milwaukee, as in other cities, was the racially restrictive covenant. Black attorney George Brawley conducted a study in the early 1940s on plats filed with the Milwaukee County Register of Deeds Office; he found that an estimated 90 percent of the plats filed after 1910 contained some restriction prohibiting the sale of property to blacks. Throughout the city, "gentlemen's agreements"—not to rent or sell property to blacks outside a sharply delineated area—supplemented the restrictive covenants. Zoning legislation also militated against the acquisition of better housing for blacks. A 1920 ordinance zoned the entire southern half of Milwaukee's black district for commercial and light manufacturing. The law allowed no new residential structures in the area until World War II. Landlords sought to squeeze as much profit as possible from these old structures, many of which were built during the Civil War and Reconstruction.[53]

The segregation of Milwaukee blacks also partly resulted from the demands of blacks themselves. The CBLA, for example, consistently struggled to capture the black housing market. Black ministers, with either full or supplemental incomes from serving churches in the Afro-American community, were reluctant to attack the ghettoization process. Aspiring politicians, for their part, hoped to benefit from the growing concentration of black voters in the Sixth Ward. A plethora of black professional and business people expected to expand their incomes by catering to the growing Afro-American population. Finally, black workers, because of racial discrimination in the labor and housing markets, frequently acquiesced in the efforts of bourgeois blacks to build a separate Afro-American social, economic, institutional, and cultural life. Moreover, since the black proletariat was forced to build its own distinct institutions and organizations, it had a vested interest in segregation apart from those of middle-class blacks. These internal pressures reinforced the economic factors associated with the proletarianization of Milwaukee blacks and heightened the process of ghetto formation.[54]

As it had struggled for jobs, so the black community vigorously fought to secure better housing. From the outset of the migration, Afro-Americans sought to meet the housing needs of the newcomers, mainly black industrial workers. Under the leadership of a black Catholic, Laura Duncan, St. Benedict the Moor, a Catholic institution of the Capuchin order, expanded its "Home for Colored Working Girls and Women Strangers in the city." Rev. Jesse S. Woods, as noted earlier, also established the Booker T. Washington Social and Industrial Center. The Milwaukee Urban League, founded in 1919, soon superseded the BTWSIC as the most consistent advocate of better housing for blacks.[55] Much as it mediated between black workers and employers, the MUL acted as an intermediary between landlords and tenants. "Our housing program has been largely one of cooperation between landlord and tenant," the league's 1927 annual report stated. Several short housing surveys represented the central thrust of the league's work in the housing field. These studies sought to bring conditions of unsanitary and inadequate housing to the attention of influential city officials as well as private social work agencies, mainly for the purpose of condemning and razing unsanitary buildings where blacks resided. In 1930, the MUL's pressure on city officials led to the elimination of "Noah's Ark," the most hazardous of these structures, and "Cat Fish Row." Available statistics showed that 22 percent of all recorded crimes committed by blacks in Milwaukee took place in Noah's Ark. The removal of such units, however, simply led to greater crowding within available structures.[56]

The activities of black realtors represented a growing entrepreneurial response to housing discrimination (see discussion in Chapter 3). These realtors included the Leon C. Pleasant Real Estate Office, the McDonald Realty, and a few others. The most outstanding business answer to the tightening housing market was the establishment of the Columbia Building and Loan Association in 1925. Financing of housing by the CBLA reflected a slow shift toward better housing among the city's small black professional and business elite. The CBLA enabled the movement of a few Afro-Americans to better areas on the edges of the expanding black district. The Halyards, founders of the association, moved some distance north and west of the main settlement.

While the foregoing housing struggle mainly reflected the verbalizations and actions of middle-class blacks, some Afro-American workers participated in such activities. William Bryant, president of Asphalt Local 88, became a founding member of the CBLA. Bryant, a skilled electrician and mason, established a building contracting firm. He hired black workers to carry out repairs on housing financed by the CBLA.[57]

Few black workers, however, could participate in the ghetto as entrepreneurs or even as employees of all-black firms. Nevertheless, black workers and the middle class developed close ties as a result of racial discrimination in both the labor and housing markets. The expanding demographic and economic base provided by factory wages, supplemented by income from domestic service, enabled businesses such as real estate and contracting to emerge and serve an increasingly segregated, Afro-American, urban-industrial working class. Thus, the process of proletarianization underlay the entrepreneurial response to black housing.

The period between 1915 and 1932 witnessed the emergence of Milwaukee's black industrial working class. Labor shortages during World War I, destructive conditions in southern agriculture, and the legislative curtailment of European immigration were the chief factors promoting the entrance of blacks into the industrial work force. Conversely, antagonistic racial attitudes and practices of labor unions and industrialists obstructed Afro-American movement into factory employment. Sporadic shifts in the larger urban economy intersected with the foregoing factors in sustaining a vulnerable industrial foothold for Afro-Americans. Although the external forces promoting the transformation of Afro-Americans into an industrial proletariat were compelling, blacks played a dynamic role in shaping their own urban economic experience. Both inconspicuous and highly visible mechanisms characterized the response of blacks to the industrial system.

Proletarianization also conditioned the struggle for better housing facilities. Unlike many northern cities, however, Milwaukee did not witness the emergence of a sharply defined black ghetto. Neither did the racial violence that often erupted in other cities surface in Milwaukee. Nevertheless, the making of Milwaukee's black working class dramatically transformed both the pattern of race relations and the internal structure of black urban life. It laid the demographic and financial basis for the emergence of a new black professional and business elite and precipitated greater class differentiation within the Afro-American population. The emergence of the new black middle class is the subject of the next chapter.

## NOTES

1. Douglas C. North, *Growth and Welfare in the American Past: A New Economic History* (1966; rept. Englewood Cliffs; N.J.: Prentice Hall, 1974), pp. 43–44, 155–57; Gabriel Kolko, *Main Currents in Modern American History* (New York: Harper and Row, 1976), pp. 11–56; John Higham, *Strangers in the Land: Patterns of American Nativism, 1860–1925* (1955; rept. New York: Atheneum, 1963), chapters 8–11; Philip S. Foner, *History of the Labor Movement in the United States,* vols. 1–4 (New York: International Publishers, 1947–65); Joseph G. Rayback, *A History of American Labor* (1959; rept. New York: Free Press, 1966), pp. 290–313.

2. For general perspectives on these issues in other cities see: Kenneth L. Kusmer, *A Ghetto Takes Shape: Black Cleveland, 1870–1930* (Urbana: University of Illinois Press, 1976), pp. 190–205; Allan H. Spear, *Black Chicago: The Making of a Negro Ghetto, 1890–1920* (Chicago: University of Chicago Press, 1967), pp. 129–46; Gilbert Osofsky, *Harlem: The Making of a Negro Ghetto* (1963; rev. ed. New York: Harper Torchbooks, 1971), pp. 127–49; Sterling D. Spero and Abram L. Harris, *The Black Worker: The Negro and the Labor Movement* (1931; rept. New York: Atheneum, 1968); Florette Henri, *Black Migration: Movement North, 1900–1920* (Garden City, N.Y.: Anchor Press/Doubleday, 1975), pp. 132–73; St. Clair Drake and Horace R. Cayton, *Black Metropolis: A Study of Negro Life in a Northern City,* vol. 1 (1945; rev. New York: Harcourt, Brace, and World, 1962), pp. 58–83; Gunnar Myrdal, *An American Dilemma: The Negro Problem and Modern Democracy,* vol. 1 (1944; rept. New York: Pantheon Books, 1972), pp. 291–96.

3. Ray Hughes Whitbeck, *The Geography and Economic Development of Southeastern Wisconsin* (Madison: State of Wisconsin, 1921), pp. 90–117; Bayrd

Still, *Milwaukee: The History of A City* (1948; rept. Madison: State Historical Society of Wisconsin, 1965), pp. 476–79.

4. Justin Galford, "The Foreign Born and Urban Growth in the Great Lakes, 1850–1950: A Study of Chicago, Cleveland, Detroit, and Milwaukee" (Ph.D. diss., New York University, 1957), pp. 267–88; Still, *Milwaukee*, pp. 453–75, 560–61.

5. Thomas W. Gavett, *Development of the Labor Movement in Milwaukee* (Madison: University of Wisconsin Press, 1965), pp. 114–51; Still, *Milwaukee*, p. 497.

6. Still, *Milwaukee*, pp. 515–68.

7. Henri, *Black Migration*, pp. 49–80; Emmett J. Scott, *Negro Migration During the War* (1920; rept. New York: Arno Press, 1969); Louise Venable Kennedy, *The Negro Peasant Turns Cityward: Effects of Recent Migrations to Northern Cities* (New York: Columbia University Press, 1930); Spear, *Black Chicago*, p. 29; "The Colored Man Comes North," *Milwaukee Journal*, 19 Aug. 1917.

8. George A. Davis and O. Fred Donaldson, *Blacks in the United States: A Geographic Perspective* (Boston: Houghton Mifflin, 1975), pp. 53–93; Henri, *Black Migration*, pp. 49–80; "The Colored Man Comes North," *Milwaukee Journal*, 19 Aug. 1917; "Let the Exodus Continue," *Wisconsin Enterprise Blade*, 16 Nov. 1916; "Special Notice," *Blade*, 29 Aug. 1918.

9. Scott, *Negro Migration*, pp. 111–18; Henri, *Black Migration*, pp. 53–56; Richard Walter Thomas, "From Peasant to Proletarian: The Formation and Organization of the Black Industrial Working Class in Detroit, 1915–1945" (Ph.D. diss., University of Michigan, 1976), pp. 6–7. Also see n. 2 of this chapter for sources discussing a similar change in other northern cities. For full references on the demographic characteristics of Milwaukee's black population between 1915 and 1930, see Joe William Trotter, Jr., "The Making of an Industrial Proletariat: Black Milwaukee, 1915–1945" (Ph.D. diss., University of Minnesota, 1980), tables 3.2 through 3.4.

10. Interview with James A. Fields, 27 Aug. 1979; Still, *Milwaukee*, pp. 572–73; Spear, *Black Chicago*, pp. 129–30; August Meier and Elliott Rudwick, *Black Detroit and the Rise of the UAW* (New York: Oxford University Press, 1979), pp. 1–22; Thomas, "From Peasant to Proletarian," pp. 2–32; Scott, *Negro Migration*, pp. 111–18.

11. Scott, *Negro Migration*, pp. 101–13; Thomas R. Buchanan, "Black Milwaukee, 1890–1915" (master's thesis, University of Wisconsin–Milwaukee, 1968), pp. 4–5; interview with Ardie A. Halyard, 14 Aug. 1979.

12. Scott, *Negro Migration*, pp. 113–15. Scott actually based his analysis of migration to Milwaukee on a larger study entitled *Report on the Migration to Chicago* by Charles S. Johnson. The Library of Congress has rough

drafts of chapters from the study, but the original data on Milwaukee are not available. Neither is the original study in the Charles S. Johnson papers at Fisk University nor at the University of Chicago where Johnson was a graduate student at the time.

13. J. Harvey Kerns to T. Arnold Hill, "Observations on the Industrial Campaign," 16 Nov. 1927, Ser. 4, Box 31, National Urban League Papers: Milwaukee Branch Files (Manuscript Division, Library of Congress); Scott, *Negro Migration,* pp. 113–15;

14. Interview with John Williams, 10 Aug. 1979; interview with Lawrence E. Miller, 30 Aug. 1979; interview with Calvin Birts, 18 Aug. 1979.

15. Kerns to Hill, "Observations on the Industrial Campaign."

16. For general discussions of these issues, see William H. Harris, *The Harder We Run* (New York: Oxford, 1982), Chapter 2, and Philip S. Foner, *Organized Labor and the Black Worker* (New York: Praeger 1974). Kerns to Hill, "Observations on the Industrial Campaign."

17. For a summary of Johnson's survey, see Scott, *Negro Migration,* p. 115.

18. Frank J. Weber, "Shortage of Labor," Box 3, Federated Trades Council of Milwaukee Papers (University of Wisconsin–Milwaukee, Area Research Center).

19. Daniel W. Hoan, "Work Among Language and Racial Groups," Box 26, File 98, Daniel Webster Hoan Papers, 1910–53 (Milwaukee County Historical Society); Milton Cantor, *The Divided Left: American Radicalism 1900–1975* (New York: Hill and Wang, 1978), pp. 3–15; Scott, *Negro Migration,* p. 116.

20. Interview with James A. Fields, 27 Aug. 1979.

21. "Strikes and Labor Disputes, 1917–1938," Box 22, File 82, Hoan Papers; Daniel W. Hoan to Richard Charlton, 8 Oct. 1919; Charlton to Hoan, 11 Oct. 1919, Box 22, File 98, Hoan Papers.

22. Eugene Cooney to Hoan, 26 July 1922, Box 22, File 82, Hoan Papers; Hoan to H. E. Byram, 27 July 1922, and William H. Finley to Hoan, 29 July 1922, Box 22, File 82, Hoan Papers.

23. Gavett, *Development of the Labor Movement in Milwaukee,* pp. 138–40; Elliott Rudwick, *Race Riot at East St. Louis, July 2, 1917* (Carbondale: Southern Illinois University Press, 1964); Spear, *Black Chicago,* pp. 158–66; William M. Tuttle, "Labor Conflict and Racial Violence: The Black Worker in Chicago, 1894–1919," *Labor History* 10, no. 3 (Summer 1969): 408–32, Allan Spear, "The Origins of the Urban Ghetto, 1870–1915," in Nathan I. Huggins, Martin Kilson, and Daniel M. Fox, eds., *Key Issues in the Afro-American Experience,* vol. 2 (New York: Harcourt Brace Jovanovich, 1971), pp. 153–66. Spear argues in this essay that nearly "every overt racial clash in the North in the early twentieth century involved conflict between blacks and workingclass whites. . . . In many instances labor disputes led directly to attacks on black workers by white

strikers and their sympathizers." "Milwaukeeans Frown upon Strike-breakers: Colored Population of City Resent Importation of Colored Men From Other Sections; Think it Bad Move of Railroads," *Blade,* 12 Aug. 1922; *Milwaukee City Directory* (Milwaukee: Wright's City Directory, 1922).

24. "Victim of Circumstances," *Blade,* 5 Aug. 1922.

25. Robert W. Wells, "Negro Migration Came Late," *Milwaukee Journal,* 8 Nov. 1967.

26. Interview with Ardie A. Halyard, 14 Aug. 1979; J. Harvey Kerns, "Industrial Outlook and the Negro of Milwaukee," *Blade,* 3 Sept. 1927.

27. Milwaukee Urban League Monthly Report, Apr. 1928 (Milwaukee Public Library).

28. Interview with James A. Fields, 27 Aug. 1979; John Gurda, "Change at the River Mouth: Ethnic Succession on Milwaukee's Jones Island, 1700–1922" (master's thesis, University of Wisconsin–Milwaukee, 1978).

29. MUL Monthly Reports, Mar. 1928 and Jan. 1928; Still, *Milwaukee,* pp. 478–79.

30. MUL Monthly Reports, Mar. 1925 through Dec. 1932.

31. MUL Monthly Reports, Feb. 1931, May 1931, Apr. 1932, Dec. 1928, June–July–Aug. 1929, and Apr. 1930.

32. Kusmer, *A Ghetto Takes Shape,* pp. 190–205; Spear, *Black Chicago,* pp. 151–66; Drake and Cayton, *Black Metropolis,* vol. 1, pp. 214–62. For full reference to comparative employment patterns of black workers see Trotter, "The Making of an Industrial Proletariat," Table 3.11 A-1 and 3.11 A-2.

33. Scott, *Negro Migration,* pp. 116–17; Herbert G. Gutman, *Work, Culture, and Society in Industrializing America: Essays in American Working Class and Social History* (1966; rept. New York: Random House, 1977), pp. 3–78; David Montgomery, *Workers' Control in America: Studies in the History of Work, Technology, and Labor Struggles* (Cambridge: Cambridge University Press, 1979), pp. 1–8.

34. Interview with Lawrence E. Miller, 30 Aug. 1979; Scott, *Negro Migration,* p. 117; William F. Kirk, "Labor Turnover in Milwaukee," *Monthly Labor Review* 8, no. 4 (1919): 53–70.

35. Gutman, *Work, Culture, and Society,* pp. 14–19; Scott, *Negro Migration,* pp. 117–18, n. 1.

36. S. R. Banks to the Colored Workingmen's Liberty Club, letter reprinted in *Blade,* 25 Oct. 1917; *Blade,* 27 Mar. 1926.

37. Interracial Committee of Council of Social Agencies, "Survey of the Negro Population of Milwaukee, Wisc. 1928," Ser. 6, Box 59, NUL Papers; "Summary of the Findings of the Unit Survey," Box 20, United Community Services of Greater Milwaukee Papers, 1903–66 (University of Wisconsin–Milwaukee, Area Research Center).

38. William Bryant, president of Local 88, presented the resolution to the Federated Trades Council at its first meeting in June 1925; *Blade,* 13 June 1925.

39. "Federated Trades Council of Milwaukee Boosts American Negro Labor Congress," *Blade,* 20 June 1925; Spero and Harris, *The Black Worker,* p. 425.

40. James W. Ford to James Weldon Johnson, 23 Feb. 1928, Box G-219, National Association for the Advancement of Colored People Papers (Manuscript Division, Library of Congress); Progressive Labor League of Milwaukee Circular Letter, ca. 25 Feb. 1928, Box G-219, NAACP Papers.

41. *Blade,* 22 Nov. 1917, 28 Mar. 1918, 23 May 1918, 18 July 1918, 22 Aug. 1918, 29 Aug. 1925; interview with John Williams, 10 Aug. 1979; interview with Ernest Bland, 8 Aug. 1979.

42. "Labor Unions," *Blade,* 2 Aug. 1917, 5 Aug. 1922, 20 June 1925.

43. Nancy Weiss, *The National Urban League, 1910-1940* (New York: Oxford University Press, 1974), pp. 206-9. T. Arnold Hill to James H. Kerns, 25 June 1925, and Kerns to Hill, 16 Nov. 1927, Ser. 4, Box 31, NUL Papers; *Blade,* 3 Sept. 1927; MUL Monthly Report, Apr. 1928.

44. MUL Monthly Reports, Nov. 1927, Feb. 1929, and MUL Annual Report, period ending 30 Sept. 1927; "Statement of the Activities of the Branch for the Year Ending November 15, 1928," Box G-219, NAACP Papers.

45. MUL Monthly Reports, Nov. 1927, Mar. 1925, Dec. 1926, Oct. 1927; T. Arnold Hill to H. E. Reinsrider, 1 Nov. 1927, Frank Persons to T. Arnold Hill, 4 Nov. 1927, and William V. Kelley to T. Arnold Hill, 13 Jan. 1930, Ser. 4, Box 31, NUL Papers; MUL Monthly Reports, Mar. 1927, Dec. 1927, Jan. 1928, Feb. 1928, Feb. 1929, June–July–August 1929, and Nov. 1930.

46. Wells, "Negro Migration Came Late"; Council of Social Agencies, "Survey of the Negro Population of Milwaukee, Wisc. 1928," NUL Papers.

47. Karl E. and Alma F. Taeuber, *Negroes in Cities: Residential Segregation and Neighborhood Change* (Chicago: Aldine, 1965), pp. 28-68; Spear, *Black Chicago,* pp. 22-23; Osofsky, *Harlem,* pp. 107-9; Kusmer, *A Ghetto Takes Shape,* pp. 166-71. Kusmer argues that "it was not suburbanites who were chiefly responsible for the shaping of the black ghetto during the post-war years. The suburban housing market was simply too expensive for the vast majority of black Clevelanders. A much more important factor in commanding and channeling the black population was the staunch resistance of certain ethnic groups." In Milwaukee such ethnic lines were not as sharply drawn, but there was clearcut competition between blacks and whites of low socioeconomic status.

48. Scott, *Negro Migration,* p. 118; "Who is to Blame?" *Blade,* 7 Feb. 1925.
49. "Housing of Negroes: Milwaukee Problem," *Blade,* 16 Oct. 1926; Edith Elmer Wood, *Slums and Blighted Areas in the United States* (Washington: Federal Administration of Public Works, Housing Bulletin No. 1, 1935); "Summary of the Findings of the Unit Survey," Box 20, UCS Papers.
50. Wm. V. Kelley to Hill, 11 May 1931, Ser. 4, Box 31, NUL Papers.
51. Council of Social Agencies, "Survey of the Negro Population of Milwaukee, Wisc. 1928," NUL Papers; United States Bureau of the Census, *Fifteenth Census of the U.S.: 1930. Population, vol. 6: Families* (Washington: Government Printing Office, 1932); "Housing of Negroes," *Blade,* 16 Oct. 1926; "Report of the Brief Housing Study Made in Summer of 1929," Box 20, UCS Papers.
52. Vivian Lenard, "From Progressivism to Procrastination: The Fight for the Creation of a Permanent Housing Authority for the City of Milwaukee, 1933–1945" (master's thesis, University of Wisconsin–Milwaukee, 1967), pp. 38–43; "Garden Homes Housing Project, Milwaukee, Wisconsin," Box 19, File 73, Hoan Papers; Still, *Milwaukee,* pp. 40–41.
53. "Proposes City Negro District: Real Estate Board to Study Plans for Redistricting Blacks," *Milwaukee Journal,* 16 Sept. 1924; Paula Lynagh, "Milwaukee's Negro Community" (Milwaukee: Citizens Governmental Research Bureau, 1946), pp. 17–18; "Housing of Negroes: Milwaukee Problem," *Blade,* 16 Oct. 1926.
54. See chapters 3 and 4 for the manner in which black business and professional people, politicians, and ministers benefitted from the ghettoization process.
55. *Blade,* 22 Feb. 1917, 28 Feb. 1925, and 22 Nov. 1917.
56. MUL Annual Report, period ending 30 Sept. 1927; William V. Kelley, "The Story of the Milwaukee Urban League" (Newspaper Clippings File of the Milwaukee Urban League, ca. 1945).
57. "Columbia Building and Loan Assn' Opens Books: $5,000 Worth of Stock Sold on First Day," *Blade,* 13 June 1925, 10 Jan. 1925, 12 June 1926, 17 July 1926; interview with Ardie A. Halyard, 14 Aug. 1979.

# 3

## Emergence of
## the New Middle Class

Despite low wages, poor working conditions, and inadequate housing, the expanding Afro-American, urban-industrial working class constituted the demographic and financial foundation from which a larger and stronger, though still weak, black middle class emerged between 1915 and 1932. As in other northern cities, a tiny business and professional elite dominated this class. Although less than elsewhere, the great migration to Milwaukee stimulated the dream of a Black Metropolis, a city within a city, that would fundamentally cater to the needs of Afro-Americans. The competitive conflict that underlay the struggle for jobs and housing also characterized the search for entrepreneurial and professional opportunities. As in jobs and housing, blacks were relegated to the least skilled and less remunerative professional and business pursuits.

Nevertheless, the dream of a Black Metropolis signaled the decline of an earlier business and professional elite based primarily upon service to a white clientele. The new middle class, under the leadership of its small elite, would seek to reconcile its philosophy of economic self-help and racial solidarity with the ideological outlook of the old elite. The forceful thrust for the full integration of blacks into the socioeconomic and political life of the city would increasingly gain its support. Conversely, the old elite would incorporate aspects of the racial self-help philosophy and behavior.[1] Both groups recognized the economic opportunities inherent in the expanding black population.

Milwaukee was considered an excellent place for the initiation of black enterprises. A visitor to the city in 1925 remarked that after "surveying your beautiful city for three days, it has struck me wonderfully as a city of opportunities. . . as a Negro business center."[2] Optimism regarding Milwaukee as a black business center arose primarily from a deepening awareness of the material potential of factory wages, though income derived from domestic service comprised a significant supplement to that gained through Afro-American industrial employment. The growing black population, increasingly concentrated in a sharply circumscribed area of the city, formed the basis of Afro-American business and professional expansion during the 1920s.

The number of blacks engaged in professional, business, and clerical occupations increased from 80 in 1910 to 301 by 1930. This included an increase of 120.7 percent between 1920 and 1930. Black proprietors led the list with 3.5 percent of the total labor force in 1930. Professional people (3.4 percent) and clerical workers (1.2 percent) followed (see Table 3.1). With their small percentages in business and professional pursuits from the beginning of the period, the number of Afro-American proprietors and professionals expanded at a rate faster than that of the city at large.

Afro-Americans were almost completely excluded from clerical occupations. Although black women acquired more clerical positions than did men during the 1920s, these pursuits constituted the lowest percentage (3.2) of black women in the labor force. The almost total absence of Afro-American women as telephone operators in the rapidly expanding communications industry reflected their depressed status in the clerical field. Black women found positions only slowly and primarily as a consequence of expanding black enterprises or city agencies such as the Public Health Department which were committed to serving black clients (see tables 3.1, 3.2, and 3.3).

While a small number of black business establishments had developed by 1915,[3] blacks in the city did not yet have a funeral business, a building and loan association, or a community drug store. The community had only one struggling and irregular weekly newspaper, the *Milwaukee Enterprise,* which later merged with the *Wisconsin Weekly Blade* to form the *Wisconsin Enterprise Blade.* By the mid-1920s, chiefly under the impact of demand for factory labor occasioned by World War I and its aftermath, black businesses expanded to include several hotels, a drug store, real estate agencies, funeral homes, a more

Table 3.1. Total Black Professional, Business, and Clerical Occupations, 1910–30

| Category | 1910 Number | 1910 Percent | 1920 Number | 1920 Percent | 1930 Number | 1930 Percent | Percent Increase 1910–20 | Percent Increase 1920–30 |
|---|---|---|---|---|---|---|---|---|
| Total Labor Force | 623 | 100.0 | 1,277 | 100.0 | 3,638 | 100.0 | 104.9 | 184.8 |
| Professional | 26 | 4.1 | 25 | 3.5 | 126 | 3.4 | 72.0 | 180.0 |
| Proprietary | 40 | 6.4 | 55 | 4.3 | 120 | 3.5 | 37.5 | 57.3 |
| Clerical | 14 | 2.2 | 31 | 2.4 | 46 | 1.2 | 121.4 | 48.3 |
| Total | 80 | 12.8 | 131 | 10.2 | 301 | 8.2 | 63.7 | 120.7 |

Source: See appendixes 3, 4, and 5.

Table 3.2. Black Professional, Business, and Clerical Occupations by Sex, 1910–30

| Category | 1910 Number | 1910 Percent | 1920 Number | 1920 Percent | 1930 Number | 1930 Percent | Percent Increase 1910–20 | Percent Increase 1920–30 |
|---|---|---|---|---|---|---|---|---|
| Male: Total Labor Force | 438 | 100.0 | 988 | 100.0 | 2,797 | 100.0 | 125.5 | 183.0 |
| Professional | 22 | 5.0 | 41 | 4.1 | 97 | 3.4 | 86.3 | 136.5 |
| Proprietary | 26 | 5.9 | 36 | 3.6 | 67 | 2.3 | 38.4 | 86.1 |
| Clerical | 10 | 2.2 | 17 | 1.7 | 19 | 0.6 | 70.0 | 11.7 |
| Total | 58 | 13.1 | 94 | 9.4 | 183 | 6.3 | 62.0 | 94.6 |
| Female: Total Labor Force | 185 | 100.0 | 289 | 100.0 | 841 | 100.0 | 56.2 | 191.0 |
| Professional | 4 | 2.1 | 4 | 1.3 | 29 | 3.4 | 0.0 | 625.0 |
| Proprietary | 14 | 7.5 | 19 | 6.4 | 62 | 7.3 | 35.4 | 226.3 |
| Clerical | 4 | 2.1 | 14 | 4.8 | 27 | 3.2 | 250.0 | 92.8 |
| Total | 22 | 11.7 | 37 | 12.5 | 118 | 13.9 | 68.1 | 218.9 |

Source: See appendixes 3, 4, and 5.

regular black weekly, and a building and loan association. These establishments emerged in conjunction with a number of small restaurants, cafes, hotels, rooming houses, commercial laundries, and other, even smaller, more traditional operations such as shoe-shine parlors. Located in one block on Sixth Street between Vliet and Cherry in 1918, black businesses gradually moved, as did the community, further north and west during the 1920s. A 1929 socioeconomic survey of the black population showed that Afro-American enterprises had moved, with the expanding ghetto, west to Seventh Street and north to Walnut Street. An estimated 150 establishments of various kinds emerged by the late 1920s.[4]

These businesses represented a fundamental shift from the prewar pattern of black enterprises. As shown in Chapter 1, before World War I black businesses catered mainly to white customers or, as often happened in Milwaukee, to both blacks and whites. Between 1915 and 1932, there was a decided shift toward enterprises serving an exclusively or nearly all-black clientele. This process reflected the emergence of the new black middle class in Milwaukee. That process began before the war in larger cities such as Chicago, though it proceeded more slowly in cities like Cleveland than in Chicago; in Milwaukee, the new middle class fully emerged in the 1920s.[5]

Unlike the new white middle class, characterized by salaried managers, professionals, and white collar service workers, the new black middle class resembled the old nineteenth-century petit bourgeoisie.[6] The most successful members of the new Afro-American bourgeoisie were owners of small businesses as well as doctors and lawyers. The new black middle class in Milwaukee, as elsewhere, received its greatest expression in the development of black business, though the expansion of blacks in the professions proceeded somewhat more rapidly and comprised an integral component of this class. Many of these people were indeed professionals with business interests. Although the numbers of black men and women proprietors were nearly equal in 1910, black men significantly outnumbered women in business in 1920; by 1930, the number of males in business exceeded females by only five, reflecting the impact of the Depression on black enterprises. Inequality in entrepreneurial opportunities between black men and women also existed in the types of businesses they might operate. Women were largely rooming and boarding house-keepers, restaurant and cafe owners, and operators of beauty shops. Afro-American men owned grocery stores, funeral establishments,

Table 3.3. Selected Clerical Occupations by Ethnicity and Sex, 1920 and 1930

| Category 1920 | Blacks | | Foreign-born Whites | | American-born Whites Foreign-born/Mixed Parentage | | American-born Whites American-born Parentage | |
|---|---|---|---|---|---|---|---|---|
| | Number | Percent | Number | Percent | Number | Percent | Number | Percent |
| Male | | | | | | | | |
| Clerks in stores | 1 | 5.8 | 141 | 4.6 | 504 | 4.2 | 300 | 3.7 |
| Commercial travelers | 1 | 5.8 | 272 | 9.0 | 872 | 7.4 | 676 | 8.5 |
| Real Estate agents and off. | 1 | 5.8 | 143 | 4.7 | 301 | 2.5 | 148 | 1.8 |
| Salesmen (stores) | 3 | 17.6 | 731 | 24.2 | 2,145 | 18.2 | 1,526 | 19.2 |
| Agents | 1 | 5.8 | 117 | 3.8 | 485 | 4.1 | 460 | 5.8 |
| Bookkeepers and Cashiers | 2 | 11.7 | 182 | 6.0 | 1,147 | 9.7 | 658 | 8.3 |
| Clerks (except stores) | 8 | 47.0 | 994 | 33.0 | 4,641 | 39.5 | 2,954 | 37.3 |
| Total* | 17 | 100.0 | 2,580 | 85.6 | 10,096 | 86.0 | 6,722 | 84.9 |
| Female | | | | | | | | |
| Clerks (stores) | 2 | 14.2 | 126 | 10.6 | 814 | 8.5 | 445 | 6.4 |
| Saleswomen | 2 | 14.2 | 337 | 28.5 | 1,536 | 16.1 | 789 | 11.5 |
| Bookkeepers | 2 | 14.2 | 163 | 13.8 | 1,462 | 15.3 | 1,013 | 14.7 |
| Clerks (except stores) | 6 | 42.8 | 195 | 16.5 | 2,163 | 22.7 | 1,646 | 24.0 |
| Stenographers and Typists | 2 | 14.2 | 259 | 21.9 | 2,701 | 28.3 | 2,293 | 33.4 |
| Total* | 14 | 100.0 | 1,080 | 91.6 | 8,676 | 91.1 | 6,186 | 90.3 |

*These figures are based upon an internal analysis of clerical occupations alone.

| Category 1930 | Blacks | | Foreign-born Whites | | American-born Whites/All | |
| --- | --- | --- | --- | --- | --- | --- |
| | Number | Percent | Number | Percent | Number | Percent |
| Male | | | | | | |
| Commercial travelers | 1 | 5.2 | 183 | 5.0 | 1,235 | 4.4 |
| Real Estate agents and officers | 1 | 5.2 | 372 | 10.3 | 1,071 | 3.8 |
| Salesmen | 7 | 36.8 | 1,231 | 34.1 | 8,443 | 30.1 |
| Clerks (except stores) | 9 | 47.3 | 1,021 | 28.3 | 10,025 | 35.7 |
| Stenographers and Typists | 1 | 5.2 | 8 | 0.2 | 169 | 0.6 |
| Total* | 19 | 100.0 | 2,815 | 78.1 | 20,942 | 74.6 |
| Female | | | | | | |
| Clerks (stores) | 3 | 11.1 | 175 | 11.6 | 1,510 | 6.4 |
| Saleswomen | 8 | 29.6 | 460 | 30.6 | 3,719 | 15.8 |
| Telephone Operators | 1 | 3.7 | 108 | 7.1 | 1,877 | 7.9 |
| Bookkeepers | 4 | 14.8 | 168 | 11.1 | 3,074 | 12.0 |
| Clerks (except stores) | 8 | 29.6 | 277 | 18.4 | 5,818 | 24.7 |
| Stenographers and Typists | 3 | 11.1 | 281 | 18.6 | 7,013 | 29.8 |
| Total* | 27 | 100.0 | 1,469 | 97.7 | 23,011 | 97.8 |

*These figures are based upon an internal analysis of clerical occupations alone.

Source: See appendixes 4 and 5.

building and loan associations, and drug stores in addition to restaurants, cafes, and barber shops. Black women, however, did play a vital role in enterprises headed by men (see Table 3.4).

Afro-Americans established all of their larger and most profitable businesses in the wake of the migration, increasing spatial concentration, and black transition to the industrial work force. Daniel W. Raynor began conducting funerals in Milwaukee by 1919 and received congratulations for "excellent arrangements." By 1925, Raynor and his wife, Nellie B. Raynor, succeeded in establishing a thriving funeral business at 414 Cherry Street. Raynor later formed an association with his foster son, E. H. Reed, renamed the business Raynor and Reed's Funeral Home, and sustained operations into the early 1930s. Two other funeral businesses emerged during the period, those of Carl F. Watson and Emile O'Bee. Watson, born in Jacksonville, Illinois, worked full time in the funeral business in Chicago and prepared funerals in Milwaukee on a commuter basis. He helped establish the O'Bee Funeral Home in 1925 and by 1930 initiated his own funeral business in the city.[7]

The most important retail establishment to open during the period was the Community Drug Store. Corporately owned and billed as the only store of its kind owned and operated by blacks in the state, Community opened in 1925 at the corner of Seventh and Cherry streets. Officers of the store included some of the leading members of the emerging professional and business elite: Dr. Edgar Thomas, president; attorney George DeReef, vice-president; J. Harvey Kerns, secretary; and Charles Pearson, treasurer. Attorney A. B. Nutt, Rev. Fountain W. Penick, pastor of Mt. Zion Baptist Church, W. W. McFarland, owner of a car washing service, and Dr. P. Jay Gilmer served as board members. Roy Peoples, a common laborer, was also a board member, thereby demonstrating how racial discrimination in the socioeconomic life of the city cemented a continuing bond between black workers and the middle class. Based on a capital stock of $10,000 with shares at $10 each, the business was furnished with "modern equipment" designed by the Northwestern Furniture Company. The black contractor, J. W. Bryant, installed the electrical equipment and Dr. P. Jay Gilmer, a pharmacy and M.D. graduate of the University of Pittsburgh Medical School, supervised the day-to-day operations of the store.[8]

As the black population expanded and racial barriers in the city's restaurant, hotel, and housing market intensified, black entrepreneurs found the Afro-American market in these areas quite appealing. The most dynamic expansion of black business enterprise responded to demands for housing as well as for cultural, recreational, and food services. Although a few prewar establishments such as the Turf Hotel shared the hotel patronage, several new hotels emerged during and following the war. While most of these establishments served working-class blacks, some Afro-American lodging and eating places geared their services to the emerging new elite and to whites as well.

The Alberta Villa, the most significant hotel to begin business in the immediate wake of the migration, opened in 1917 under the ownership of Hollis B. Kinner. Born in Georgia, Kinner came to Milwaukee in 1897. He joined his brother who had operated a restaurant in prewar Milwaukee on North Third Street. Kinner would open a sausage firm in 1929, despite the deepening economic depression, that would thrive during the 1930s, but for most of the 1920s Kinner operated a commercial laundry and the Alberta Villa.[9] The *Blade* described the hotel, a converted private residence of an old German family at the corner of Fifth and Galena streets, as the greatest enterprise that Milwaukee "has yet witnessed and one which indicates clearly the advance which some of our citizens are making toward real service and efficiency." The paper went on to describe the firm in some detail and hailed it as a step toward better housing for visitors as well as for local blacks.[10]

Following a brief lull during the postwar economic retrenchment, 1919 to 1922, expansion in hotels, boarding houses, and restaurants continued through the later 1920s. As each establishment opened its doors for business, the *Blade* roundly applauded the achievement as another step toward self-sufficiency and development of the black urban economy. In its 17 April 1926 issue, for example, the *Blade* announced the opening of the Angel Food Tea Shop, another major hotel serving blacks. The headline proclaimed: "Milwaukee to Have a $25,000 Tea Room and Hotel at 515 Galena Street." Several distinguished black guests visited the restaurant while in Milwaukee. Congressman Oscar DePriest of Chicago wrote in the guest book: "Everyman should have an equal chance." Some white notables also dined at the establishment: "Next to home," the movie actress Mae West wrote, "this is the best. Take my word."[11]

The Columbia Building and Loan Association (CBLA) emerged as the most successful of the new black businesses. Wilbur Halyard and his wife, Ardie, spearheaded the formation of the CBLA. The

Table 3.4. Selected Proprietary Occupations by Ethnicity and Sex, 1920 and 1930

| Category | Blacks | | Foreign-born Whites | | American-born Whites Foreign-born/Mixed Parentage | | American-born Whites American-born Parentage | |
|---|---|---|---|---|---|---|---|---|
| | Number | Percent | Number | Percent | Number | Percent | Number | Percent |
| **1920** | | | | | | | | |
| **Male** | | | | | | | | |
| Restaurant, Cafe, Lunch. | 6 | 16.6 | 111 | 2.0 | 57 | 0.9 | 33 | 1.0 |
| Retail Dealers | 17 | 47.2 | 2,753 | 51.0 | 2,225 | 37.8 | 900 | 27.8 |
| Barbers, Hairdressers | 13 | 36.1 | 323 | 5.9 | 329 | 5.6 | 188 | 5.8 |
| Total* | 36 | 100.0 | 3,187 | 58.9 | 2,611 | 44.3 | 1,121 | 34.6 |
| **Female** | | | | | | | | |
| Boarding and Lodging House | 15 | 78.9 | 234 | 43.5 | 389 | 49.1 | 173 | 54.5 |
| Barbers, Hairdressers | 4 | 21.0 | 19 | 3.5 | 90 | 11.3 | 66 | 20.8 |
| Total* | 19 | 100.0 | 253 | 47.0 | 479 | 60.4 | 239 | 75.3 |
| **1930** | | | | | American-born Whites/All | | | |
| **Male** | | | | | | | | |
| Manufacturers | 2 | 2.9 | 455 | 7.8 | 742 | 5.7 | | |
| Building and Contractors | 2 | 2.9 | 351 | 6.0 | 957 | 7.4 | | |
| Garage Owners, Mgr., Off. | 2 | 2.9 | 40 | 0.6 | 241 | 1.8 | | |
| Truck, Transfer, and Cab | 3 | 4.4 | 41 | 0.6 | 176 | 1.3 | | |
| Bankers, Brokers, and Money Lenders | 1 | 1.4 | 90 | 1.5 | 791 | 6.1 | | |

| | Blacks | | Foreign-born Whites | | American-born Whites/All | |
| --- | --- | --- | --- | --- | --- | --- |
| | Number | Percent | Number | Percent | Number | Percent |
| Retail Dealers | 25 | 37.3 | 3,382 | 58.0 | 4,875 | 38.0 |
| Undertakers | 3 | 4.4 | 25 | 0.4 | 153 | 1.1 |
| Restaurant, Cafe, and Lunch. | 6 | 8.9 | 340 | 5.8 | 267 | 2.0 |
| Officials and Inspectors | 2 | 2.9 | 19 | 0.3 | 139 | 1.0 |
| Barbers, Hairdressers | 21 | 31.3 | 413 | 7.0 | 914 | 7.1 |
| Total* | 67 | 100.0 | 5,178 | 88.9 | 9,255 | 72.1 |

*These figures are based upon an internal analysis of proprietary occupations alone.

| Category | Blacks | | Foreign-born Whites | | American-born Whites/All | |
| --- | --- | --- | --- | --- | --- | --- |
| 1930 | Number | Percent | Number | Percent | Number | Percent |
| Female | | | | | | |
| Boarding and Lodging House | 24 | 38.7 | 302 | 47.7 | 739 | 35.2 |
| Retail Dealers | 4 | 6.4 | 217 | 34.3 | 510 | 24.3 |
| Restaurant, Cafe, Lunch. | 12 | 19.3 | 43 | 6.8 | 95 | 4.5 |
| Barbers, Hairdressers | 22 | 35.4 | 62 | 9.8 | 687 | 32.8 |
| Total* | 62 | 100.0 | 624 | 98.7 | 2,031 | 96.9 |

*These figures are based upon an internal analysis of proprietary occupations alone.

Source: See appendixes 4 and 5.

Halyards were born, respectively, in South Carolina and Georgia and graduated from Morehouse College and Atlanta University. They married in 1920 and migrated, during the same year, to Beloit, Wisconsin, where they conducted a housing camp for white workers at the Fairbanks-Morse Corporation. During the economic depression of 1921–22, the Halyards found that their services were no longer required. They heard of the severe housing problems of blacks in Milwaukee and believed the city offered an opportunity for enterprising blacks in the housing field. They came to Milwaukee in 1923 and began procedures for establishing a building and loan association. Columbia was organized by the fall of 1924 and began operations in January 1925. Founding officers of the corporation included Daniel W. Raynor, president; Wilbur Hayard, secretary; Rev. Eugene Thompson, pastor of St. Mark AME Church, vice-president; and Dr. L. T. Gilmer, treasurer. Attorney George DeReef; C. L. Johnson, owner of a tailoring business; F. G. Alleyne, a coal and wood proprietor; William Wims, a chiropractor; and J. W. Bryant served as board members.[12]

Beginning with an authorized capital of $5,000,000, the corporation had two basic goals. It aimed to promote the "saving habit by providing each member with a place to invest their funds" where a profitable return could be guaranteed. It also sought to enhance home ownership by loaning its funds to members who desired "to build or purchase a home or pay off an existing mortgage on monthly payments."[13] The association drew upon both the small savings of numerous working-class blacks and the earnings of the expanding black business and professional class serving mainly Afro-American customers. The loan policies of the company, as with most financial institutions, emphasized stability of income and occupation as well as evidence of the saving habit. Most of the assistance offered by Columbia consequently accrued to the small business and professional elements.[14]

CBLA sustained a steady campaign of promotion into the early years of the Depression. It made consistent appeals to the proletarian as well as to the emerging professional and business base among blacks to "Let Your Rent Pay For Your Home." Under the impact of the Depression, its appeal to black workers became desperate: "Heads of various industries in Milwaukee give preference to individuals who practice the virtues of Thrift and Frugality."[15] Despite its increasing difficulties by the late 1920s, the CBLA remained the most successful enterprise to emerge during the era. As late as 1932, its officers and board of directors remained constant. The association's assets had grown to nearly $73,000, and about thirty mortgage loans, amounting to $62,000, had been granted. The company owned $6,900 worth of property.[16]

However successful the CBLA and other black businesses may have been, Afro-American enterprises never reached their proportionate share (1.2 percent) of the city's businesses. According to the United States Census of Business for 1939, there were only forty-eight black-owned retail establishments in the entire state in 1929. The black population in the state made up 0.3 percent of the total but owned only 0.1 percent of all retail businesses. An estimated 80–90 percent of these businesses were in Milwaukee, the largest center of black population in the state.[17] These businesses accounted for less than the Afro-American proportion of the population in payroll, sales, and all other categories of business operations, except the number of active proprietors not on the payroll. Most were single proprietor or family owned and operated enterprises. According to the *Blade,* blacks in Milwaukee had an estimated $300,000 worth of investments in businesses of all types in 1926. This compared favorably to the approximately $200,000 worth of investments on the eve of World War I, yet it was an infinitesimal proportion of the total business investments for the city as a whole, where the capital employed in industry alone amounted to $136,775,336 in 1929.[18]

Thus, while migration and industrial wages expanded the market for black business, as elsewhere these did not remove the barriers that previously had thwarted Afro-American business development: lack of capital, inability to secure credit, and competition from better-financed white companies.[19] The most successful black businesses leaned heavily upon initial white support, a degree of political influence, and supplemental full-time or part-time employment, or, as often happened, the wife worked to support the husband until the business got on its feet. Wilbur Halyard received support from his wife's full-time position at Goodwill Industries as he made contacts for the CBLA. Ardie Halyard took the job anticipating only a few months employment but actually worked twenty years in support of the business. She also served about eighteen years as an unpaid bookkeeper for the firm. Yet none of the men would entertain the notion of having a woman serve on the board of directors.[20]

The experience of the Halyards also demonstrated that at least the larger and most successful black firms required a degree of white support and political influence. The Halyards entered the city with a letter of recommendation to Mayor Hoan from J. F. Crawford, a white professor at Beloit; Crawford highly recommended Wilbur Halyard for assistance in establishing a "co-operative organization of colored people" in the city.[21] Mayor Hoan favorably responded to Crawford's letter, granted Halyard an interview, and extended essential support. The experience of the Halyards equally illustrated the necessity for viable political contacts on other levels of government as well. According to an interview with Ardie Halyard, a state charter for the company became bogged down in red tape and was not secured until Samuel Banks, a black aide to Governor Phillips, intervened on the company's behalf.[22]

The career of another black businessman, Clarence L. Johnson and his wife, Cleopatra, duplicated many of the problems that confronted the Halyards. C. L. Johnson was born in Dalton, Georgia, and both he and his wife graduated from Tuskegee Institute. Like the Halyards, the Johnsons migrated to Beloit, Wisconsin, and found employment with the Fairbanks-Morse Corporation, which had vigorously recruited southern blacks for foundry work during the war. The Johnsons came to Milwaukee in 1920 when the plant curtailed production and started laying off workers. Tailors by trade, Johnson and his wife opened a tailoring business in 1921. Cleopatra worked full-time at Johns-Manville Company while her husband established the business.[23]

The Johnsons faced initial difficulties because white property owners refused to rent them quarters in which to open the enterprise. It was only through the intervention of a white salesman that they secured a place. The salesman leased the shop at 130 Sycamore (Michigan) Street in his name and allowed the Johnsons to occupy the building in order to conduct their business. When the owner discovered the arrangement, according to Johnson, "he ranted and swore." After securing new pressing equipment through the help of other whites, the Johnsons soon developed a relatively successful business that employed twelve persons, blacks and whites.[24]

Most black business efforts experienced serious difficulties since few blacks who desired to enter business could overcome the initial obstacles: lack of capital, few influential and cooperative white contacts, lack of political influence, and stiff competition from better-financed white chain establishments. Carl Watson, the black funeral director, noted how the Community Drug Store had to struggle against great odds when Walgreen Drug stores expanded throughout the city.[25] Under the impact of the Depression, the foregoing combination of constraints on black business intensified. For example, in 1931, when C. L. Johnson, as a means of employing unemployed black men, sought to establish a car parking service in downtown Milwaukee, his plans were blocked by a hostile reaction from potential white customers.[26] Johnson's difficulties not only highlighted the importance of white assistance in developing black enterprises, but also demonstrated the narrowing opportunities to build businesses catering mainly to whites.

The dream of a black city within the city also included the practices of black professionals as well as their business activities. Similar to black business people, Afro-American professionals moved toward a clientele rooted primarily in the expanding black, urban-industrial working class rather than in the white population. The numbers of blacks in the professions expanded at a faster rate than those in business and clerical positions, increasing by 180.0 percent between 1920 and 1930, compared to 57.3 and 48.3 percent for proprietors and clerical employees. In the wake of the migration, black professionals nearly equaled the number of black proprietors (see Table 3.1).

Changes in black professional positions in the city were not uniform for either the specific occupations involved or for men and women. Most of the gains reflected an expanded number of black men in the professions. The number of black professional men increased by 86.3 percent, twenty-two to forty-one, between 1910 and 1920. This contrasted with the failure of black women to increase their numbers in the professions at all during the same decade. Black women did expand their numbers in the professions from four in 1910 and 1920 to a modest twenty-nine in 1930; by then black professional men numbered nearly one hundred. The discrepancy between men and women was even greater than the figures indicate. Black women disproportionately concentrated in the less-skilled professions such as musicians and teachers of music, the acting field, and social work. Black men occupied similar fields, but they monopolized the ministry and positions as doctors and lawyers (see Table 3.5).

On the other hand, the expansion of black professional men was far less than the foregoing analysis suggests. Physicians increased by only two, from four to six, during the period. Attorneys fared even worse. There was an actual decline in the number of blacks in the legal pro-

Table 3.5. Selected Professional Occupations by Ethnicity and Sex, 1920 and 1930

| Category 1920 | Blacks | | Foreign-born Whites | | American-born Whites Foreign-born/Mixed Parentage | | American-born Whites American-born Parentage | |
|---|---|---|---|---|---|---|---|---|
| | Number | Percent | Number | Percent | Number | Percent | Number | Percent |
| Male | | | | | | | | |
| Authors, Eds., Reporters | 1 | 2.4 | 37 | 3.4 | 61 | 2.4 | 78 | 3.5 |
| Clergymen | 6 | 14.6 | 129 | 11.9 | 133 | 5.2 | 59 | 2.7 |
| Dentists | 2 | 4.8 | 28 | 2.5 | 199 | 7.8 | 156 | 7.1 |
| Draftsmen | 1 | 2.4 | 104 | 9.6 | 418 | 16.5 | 299 | 13.6 |
| Lawyers, Judges, Justices | 2 | 4.8 | 43 | 3.9 | 258 | 10.0 | 284 | 13.0 |
| Musicians and Teachers of Music | 22 | 53.6 | 144 | 13.3 | 180 | 7.1 | 96 | 4.3 |
| Photographers | 1 | 2.4 | 39 | 3.6 | 84 | 3.3 | 54 | 2.4 |
| Physicians and Surgeons | 5 | 12.1 | 104 | 9.6 | 286 | 11.2 | 219 | 10.0 |
| Teachers (school) | 1 | 2.4 | 97 | 8.9 | 176 | 6.9 | 159 | 7.2 |
| Total* | 41 | 100.0 | 725 | 67.0 | 1,795 | 70.8 | 1,404 | 64.2 |
| Female | | | | | | | | |
| Musicians and Teachers of Music | 3 | 75.0 | 29 | 7.1 | 249 | 12.0 | 198 | 12.4 |
| Religious, Charity, Welfare | 1 | 25.0 | 54 | 13.2 | 95 | 4.5 | 71 | 4.4 |
| Total* | 4 | 100.0 | 83 | 20.3 | 344 | 16.5 | 261 | 16.8 |

*These figures are based upon an internal analysis of professional occupations alone.

| Category 1930 | Blacks | | Foreign-born Whites | | American-born Whites/All | |
|---|---|---|---|---|---|---|
| | Number | Percent | Number | Percent | Number | Percent |
| Male | | | | | | |
| Actors and Showmen | 5 | 5.1 | 27 | 2.0 | 179 | 3.0 |
| Authors, Eds., Reporters | 1 | 1.0 | 39 | 2.9 | 191 | 3.2 |
| Chemists, Assayers, Metallurgists | 2 | 2.0 | 45 | 3.4 | 295 | 4.9 |
| Clergymen | 15 | 15.4 | 137 | 10.4 | 276 | 4.6 |
| Dentists | 6 | 6.1 | 44 | 3.3 | 505 | 8.5 |
| Lawyers, Judges, Justices | 3 | 3.0 | 86 | 6.5 | 684 | 11.5 |
| Musicians and Teachers of Music | 58 | 59.7 | 102 | 7.7 | 404 | 7.4 |
| Physicians | 6 | 6.1 | 112 | 8.5 | 615 | 10.3 |
| Technical Engineers | 1 | 1.0 | 264 | 20.1 | 1,328 | 15.7 |
| Total* | 97 | 100.0 | 856 | 65.2 | 4,513 | 69.1 |
| Female | | | | | | |
| Actresses and Showwomen | 8 | 27.5 | 6 | 1.3 | 53 | 0.9 |
| Musicians and Teachers of Music | 9 | 31.0 | 14 | 3.2 | 61 | 1.0 |
| Religious Workers | 2 | 6.8 | 36 | 8.2 | 116 | 2.0 |
| Social Workers | 5 | 17.2 | 14 | 3.2 | 177 | 3.0 |
| Teachers and Lab. Assts. | 3 | 10.3 | 194 | 44.4 | 2,937 | 51.2 |
| Nurses (trained) | 2 | 6.8 | 131 | 30.0 | 1,475 | 25.7 |
| Total* | 29 | 100.0 | 395 | 90.5 | 4,819 | 84.1 |

*These figures are based upon an internal analysis of professional occupations alone.

Source: See appendixes 4 and 5.

fession from four in 1910 to three in 1930. This trend in the top professional jobs paralleled that of other northern cities during the era. The
competitive confrontation of blacks and whites in search of greater
professional opportunities undoubtedly underlay the trend. The total
number of lawyers in the city increased by 57.4 percent between 1910
and 1930, rising from 491 to 773 during the period. Likewise, though
less dramatically, the number of physicians also increased to serve the
growing Milwaukee population. In the face of these changes, black
lawyers and physicians, finding it increasingly difficult to retain white
clients, turned toward the growing black population for support.[27]

The greatest expansion among black professionals took place
within a few limited, less-skilled, and less-profitable occupations.
Musicians and teachers of music registered the most dramatic expansion. When men and women are counted, blacks engaged in music increased by 78.5 percent, fourteen to twenty-five, between 1910 and
1920. By 1930, there were sixty-seven Afro-American musicians in the
city, an increase of 168.0 percent over the previous decade (see Table
3.5). The expansion of blacks into music and show business professions was a response to the expanding cultural and entertainment
needs of the local black community. On the other hand, opportunities
for black entertainers grew partly from the popularity of the black
community as a place for white entertainment.[28] As the Harlem
image of blacks rapidly spread across the urban North, Milwaukee
whites increasingly turned to local black entertainment spots. These
establishments centered around W. Juneau Avenue and W. Vliet
streets between North Sixth and North Seventh streets. The demand
for music in these places augmented the ranks of black musicians.[29]

Afro-American musicians included those who played in and
directed bands as well as those who offered lessons for a fee in their
homes. W. A. Barbour, one of the most outstanding black musicians
to emerge in the wake of the migration, directed, played, and taught
music. Barbour frequently advertised his services in the *Blade* as a
teacher of music and director of large bands for social gatherings. The
most well known black female musician in the city, Gladys Sellers-
Smack, received billing as "Wisconsin's only dramatic soprano."
Sellers-Smack had studied at Madame Azalia Hackley's Conserva-
tory and now offered lessons in her home at 315 4th Street.[30]

Other blacks found employment in professional bands. The most
important of these during the early years had been John H. Wickcliffe
and his Famous Ginger Jazz Band. Comprised of well-trained musicians, the band was billed as the only "Race combination" to play at

the Schlitz Gardens, a beer hall that otherwise restricted black admission. Although originally based in Chicago, the group played in Milwaukee so often that several of its members came from the local black population, and some of those from Chicago took up residence in Milwaukee. Roy Wolfscale, the band's leader, and his wife were among those who moved to Milwaukee.[31] Some musicians built their careers by catering almost exclusively to whites, especially during the early migration years. David Johnson, whose father was a well-known violinist from Chicago, conducted an orchestra composed of more than twenty students, only two of whom were black.[32] Probably the most prominent black musician to emerge during the period was J. Howard Offutt, who came to Milwaukee in 1928. After receiving musical training in voice at the Mandy School of Music in Chicago, Offutt arrived in the city to direct the choir at St. Mark AME church. His impact on the musical life of the city increased in 1932 when he organized the Coleridge-Taylor Singers; named after the famous African-English composer, the group expressed a variety of musical experiences: classics, patriotic, semiclassics, spirituals, and folk songs.[33]

In numbers, clergymen ranked next to musicians. With only three black ministers in 1910, the city had six in 1920 and fifteen by 1930. Only a few of these men received seminary training. Besides black musicians, ministers, and a few physicians and lawyers, Afro-American professionals in the city were few indeed (see Table 3.5). Only four persons stood out as journalists during the period: R. B. Montgomery, James D. Cooke, S. H. Lane, and J. Anthony Josey. None of these men was a trained journalist. Montgomery, as noted in Chapter 2, edited and published the *Wisconsin Weekly Advocate* between 1898 and 1915. Apparently seeking both to expand the paper's midwestern appeal and escape some of the competition engendered by other black weeklies in the city, Montgomery continued his residence in Milwaukee but shifted the paper to Minneapolis, Minnesota, and changed its name to the *National Advocate*. The paper carried a weekly Milwaukee column as a means of retaining local readers.[34]

J. D. Cooke published the *National Defender* from 1905 to 1919. Cooke then moved the paper to Gary, Indiana, the seat of an expanding black industrial population, where it combined with *The Sun,* which Cooke had started in 1910. The paper continued publication as the *National Defender and Sun* until 1920, when it became the *Gary Sun.* The *Milwaukee Enterprise* began publication under the editorship of

S. H. Lane and attorney George DeReef in 1916. The paper published irregularly until about 1925 when it merged with the *Wisconsin Weekly Blade,* a Madison-based weekly under editor and publisher J. A. Josey. Of all the papers to emerge during and following the migration, only papers under Josey's editorship published with any degree of regularity.[35]

Josey was born in Augusta, Georgia, and graduated from Atlanta University. He spent two years at the University of Wisconsin Law School before initiating publication of the *Weekly Blade* in 1916. Josey resided in Madison until 1925 when he moved to Milwaukee and continued his newspaper work under the paper's new name, *Wisconsin Enterprise Blade.* The paper was strongly Republican in its political orientation and persisted as such, at least on national issues, throughout the period. As editor of the *Blade,* Josey took a position on almost every issue of importance in the lives of Afro-Americans in the city.[36]

Several local correspondents for national and regional black newspapers augmented the local black press. Milwaukee blacks served as agents for such papers as the *Chicago Defender,* the *Chicago Sunday Bee,* Cooke's *National Defender and Sun,* and the Madison-based *Wisconsin Weekly Blade.* During the early years of the migration, H. B. Kinner, owner of the Alberta Villa and laundry operator, and Genevieve Reuben, a young woman from Kansas City, gained prominence as local correspondents.[37]

The forceful thrust of black Milwaukeeans to establish themselves in businesses and professions gained organized expression in the formation of the Milwaukee Negro Business League (MNBL). The MNBL was a local chapter of the National Negro Business League, an organization formed under Booker T. Washington's leadership in 1900. Although Milwaukee's branch had been organized during the migration years,[38] by 1925 a special meeting was needed to reinvigorate the unit. The meeting, held at the Urban League office, attracted about forty-five Afro-American business and professional people. The gathering developed out of the general need for "closer cooperation and mutual encouragement." All forty-five persons at the 1925 session repledged themselves to support the MNBL. New officers and board members were elected. Officers included H. B. Kinner, president; George DeReef, vice-president; Dr. B. Nichols, a chiropractor, secretary; and J. H. Kerns, auditor.[39] Milwaukee's Negro Business League immediately launched plans to hold a black business exhibit. The exhibit, held between 6 and 9 May 1926, aimed to depict the business progress of local blacks during the decade 1916 to 1926, encourage Afro-Americans already in business, and "advertise opportunities" available for those who desired to enter business.[40]

As noted in Chapter 2, the persistence of white racial hostility promoted a convergence of interests between black workers and the middle class. That intersection of interests was highlighted when black musicians formed Musicians' Local No. 587 in 1924. Local 587 developed as "a separate self-governing and self-operating" body of union musicians "because of the need of an Independent Body of Musicians, operating under the jurisdiction of the American Federation of Musicians, to take care of the Colored, Union Musicians who had migrated into the Milwaukee, Wisconsin Jurisdiction to play music." Although existence of the union accorded with the AFL practice of permitting separate black locals in those fields where Afro-Americans were too numerous to exclude totally, it also represented ways in which blacks sought to utilize separate locals to help fashion their experience in an often hostile environment. As early as January 1925, the local had established sick and disability assistance as well as death benefit funds for its members. The membership in 1925 included about seventy-five musicians, several part-timers. Many of these musicians would leave the city when the Depression hit in the late 1920s. The organization elected Frank Weaver, a cellist-banjo specialist, as its first president. Other charter members included Georgia Hooper, pianist; Jack Mhore, pianist; Ruth Mhore, pianist-composer; Webster Owsley, drummer; and others.[41]

Just as Afro-Americans were confined to the bottom of the industrial work force, they were relegated to the least profitable and prestigious businesses and professions as well. This obtained despite their voluminous rhetoric of business and professional expansion and modest strides toward that end. The number of black professional and business people, especially business, compared poorly to those in the city as a whole. Afro-American men had 2.3 percent of their numbers in proprietary capacities in 1930 compared to 9.7 percent for all men. The foreign born had a larger percentage of their numbers in businesses than either blacks or American-born whites.

Blacks conducted a narrow range of businesses such as restaurants, cafes, barbershops, and small retail establishments, while other groups operated manufacturing, building and construction, banking, wholesale as well as retail establishments, and a variety of other business firms on a larger scale. In 1920, for example, all black male proprietors could be found in restaurants, small retail business, and barbering, compared to 58.9 percent of immigrants and 34.6 percent of American-born whites (see Table 3.4). Although there was a significant shift in the number and types of black businesses during the 1920s, blacks nevertheless remained restricted to a small number of enterprises. In 1930, 77.5 percent of all black businessmen concentrated in barbering, small retail business, and restaurants. This compared to 47.1 percent for American-born whites.

All women, black and white, operated within a limited scope of business enterprises, yet Afro-American women found even fewer businesses open to them. Considering business enterprises alone (as a separate category), in 1920 all black female proprietors operated beauty shops or boarding and lodging houses. American-born white women had 75.3 percent of their numbers in these businesses. By 1930, black women became involved in a more diversified range of businesses, but the majority of black females continued to operate boarding and lodging houses and beauty parlors, while white women found more opportunities in small retail trade establishments (see Table 3.4).

Afro-Americans likewise found limited access to the professions. Blacks concentrated mainly in the ministry, music, and teaching of music. Afro-American men had 53.6 percent of their professional people in music and teaching of music in 1920. Their white immigrant counterparts had only 13.3 percent of their numbers so engaged; American-born whites had still fewer (4.3 percent) persons in the music field. There was no appreciable shift in the pattern by 1930. Whites, though the edge was distinctly in favor of the American-born, had their numbers more evenly distributed among the more remunerative and prestigious professions such as law and medicine (see Table 3.5).

Blacks had more of their numbers employed as musicians and teachers of music than as show people, in part because, unlike blacks in some larger northern cities, Afro-Americans in Milwaukee failed to develop and sustain a community theater. With the exception of periodic dramatic productions at the Urban League social center during the early 1930s, nothing comparable to the Karamu Theater of Cleveland or the Apollo and Lafayette theaters of New York emerged in Milwaukee.[42]

As with business enterprises, few professions admitted black women. Only four Afro-American women occupied professional positions in 1920 and they served as music and religious or charity workers. Taking the professions alone as an occupational category, neither American-born white women nor immigrant women had more than 20 percent of their numbers in music and religious or charity work. Although the number of professions open to black women diversified during the 1920s, the majority of black females still concentrated in the less economically viable positions of religious and social work, acting, and music, while other women found most of their numbers in the better positions of teaching and nursing. In 1930, there were only 17.1 percent of all Afro-American professional women in teaching and nursing compared to 74.4 percent for immigrant women and 76.9 percent for American-born white women (see Table 3.5).

Like their counterparts in business, black men and women who managed to enter the professions and survive found the returns for their labor below that of comparable white practitioners.[43] To be sure, black professionals, like those in the larger society, sought to distinguish their "social service" function, especially the securing of equality before the law and tending to the health needs of the community, from what Talcott Parsons has called the peculiarly "market-oriented business groups." But probably more than in the larger social system, in part because of their small numbers, black business and professional people, under the process of proletarianization, merged business and social service functions in a manner suggested by C. Wright Mills: "When we speak of the commercialization of the professions or the professionalization of business, we point to the conflict or the merging of skill and money. Out of this merging, professions have become more like businesses, and businesses have become more like professions. The line between them has in many places become obscured."[44]

Afro-Americans in Milwaukee compared favorably to blacks in other northern cities in the percentage of their numbers in business and professions (see Table 3.5), yet blacks in Milwaukee were actually more limited in their business and professional development than blacks in larger cities. Afro-Americans in cities such as Chicago, New York, Philadelphia, and to a lesser extent Cleveland had a greater prewar variety and number of businesses than blacks in Milwaukee; the migration, increasing spatial concentration, and the shift of blacks into the industrial work force promoted further diversification and expansion. In Chicago, for example, there was a notable breakthrough

in the insurance field. Banks and real estate agencies also operated on
a grander scale in these other northern cities. There were no black
realtors in Milwaukee comparable to the Afro-American Realty Company of Harlem or the Cleveland Realty Housing and Investment
Company. Such companies played a vital role in the transfer and rental of ghetto properties. Although the Columbia Building and Loan
Association and black realtors in Milwaukee extended their influence
over the housing market available to blacks, the small demographic
and economic base of the black population imposed fundamental re-
straints on their efforts. Moreover, the CBLA's corporate structure
placed limitations on its acquisition and holding of property for specu-
lative purposes.[45]

Differences in the type, scale, and success of black enterprises in
larger cities generated three sharp contrasts to the experience of blacks
in Milwaukee. First, the development of larger banking, insurance,
and real estate enterprises in other northern cities promoted greater
economic exploitation there than in Milwaukee. Kusmer has noted,
for example, that the Cleveland Housing and Realty Company, like
its white counterparts, charged exorbitant rents for ghetto housing. In
his comprehensive study of black banking institutions, Abram L.
Harris found that interest rates on many loans to black wage earners
were as excessive as those of the loan shark and pawn broker. Such
large-scale intraracial exploitation did not develop in Milwaukee. On
the other hand, however, since black clerical and professional
employees in other cities found jobs in expanding enterprises serving
Afro-American clientele, the failure of black businesses to diversify
and expand as much in Milwaukee placed greater limits on black
employment.[46]

Finally, contrasts in the growth of black businesses would make the
division between the old and new elites less distinct in Milwaukee
than elsewhere. Additonally, the lines between the old and new elites
in Milwaukee blurred partly because of the latter's later emergence, in
conjunction with the tremendous northward migration and the
dynamic shift of blacks into the industrial work force. The individuals
who staffed and/or owned Milwaukee's black enterprises were of old
as well as new elite ideological persuasions, yet, as elsewhere during
the 1920s,[47] the "New Negro" surfaced as most of these individuals
sought to reconcile the paradoxical currents of integration and civil
rights protest with a philosophy and practice of racial self-help and
solidarity. The lives of the most influential black professional and

business people reflected these ideological forces, and the efforts to reconcile them.

Unlike other northern cities, Milwaukee had no lawyers with a long prewar practice when the migration got underway. William T. Green, the active prewar black lawyer, died in 1911 and left the city without a practicing black attorney. James G. Thurman, George DeReef, and James W. Dorsey were the three active lawyers during the period. None of them arrived in Milwaukee before 1913. Thurman, the oldest of the three, came to Milwaukee around 1915 from a practice in Superior, Wisconsin. Admitted to the Wisconsin state bar through the efforts of William T. Green, Thurman had practiced for about eighteen years when he arrived in Milwaukee. He apparently developed a practice among whites and sustained much of this business until his death in 1927. With the exception of occasional participation in black protest meetings and active war work (he was an active member of the committee to form a Wisconsin battalion of black infantry troops), Thurman played a minor role in the affairs of the local black population.[48]

DeReef and Dorsey, on the other hand, were younger men who explicitly exploited the potential for professional advancement within the expanding black population. They conducted extensive social, political, and community service activities in conjunction with their law practices. Born in Missoula, Montana, in 1897, Dorsey attended Montana State University Law School and spent a short period of time in Minneapolis and St. Paul before coming to Milwaukee in 1928. He entered his practice as a junior partner of George DeReef, who apparently "taught him many of the intricacies of law practice, and gave him some sound advice." Dorsey established his practice under the conditions of increasing economic depression, but his influence lay mainly in the period after 1932.[49]

It was DeReef more than any other single attorney who left his mark upon the social, economic, and political life of blacks during the period. His career vividly reflects ways in which the ideology of self-help and racial solidarity overlapped with an emphasis on racial protest and integration. DeReef, originally from Charleston, South Carolina, and a descendant of a prominent slave-holding family, came to Milwaukee from a law career in Washington, D.C. He graduated from the Howard University law program in 1905 and arrived in Milwaukee in 1913. The attorney established an office in space formerly occupied by W. T. Greene at 217–18 Empire Building.

DeReef participated in a broad range of programs reflecting the idea of building up from within the black population. He was part-owner of the *Milwaukee Enterprise,* later the *Wisconsin Enterprise Blade,* and a member and officer of the CBLA and the MNBL. On the other hand, as part of his active involvement in the Milwaukee NAACP, he vigorously fought manifestations of segregation in the city's public institutions. In 1919, for example, he staunchly opposed the organization of a black Soldiers and Sailors Club for veterans of World War I.[50]

If the division between the new and old elites was drawn at all sharply in Milwaukee, it was so drawn between black medical practitioners. Unlike attorneys, some black physicians and dentists had long prewar practices. These men managed to continue much of their earlier service to a white clientele into the 1920s. Their articulation of earlier integrationist ideas was more clearcut. The emergence of new black doctors with a predominantly black clientele increasingly challenged the ideological stance of these older physicians, defined as "a social and ideological grouping in the black community" rather than simply as chronologically older men. The new men did not hesitate to advocate separate black institutions as a means of uplifting the race. Nevertheless, in the cauldron of the 1920s, the old and new elites gravitated toward each other's socioeconomic and political perspectives.

Dr. Allen L. Herron was the most important prewar physician to continue his practice during and following the war. Born in Marshall, Texas, in 1865, Dr. Herron received a degree in medicine from Howard University and came to Milwaukee in 1900. He practiced in the city until his death in 1956 at the age of 93. Dr. Herron sustained a clientele, at least before 1930, that was over 90 percent white. Another prewar practitioner, Dr. Clifton A. Johnson, a dentist, functioned with a largely white clientele from the turn of the century through 1934. The *Blade* remarked during the migration years that Johnson was considered one of the best dentists in the state and had a "larger practice among the other race than his own."[51]

These medical practitioners were joined, indeed challenged, by new physicians and dentists with links more directly to the expanding black population. The most active of these was Dr. P. Jay Gilmer, the physician, pharmacist, and *Blade* columnist, who arrived in Milwaukee in the wake of the great migration. Gilmer became one of the most forceful spokesmen for the concept of economic self-help and racial solidarity. His articles in the *Blade* appeared under such titles as

"Thrift and the Negro," in which he stressed the saving habit among blacks and outlined the problems of black businesses as too little finance, very small stock, and selling on credit. He concluded that blacks needed to "study thrift, pay cash, save money," and make it easier for black business people to succeed. Gilmer, as noted earlier, was one of the founding members of the Community Drug Store and headed its practical operations. On the other hand, as an individual and as president of the local NAACP around 1927, Gilmer sought to break down racial barriers in the economic, social, and political life of the city.[52]

Dr. Gilmer's heavy emphasis on economic self-help and racial unity was supported by other black physicians and dentists who came to Milwaukee during the migration and its aftermath. Dr. Edgar Thomas, for example, born in Mt. Gilead, North Carolina, and a graduate of Howard University Medical School, came to the city in 1923 and began a practice that catered primarily to blacks. Dr. Thomas became president of the Community Drug Store and sought to link his economic self-help and racial unity philosophy to an ideology of civil rights protest when he served as president of the NAACP between 1923 and 1925. New black dentists in the city augmented the efforts of Gilmer and Thomas to exploit the increasing economic and professional opportunities inherent in the expanding black population. Dr. Alden McDonald, for example, opened the McDonald Realty Company and hired a black minister, Rev. W. A. T. Miles, to aid in selling, renting, and managing his properties.[53]

As if to counter the influence of P. Jay Gilmer and others, another black doctor, Ludie T. Gilmer, no relation to P. Jay Gilmer, came to Milwaukee in 1923. Although a younger man and entering the city in the wake of the migration, L. T. Gilmer augmented the forces of the old elite. Gilmer, born in Alabama in 1895, came to Milwaukee from Beloit. He was light-skinned and deprecated the idea of serving a mainly black clientele, yet even his career represented attempts to reconcile the opposing crosscurrents of separation and integration. He eventually developed a practice among blacks and whites at two separate offices. Gilmer also became treasurer of the CBLA, the archetypical black enterprise in the city, and simultaneously played a prominent role in the black Cream City Medical Society, an organization of black physicians, though theoretically open without racial restrictions.[54]

The Cream City Medical Society was formed in 1927 under the

leadership of Dr. Richard Herron, son of Dr. A. L. Herron. The organization opposed segregated black institutions and services. For example, when Rev. Cecil Fisher received appointment as "Colored Social Worker and Probation Officer," the society turned down his invitation to participate in a Negro Health Week program. The organization's official response to Fisher's invitation highlighted the ambiguities inherent in its ideological position:

> The matter was thoroughly discussed at a regular meeting and the body concluded that the program of "Negro Health Week" is not necessary in Milwaukee in so far as there is an observance of "National Health Week" which is participated in by all peoples of these United States regardless of race or color....The body also feels that the practice of continually isolating the Negro in such activities has a tendency to create a racial barrier and fosters the inference that Negroes are basically, physically and socially different if not inferior to other races.[55]

Efforts to reconcile the conflicting tendencies within the black middle class took their sharpest, most articulate, and consistent focus in the pronouncements of J. Anthony Josey, editor of the *Blade*. Unlike R. B. Montgomery, who before World War I adhered rather single-mindedly to the economic self-help model of Washington, Josey linked his belief in black business to an ideology of civil rights protest in accord with the emergent "New Negro" movement. Even Montgomery shifted toward an ideology of protest in the postwar era, serving as president of the local NAACP for a short period and embarking upon a vigorous antilynching campaign.

The *Blade* opened in 1916 with a strong attack on Washington's legacy of leadership and philosophy: "The Negro who is thought to be a leader is telling his people to 'learn to work, get property, own homes,' etc. — The Negro seekers of notoriety who in the lobbies of the Capitol, in the anterooms of the city council begging for crumbs, would shine brighter as a beacon light if from the pulpit and platform they would preach and teach the people the power of the Ballot."[56] Initial rhetoric from the *Blade* was militant and appeared to explicitly link its orientation to the strong abolitionist tradition emerging from the struggle against slavery: "It will not be the mission of The BLADE to PULL DOWN but rather LIFT UP....THE BLADE will cut but only into the rank of ignorance and error, and for the purpose of opening up a path of truth and right."[57]

Josey identified himself and the *Blade* with national postwar black militance when he reprinted W. E. B. DuBois's famous NAACP *Crisis* editorial, "We Return Fighting," in June 1919: "This is the country to which we soldiers of Democracy return. . . .We return—We return From Fighting. We Return Fighting. Make way for Democracy. We saved it in France, and by the Great Jehovah, we will save it in the United States of America or know the reason why."[58] The *Blade's* editor vigorously fought the separation of blacks and whites in the city's public institutions during the 1920s and early 1930s. He objected to the county's appointment of a black social worker and probation officer, whose duties were to be restricted to serving black clients, and he vehemently opposed the Milwaukee Urban League's acquisition of a social center to serve only blacks. He believed that each instance of segregation in public life was a step toward introducing southern-brand Jim Crow attitudes into "free Wisconsin."[59]

The *Blade's* editor struggled to bring civil rights protest into accord with business expansion and racial solidarity. Josey's promotion of black enterprise was highly ambitious and often reflected much of Washington's and Montgomery's earlier emphasis on self-help. In its first year of publication, for example, the *Blade* criticized the forceful civil rights struggle developing around the NAACP. Josey stressed the values of wealth and education and encouraged blacks to follow the line of least resistance: "Let the Negro go ahead along the line on which he is not hampered. Let him increase in wealth, his knowledge, his worth. Let him rely more upon himself and develop more within himself."[60]

Throughout the period, Josey spearheaded a verbal campaign in support of black enterprises. His promotion of black business developed around three basic beliefs. Support of black enterprises was a sign of racial unity. Successful businesses would create employment for blacks, especially youth. And enterprises catering to a black clientele were an alternative or answer to racial proscription by the larger white business and professional community. From its inception, the *Blade* hammered out these themes of business encouragement and support. In a 9 November 1916 editorial, Josey wrote: "We must. . .instill the idea of appreciation and honesty and efforts of those who lift themselves by their bootstraps above natal conditions. In this way we multiply avenues of employment for the people of our own race. When we can have businesses like the other races, employing our boys and girls, we shall have made a long step in the solution of the [race] problem."[61]

By the mid 1920s, the *Blade* became even more enthusiastic about the possibilities of black business. Josey moved the paper from Madison to Milwaukee in accord with this belief. The editor vigorously sought to transform Milwaukee into a center of black enterprise: "The men and women who are conducting business houses in Milwaukee are worthy of our support. With our help they can develop into powerful institutions that will give employment to thousands of our boys and girls. Without our assistance they will dry up and die. Boosting Milwaukee Business should be our slogan. Here is where we work, sleep and eat."[62] The same editorial lauded those "brave souls" who had "gone forward and succeeded" in setting up "race" enterprises. Such success, it was believed, would "encourage other young men to venture into business."[63]

The *Blade* coupled its advocacy of black business with criticisms of Afro-Americans for their failure to support race enterprises. The editor was particularly critical of those who criticized relatively successful business people and urged them to "hang up the little hammer and pick up the big horn and blow about bigger business." Attacks against blacks for lack of business unity were often scathing. In a 5 September 1925 editorial, Josey argued that, despite rhetoric to the contrary, many blacks "too many by far — deep down in their hearts" believed in "the superiority of the white man over other people." Josey took his argument to the extreme when he concluded that lack of racial unity was "apparently peculiar to people of color." The editor, however, placed part of the blame on black business people for their failure to buy advertising space in the paper. "Colored business men often complain because Negroes do not patronize them, and in nine cases out of ten they are to blame. The Negro trade does not know the Negro merchant is in business. Advertisement is a business builder, a business getter."[64]

Josey linked his criticism of black business people to a campaign urging blacks to support those establishments advertising with the paper. "Advertisements in this paper are a bid for your trade and a guarantee of decent treatment. Don't force your money on those who don't want it."[65] Over time, the *Blade* modified its emphasis on racial solidarity and self-help, partly because several white businesses supported the paper through advertisements. "Many white men in business are fair and courteous to their customers — black and white — and merit the patronage of their Colored patrons." But Josey staunchly maintained the need for equal consideration of black businessmen. "What we do mean to say, and we insist upon it, is that no man, merely because he is white, is better prepared or more able to serve than others who happen to be black. If you can't feel a preference for your own race...don't boycott him for that reason."[66]

A new black middle class fully emerged in Milwaukee by the mid-1920s. The Afro-American industrial proletariat, though itself weak, constituted the demographic and economic bedrock from which the new black bourgeoisie and its small elite derived its existence. Developing on such a precarious foundation, the new middle class was likewise fragile. Just as Afro-Americans were relegated to the bottom of the industrial work force, they were also confined to the less remunerative and prestigious businesses and professions, yet, though not as forcefully as elsewhere, blacks in the city entertained the notion of a black city within the city. As Ardie Halyard has recently recollected, while there was much talk of the dream, "few could realize it" through the development of viable enterprises.[67] Exploiting the expanding potential of black industrial and domestic service wages, Afro-American business and professional people aggressively worked to develop enterprises that would cater mainly to the needs of blacks.

The emergence of the new black middle class marked a growing conflict between those business and professional people catering primarily to a black clientele and those who wished to serve white and black patrons on an equal basis; it was a conflict that moved increasingly toward resolution as persons of old and new elite persuasions struggled to incorporate elements of both outlooks. To be sure, the often painful and imperfect reconciliation of these forces would open the way for abrasive conflicts within the middle class; nevertheless, this class became more unified. Thus, the most fundamental class division within the black population was increasingly that between the expanding urban-industrial working class, augmented by domestic service workers, and the growing, though small, black bourgeoisie.

Although the persistence of racial antagonism against blacks promoted and sustained a convergence in the interests of black workers and the middle class, objective differences in their access to economic, social, and political benefits would foster a tenuous rather than a solid racial unity. These growing class tensions within the black population would find frequent expression in the response of Afro-Americans to their larger urban-industrial experience, especially the most oppressive aspects of the black proletarianization process. Growing stratification within the black population would intersect with the expansion of white racial hostility in creating two conflicting but converging modes of consciousness and behavior, class and race. The complex interplay of these processes in the development of black institutional life, politics, and race relations is explored in the following chapter.

NOTES

1. Kenneth L. Kusmer, *A Ghetto Takes Shape: Black Cleveland, 1870–1930* (Urbana: University of Illinois Press, 1976), chapters 9, 10, and 11; Allan H. Spear, *Black Chicago: The Making of a Negro Ghetto, 1890–1920* (Chicago, University of Chicago Press, 1967), chapters 3 and 4; St. Clair Drake and Horace R. Cayton, *Black Metropolis: A Study of Negro Life in A Northern City,* vol. 1 (1945; rev. New York: Harcourt, Brace, and World, 1962), especially pp. 77–97.
2. *Wisconsin Enterprise Blade,* 12 Sept. 1925.
3. "Milwaukee and Her Progressive Citizens," *Blade,* 4 Jan. 1917.
4. *Blade,* 9 May 1918; Interracial Committee of the Council of Social Agencies, "Summary of the Findings of the Unit Survey," Box 20, United Community Services of Greater Milwaukee Papers, 1903–6 (University of Wisconsin–Milwaukee, Area Research Center).
5. Spear, *Black Chicago,* p. 71; Kusmer, *A Ghetto Takes Shape,* pp. 235–74. Kusmer (and Spear as well) places rather singular emphasis on the expansion of the ghetto as the basis of black business expansion: "The consolidation of the ghetto led to increased opportunities for black businessmen" (Kusmer, p. 235).
6. John C. Leggett, *Class, Race, and Labor: Working-Class Consciousness in Detroit* (New York: Oxford University Press, 1968), pp. 34–42; C. Wright Mills, *White Collar: The American Middle Class* (1951; rept. New York: Oxford University Press, 1956), pp. 63–76.
7. *Blade,* 20 Nov. 1919, 10 Jan. 1925, 17 July 1926, 16 Jan. 1932; interview with Carl F. Watson, 5 Aug. 1979.
8. "Grand Opening of the Community Drug Store," *Blade,* 17 Oct. 1925; *Milwaukee City Directory* (Milwaukee: Wright's City Directory, 1924 and 1926).
9. "Kinner Firm to Mark 30 Years in City," 21 July 1959 (Newspaper Clippings File: Milwaukee Public Library); *Blade,* 29 Nov. 1917; "The Alberta Villa," *Blade,* 22 Mar. 1917.
10. *Blade,* 22 Mar. 1917.
11. "Milwaukee to Have a $25,000 Tea Room and Hotel at 615 Galena Street," *Blade,* 17 Apr. 1926; "William K. Heards," *Echo: Bicentennial Issue* 21, no. 27 (1976): 31–32.

12. Interview with Ardie A. Halyard, 14 Aug. 1979; *Milwaukee City Directory* (Milwaukee: Wright's City Directory, 1926).
13. Interview with Ardie A. Halyard, 14 Aug. 1979; "Columbia Building and Loan Ass'n Opens Books: $5,000 Worth of Stock Sold on First Day," *Blade,* 10 Jan. 1925; Mary Ellen Shadd, ed. *Negro Business Directory of the State of Wisconsin* (Milwaukee, 1950), p. 40.
14. "Columbia Building and Loan Association; New and Permanent Office, 486–8th St.: The Objects and Purposes of Building and Loan Associations," *Blade,* 4 Apr. 1925.
15. Ibid.; *Blade,* 27 Mar. 1929.
16. "Seventh Annual Statement at the Close of Business Dec. 31, 1932," Box G-219, National Association for the Advancement of Colored People Papers (Manuscript Division, Library of Congress).
17. United States Bureau of the Census, *Sixteenth Census of U.S.: 1940 Census of Business, vol. 1, Retail Trade, 1939* (Washington: Government Printing Office, 1941), p. 754.
18. Ibid.; "The Business League's Ten Years of Progress," *Blade,* 1 May 1926; Bayrd Still, *Milwaukee: The History of a City* (1948; rept. Madison: State Historical Society of Wisconsin, 1965), pp. 476–96, 576–77.
19. For an important seminal discussion of the problems of black business, see Abram L. Harris, *The Negro as Capitalist: A Study of Banking and Business among American Negroes* (Philadelphia: American Academy of Political and Social Sciences, 1936), especially pp. 46–61.
20. Interview with Ardie A. Halyard, 14 Aug. 1979.
21. J. F. Crawford to D. W. Hoan, 19 Jan. 1923, Box 26, File 98, Daniel Webster Hoan Papers, 1910–53 (Milwaukee County Historical Society).
22. D. W. Hoan to Wilbur Halyard, 17 May 1923, Box 26, File 98, Hoan Papers; interview with Ardie A. Halyard, 14 Aug. 1979.
23. Interview with Clarence L. Johnson, 15 Aug. 1979; "Fiftieth Wedding Anniversary of Mr. and Mrs. Clarence L. Johnson," 21 Mar. 1969, St. Mark African Methodist Episcopal Church, Milwaukee.
24. "Two is a Team," *Echo* 21, no. 27 (1976): 10–11.
25. Interview with Carl F. Watson, 5 Aug. 1979.
26. "Post Profile: Clarence L. Johnson," *Milwaukee Post,* 28 Jan. 1964.
27. Kusmer, *A Ghetto Takes Shape,* p. 191; Still, *Milwaukee,* pp. 578–79.
28. Gilbert Osofsky, *Harlem: The Making of a Ghetto, 1890–1930* (1963; rev. ed. New York: Harper Torchbooks, 1971), pp. 179–87; Nathan I. Huggins, *Harlem Renaissance* (New York: Oxford University Press, 1971), chapters 1 and 2.
29. "Milwaukee's 'Harlem' Is a Busy Changing Community," *Milwaukee Journal,* 26 Nov. 1939.
30. *Blade,* 4 Jan. 1917, 7 Dec. 1916.
31. Ibid.; H. Russell Austin, *The Milwaukee Story: The Making of an American*

*City* (Milwaukee: *Milwaukee Journal,* 1946), p. 145. The Schlitz Palm Garden opened in 1896 near the corner of Grand Avenue (W. Wisconsin Avenue) and North 3rd Street and closed around 1919 when prohibition occurred.

32. *Blade,* 16 Jan. 1919.
33. "J. Howard Offutt," *Echo* 21, no. 27 (1976): 23–24.
34. "Milwaukee Happenings," *National Advocate,* 7 Jan. 1921.
35. For a discussion of J. D. Cooke's *National Defender and Sun* after he moved to Gary, see Elizabeth Balanoff, "A History of the Black Community of Gary, Indiana, 1906–1940" (Ph.D. diss., University of Chicago, 1974), especially pp. 46, 248–52; Armstead Scott Pride, "A Register and History of Negro Newspapers in the United States" (Ph.D. diss., Northwestern University, 1950), pp. 166–67, 391–93; *The Milwaukee Enterprise,* 29 Dec. 1923, Box G-219, NAACP Papers (this is apparently the only extant issue of the *Enterprise* before its merger with the *Blade* in 1925); *Milwaukee City Director* (Milwaukee: Wright's City Directory, 1917, 1923, and 1924).
36. "Bronzeville Has New Mayor, and His Election is Cheered," *Milwaukee Journal,* 13 Nov. 1945; "J. Anthony Josey Still Living," *National Advocate,* 1 Apr. 1921. (This article appeared after Josey was erroneously reported dead by the *Chicago Whip.*) Several insights into Josey's activities are provided by people who knew him during the period: interviews with John Williams, 10 Aug. 1979; Bernice Copeland-Lindsay, 9 Aug. 1979; and Carl F. Watson, 5 Aug. 1979.
37. *Blade,* 18 Jan. 1917, 4 Jan. 1917, 8 Feb. 1917, 1 Mar. 1917, 7 Dec. 1916, 3 Aug. 1916; *Milwaukee Journal,* 1 Nov. 1917.
38. "The Business League's Ten Years of Progress," *Blade,* 1 May 1926.
39. "Negro Professional and Business Men's League," *Blade,* 7 Nov. 1925; *Milwaukee City Directory* (Milwaukee: Wright's City Directory, 1924 and 1926).
40. *Blade,* 1 May 1926.
41. *Blade,* 31 Jan. 1925; Shadd, *Negro Business Directory,* p. 74.
42. Kusmer, *A Ghetto Takes Shape,* pp. 216–19; Osofsky, *Harlem,* pp. 108–9; James Weldon Johnson, *Black Manhattan* (1930; rept. New York: Atheneum, 1968), pp. 170–82; Nathan I. Huggins, *Harlem Renaissance,* p. 291.
43. Carter G. Woodson, *The Negro Professional Man and the Community* (1934; rept. New York: Johnson Reprint Corporation, 1970), pp. 322–33.
44. Talcott Parsons, "Professions," in David L. Sills, ed., *International Encyclopedia of the Social Sciences,* vol. 12 (Macmillan and the Free Press, 1968), pp. 537–47; Mills, *White Collar,* pp. 136–37.
45. Spear, *Black Chicago,* pp. 112–13, 181–82; Harris, *The Negro as Capitalist,*

pp. 48–49, 144–64, 191–99; Kusmer, *A Ghetto Takes Shape,* pp. 192–95; Osofsky, *Harlem,* pp. 92–104, 117–123.

46. Harris, *The Negro as Capitalist,* p. 175; Kusmer, *A Ghetto Takes Shape,* pp. 192–95.

47. Kusmer, *A Ghetto Takes Shape,* p. 236; Osofsky, *Harlem,* pp. 159–87; Huggins, *Harlem Renaissance,* pp. 52–83; Spear, *Black Chicago,* pp. 197–200.

48. *Blade,* 27 June 1918, 11 July 1918, 4 Jan. 1917, 29 June 1916, 1 Nov. 1917, 22 Nov. 1917.

49. "A Salute to James Weston Dorsey," Box 1, James W. Dorsey Papers, 1930–66 (Milwaukee County Historical Society).

50. *Blade,* 4 Jan. 1917; *The Milwaukee Enterprise,* 29 Dec. 1923, Box G-219, NAACP Papers; interview with Ardie A. Halyard, 14 Aug. 1979; *Blade,* 10 Jan. 1925, 7 Nov. 1925, 27 June 1918, 5 June 1919.

51. "Early Negro Doctor Honored by Shriners," *Milwaukee Journal,* 21 Aug. 1968; "Spirit of '76: Early Negro Doctors," *Echo* 21, no. 27 (1967): 43–44; *Blade,* 4 Jan. 1917, 11 July 1918; Kusmer, *A Ghetto Takes Shape,* p. 115, n. 2.

52. *Blade,* 17 Oct. 1925; "Thrift and the Negro," *Blade,* 1 Oct. 1927; "Where We See Prosperity," *Blade,* 17 Apr. 1926, 17 July 1926; James Weldon Johnson, national secretary, to P. J. Gilmer, 27 Feb. 1928; P. J. Gilmer to J. W. Johnson, 3 Mar. 1928, Box G-219, NAACP Papers.

53. "Spirit of '76: Dr. Edgar Thomas," *Echo* 21, no. 27 (1976): 43–44; *Blade,* 17 Oct. 1925; Edgar Thomas to Robert Bagnall, NAACP director of branches, 23 Jan. 1924, Box G-219, NAACP Papers; *Blade,* 17 July 1926.

54. Interview with Ardie A. Halyard, 14 Aug. 1979; "Negro Doctor Refused Burial in Memorial Park Grave," *Milwaukee Sentinel,* 17 Jan. 1946; *Blade,* 10 Jan. 1925; Shadd, ed. *Negro Business Directory,* p. 37.

55. Cream City Medical Society to Rev. C. A. Fisher, 30 Mar. 1931, Folders 1–3, Cecil A. Fisher Papers, 1921–66 (University of Wisconsin–Milwaukee, Area Research Center).

56. R. B. Montgomery to James Weldon Johnson, 15 Nov. 1923 and 28 Nov. 1923, Box G-219, NAACP Papers; "Leaders," *Blade,* 8 June 1916.

57. "Leaders," *Blade,* 8 June 1916.

58. *Blade,* 5 June 1919.

59. "Colored People's Exhibit at State Fair," 28 Feb. 1918; "A Friendly Protest," *Blade,* 22 Nov. 1917; "A Citizen," *Blade,* 3 Jan. 1918.

60. "For God's Sake Stop Whining," *Blade,* 14 Dec. 1916; "Being Jealous," *Blade,* 9 Nov. 1916.

61. "Being Jealous," *Blade,* 9 Nov. 1916.

62. "Boost Milwaukee Business," *Blade,* 24 Sept. 1927.

63. *Blade,* 25 Aug. 1928.

64. "Patronizing Our Own," *Blade,* 5 Sept. 1925.

65. *Blade,* 9 Jan. 1919, 6 Feb. 1919.

66. *Blade,* 5 Sept. 1925.

67. Interview and follow-up interview with Ardie A. Halyard, 14 Aug. 1979; 9 July 1981.

# 4

## Race Relations, Politics, and Institutions

Changes in the Afro-American class structure — discussed in preceding chapters — intersected with a shifting pattern of race relations
and dramatically transformed black politics and institutional life.
Racial tensions in Milwaukee did not end with the struggle for jobs,
housing, business, and professional opportunities. The competitive
interplay between blacks and whites surfaced in a broad spectrum of
public and private institutions and services as well as in politics.[1] As
they joined together to combat racial discrimination in other areas of
their lives, so black workers and the bourgeois elite joined forces to
resist racial discrimination in the broader institutional and political
life of the city. In practice, though, the different class interests of the
black business and professional elite on the one hand and those of
black industrial workers on the other hampered the thrust for racial
unity. The dynamic interaction of these different class interests
underlay many of the intraracial conflicts that convulsed the Afro-
American urban community. These internal cleavages, accompanied
by divisions within the black middle class, would find frequent expression in the development of Afro-American civil rights activities, electoral politics, and institutional life. Despite painful class divisions, the
expansion of Afro-American institutions and political activities
potently demonstrates how Milwaukee blacks collectively forged a
creative response to their often hostile urban-industrial experience.
Let us first turn to the changing pattern of race relations as a backdrop

to the Afro-American response to racial discrimination in the larger institutional and political life of the city.

Racial hostility following World War I increasingly blocked Afro-American access to theaters, restaurants, health services, recreational facilities, and a variety of other amenities and necessities. William V. Kelley, executive secretary of the Milwaukee Urban League, later summarized the increasing rift between blacks and whites in the social and political life of the city: "Whereas, in the early days of the migration, the average Milwaukeean was possessed of a kindly interest in Negroes born of curiosity. This soon gave way under the impact of economic pressure to a quiet, but telling indifference and in many instances to open resentment and unmistakable color prejudice."[2]

Racially biased and stereotypical reports of blacks in local newspapers mirrored and implicitly supported unequal treatment of Afro-Americans in other areas of urban life. Although the *Milwaukee Journal* initially supported local blacks, from about 1919 through the 1920s, members of the black community justly criticized the paper for racist reporting. Indeed, the *Journal* rigorously and graphically depicted black crime and underplayed Afro-American achievement. Thus, in a 1919 issue, the *Journal* headlined a story of a black charged with arson and loss of life: "STEAMER BURNS; LIVES LOST, Negro Charged with Setting Fire to Passenger Ship Virginia." On the following day a second headline announced the heroic efforts of two persons to save a victim of the fire: "THROUGH FLAMES TO SAVE SHIP VICTIM." The headline failed to mention that the two "heroic" persons were blacks. Only some distance into the article was their race identity made known.[3]

Other leading Milwaukee newspapers, especially the *Milwaukee Sentinel,* pursued similarly biased formats. The *Sentinel* presented headlines and stories, particularly of alleged interracial sex incidents, in a manner that would produce public outrage against blacks. Such reporting became so virulent by 1921 that it provoked the Milwaukee branch of the NAACP to publish a tract protesting such racially slanted treatments.[4] In an equally hostile vein, the *Wisconsin News* attributed Milwaukee's rising crime rate to the migration of blacks to the city.[5]

In Milwaukee, although to a lesser degree than in larger northern cities, the intent of the state's civil rights law was also subverted by various devices of subterfuge: harassment, outright refusal of service, poor service, and overcharging. Blacks faced the most blatant forms of discrimination in local restaurants and theaters. In the midst of the migration, the Butterfly Theater initiated a discriminatory policy against blacks. The theater's box office refused to sell tickets to blacks, informing them that the house was not "catering to Colored patrons" or that the house was "sold out." Another theater, the Davidson, began a similar policy in 1919. Rather than seeking to exclude blacks totally, as the Butterfly aimed to do, the Davidson sought to relegate Afro-Americans to separate seats in the balcony. Restaurants also exhibited an increasing reluctance and refusal to serve black patrons. Such refusal sometimes involved nonwhite establishments catering mainly to whites. In 1920, for example, blacks filed a racial discrimination suit against the Chinese restaurant of Moy Wah Fon and Moy Yee, partners in the chop suey business, which denied service to Afro-Americans by simply ignoring their presence and serving whites only.[6]

Afro-Americans complained of discriminatory policies of restaurants and theaters throughout the 1920s. As such complaints became more frequent, discrimination in such places became more subtle but even more effective. "The practice here is not to refuse admission to Colored people, because we have already established our rights in that respect," the Milwaukee NAACP reported, "but before selling the ticket, and often as the person goes in, he is told that the management does not cater to Colored people, or 'your people' as the case might be." Efforts to subvert the meaning of the Civil Rights Act precipitated a movement by blacks and their white allies to strengthen the Wisconsin statute; proposed revisions aimed to spell out more clearly and extend the instances of discrimination contained in the law. By 1931, the Wisconsin legislature passed an improved law, which, in addition to clarifying prior items, clearly outlawed the practice of overcharging black customers as a means of discouraging their patronage.[7] While some Afro-Americans brought discrimination suits under the Civil Rights Act and occasionally won, most simply did not have the financial resources or often the resolve to sustain legal actions against discriminating establishments.

Although increasing racial discrimination was most evident in the press, restaurants, and theaters, it became more prominent in a variety of other institutions: health care organizations, life insurance companies, public utilities, and official government bodies, notably social welfare and law enforcement agencies. In 1918, Muirdale Sanitarium, a state institution located in Milwaukee County, initiated a policy of separating black and white tuberculosis patients. Treatment of black patients, even during an emergency, at any other than the Milwaukee County Hospital was rare. Mayor Daniel W. Hoan presented the most potent evidence of racial discrimination in the city's health institutions. In a 1931 letter to the Julius Rosenwald Fund, Hoan supported efforts to establish a separate hospital for blacks in the city: "We feel that this is a most worthy and opportune work for our Colored people. An up-to-date hospital where these people are made to feel welcome is no doubt a project which deserves our warmest consideration." Various life insurance companies and public utilities either refused to serve blacks or enforced discriminatory rates. The Bell Telephone Company, according to an NAACP complaint, charged Afro-Americans "an additional fee to have a telephone installed on the basis that Colored people did not pay their bills."[8]

Blacks in Milwaukee had several abusive experiences, even if less abrasive than elsewhere, with police, the courts, and the law in general. The relationship of blacks to the police had a contradictory character: Afro-Americans were both overpoliced and underprotected in their lives and property. Police intensified their harassment of interracial couples in the wake of the migration, and such abuses recurred frequently during the 1920s. As noted in Chapter 2, law enforcement officials singled blacks out for harsh treatment during the economic retrenchment of 1921–23. The police arrested several Afro-Americans for vagrancy, who were placed on road work for the county and ordered out of town at the end of their service. In 1929, the NAACP complained to the mayor that a police captain referred to a black physician as a "nigger doctor" and severely reprimanded a white auto accident victim for enlisting his services. At the same time, there was a lack of adequate police protection in the black community. As part of a campaign for more public service jobs for blacks, the *Blade* periodically carried an editorial entitled "A Colored Man For Detective," in which the need for black policemen and detectives was expressed and justified. During the 1920s, an interest in black police officers intensified, especially in respect to the safety of black women. "On several occasions some of our best women have been molested in broad daylight," the *Blade* protested.[9]

The shifting racial climate in the city was dramatically revealed in 1932 when Mayor Hoan addressed a Socialist party convention. Before an audience of 6,000 delegates in the Milwaukee auditorium, the mayor prefaced his speech to the gathering with a "Darky Story." The racial stereotypes and anti-black content of the story provoked black delegates to write a letter of protest: "Realizing that all humanity must share in the future industrial democracy of the world, it was a surprise and a shock to hear the Mayor in the presence of 6,000 workers, men and women from every nook and corner of this country, tell a 'Darky Story' to the discomfiture and shame of 10,000 [black] citizens of Milwaukee who have supported him almost one hundred per cent for mayor of this city."[10] Although the "Darky Story" was uncharacteristic of the mayor's basic relationship with blacks and although he earnestly apologized, his words clearly symbolized a historical process, a sharp upswing in racial proscription against blacks, that had grown deeper since the onslaught of the migration and the increasing shift of Afro-Americans into the industrial work force.

Afro-Americans in Milwaukee were not passive recipients of the increasing racial animosity directed against them. In response to widespread racial discrimination in the social and political life of the city, Milwaukee blacks vigorously expanded their civil rights protests, electoral politics, and separate institutions. Blacks particularly accelerated their demands for equal socioeconomic and political treatment. Between 1916 and 1920, Milwaukee blacks joined other Wisconsin blacks in a series of "Race Conventions." These sessions aimed to assess the state of the "Race" in various parts of the state as a first step toward developing political, economic, and social advancement strategies. Before its demise in the 1920s, the Race Convention had briefly succeeded in creating greater unity among blacks throughout the state in their fight against racial discrimination.[11]

As early as 1918, Afro-Americans protested the absence of black jurors in Milwaukee county courts. Attorney DeReef initiated the action when he addressed a letter to the Milwaukee County Jury Commission. DeReef noted that county courts had impaneled more than 3,000 jurors over the previous decade. None of the estimated 1,500 blacks had been chosen, yet, DeReef noted, nearly 300 black men of draft age had registered with "more than a score of them sent away to 'make the world safe for democracy.' " Within a year, Afro-Americans began serving on county juries.[12]

Using the Milwaukee Urban League as a political instrument, Afro-Americans pushed for greater access to social services within the city. Public and private agencies responded to these demands through an expanded network of segregated social services to blacks. During the 1920s, social work agencies funneled greater services to Afro-

Americans through the Milwaukee Urban League. Although its function was mainly employment, the MUL played a pivotal role in the work of various public and private agencies within the black community: the County Department for Outdoor Relief, Family Welfare Department, County Health Department, Juvenile Court, and the public schools.

Segregated social work expanded by the late 1920s, when Afro-Americans intensified their pressure on municipal agencies to hire black workers to serve the increasingly segregated black population. In 1930, the Milwaukee County Board of Supervisors, responding to such political pressure, created the position of "Social Worker (For Colored People)." In a formal resolution, a cross section of several black business and professional people lauded the board's creation of the position: "Resolved: That we extend to the County Board of Supervisors, the County Civil Service Commission and to Mr. Geo. J. Herrman, Sup. 6th Ward our profound gratitude to you in the creating of the position of Colored Probation Officer and Welfare worker to work among Colored people of this city feeling that this position was made for the welfare of our people and for no other reason. We are thankful and hope that in no manner either by insinuation from any source or protest will affect its continued existence." The Milwaukee Health Department hired a "Special Colored nurse" who worked "with Colored people only, under the direction of the city field nurses." Other public departments — police, school board, and outdoor relief — followed suit. Among private social welfare and recreational agencies, the Family Welfare Association and the Young Women's Christian Association (YWCA) took the lead in serving blacks in segregated subdepartments of larger programs. These institutional developments represented a northern variant of what Howard Rabinowitz has called, in the southern context, "from exclusion to segregation."[13] Milwaukee blacks increasingly accepted segregated services as preferable to the pattern of de facto exclusion.

Milwaukee blacks also used their growing political potential to seek racial, social, economic, and political justice in national, state, and local affairs. In local elections, blacks exercised a decided independence in their voting patterns. Mayor Hoan won the Sixth Ward's vote by large margins during the entire period. When Republicans and Democrats began the process of "fusion" politics, whereby the two parties joined forces in order to dismantle Socialist influence in city government, Afro-Americans stood firmly for the Socialists. "As for the Socialists we are yet to be convinced they are all rascals," the *Blade* declared.[14]

The question of aldermanic representation on the city council constituted the most important political item for blacks at the city level. Afro-Americans in Milwaukee hoped to influence the municipal patronage system to their benefit as did white ethnic groups and, increasingly, Afro-Americans in other cities. The tremendous influx of blacks during World War I, their increasing spatial concentration, and their transition to the urban-industrial work force heightened a similar process in Milwaukee. Yet, as late as June 1924, attorney DeReef planned to garner significant white support when he filed nomination papers as a Republican candidate for Wisconsin's Sixth District Assembly seat encompassing the Sixth Ward. The increasing racial hostility that accompanied postwar black expansion in the city assured almost certain defeat. DeReef failed to advance beyond the primary. Thus, like their counterparts in other cities, blacks turned vigorously toward ward-level positions.

As early as 1918, Milwaukee blacks opposed efforts of reform elements to replace ward aldermen by aldermen-at-large. While the movement to eliminate ward aldermen was defeated by popular city-wide opposition, blacks supported the ward aldermanic form because, as the *Blade* put it, "If this form is retained you may hope someday to do what your people have done in the 2nd Ward of Chicago, where they have already one alderman and will soon have another." Although Afro-Americans failed to elect an alderman during the period, they waged vigorous struggles to secure such representation in the aldermanic primaries of 1928 and 1932. In these elections there was a tremendous appeal to racial unity, as reflected in campaign literature: "Do you want a Colored Alderman? Will you honestly use your influence to give our people a representative? Will you honestly aid in making a success of the first real honest effort made in Milwaukee, to secure civic and political recognition for our group."[15]

In the series of national elections between 1916 and 1932, Milwaukee blacks supported the Republican party. The Democratic party was consistently excoriated by the *Blade* as the party of disfranchisement, segregation, and white racism. Any blacks who supported the so-called Democracy were likewise severely condemned. Despite such staunch support for the Republican party during most of the period, however, Afro-Americans in Milwaukee never advocated blind loyalty to Republicans. Support of Republicans was explicitly linked to a struggle for "representative and prominent positions" in the management of Republican campaigns and a proportionate share of patronage positions. By 1932, the *Blade* notwithstanding, rising black unemployment precipitated a shift to the Democratic party, as a more useful ally than the Republican party for promoting the interests of Afro-Americans in national contests. In greater numbers than blacks in larger northern cities, blacks in Milwaukee voted for Franklin D. Roosevelt in the presidential election of 1932. Black precincts in Milwaukee extended 55 percent of their votes to Roosevelt. Not until 1936 did such high percentages of blacks in other northern cities shift their votes to the Democratic party.[16] The strong local tradition of voting for Socialists may have sensitized Milwaukee's small black population for a shift to the broad social programs of the Democrats earlier than elsewhere.

In addition to civil rights protest and electoral activities, Afro-Americans responded to growing racial discrimination in the social life of the city by expanding their separate institutional life. These activities not only included the expansion of business and professional organizations, as noted in Chapter 3, but the growth of black religious institutions as well. St. Mark African Methodist Episcopal, Calvary Baptist, and St. Benedict the Moor Mission and School were the major churches serving blacks when World War I got underway. By 1930, Milwaukee blacks had established at least thirteen new churches, mostly Baptist and Holiness or Spiritualist denominations. Although under-financed and ill-equipped, Afro-American churches served remarkably well the religious and social needs of black residents. Churches linked local blacks closely to each other and to a national black community. The establishment of the local black ministerial alliance in 1926 reflected efforts of religious leaders to enhance unity among black churches. They often shared each other's pulpits and took an active role in several civic, political, and social developments within the black community. A closer bond between local blacks and Afro-Americans in other parts of the country and surrounding states developed through the sponsorship of national and regional speakers. For example, Kelly Miller, mathematics professor and later dean of Howard University, and W. A. Fountain, president of Morris Brown College (and later AME bishop), visited the city under the auspices of St. Mark AME church.[17]

Afro-Americans indeed waged a relentless struggle against racial discrimination in the social, institutional, and political life of the city, yet increasing social class differentiation among blacks impeded racial unity in the forceful thrust for socioeconomic and political rights. Such divisions manifested themselves in the growing dichotomy between the new black middle class and the old elite on the one hand, and the expanding industrial working class on the other. The black population in Milwaukee, though less sharply than in other northern cities, became more stratified among upper, lower, and middle classes between World War I and the Depression. An MUL and Council of Social Agencies survey of the black population in 1928 identified three rather distinct classes among blacks. At the top were "old settlers" of twenty-five to forty-five years residence. Some of these people had even intermarried with the general white population. They had few contacts with the newer migrants and represented the persistence of the rapidly declining old elite who catered to an almost exclusively white clientele. The social exclusiveness of this class continued to draw comments during the 1920s; the *Blade* attacked their lingering elitism and ideological outlook in an editorial: "There is a bunch of self-chosen 'exclusives' in this city, who regard themselves as the 'elects' of society, and who believe that mankind was made to serve them, and they were not made to serve mankind. They yell loudest, and largest about discrimination, and do absolutely nothing to abate it. They do not contribute to any race enterprises or institutions."[18]

Although light skin color, which characterized the old elite of the prewar era, declined as a factor in black class divisions, it persisted as an important divisive force throughout the period. Under the impact of the Depression and the competition among blacks for scarce jobs, it apparently received renewed emphasis. The *Blade* delivered strong editorials against such invidious distinctions as late as 1932. Members of the old elite, their exclusiveness notwithstanding, eventually merged with the broader-based new black business and professional elite, who owed their existence to the expanding Afro-American population. Providing business and professional services primarily to blacks, the new elite was joined by a small number of clerical workers in making up the larger Afro-American middle class. The black bourgeoisie represented the most verbal influence in black economic, social, political, and institutional life. These people designated themselves the "Better Class" and astutely cultivated white allies for their programs of racial uplift and institution-building.

As the old elite tended to disparage the new middle class as well as working-class blacks, the new middle class also adopted an exclusive attitude toward the expanding Afro-American proletariat. Although itself a part of the new elite, the *Blade* sometimes criticized its class bias: "Quite frequently groups of our people band themselves together and. . .'high hat' those without professional standing and bear down hard upon the struggling mass of common people, yet they say they are the class — 'The Better Class,' if you please."[19] The largest class of blacks, the lower class, was mainly made up of unskilled and semi-skilled factory laborers, female domestics, prostitutes, and other similar members of the so-called floater class. At the core of the lower class, however, was the expanding population of skilled, unskilled, and semiskilled urban industrial workers.

Internal class divisions were not mute. These cleavages found ex-pression on several levels: civil rights activities and demands for greater access to public institutions, parallel institutional develop-ment within the black community, and participation in electoral politics. Civil rights protest took place in the work of the Milwaukee NAACP and various attempts to organize separate black departments under the auspices of citywide public agencies. Organized in 1915, the Milwaukee NAACP experienced a painful reorientation between 1918 and the early 1920s toward the new middle class and, to a lesser degree, toward the expanding urban industrial working class. L. H. Palmer, the prewar grocer, realtor, and former black Wisconsin assemblyman, emerged as the chief spokesman of the NAACP in 1918. He cooperated with the national leadership in reversing the policy of segregating black and white tuberculosis patients at the Muirdale Sanitarium. But Palmer and the old elite, with their staunch emphasis on integration and protest, were gradually dis-placed by persons representing decidedly new elite or "New Negro" philosophical orientations.[20]

Conflicts within the black elite expressed themselves most clearly in the controversy over the establishment of separate black units of public institutions. These conflicts reflected a variety of factors: divergent ideological orientations, opposing relationships with the ex-panding working class, and sometimes personal rivalries within the black middle class. At base, however, these divisions represented con-tradictory crosscurrents attendant on New Negro efforts to reconcile two different ideological orientations: integrationist protest and separate or parallel institutional development. In June 1919, internal dissension arose over the War Camp Community Service proposal to institute a segregated black Soldiers and Sailors Club for veterans of World War I. President of the Milwaukee NAACP, Horace Preston, favored the club and sought to have the NAACP membership endorse it. Since white veterans discriminated against blacks in their activities, black veterans also supported the separate club idea. Rev. J. S. Woods and attorney George DeReef, vice-president of the branch, led the opposition; DeReef presented a resolution which suggested that "plans for the said club be so amended as to make it a club for soldiers and sailors of the community here located without regard to their race identity." Efforts to defeat the club failed when Preston tabled the DeReef resolution and prevented further deliberations. A separate Soldiers and Sailors Club became functional under the auspices of the War Camp Community Service in July 1919.[21]

The emergence of the working class-oriented Milwaukee Universal Negro Improvement Association (UNIA) or Garvey Movement exacerbated conflicts within the black middle class. In contrast to the national Garvey Movement, which had reached its peak during the early 1920s and had declined with Garvey's deportation as an "undesirable alien" in 1924, the UNIA in Milwaukee reached its peak in the early 1930s. By 1932, the Milwaukee branch of the UNIA had grown from no more than 100 members in 1922 to an estimated 400. This was partly because of the city's expanding Afro-American demographic and economic base, but it was also due to the energetic leadership of Rev. Ernest Bland. Born in Atoka, Tennessee, in 1903, Bland came to Milwaukee in 1922. He joined the Socialist party shortly after his arrival and retained his affiliation as he became active in the local Garvey organization. The Milwaukee UNIA, like the national organization, had a band, which staged several colorful parades, a black legion, and a Liberty Hall at Third and Walnut streets. Moreover, as a means of enhancing its membership and influencing the affairs of the local black community, the UNIA developed several civic organizations which contacted city, county, state, and even national government officials in pressing for equitable treatment of Milwaukee blacks. Lower-class black ministers were particularly active among the Garvey forces. These included Rev. E. W. Thomas, a storefront Holiness minister, and Rev. Earl Little, father of Malcolm X, the renowned 1960s black nationalist.[22]

Under the weight of internal conflicts within the middle class and the growing Garvey Movement, in 1923 the Milwaukee NAACP split into two opposing factions. Attorney DeReef, who had become president of the NAACP branch around 1920–21, sought to use the organization mainly to protect and enhance the local interests of the expanding business and professional elite. His leadership was challenged in 1923 by R. B. Montgomery, the vocal prewar editor of the *Advocate,* who used his influence with the Republican party to gain brief control of the Milwaukee branch. After moving his paper to Minneapolis, Montgomery shuttled between the two cities and worked vigorously to develop a national constituency. He aimed to use the NAACP as a vehicle for articulating such national issues as disfranchisement and lynchings. Montgomery invited U. S. Representative L. C. Dyer of Missouri, sponsor of the Dyer Anti-Lynching Bill then before Congress, to speak in Milwaukee. Dyer criticized the local NAACP for inactivity on this important national legislation and urged a reorganization of the branch. Montgomery exploited the interest generated by Dyer and became temporary president of a second branch. Robert Bagnall, director of NAACP branches, authorized Montgomery's actions. Meanwhile, unlike his efforts in the struggle over the Soldier and Sailors Club, DeReef gravitated toward a closer alignment with the interests of the black working class. The DeReef faction reorganized and elected Rev. E. W. Thomas, a Garveyite, as president. When Thomas became president of the opposing branch, Montgomery was incensed; in a letter to Bagnall he referred to Thomas as a "storefront preacher" who "does not amount to very much" and who "is a member of the Garveyite Association and is doing all he possibly can to break up your Association here in Milwaukee."[23]

The national office intervened and resolved the split through an arrangement suggested by James Weldon Johnson, the national secretary. Dr. Edgar Thomas (no relation to Rev. E. W. Thomas), a newly arrived physician and surgeon, became president, with both Montgomery and E. W. Thomas agreeing to step down. Resolution of the split firmly established the NAACP as an instrument of the expanding new business and professional class. Dr. Thomas exhibited a range of anti-working class biases. He was particularly critical of the Universal Negro Improvement Association. "There is quite a Garvey following here in the city," he wrote to Bagnall, "and it goes without saying that they are against the N.A.A.C.P. They as usual consist of that ignorant class." In another instance Thomas related how the organization would grow on the basis of the so-called better class that would organize what he repeatedly called the "ignorant" newcomers from the

South. By 1924, the new elite dominated the roster of NAACP members. Such people as Wilber and Ardie Halyard emerged as top contributors. Although a few working-class blacks paid membership dues, ministers of the largest churches, lawyers, funeral direetors, and several other business and professional people characterized the membership lists.[24]

Some intraracial conflicts deteriorated into personality differences with little direct relevance to contending ideological or class commitments. When the Milwaukee Urban League gained a social center for recreational work among blacks, for example, a personal dispute erupted between J. A. Josey and William V. Kelley. Born in Nashville, Tennessee, Kelley served as industrial secretary of the St. Louis Urban League before arriving in Milwaukee in 1928. Kelley immediately became an important figure within the local black community. Josey disliked the idea that virtually all public and private social welfare agencies cleared any matters impinging on black socioeconomic life through the MUL. The editor also found Kelley's broad contacts with and speeches before white audiences too conciliatory. The *Blade*'s editor linked the social center with all of the foregoing criticisms and initiated a strong "Kelley Must Go" campaign. He attacked the social center as a firm step toward Jim Crow treatment of blacks in other areas of the city's life. While Milwaukee's black Ministerial Alliance joined the *Blade* in opposing the center, Josey nevertheless failed in his efforts to stop the social center and remove Kelley as executive secretary of the MUL.

Despite several such divisive controversies, the ideological gap within the middle class grew smaller by the late 1920s. Josey's career, for example, actually represented attempts to reconcile divergent ideologies within the black bourgeoisie. The editor was both a strong integrationist and one of the most consistent advocates of racial self-help and solidarity. Even in regard to public institutions, where his integrationist attitude was most rigid, Josey could bend. When the opportunity arose to hire black teachers in predominantly black schools, Josey enthusiastically supported the appointments.[25]

Although certain bourgeois factions allied with the interests of the black working class, it was the division between the black urban-industrial working class and the small Afro-American bourgeoisie that increasingly constituted the most significant class division within the black urban community. The great migration and attendant changes in the Afro-American class structure placed a tremendous challenge before established institutions, which had neither the time nor the resources to accommodate the rapid influx of rural migrants into the industrial city. In the process, a conservatism, resistance, and antimigrant attitude often developed among old residents, reflected in different modes of behavior and institutional life. Although several new black business and professional people entered the city, they usually augmented the new middle class or joined the old elite. The majority of newcomers were unskilled male industrial workers and female domestic service employees. Thus, the dichotomy between newcomers and old residents was mainly a division between the emerging Afro-American industrial working class and the small, and increasingly unified, black middle class. Fundamentally new Afro-American institutions emerged to meet the needs of the rapidly differentiating social class structure.

Established institutions differed in their characteristics and appeal to the migrants. Functioning with white priests and mission school-teachers, St. Benedict grew from an enrollment of about three black families in the prewar era to nearly fifty families in 1918. The school moved from an enrollment of a few local black youth to an enrollment of sixty-five black children from almost as many cities throughout the country. In addition to the mission and school, St. Benedict developed programs that appealed to black working class women: a day nursery for employed black mothers and a settlement house for young Afro-American women. By the early 1930s, the institution deepened its local social welfare role by establishing St. Anthony's Hospital, a facility designed primarily but not exclusively to meet the mounting medical needs of blacks. At the same time, St. Benedict expanded its appeal to a national black Catholic constituency.

Differences also marked St. Mark AME and Calvary Baptist, where the vast majority of Afro-Americans worshipped. As the oldest black church in the city, St. Mark entered the migration era under outstanding prewar community and church leaders like Rev. Jesse S. Woods and Lucien H. Palmer. Although the church retained its middle-class orientation, by the mid-1920s, newcomers had somewhat modified the exclusiveness of the church, especially its emphasis on "light skin-color." On the other hand, from its early twentieth-century inception through the early migration years, Calvary Baptist had represented the "newcomers" church. Calvary faced greater financial difficulties and alloted considerably more time to fund raising activities than did St. Mark. Some of these benefits conspicuously solicited the financial support of white Baptists. In decorum, too, the two churches differed. St. Mark conducted emotionally and physically subdued services; it exhibited a decided impatience with those who aimed to carry on a shouting tradition. Members of Calvary, by contrast, expressed themselves more freely as "the spirit" moved them. Such expression was often encouraged by the pastor, who himself displayed similar behavior. "So full of the Holy Ghost was the pastor," reported the *Blade* about a sermon at Calvary, "that we could see Christ the Word in flesh and spirit and all hearts were touched. Many shouted and wept for joy." Thus, the mode of worship at Calvary appealed to most newcomers, and the church also expanded its recreational and social facilities to serve the increasing migrant population. It was St. Mark, however, with its sounder economic base, that instituted the most practical programs for newcomers: an industrial employment bureau, several clubs for males and females of various ages, and a new religious social center.[26]

Despite heroic efforts by established institutions like St. Mark, Calvary, and St. Benedict, as the migration accelerated, old institutions proved unable to adequately accommodate the influx. Black religious leaders consistently pinpointed lack of space, personnel, and finances as obstacles to the implementation of necessary religious and secular activities. Old residents soon evinced an unmistakable animosity toward the newcomers. This conflict reflected deepening class divisions accompanying the increasing proletarianization of the black population. Established families keenly felt that the newcomers undermined their status and opportunities. They did not oppose migrants per se; rather, they opposed the unskilled, uneducated, and poor. Business and professional blacks found more ready acceptance. Dr. L. T. Gilmer, originally from Alabama and a newcomer to the city, for example, soon adopted the stance of the old residents. He asserted that newcomers from the South should be stopped at the city limits and turned back by local authorities.[27]

Southern blacks frequently complained about the cold treatment accorded them by old residents. "Instead of the Colored Northern citizens trying to help lift up your Colored neighbor," wrote one black female newcomer, "you run him down." In response to these tensions with old residents, newcomers often vowed, as did the foregoing woman, to make their own impact on the social, especially religious, life of the community: "We shall prove to you that we are good worthy law-a-biding citizens. . . . We shall prove to be citizens in helping to make Milwaukee one of the greatest religious cities of Wisconsin." Indeed, the rapid proliferation of new churches added substance to their comments and resolve. Baptist churches like Galilee (later Greater Galilee), Mt. Zion, and St. Paul (later Tabernacle) emerged between 1917 and 1922. Others like Mt. Olive Baptist and the Church of God in Christ began services between 1924 and 1925. A Seventh Day Adventist and St. Matthew Colored Methodist Episcopal (CME) church also developed during the period. If financial difficulties and problems of space and personnel plagued established churches, such hardships were endemic for the new bodies. When Galilee opened its doors in 1920, it immediately sought to erect a $40,000 church edifice to meet the "crying needs" of its "growing congregation." The church had 462 members by the mid-1920s.[28]

Of all the new churches to emerge during the period, the storefront Holiness church depicted most clearly the profound changes in the Afro-American class structure. By the mid-1920s, the Holiness "big summer camp meetings" became prominent. The black Pentecostal church in Milwaukee was led by Elder J. R. Anderson. As in other cities, this institution developed among working-class newcomers with the least economic means of subsistence. Recent oral interviews conducted by Joe Savage of WMVS Television in Milwaukee reveal the roots of Pentecostalism among blacks in the city. A Holiness minister's wife, Idella Blakely, provides a graphic description of how her mother and father, a foundry worker, made room in their home for the first Afro-American Holiness church services before the congregation moved on to a vacated fish market:

> Pentecostalism started in my father's home. In the year 1924–25, a Rev. Anderson came to the city and had no place to stay, and my father and mother took him in, and he began to preach the word of God. We as children were taken out of our beds, put in bathrooms, under the beds, anyplace, so they had a place to stay, because he had a large family. The neighbors heard of this minister that was in town, and many came to our home and received salvation. In the early part of 1926, they moved to a fish market on. . .6th and Vliet Street. . . .The odor of fish was so very strong, that we had to use all kind of soap and water and everything to get it out, but we insisted on having a place to serve. . . .My mother and father were so consistent in working and helping. My father was working in a foundry at the time, and he would come in the evenings, and work until [late] at night to try and get this place ready. And many souls came to God thru it.[29]

The Church of God in Christ offered the most emotionally and physically uninhibited meetings of any church in the city. Services emphasized shouting, faith healing, speaking in tongues, and the casting out of devils.

Like the churches, the persistence of old and the emergence of new fraternal organizations, lodges, and social service clubs sensitively mirrored the growing stratification of the black community. Three major lodges established by the prewar elite persisted into the 1920s: the Masonic Widows Son Lodge, the Knights of Pythias (Pride of Milwaukee), and the United Order of Odd Fellows. The rise of social welfare organizations like the MUL undermined the earlier material and mutual aid functions of these organizations. In the 1920s, established fraternal organizations turned increasingly toward a more restricted social, recreational, and supportive role in the community. They raised money for such organizations as the NAACP, MUL, and the churches; above all, these organizations provided members a medium for cultural expression and mutual social interaction. Lawrence E. Miller, a resident of Milwaukee since 1921 and later member of Widows Son, has described how, because of the stringent membership rules and practices governing old organizations, new lodges emerged to meet the needs of the changing class structure. In 1925, several newcomers banned together and formed the Blazing Star Chapter of the Prince Hall Masons. New elite in its leadership, membership, and orientation, Blazing Star was nevertheless more receptive to blacks from the expanding industrial working class than Widows Son. Elks Lodge Number 423, established around the same time, was even more decidedly working class in its membership and orientation.

Black women's organizations were particularly sensitive to changes in the Afro-American class structure, as well as to changes in the functions of black institutions. More than male organizations, middle-class black women's groups conducted supportive "charity work" for social welfare, civil rights, and religious organizations. Like male lodges, though, their chief function turned increasingly toward cultural expression and entertainment for members, a goal vividly reflected in the name of the most important new club to emerge by the mid-1920s: the Pleasant Company Needle Craft Club. The founding women of this club were the spouses of such men as Dr. P. Jay Gilmer, J. H. Kerns, J. A. Josey, and the wives of various ministers. To be sure, the older clubs, e.g., the Woman's Improvement Club, also had recreational, social, and cultural components, but prewar women's clubs, without the benefit of such organizations as the Urban League and NAACP, exhibited greater urgency, broader scope, and more intense involvement with the socioeconomic and political issues of the day.[30]

The activities of black working-class women, though more casual and informal, suggest an urgent orientation to the socioeconomic problems of the postwar era. Material or economic aid continued to weigh heavily among their primary activities. A glimpse of their work is revealed in Mrs. Blakely's description of her mother's role in the Church of God in Christ:

> My father started first in the ministry, and my mother thru his consistent urging and his hard work, was drawn into the ministry. She was a great gospel singer and great expounder of God's word. She helped many people, those that had no homes to live in, those that had no food, those that had no clothes. She went around the street gathering up wayward children. We reared two children that, she adopted them, two, we didn't adopt, we just raised them. My mother's home was always open to all strangers...when my father would be at work, these people would come to the home...and she really pushed, when my father would come home, she would have a house full, we would go from home to home, and sing and pray and administer the word of God. We'd wash dirty clothes. We'd take food and feed them, and every day every evening, we'd bring like 6, 7, 8 souls into God.[31]

The foregoing suggests a different social orientation for the wives of black industrial workers. Although integrally linked to cultural, social, and entertainment aspects, the goals of material relief and assistance seem to have been predominant. These women also conducted their work without the aid of as much formal education or the formalized instruments, a plethora of long-lasting women's clubs, that characterized the efforts of their middle-class counterparts.

Black institutions within Milwaukee's small Afro-American community developed in marked contrast to those of blacks in larger centers of Afro-American population. With fewer institutions at the outset of the period, Milwaukee blacks also moved less rapidly toward greater institutional diversity than blacks in Cleveland, Chicago, and other cities. As a consequence, class divisions in Milwaukee — themselves less prominent than elsewhere — found less institutional expression. Social stratification in the city's black institutional life usually involved one or two major institutions (e.g., St. Mark and Calvary versus the Holiness Church) rather than distinct clusters of several middle- and working-class institutions that prevailed among Afro-Americans in larger northern cities.[32]

Local politics also revealed internal divisions within Milwaukee's black population. Although efforts to elect a black alderman from the Sixth Ward in 1928 and 1932 failed as a result of white resistance and the small demographic base of the black population, internal cleavages along class lines also undermined these efforts at political representation. In the primary of 1928, Carlos Del Ruy, the Progressive Labor League's candidate, failed to obtain the endorsement of black business and professional people in the city. Dr. P. Jay Gilmer, then president of the local NAACP, took a cautious stand against any activity involving the Communist party and claimed that such involvement would split the black votes. James W. Ford, national organizer of the ANLC, decried this lack of racial unity and pointed to its genesis in the class interests of the black bourgeoisie: "Dr. Gilmer has made a serious error and placed the NAACP in an embarrassing position when he states that the situation has split the Colored vote. We are to presume that he means split the Colored workers from the Colored professional and business groups." Del Ruy's bid for office reflected a growing conviction that neither whites nor middle-class blacks could adequately represent the interests of Afro-American workers.[33]

Intraracial class conflicts that characterized the struggle for a black alderman in 1928 lessened under the deepening crisis of unemployment and suffering engendered by the Depression. In the election of 1932, Afro-Americans exhibited a high level of racial and class unity in their efforts to elect a black alderman. This unity, however, was not achieved without manifestations of conflict both within the black middle class and between the bourgeoisie and the Afro-American proletariat. The cleavage within the middle class was partly generational and ideological as well as economic and political. J. A. Josey and similar black Republicans believed that the white incumbent alderman Samuel Soref had responded adequately to stepped-up pressure from local blacks for increased political patronage and unemployment relief: "The laboring and unemployed men has no more devoted friend than Alderman Soref," Josey editorialized in the *Blade*. "Soref is directly responsible for two Colored girls teaching in the Public Schools in Milwaukee."[34]

On the other hand, a growing number of younger blacks believed that even more could be accomplished through a black elected official. Those endorsing the drive for a black alderman formed the Federated Council of Clubs (FCC) in the winter of 1932. This coalition, an alliance of black Republicans, Socialists, and Garveyites, gave the campaign for a black alderman its remarkable intraracial and inter-class unity among black workers, business, and professional people. Such an alliance of diverse factions, mainly a result of the deepening economic depression and racial antagonism, was also partly a conse-quence of the small demographic base, where ideological exclusive-ness could easily undermine possible political gains. All of the various elements, however, expected concrete class-related benefits from the alliance. The Lincoln Regular Republican Club and the Progressive Worker's Club, the Republican components, included such men as T. L. Johnson, operator of a small tailor shop and founder of the Pro-gressive Worker's Club (not related to the other well known tailor and political activist C. L. Johnson), and attorney George Hamilton. Although William V. Kelley avoided direct endorsements of political factions, by providing convenient meeting space at the offices of the MUL, he subtly placed his weight behind the rising new group of young Republicans. Moreover, as noted earlier, Josey and Kelley fre-quently opposed each other on a variety of issues. The new group of black Republicans sought to capitalize on the voting potential of the expanding black population in the interests of Afro-American business and professional people. Moreover, these two groups aimed to uproot the traditional black Republican organization (centered around J. A. Josey and the *Blade*) by a forceful appeal to the needs of black workers. The UNIA, for its part, desired to elect an Afro-American alderman as part of its practical response to increasing unemployment among the masses of black workers. Leading Garvey-ites, however, like Ernest Bland and Carlos Del Ruy, were also Socialists. They recognized the racial barriers to class unity and sought race unity in efforts to overcome such barriers.[35]

Indeed, the mass-based Milwaukee UNIA constituted the strong-est element in the push for a black alderman. Rooted deeply in the black working class, the Garvey Movement provided the central political and cultural symbolism designed to mobilize the expanding proletarian electorate. The UNIA used the concept of a "Black Moses" to engender support for the FCC aldermanic candidate. Following a bloc voting strategy in its thrust for a black alderman, the FCC held an elimination meeting, for black candidates only, at the UNIA's Liberty Hall in mid-February 1932. Of the three candidates attending the meeting, only one, attorney George Hamilton, agreed to the procedure, whereby a popular vote would eliminate all but one candidate, with other aspirants agreeing to abandon their campaigns in support of the victor. The FCC endorsed Hamilton and conducted his campaign around the slogans "Only Candidate Endorsed by Federated Council of Clubs" and "Lower Taxes." While one of the other two candidates soon dropped out of the race, C. L. Johnson, the well-known tailor and churchman, vigorously campaigned against Hamilton, claiming that Hamilton's endorsement unfairly curtailed freedom of choice among black voters. The *Blade* bitterly opposed the FCC and the UNIA and launched derisive attacks against both the slogan of a "Black Moses" and the exclusion of white alderman Soref from the candidate selection process: "The Council could not afford any other candidates to be present because none other than the Black Moses of the Federated Council of Clubs can bring a Colored Fire Department to Milwaukee, none but he can give us workers, policemen, and detectives, he will even give us black trees, black flowers and most of all a black and dismal place to live in."[36]

While both Hamilton and Johnson lost in the spring primary, they made strong showings that highlighted a process of both intraracial unity and disunity within the black community. Hamilton received the largest number of votes with 667 (13.7 percent) to Johnson's 437 (8.6 percent). White candidates Samuel Soref (46.0) and Ernst C. Schultz (17.0) received the first and second highest percentage of total votes. Had blacks indeed concentrated their votes on one candidate, they would have topped the second highest contender and won a position on the ballot during the spring election, but greater black unity would likely have provoked more white unity. Although most blacks extended customary support to Alderman Soref following the primary, a few Afro-Americans, such as Ernest Bland and Carlos Del Ruy, sided with the Socialists in an attempt to elect Ernst C. Schultz. Despite a level of black support, the Socialist candidate lost to Soref by more than 500 votes.[37] Black support of the Socialist candidate after the primary accented an enduring division between Afro-American workers and the middle class despite the onslaught of the Depression and the persistence of racial hostility in the social, economic, and political life of the city.

The role of the Garvey Movement in Milwaukee lends support to interpretations of the UNIA that emphasize its class as well as racial aspect. Developing within a strong Socialist context, key members of the Milwaukee UNIA were also Socialists. Through the creation of several civic organizations, local Garveyites intimately participated in the socioeconomic and political affairs of the black community, i.e., civil rights protest activities and electoral politics. The rhetoric of emigration, over-emphasized in accounts from larger cities, found little expression in Milwaukee. Indeed, as noted in Chapter 3, the Milwaukee UNIA spearheaded efforts of local blacks to block the importation of Afro-American strikebreakers during the postwar economic slump of 1921–22.

If Afro-Americans were fragmented internally, it was partly because they did not face a uniformly hostile urban environment. Despite the discriminatory treatment accorded blacks in the socioeconomic, political, and institutional life of the city, a great deal of interracial cooperation persisted and in some respects intensified. The most clear-cut and consistent evidence of interracial cooperation developed around the programs of the Milwaukee Urban League and, to a lesser degree, the NAACP. Milwaukee's Central Council of Social Agencies, the chief instrument for social services in the city, strengthened black-white cooperation when it supported the establishment of a local branch of the National Urban League. Following a social survey of Milwaukee's black community by Charles S. Johnson, graduate student at the University of Chicago and later head of the Social Science Department at Fisk University, the league began operating on 1 October 1919. The MUL's organizational framework largely conformed to the NUL's policy of establishing an interracial board, which formulated policy, and a black staff. White board members included industrialists Walter Stern and Edward Frost, who supported the organization almost entirely for a three-year probationary period before the MUL became a member of the Community Fund in 1922. Black board members consisted of professional people such as Dr. T. A. Boger and Dr. Rankford Holley. White officers included Dr. Charles H. Beal, pastor of the Grand Avenue Congregational Church, president; Lenora Rosing, executive secretary of the Central Council of Social Agencies, treasurer; and Edward Frost, vice-president. Mabel Raimey, a stenographer and secretary to the board, and attorney Ambrose Nutt, first executive secretary of the Milwaukee branch, were black founding officers of the organization. From its beginning through the 1920s and early 1930s, the MUL vigorously promoted interracial cooperation through several devices: public speeches, newspaper articles, and special programs of various types.[38]

Although the evidence is scanty, white board members were certainly not equally interested in blacks. Businessmen like Frost and Stern undoubtedly had vested interests in the MUL, since it served as an instrument for labor recruitment during a period of labor shortage. Both men probably depended to a degree on blacks to man their local plants. On the other hand, the minister, Dr. Beal, and probably the social worker, Lenora Rosing, were more altruistic in their support of local black welfare programs. Ardie Halyard has described Dr. Beal as a "liberal man" who sincerely "helped to integrate" black newcomers into the city of Milwaukee. Not only his service on the MUL board, but also his church, became an important source of support for local blacks. Whatever the specific motives of whites may have been, however, their interest in blacks was intricately intertwined with the racial and class context of the period. Operating from a set of bourgeois values, the MUL's interracial program aimed to encourage whites, mainly industrialists and professional people, to view blacks in class rather than simply in racial terms, with emphasis on the so-called more progressive and ambitious middle class.

> With the belief that Interracial acquaintance promotes Interracial tolerance and goodwill, no opportunity for work in that direction is allowed to escape. Following a well established custom, the League sponsored a "pre-Thanksgiving Dinner" at its rooms last November, at which time more than (60) persons of both races had an opportunity to get acquainted.... Many of these visitors had for the first time, an opportunity to see not only the Negro they had heard about, but also the more progressive and ambitious types.[39]

In contrast to the MUL, the NAACP drew more directly upon an Afro-American constituency, yet, like the MUL, the NAACP encouraged the membership and participation of leading white citizens. A founding membership of thirty-two included only three whites, who nonetheless served in influential positions of the organization. One of the founding members, Alice J. Kaine, widow of the philanthropist Jonathan Kaine, served as treasurer, and both Mayor Hoan and his assistant, Otto Hauser, pastor of the First German Baptist Church and later of Immanuel Baptist Church, accepted positions on the board at various times during the period. Other influential white members included Walter Stern and Emma W. Quarles, wife of at-

torney and local philanthropist Charles Quarles. Such white participation, though less significant than in the MUL, pinpointed the
importance of white support in the vigorous civil rights struggle of
local blacks.

Like white participants in the MUL, white members of the
NAACP reflected the complex blending of vested economic and
political interests with altruistic concern for Afro-American social
welfare. Walter Stern's support of the NAACP suggests a more
ambiguous relationship than the above emphasis on his economic
interests in the MUL suggests. Although the MUL proved to be an effective recruiter of low-wage black labor for area industries, Stern
nevertheless chose to support the civil rights activities of the
Milwaukee NAACP as well. On the other hand, providing initial
financial and moral support, individuals like Mrs. Quarles exhibited
a more uniform philanthropic interest in local blacks. Conversely,
Mayor Hoan gave attention to local blacks largely for political
reasons. The Sixth Ward, and blacks in particular, voted overwhelm-
ingly for Hoan in muncipal elections. Thus, Hoan often extended his
support of blacks beyond membership on the NAACP board to concrete economic and political matters. As noted in Chapter 3, Wilbur
and Ardie Halyard, founders of the Columbia Building and Loan
Association, entered the city in 1923 through a strong letter of recommendation to Mayor Hoan, who in turn placed his support behind
their business activities. Hoan also took a firm stand, under the
urging of local blacks and their white allies, against the Ku Klux Klan
and closed the Milwaukee auditorium to Klan meetings in 1922. The
Klan thus did not figure as prominently in race relations in Milwaukee as in several other northern cities.[40]

Proletarianization of Milwaukee's Afro-American population between World War I and the Depression unleashed forces that
heightened intra- and interracial antagonisms. The competitive interplay of blacks and whites in the job and housing markets created tensions, though not of the violent intensity evident in larger cities, that
affected race relations in nearly every aspect of the city's social, economic, and political life. As in their struggle for jobs and housing,
Afro-Americans mounted and sustained vigorous protests against
racial discrimination in virtually all of its manifestations.

Despite evidence of racial unity in their response to racial and class
injustice, however, the socioeconomic and political struggles of Afro-

Americans were fraught with intraracial class divisions. The processes that enabled blacks to extend their institutional, economic, and political potential also promoted greater social class differentiation. Distinctions between the new black middle class and the old elite, on the one hand, and the expanding urban-industrial proletariat on the other became more sharply drawn. The persistence of white racial hostility, intensified by the industrial proletarianization of Afro-Americans, held racial and class consciousness among Milwaukee blacks in a delicate balance. Although the trend toward racial animosity against blacks would continue into the mid-1930s, the organizing efforts of the Congress of Industrial Organizations and the government-directed movement of blacks into defense industries would significantly modify inter- and intraracial relations. These processes will be examined in chapters 5 and 6.

## NOTES

1. Alan Spear, "The Origins of the Urban Ghetto, 1870–1915," in Nathan I. Huggins, Martin Kilson, and Daniel M. Fox, eds. *Key Issues in the Afro-American Experience* (New York: Harcourt Brace Jovanovich, 1971), pp. 153–66. For general discussions of competitive race relations in the United States, see Pierre van den Berghe, *Race and Racism* (New York: John Wiley and Sons, 1967), pp. 25–34, and William J. Wilson, *The Declining Significance of Race: Blacks and Changing American Institutions* (Chicago: University of Chicago Press, 1978), especially Chapter 5.
2. Milwaukee Urban League Monthly Report, May 1939.
3. *Milwaukee Journal,* 27 and 28 May 1919.
4. Milwaukee National Association for the Advancement of Colored People, "The Genesis of Race Riots, Mob Violence and Lynchings: One Reason for NAACP," Box G-219, NAACP Papers.
5. Excerpts reprinted in the *Wisconsin Enterprise Blade,* 17 May 1919. For black protests against racist reporting, see *Blade,* 27 June 1918, 18 July 1918, 5 June 1919, 25 July 1926, 22 Apr. 1932.
6. "Butterfly Theatre Refuses Race Admission," *Blade,* 4 Jan. 1917; *Blade,* 10 July 1919, 28 Aug. 1919; "Jim Crowism in Milwaukee," *National Defender and Sun,* 24 Mar. 1917; *Milwaukee Sentinel,* 26 May 1920; George H. DeReef to Mary White Ovington, chair of NAACP national board of directors, 26 May 1920, Box C-227, NAACP Papers; "Cases handled by the Milwaukee Branch of the NAACP, 1924," Box G-219, NAACP Papers.
7. DeReef to Ovington, 26 Feb. 1920, Box C-227, NAACP Papers;

"Revised Statute, Section 4398c," Box C-227, NAACP Papers; *Blade,* 28 Aug. 1919; *Milwaukee Sentinel,* 26 May 1920; DeReef to Ovington, 26 May 1920, Box C-227, NAACP Papers; *Wisconsin Session Laws: Including All of the Acts and Certain Resolutions, 1931* (Madison: 1931), p. 20.

8. NAACP field secretary to L. H. Palmer, 10 July 1918; L. H. Palmer to John R. Shillady, 27 June 1918, Box G-219, NAACP Papers; *Blade,* 27 June 1918; Daniel W. Hoan to Julius Rosenwald Fund, 30 Apr. 1931, and Michael M. Davis, director of medical services of the Rosenwald Fund, to Hoan, 4 May 1931, Box 26, File 98, Daniel W. Hoan Papers, 1910-53 (Milwaukee County Historical Society). When blacks did obtain hospital care outside the Milwaukee County Hospital, it occasioned enthusiastic and exaggerated comments from the black press: "No Color Line at Mt. Sinai," *Blade,* 1 Sept. 1928; P. Jay Gilmer to Robert S. Abbott, editor, *Chicago Defender,* 10 Nov. 1927; Gilmer to district manager, Metropolitan Life Insurance Company, 1 Nov. 1927, Box G-219, NAACP Papers; "Statement of the Activities of the Branch for the Year Ending 15 November 1928," Box G-219, NAACP Papers; *Blade,* 2 Nov. 1928.

9. Thomas R. Buchanan, "Black Milwaukee, 1890-1915" (master's thesis, University of Wisconsin-Milwaukee, 1968), pp. 86-88; Robert Wells, "Negro Migration Came Late," *Milwaukee Journal,* 8 Nov. 1967; Wilbur Halyard to Daniel Hoan, 22 Feb. 1929, and Milwaukee Police Department, office of the inspector, to J. G. Laubenheimer, chief of police, 11 Mar. 1929, Box 26, File 98, Hoan Papers; "A Colored for Detective," *Blade,* 25 July 1925; *Blade,* 23 Apr. 1932, 7 Nov. 1925, 4 Jan. 1917; Marie Burgette, secretary Milwaukee NAACP, to May Childs Nerney, national secretary NAACP, 28 June 1915, Box G-219, NAACP Papers; "Police Women Needed in this Community," *Blade,* 23 Apr. 1932.

10. Roy Schultz, Dr. C. F. Turney, and Alfred Taylor to Hoan, 24 May 1932, and Mayor Hoan to Schultz, Turney, and Taylor, 4 June 1932, Box 26, File 98, Hoan Papers.

11. "A Great Gathering of Representative Negroes of the State at Oshkosh, Wisconsin . . . Meeting a Success — Next Meeting at Milwaukee," *Blade,* 29 June 1916, 2 Aug. 1917, 26 June 1919.

12. George DeReef, "Milwaukee County Jurors," *Blade,* 25 Apr. 1918; "Victory for Blade: Colored Man Serving on Milwaukee Jury," *Blade,* 27 Feb. 1919; *Milwaukee Sentinel,* 10 Feb. 1919.

13. William V. Kelley, "The Story of the Milwaukee Urban League" (Milwaukee: Newspaper Clippings File of the Milwaukee Urban League, ca. 1945); MUL Monthly and Annual Reports, "Summary of the Findings of the Unit Survey," Box 20, United Community Services of Greater Milwaukee Papers, 1903-66 (University of Wisconsin-Milwaukee, Area Research Center); "Milwaukee County Civil Service Commis-

sion; Job Description: Social Worker (For Colored People)"; "Resolutions from the Colored People of Milwaukee...Concerning...the Position of Colored Probation Officer and Welfare Worker," Folders 1–3, Cecil A. Fisher Papers, 1921–66 (University of Wisconsin–Milwaukee, Area Research Center); *Blade,* 8 Sept. 1928; "Calvin Moody," *Echo: Bicentennial Issue* 21, no. 27 (1976): 29–30; for black Outdoor Relief Department employee, see *Blade,* 8 Sept. 1928; interview with Bernice C. Lindsay, 9 Aug. 1979; Howard Rabinowitz, *Race Relations in the Urban South, 1865–1890* (1978; rept. Urbana: University of Illinois Press, 1980), pp. 125–226.

14. Milwaukee Board of Election Commissioners, *Biennial Reports, 1916 through 1932* (Milwaukee Legislative Reference Bureau); "Fusion in Milwaukee," *Blade,* 24 Oct. 1918.

15. *Blade,* 28 Mar. 1918; Progressive Labor League of Milwaukee circular letter, 5 Mar. 1928, Box G-219, NAACP Papers; James W. Ford to James Weldon Johnson, 23 Feb. 1928, Box G-219, NAACP Papers.

16. "Our Anchor Is in the Republican Party," *Blade,* 21 Sept. 1916; "The Party of Human Liberty," *Blade,* 9 Apr. 1932; Milwaukee County Board of Election Commissioners, *Biennial Reports, 1916 through 1932* (Milwaukee Legislative Reference Bureau); Keith Robert Schmitz, "Milwaukee and its Black Community, 1930–1942" (master's thesis, University of Wisconsin–Milwaukee, 1979), pp. 57–60; Oscar Glantz, "The Negro Voter in Northern Industrial Cities," *Western Political Quarterly* 13 (1960): 999–1010, n. 2.

17. United States Bureau of the Census, *Religious Bodies, 1916, pt. 1* (Washington: Department of Commerce, 1916), pp. 556–57, 576–77; Charles E. Hall, *Negroes in the United States, 1920–1932* (1935; rept. New York: Arno Press, 1969), p. 536; "Milwaukee and Her Progressive Citizens," *Blade,* 4 Jan. 1917, 4 Sept. 1927, 10 July 1919, 7 Sept. 1916, 11 Jan. 1917, 18 Jan. 1917, 13 Sept. 1917, 25 Jan. 1917, 15 Mar. 1917, 14 June 1917, 22 Nov. 1917, 21 Mar. 1918, 10 Jan. 1925, 18 July 1925, 24 Jan. 1925, 10 Sept. 1932. Mary Ellen Shadd, ed., *Negro Business Directory of the State of Wisconsin* (Milwaukee, 1950), pp. 11–26; Rev. Berchmans Bittle, *A Herald of the Great King* (Milwaukee: St. Benedict the Moor Mission, 1933), pp. 84–127, an orthodox Catholic perspective on the role of Father Stephen Eckert, a white priest, in developing the programs of St. Benedict; Schmitz, "Milwaukee and its Black Community, 1930–1942," pp. 23–25. Bicentennial Project Committee, "Black Heritage–Wisconsin, 1776–1976" (Milwaukee, 1976), p. 25; "St. Mark Burns Mortgage," Folders 1–3, Fisher Papers; "Church of the Anvil: St. Mark AME" (Milwaukee, 1969); "Calvary Saga," *Echo* 21, no. 27 (1976): 13; "Dedicatory Program: Calvary Baptist Church History" (Milwaukee, n.d.); interview with Ernest Bland, 8 Aug. 1979.

18. Interracial Committee of Council of Social Agencies, "Survey of the Negro Population of Milwaukee, Wisc. 1928," Ser. 6, Box 59, National Urban League Papers; "Exclusive Negroes," *Blade,* 31 July 1926.

19. "Inter-Racial Divisions," *Blade,* 16 Apr. 1932; "Who Are Our Better Class?" *Blade,* 6 Feb. 1932.

20. "Application: NAACP—Milwaukee Branch, January 23, 1915," Box G-219, NAACP Papers. For a discussion of the "New Negro" in the Milwaukee context, see Chapter 3.

21. "Milwaukee NAACP Holds Warm Meeting," *Blade,* 5 June 1919; "Colored Soldiers, Sailors, and Marines to Have Club," *Milwaukee Journal,* 11 June 1919; "Black Soldiers Club," *Blade,* 10 July 1919; field secretary NAACP to L. H. Palmer, 10 July 1918, and Palmer to John Shillady, 27 June 1918, Box G-219, NAACP Papers; "Community Soldiers Club," *Blade,* 15 Aug. 1919.

22. Interview with Ernest Bland, 8 Aug. 1979; Alex Haley and Malcolm X, *The Autobiography of Malcolm X* (New York: Grove Press, 1964), pp. 1–5; follow-up interview with Ernest Bland, 29 Sept. 1982.

23. R. B. Montgomery to James Weldon Johnson, 14 Sept. 1923, 15 Oct. 1923, 25 Oct. 1923; Johnson to Montgomery, 27 Oct. 1923; Robert Bagnall, director of NAACP branches, to Johnson, 13 Nov. 1923; Bagnall to Montgomery, 29 Oct. 1923; Montgomery to J. E. Springarn, national treasurer NAACP, 25 Nov. 1923, Box G-219, NAACP Papers; R. Bagnall to DeReef, 5 Nov. 1923; DeReef to Bagnall, 30 Oct. 1923; Rev. E. W. Thomas to NAACP national headquarters, 7 Nov. 1923; Montgomery to Bagnall, 2 Jan. 1924; Montgomery to Johnson, 2 Jan. 1924, Box G-219, NAACP Papers.

24. Bagnall to Montgomery, 13 Dec. 1923; Bagnall to Rev. E. W. Thomas, 12 Dec. 1923; Montgomery to Bagnall, 28 Dec. 1923, Box G-219, NAACP Papers; Edgar Thomas to Bagnall, 23 Jan. 1924 and 20 Feb. 1924; "Pledges of Milwaukee Branch—April 24, 1924", and "Membership Lists and Dues, 1927, 1928, and 1929," all in Box G-219, NAACP Papers.

25. "Negroes Regret Slaves Were Set Free, He Asserts," *Blade,* 9 Apr. 1932; "A Noble Experiment," *Blade,* 6 Feb. 1932; "Social Center Explained," *Blade,* 13 Feb. 1932; "Wm V. Kelley Exec. — Sec'y Urban League Must Go: Tell White Students Negroes Regret Proclamation," *Blade,* 13 Feb. 1932; Schmitz, "Milwaukee and Its Black Community," pp. 98–105; "Truth Will Out," *Blade,* 5 Mar. 1932; "Seeking Glory," *Blade,* 16 Jan. 1932.

26. See n. 17.

27. Interview with Bernice Lindsay, 9 Aug. 1979.

28. *Blade,* 18 July 1918, 10 May 1917; Shadd, ed., *Negro Business Directory,* pp.

11–26; *Blade,* 4 Aug. 1928, 28 Feb. 1925; "A Brief History of St. Matthew Christian Methodist Episcopal" (Milwaukee: Personal Collection of Louise Bracey, Feb.–Mar. 1958). The church's name was later changed from "Colored Methodist" to "Christian Methodist." "Tabernacle Community Baptist Church: History" (Milwaukee, 1971).

29. *Blade,* 14 Feb. 1925 and 4 Apr. 1925; Joe Savage, "Good News, Chariots Coming: The Black Church in Milwaukee" (Milwaukee: Transcript WMVS Television Channel 10, ca. 1979).

30. Interview with Lawrence E. Miller, 30 Aug. 1979; *Blade,* 4 Jan. 1917, 15 Aug. 1918, 29 Mar. 1919, 29 Aug. 1925, 26 June 1926; Buchanan, "Black Milwaukee," pp. 114–19; interview with Ernest Bland, 8 Aug. 1979; "Blazing Star Lodge No. 4: List of Officers, 1925–1978" (Milwaukee, 1979); "Mrs. Horton Makes Annual Address," *Blade,* 18 Oct. 1917; Virginia W. Williams, "Negro History Makers in Milwaukee," *Milwaukee Star,* 13 Nov. 1965.

31. Savage, "Good News."

32. Allan H. Spear, *Black Chicago: The Making of a Negro Ghetto, 1890–1920* (Chicago: University of Chicago Press, 1967) pp. 99–126; Kenneth L. Kusmer, *A Ghetto Takes Shape: Black Cleveland, 1870–1930* (Urbana: University of Illinois Press, 1976), pp. 235–74.

33. Milwaukee County Board of Election Commissioners, *Biennial Reports, 1928–1932* (Milwaukee Legislative Reference Bureau); P. Jay Gilmer to James Weldon Johnson, 3 Mar. 1928, Box G-219, NAACP Papers.

34. *Blade,* 30 Jan. 1932, 5 Mar. 1932; interview with Ernest Bland, 8 Aug. 1979; "The Copyright Leader," *Blade,* 13 Feb. 1932.

35. Interview with Ernest Bland, 8 Aug. 1979; "The Black and White Revue," *Blade,* 13 Feb. 1932; follow-up interview with Ernest Bland, 29 Sept. 1982.

36. *Blade,* 12 Mar. 1932; interview with Ernest Bland, 8 Aug. 1979; "What Next? Same Old Trick," *Blade,* 27 Feb. 1932; "Eliminators Admit There was No Elimination," *Blade,* 5 Mar. 1932; "Truth Will Out," *Blade,* 5 Mar. 1932; "Eliminators," *Blade,* 5 Mar. 1932.

37. Interview with Ernest Bland, 8 Aug. 1979; *Blade,* 2 Apr. 1932; "Temporary Negro Socialist's Wing Lost in the Sixth Ward," *Blade,* 9 Apr. 1932, 5 Nov. 1932; Milwaukee County Board of Election Commissioners, *Biennial Reports, 1928–1932* (Milwaukee Legislative Reference Bureau).

38. "Statement Given by the National Urban League on the Race Conditions at the Present Time," Box 26, File 98, Hoan Papers; Kelley, "Story of the Milwaukee Urban League" (Milwaukee, ca. 1945); *Blade,* 28 Mar. 1918, 15 June 1918, 9 Oct. 1919; William V. Kelley, "Milwaukee Urban League," Ser. 4, Box 31, NUL Papers; *Milwaukee City Directory* (Milwau-

kee: Wright's City Directory, 1919, 1920, and 1925); Nancy Weiss, *The National Urban League, 1910–1940* (New York: Oxford University Press, 1974), pp. 29–70.

39. MUL Seventh Annual Report, 1 Oct. 1928 to Sept. 1929; "Urban League Gains Comments of Distinguished Milwaukeeans," *Blade,* 2 May 1925; follow-up interview with Ardie A. Halyard, 24 Sept. 1982.

40. "Application: NAACP-Milwaukee Branch, January 23, 1915," Rev. E. W. Thomas to national NAACP office, 7 Nov. 1923; LaJoyeaux H. Stanton, secretary Milwaukee NAACP, to Robert Bagnall, 10 Jan. 1927, Box G-219, NAACP Papers; *Milwaukee City Directory* (Milwaukee: Wright's City Directory, 1917, 1919, and 1927); assistant secretary NAACP to George H. DeReef, 11 May 1921, Box G-219, NAACP Papers; "Negroes Hear Truth About Hoan and Klan, 1 April 1924," Box 26, File 98, Hoan Papers; *National Advocate,* 20 Oct. 1922, 7 May 1921, 27 Oct. 1922; Kusmer, *A Ghetto Takes Shape,* p. 175.

Wilbur and Ardie Halyard founded the Columbia Building and Loan
Association in 1924. The Halyards managed a housing camp for white
workers at the Fairbanks-Morse Corporation in Beloit, Wisconsin, before
arriving in Milwaukee in 1923. They were, respectively, graduates of
Morehouse College and Atlanta University in Georgia. (Courtesy: Private Collection of Ardie A. Halyard, Milwaukee, Wisconsin)

Clarence L. Johnson and his wife, Cleopatra, established their tailoring
business in 1921. They came to Milwaukee in 1920 from Beloit, Wisconsin, where Clarence worked in a foundry at the Fairbanks-Morse Corporation. The Johnsons were graduates of Tuskegee Institute, where they
majored in tailoring. (Courtesy: Milwaukee Black Heritage Project, University of Wisconsin–Milwaukee-Extension)

Emile O'Bee established his funeral business in 1924. He was assisted in this effort by Carl F. Watson, another black funeral director of the period. (Courtesy: Black Heritage Project, University of Wisconsin–Milwaukee-Extension)

J. Harvey Kerns directed the Milwaukee Urban League between 1923 and 1927 before moving on to Omaha, Nebraska, where he directed the Omaha Urban League. He was succeeded by William V. Kelley, a graduate of Fisk University, who directed the Milwaukee Urban League through the Depression and World War II. (Courtesy: Black Heritage Project, University of Wisconsin–Milwaukee-Extension)

Millie French was one of the first two Afro-American school teachers to receive an appointment in the Milwaukee public school system. She was assigned to the Fourth Street School. (Courtesy: Black Heritage Project, University of Wisconsin–Milwaukee-Extension)

Blacks played on a baseball team sponsored by the Wehr Steel Foundry in 1935. The Wehr Steel Foundry became the scene of a major racial confrontation in 1934, when white workers walked out in an effort to remove black employees. Violence erupted when blacks served as strikebreakers. The company, however, soon reopened on an open-shop basis. (Courtesy: Black Heritage Project, University of Wisconsin–Milwaukee-Extension)

The pastor and officers of St. Mark African Methodist Episcopal church during its 75th Anniversary celebration in 1944. Founded four years after the Civil War, St. Mark was and remains the oldest black church in the city of Milwaukee. Black churches in Milwaukee expanded slowly until World War I. Only two other churches, Calvary Baptist and St. Benedict the Moor Mission and School, an interracial Catholic church of the Capuchin Order, served the religious needs of blacks before 1915. (Courtesy: Black Heritage Project, University of Wisconsin–Milwaukee-Extension)

A social function at St. Mark African Methodist Episcopal church during World War II. (Courtesy: Black Heritage Project, University of Wisconsin–Milwaukee-Extension)

LeRoy Simmons, a realtor, was elected to the Wisconsin state legislature in 1944. He was the first black to be elected to that body since 1906, when Lucien Palmer served for one term. Palmer won the election partly by camouflaging his racial identity. Simmons, however, gained the endorsement of the predominantly white Democratic party, as well as support from the growing black population. (Courtesy: Black Heritage Project, University of Wisconsin–Milwaukee-Extension)

# PART THREE

# Depression, World War II, and the Precarious Nature of Black Urban-Industrial Working Class Formation, 1933–45

# 5

## Depression, World War II, and the Struggle for Fair Employment in Defense Industries, 1933–45

The Afro-American experience during the Depression and World War II graphically continued to illustrate the tenuous nature of black urban-industrial working-class formation. From the onset of the Depression, black unemployment rapidly exceeded that of whites and persisted at disproportionately high levels throughout the period. Even as whites gradually reentered industrial jobs with the initiation of defense production by 1939–40, blacks remained largely outside the industrial workplace. The continuation of labor union discrimination, particularly from the American Federation of Labor (AFL), the racist hiring practices of employers, and the prolonged crisis in the urban economy impeded the reemployment of blacks. But the labor demands of war industries and military conscription soon exhausted available labor supplies and blacks, after the nearly complete rehiring of unemployed whites, reclaimed industrial jobs in full force.

Most blacks reentered industrial positions at the lowest rungs of the industrial ladder, yet, unlike during the World War I period, when blacks almost exclusively entered industry as unskilled laborers, Afro-Americans breached what St. Clair Drake and Horace R. Cayton have called the "job ceiling" at the level of skilled and semiskilled occupations. Despite the fragile "industrial reserve" character of the black urban economic experience, a more consolidated Afro-American proletariat emerged by 1945.[1] The reemergence of the Afro-American proletariat, though still weak, was spurred forward by several interlocking factors: the organizing efforts of the Congress of Industrial Organizations (CIO), labor shortages of World War II, the activities of various federal manpower agencies, especially the Fair Employment Practices Committee (FEPC), and the vigorous socio-economic and political efforts of blacks on their own behalf.

Black life in Milwaukee between 1933 and 1945 unfolded within the larger context of economic, social, and political changes. By the end of 1933, the city showed some degree of economic recovery as a result of New Deal relief programs and legalization of 3.2 percent beer. Optimistic economic signs, a rise in the payroll index and a decrease in business failures among other indicators, prompted the *Milwaukee Sentinel* to assert in 1936 that "Milwaukee's industry and commerce had thrown away 'their crutches and walked out of the depression sick room' at last." But the Depression was not yet over; drastic layoffs in the automotive, farm implements, and heavy machinery group came in the wake of a serious recession between August 1937 and September 1938. As late as 1939, approximately one of every five Milwaukee county families received some form of public aid.[2]

In ways similar to other cities, Milwaukee benefitted immensely from the various New Deal programs. Such federal agencies as the WPA (Works Progress, later Works Projects Administration) and others subsidized the construction of miles of sewers and streets, two low-cost housing projects, and several school buildings. Expenditures from federal relief agencies peaked in 1936 when the city received an estimated $26 million. New rules tightening the qualifications for aid and, especially, the beginning of war production markedly decreased the number of persons on WPA rolls by 1940.[3]

Economic depression severely curtailed Milwaukee's population growth and transformed political and economic relations in the city. The population increased by only 9,223 to 587,472 between 1930 and 1940, the lowest rate (1.5 percent) of growth in Milwaukee's history. Heavy labor demands during World War II, however, arrested population decline and restimulated migration to the city, especially from rural areas of the South. By 1945, according to Milwaukee Health Department statistics, the population increased by an estimated 2.6 percent (15,528) over the 1940 figure (see Table 5.1).

In Milwaukee, as in other cities, especially in the North and West, the Depression and various New Deal measures altered the relation of workers to employers and to each other. Federal protection of labor's right to collective bargaining stimulated a tremendous organizing

Table 5.1. Population of Milwaukee by Race and Nativity, 1930–45

| Year | Total Pop.* | Blacks | Percent | Foreign-born Whites | Percent | American-born Whites | Percent |
|------|-------------|--------|---------|---------------------|---------|----------------------|---------|
| 1930 | 578,249 | 7,501 | 1.2 | 109,383 | 18.9 | 459,424 | 79.4 |
| 1940 | 587,472 | 8,821 | 1.5 | 83,809 | 14.3 | 494,368 | 84.1 |
| 1945 | 603,000 | 10,200 | 1.6 | N/A | N/A | N/A | N/A |
| | | | Percentage Increase or Decrease | | | | |
| 1930–40 | 1.5 | | 17.5 | −23.3 | | 7.6 | |
| 1940–45 | 2.6 | | 15.5 | N/A | | N/A | |

*Includes a small number of other nonwhite ethnic groups.

Source: Bureau of Census, *Sixteenth Census of U.S.: 1940 Population, vol. 2, pt. 7* (Washington: Government Printing Office, 1943), pp. 680–81; Lynagh, p. 33.

thrust among Milwaukee workers, which precipitated a split within the labor movement. Against the decided opposition of the Milwaukee Federated Trades Council, the Committee for Industrial Organizations, seeking to organize all workers into mass-production unions, began its organizational drive in Milwaukee in 1936. In July 1937, officers of sixty-two CIO locals formed the Milwaukee County Industrial Union Council (IUC) and broke with the narrow, craft-oriented, AFL-dominated FTC. Emergence of a stronger labor influence introduced a complex pattern of urban Depression politics. In addition to the regular Democratic and Republican parties, there were other key contenders for control of municipal government. The Progressive wing of the Republican party separated from the regular Republicans in 1934 and actively competed with the Socialists for votes in Milwaukee County. Since this competition sometimes resulted in the election of more conservative Democrats and Republicans, often under the nonpartisan banner, Progressives, Socialists, and labor leaders (the Wisconsin Federation of Labor and the Milwaukee Federated Trades Council) organized the Farmer-Labor Progressive League or Progressive party in 1935. The Progressive party, although it barred the CIO because of its Communist links and although some Progressives such as Robert LaFollette refused to join, functioned until about 1941. At that time, the Socialists returned to the ballot as a separate party and the Progressive party steadily declined and reentered regular Republican ranks by the end of World War II. Labor organizations, representatives of the CIO, AFL, and the railroad unions, formed the United Labor Committee in 1940 and gravitated toward the Democratic party. The end of the Depression brought the end of third-party politics in Milwaukee. Socialist Mayor D. W. Hoan was among its victims. Although Democrats and Republicans consistently collaborated in attempts to unseat Hoan, they failed to do so until 1940. Following passage of the Boncel Act of 1935, giving the mayor considerable discretionary power in dealing with industrial strikes, Hoan's political base progressively eroded as manufacturers vigorously campaigned against his reelection. The city council repealed the Boncel Act, which businessmen thoroughly opposed, in 1936, and by 1940 the so-called non-partisan candidate, Carl Zeidler, defeated Hoan on a strategy that aimed to encourage business, cut taxes, and, as Zeidler put it, "pull this town out of Socialist lethargy that scares away business, keeps our men unemployed, denies our youth a chance for jobs."[4]

Within this urban milieu, Milwaukee's black population increased from 7,501 to 8,721 during the Depression decade, an increase of only 17.5 percent. Afro-Americans nevertheless expanded their numbers at a faster rate than did the city as a whole. By 1945, Milwaukee's black population reached an estimated 10,200. Despite the acute labor demands of World War II, blacks in Milwaukee, with 1.6 percent of the total population, persisted as one of the smallest Afro-American communities in northern cities (see Table 5.1). Blacks made up 8.2, 6.1, 9.2, and 9.6 percent, respectively, of Chicago, New York, Detroit, and Cleveland's populations in 1940. Black newcomers to the city, as in the pre-Depression years, arrived mainly from the states of the lower South. Chicago continued to serve as an important feeder of black migrants to Milwaukee. The route to Milwaukee via Chicago, however, was often circuitous. In its annual report for 1942–43, the Milwaukee Urban League traced the course of one migrant: "J. H. ——— was born in Canton, Mississippi. At 16 he went to Memphis, Tennessee. From Memphis he went to Sapulpa, Oklahoma. From Sapulpa he went to the army and to France. After the war [World War I] he settled in Kansas City. From Kansas City [he migrated to] Chicago and then Milwaukee at the age of 40. He has lived in Milwaukee for six (6) years."[5] While Chicago persisted as a key entrepôt for black newcomers to Milwaukee, the number arriving directly from the South gradually increased. In October 1937, the majority of 200 new job applicants with the MUL's industrial department arrived directly from the South, but by 1940, as earlier migrants established their families, the percentage of blacks born in Wisconsin significantly increased, from 10.2 percent of Milwaukee's black population in 1930 to 23.8 percent in 1940.[6]

Milwaukee blacks had entered the city's industries in significant numbers during World War I and its aftermath, but the Depression arrested, even temporarily reversed, the process of black proletarianization. White competition for even the lowest industrial jobs made blacks even more vulnerable to layoffs and firings. An MUL survey of 331 black male workers in 1933 revealed 54.6 percent unemployed and 69.1 percent receiving county aid because of unemployment or insufficient wages. The U.S. unemployment census of 1937 showed that blacks, with 1.5 percent of the population, comprised 3.9 percent of the "totally unemployed," excluding public emergency workers. Afro-Americans constituted 6.9 percent of all workers on public emergency relief projects (see Table 5.2). The 1940 census of unemployment presented an even more telling picture of Afro-American economic decline: only 49.0 percent of black men worked in private employment compared to 81.0 percent for whites. The 29.3 percent of black males seeking employment stood in sharp contrast to the 12.7 percent so classified among white workers. While the unemployment

Table 5.2. Milwaukee's Labor Force: Unemployed and Emergency Workers by Race and Sex, 1937

| | Totally Unemployed* | | Emergency Workers | | Partly Unemployed | |
|---|---|---|---|---|---|---|
| | Number | Percent | Number | Percent | Number | Percent |
| City Total | 31,554 | 100.0 | 14,063 | 100.0 | 12,984 | 100.0 |
| Male | 22,924 | 72.6 | 11,891 | 84.5 | 10,042 | 77.3 |
| Female | 8,630 | 27.3 | 2,172 | 15.4 | 2,942 | 22.6 |
| Blacks | 1,235 | 3.9 | 984 | 6.9 | 299 | 2.3 |
| Male | 679 | 2.1 | 738 | 5.2 | 234 | 1.8 |
| Female | 556 | 1.7 | 246 | 1.7 | 65 | 0.5 |
| Whites | 30,246 | 95.8 | 13,034 | 92.6 | 12,669 | 97.5 |
| Male | 22,198 | 70.3 | 11,114 | 79.0 | 9,792 | 75.4 |
| Female | 8,048 | 25.5 | 1,920 | 13.6 | 2,877 | 22.1 |
| Other Races | 73 | 0.2 | 45 | 0.3 | 16 | 0.1 |
| Male | 47 | 0.1 | 39 | 0.2 | 16 | 0.1 |
| Female | 26 | 0.0 | 6 | 0.0 | — | — |

*Persons ages 15–74 who registered in the unemployment census. Totally unemployed does not include emergency workers.

Source: Bureau of Census, *Partial Employment, Unemployment, and Occupations: 1937, vol. 3* (Washington: Government Printing Office, 1938), pp. 649–50.

statistics of black men and women were nearly identical, white women had a slightly higher percentage of their numbers in private employment and a lower unemployment rate than white men (see Table 5.3).

The number of gainfully employed Afro-American men plummeted from 2,797 in 1930 to 1,382 in 1940. The number of unskilled workers precipitously dropped by 70.1 percent from 1,557 in 1930 to 459 during the same decade; though less dramatically, the number of skilled and semiskilled black employees likewise sharply declined. Because black women were largely concentrated in domestic and personal service jobs by 1930, the Depression was relatively more harsh on female workers. The number of black women in domestic and personal service dropped by 37.0 percent; conversely, the number of all females in domestic work increased by 15.4 percent (see Tables 5.4 and 5.5, Appendix 6). Compared to black populations in other northern cities, with few exceptions, Afro-Americans in Milwaukee had more of their numbers unemployed by 1940. With a rate of unemployment comparable to Milwaukee's at the outset of the Depression, Detroit counted only 15.7 percent of its black men seeking work in 1940, compared to 29.3 percent for Milwaukee (see Table 5.6).

Employers continued to view Afro-Americans as qualified for only dirty, unpleasant, low-paying, and heavy work. "Well," said one employer when asked why he failed to employ blacks, "we don't have a foundry in our plant and that's the kind of work Negroes are best suited for." These attitudes and practices resulted partly from pressure exerted by white rank and file union members. White workers, with a backlog of unemployment, demanded retention and reemployment of whites over blacks. The growing influence of white workers indeed provided industrialists an additional rationale for excluding blacks: "We just sort of work like a family here and to bring in Negro workers would cause confusion and cause white workers to feel that their jobs had lost in dignity if being done by Negroes." Such racist beliefs and policies enabled employers to split the labor market along racial lines and foster what some analysts have called a white "labor aristocracy." White workers benefitted somewhat from both black exclusion and exploitation, but industrialists, exploiting their fears, reaped greater profits by a generally depressed wage structure. When blacks sought to gain employment in the breweries during the early 1930s, employers uniformly pointed to union opposition as the basis for black exclusion.[7]

Some companies—International Harvester Corporation, Plankin-

Table 5.3. Milwaukee's Labor Force by Race and Sex, 1940

| | Population 14 Years of Age and Over | Total in Labor Force Over 14 | | Employed Except Emergency Work | | Employed on Emergency Work | Seeking Work | |
|---|---|---|---|---|---|---|---|---|
| | | Number | Percent | Number | Percent | Percent | Number | Percent |
| Male | 231,008 | 186,135 | 80.6 | 149,939 | 80.6 | 6.4 | 24,195 | 13.0 |
| Black | 3,569 | 2,818 | 79.0 | 1,383 | 49.0 | 21.6 | 826 | 29.3 |
| White | 227,198 | 183,106 | 80.6 | 148,392 | 81.0 | 6.2 | 23,339 | 12.7 |
| Other | 241 | 211 | 87.6 | 165 | 78.2 | 7.1 | 31 | 14.7 |
| Female | 241,359 | 72,139 | 29.9 | 62,374 | 86.5 | 3.8 | 7,019 | 9.7 |
| Black | 3,381 | 1,115 | 33.0 | 539 | 48.3 | 20.9 | 343 | 30.8 |
| White | 237,850 | 70,993 | 29.8 | 61,814 | 87.1 | 3.5 | 6,668 | 9.4 |
| Other | 128 | 31 | 24.2 | 21 | 48.3 | N/A | 8 | N/A |

Source: U.S. Census Bureau, *Sixteenth Census of the United States: 1940 Population, Labor Force, vol. 3, pt. 5* (Washington: U.S. Government Printing Office, 1943), pp. 971–72.

Table 5.4. Black Occupational Change: Milwaukee, 1930–40

| Occupation | Male | | Percent Increase or Decrease | Female | | Percent Increase or Decrease |
|---|---|---|---|---|---|---|
| | 1930 | 1940 | | 1930 | 1940 | |
| Blacks | | | | | | |
| Professional | 97 | 50 | – 48.4 | 29 | 11 | – 62.0 |
| Proprietary | 67 | 69 | + 2.9 | 62 | 40 | – 35.4 |
| Clerical | 19 | 33 | + 73.6 | 27 | 28 | + 3.7 |
| Skilled | 161 | 106 | – 34.1 | 6 | 1 | – 83.3 |
| Semiskilled | 530 | 343 | – 35.2 | 152 | 111 | – 26.9 |
| Unskilled | 1,557 | 459 | – 70.5 | 32 | 20 | – 37.5 |
| Domestic | 366 | 319 | – 12.8 | 518 | 326 | – 37.0 |
| All Workers | | | | | | |
| Professional | 7,348 | 8,777 | + 19.4 | 6,194 | 6,817 | + 10.0 |
| Proprietary | 18,710 | 16,397 | – 12.3 | 2,788 | 4,067 | + 45.8 |
| Clerical | 31,665 | 26,046 | – 17.7 | 25,055 | 24,087 | – 3.8 |
| Skilled | 82,038 | 38,440 | – 53.1 | 606 | 753 | + 24.2 |
| Semiskilled | 38,426 | 31,706 | – 17.4 | 17,793 | 14,600 | – 17.9 |
| Unskilled | 29,843 | 23,014 | – 22.8 | 714 | 358 | – 49.8 |
| Domestic | 11,823 | 7,287 | – 38.3 | 10,090 | 11,648 | + 15.4 |

Source: See appendixes 5 and 6.

ton Packing Company, and the Wehr Steel Foundry—retained a corps of black workers in mainly hot and difficult jobs throughout the Depression. These employers expected staunch loyalty from their Afro-American employees in return. These demands for fidelity intensified during organizing threats from white workers. When the AFL local struck the Wehr Steel Foundry in 1934, the company warned blacks to avoid union organizations "of any kind," except those organized by the firm.[8] Such expectations aimed to link the fate of Afro-Americans to industrialists and to draw the line sharply between blacks and labor unions.

The Wehr Steel strike also unmasked the highly competitive nature of race relations in Milwaukee's labor market. Capitalizing upon its newly won federal protection under Section 7a of the National Recovery Act, the AFL organized a Wehr Steel Foundry union in 1934 and struck the plant by mid-July. The union, according to MUL records, ordered a walkout "without the knowledge" of black workers. Although the union demanded recognition by management, the chief aim of the strike was the "dismissal of Negroes from the plant." Some blacks perceived the strike as simply the first step in a grand program to remove Afro-Americans from all industrial plants. The strike

Table 5.5. Occupational Structure of Milwaukee by Racial and Ethnic Group, 1940

|  | Occupational Category | | | | | | | | | | | | |
|  | Professional | | Proprietary | | Clerical | | Skilled | | Semiskilled | | Unskilled | | Domestic | |
|  | Number | Per-cent | Number | Per-cent | Number | Per-cent | Number | Per-cent | Number | Per-cent | Number | Per-cent | Number | Per-cent |
|---|---|---|---|---|---|---|---|---|---|---|---|---|---|---|
| Male: Total Labor Force = 149,939* | | | | | | | | | | | | | | |
| Blacks | 50 | 3.6 | 69 | 4.9 | 33 | 2.3 | 106 | 7.6 | 343 | 24.8 | 459 | 33.2 | 319 | 23.0 |
| Whites | 8,727 | 5.8 | 16,328 | 10.9 | 26,013 | 17.5 | 38,334 | 25.8 | 31,363 | 21.1 | 22,555 | 15.1 | 6,968 | 4.6 |
| All | 8,777 | 5.8 | 16,397 | 10.9 | 26,046 | 17.3 | 38,440 | 25.6 | 31,706 | 21.1 | 23,014 | 15.3 | 7,287 | 4.8 |
| Females: Total Labor Force = 62,374** | | | | | | | | | | | | | | |
| Blacks | 11 | 1.8 | 40 | 7.3 | 28 | 5.1 | 1 | 0.2 | 111 | 20.5 | 20 | 3.7 | 326 | 60.4 |
| Whites | 6,806 | 11.0 | 4,027 | 6.5 | 24,059 | 38.9 | 752 | 1.2 | 14,489 | 23.4 | 338 | 0.5 | 11,322 | 18.3 |
| All | 6,817 | 10.9 | 4,067 | 6.5 | 24,087 | 38.6 | 753 | 1.2 | 14,600 | 23.4 | 358 | 0.5 | 11,648 | 18.6 |

*This figure is slightly lower than the number of occupations that the census actually specified.
**This figure is slightly higher than the number of occupations that the census actually specified.

Source: See Appendix 6.

Table 5.6. Percent Unemployment and Public Emergency Work by Race:
Selected Northern Cities, 1940

| | Seeking Work | | | | Employed on Emergency Work | | | |
|---|---|---|---|---|---|---|---|---|
| | Male | | Female | | Male | | Female | |
| City | Black | White | Black | White | Black | White | Black | White |
| Milwaukee | 29.3 | 11.8 | 30.8 | 9.4 | 21.6 | 6.2 | 20.9 | 3.5 |
| New York | 19.3 | 15.0 | 19.9 | 14.9 | 10.6 | 2.9 | 3.5 | 1.2 |
| Chicago | 16.7 | 11.1 | 24.4 | 9.3 | 18.6 | 3.1 | 11.5 | 1.7 |
| Philadelphia | 33.7 | 15.6 | 22.9 | 14.2 | 5.3 | 2.1 | 6.5 | 1.7 |
| Detroit | 15.7 | 9.6 | 19.2 | 11.7 | 17.4 | 2.7 | 10.6 | 2.2 |

Source: Richard Sterner, *The Negro's Share: A Study of Income, Consumption, Housing and Public Assistance* (New York: Harper and Brothers, 1943), pp. 239–53.

culminated in the first clear-cut case of racial violence in the city's industrial labor market. Police joined strikers in attacks on black strikebreakers, while the owner supported blacks: "The first few days of the strike brought considerable violence between the Negroes who attempted to continue on the jobs and the white pickets. . . . Police had been summoned [by management] to protect those who cared to enter but in turn joined with the strikers in overturning an automobile filled with Negro workers." Despite its antagonistic stance toward blacks, the union denied any anti-black attitudes and practices during an investigation of the strike by the National Labor Relations Board. As the strike wore on, the union attempted to attract a few black supporters, but this effort came too late and too half-heartedly to win the trust of black workers. Officials closed the plant by 13 August 1934; it reopened in mid-September as an open shop, one of the few cases in the city where an employer was able to do this.[9]

As earlier, other AFL locals either denied blacks membership or relegated them to separate all-black bodies. Few additional AFL trades were opened to blacks in the midst of the Depression; the AFL continued to carry twenty-four national and international unions that barred Afro-Americans by ritual or constitutional fiat. Even during the organizing drive of the CIO, the AFL discouraged black membership in a local butchers' and meat cutters' union. After a local packing firm hired a black butcher, he was denied union membership on the grounds that "there were [white] union butchers yet to be supplied with work." The black worker, the MUL noted, could not work at "his trade without becoming a member of the union and the union" would "not accept his membership."[10] At the outset of the period, in March

1933, "a reorganized local of bartenders, cooks, and waiters...stead-
fastly refused to accept" black applicants but "offered their assistance
in helping to organize a separate local" for Afro-Americans. In
another instance, black workers took an AFL carpenters' local to court
in an effort to break racially discriminatory barriers.

Although Afro-American unemployment persisted at deep-seated
and destructive levels until the production demands of World War II,
a great deal of economic dynamism and fluctuation punctuated the
black experience during the period. Spurts of activity related primarily to public relief benefits and, to a lesser degree, sporadic shifts in
private employment marked the otherwise pessimistic and stagnant
economic position of blacks. Despite the dramatic rise in black unemployment, for example, throughout the period a few blacks tenacious-
ly held on to the slippery rungs of the industrial ladder. In each occupational category, a significant core of black urban industrial workers
survived the Depression. A total of 908, or 65.7 percent of black men,
found employment in private industry. Fifty-eight percent of these
men worked in semiskilled and unskilled positions; only 36.2 percent
of white men occupied similar jobs. Black women were basically excluded from this narrow industrial footing; 60.4 percent of their
numbers labored in domestic service as compared to only 18.6 percent
of all females (see Table 5.5 and Appendix 6).

Direct relief work under such programs as the Federal Emergency
Relief Administration (FERA), Works Progress Administration
(WPA), and the Civil Works Administration (CWA) played an important role in the black community between 1933 and 1939, yet these
helpful programs simply underscored the critical depths to which the
black population had plunged. With less than 1.5 percent of the total
population, blacks accounted for 6.3 percent of all relief cases in 1934.
By 1935, the Sixth Ward, center of black residence in the city,
registered 36 percent of its population in receipt of general relief
compared to 14.4 percent for the city as a whole. As in other northern
cities, blacks on such projects as WPA significantly exceeded their
proportion in the general population[11] (see tables 5.2 and 5.6).

Coming as they did in the depths of the Depression, around
1933–34, public work jobs, albeit at subsistence wages, provoked
approving comments from black leaders. By Christmas 1935, the
MUL enthusiastically reported: "PWA and WPA produced at a most
opportune time, for the heads of many families in the sixth and tenth
wards, pay checks for the first time in many months. Some of them

had not experienced a payday in years. The entire neighborhood put on Christmas clothes." Employment on public emergency projects reached a peak in September 1936.[12] Expansion in private industry presented the least hopeful job prospects for blacks during the period, yet by October 1936 the MUL monthly report displayed a somewhat promising picture for private sector employment and wages.

Despite the existence of improved income through relief work and minor expansion in private industry by the mid and late 1930s, several factors accented the economic decline and suffering of the black proletariat: inadequate wages on work relief, drastic cuts in WPA appropriations, harassment by direct relief officials, and the enduring employment difficulties of black women. While blacks were disproportionately represented on such projects as WPA, as elsewhere, such aid proved inadequate to meet the needs of Afro-Americans. Milwaukee blacks justly complained that their share of WPA employment was insufficient because their needs were so much greater. In a survey of twenty-three black homes in February 1934, the MUL found that in a majority of these "the heads were employed on C.W.A. work, but there was much complaint that the $15.60 (3 days a week) earned was not sufficient for the needs of the average family." A survey of thirty-two black households in March 1936 again revealed general complaints that the $60.00 a month "did not stretch" far enough. The difficulties of Afro-Americans, with their heavy dependence on public emergency relief work, increased following retrenchment in WPA appropriations in late 1938 and early 1939; nevertheless, despite financial cuts, the WPA continued to play a significant role in the lives of Afro-Americans until World War II, for racial discrimination engendered by intense competition with unemployed whites blocked early access to defense industry jobs.[13]

The value of direct relief to Afro-Americans was undermined by administrative guidelines that permitted the harassment of black recipients, indeed probably all recipients. By the late 1930s, Josephine Prasser, a white social worker active among Sixth Ward blacks, informed NAACP national headquarters that blacks were "being harassed and worried by the Department of Relief." The department forced many single people who lived in two-room apartments to give up their "few belongings" and move into "small furnished bedrooms" with less space. Such requirements, Prasser argued, were especially designed to save on fuel during the winter months. When one elderly black woman, who paid her own rent, refused to move, the Relief

Department "stopped her food supply."[14] Some black welfare recipients did not accept the restrictions with equanimity, as Prasser noted: "You will readily understand what I mean, when I tell you that a young colored woman of Milwaukee is now serving a three month's sentence at the work house because she beat up an investigator, who it is said, is very hard on the people."[15]

As black men lost the bulk of their industrial foothold, Afro-American women found it necessary to seek domestic and personal service work in greater numbers. Despite the impact of New Deal programs, black women remained more thoroughly relegated to the bottom of the urban economy than did any other group. Coupled with racist stereotypes and practices that blocked the access of black men and women to industrial jobs, Afro-American females suffered distinctive anti-black attitudes and hiring policies. One manager of a large business asserted that black women "should aspire to becoming first class house servants and stop worrying about other types of work because they made the world's finest 'Mammies.' " Another said essentially the same thing and referred to the renowned novel and movie *Gone with the Wind* as proof.

Such discriminatory attitudes and policies, coupled with increasing competition from white women and the decline of jobs with well-to-do white families, forced black women primarily into "day work," the most unstable and low-paying category of domestic service. One person often worked for seven or eight different families during a single day. Where black females worked in close proximity to whites, the work was stratified along racial lines. At the Schroeder Hotel, for example, black women operated the freight elevator, scrubbed the floors, and generally performed the most disagreeable maid's duties. Conversely, white women worked the passenger elevator, filled all clerical positions, and carried out light maid's duties. Despite the difficulties that marked the employment experience of black women, income from female domestic service constituted a major component in the economic survival of black families during the Depression.[16]

Racial discrimination in the labor market and inadequate relief benefits for the unemployed helped to forge a closer unity between black workers and the black middle class. The activities of the MUL and the NAACP, designed to eliminate barriers to black economic survival, reflected this intraracial unity. Although Afro-Americans benefitted from New Deal relief programs, such federal help did not automatically accrue to them. Afro-Americans increased their pro-

portion of direct relief and public works jobs by exerting mass
pressure on city and county institutions. Rev. Cecil Fisher, the Afro-
American probation officer and coordinator of relief among blacks,
obtained his position through such efforts. His office constituted the
pivot around which blacks, through such organizations as the Urban
League and NAACP, pressed for greater access to material and work
relief.[17]

Middle-class leaders also fought to break down racial barriers in
local industries. The Wehr Steel strike of 1934, for example, helped to
strengthen the fragile link between the black bourgeoisie and Afro-
American workers. Although proceeding extremely cautiously, the
MUL assisted blacks in organizing a separate union despite the company's injunction to avoid non-company unions of any kind. William
V. Kelley, the MUL's executive secretary, articulated the MUL's
cautious move toward union advocacy during the strike: "I believe,
however, that many of these men can be organized into a separate unit
with men doing similar types of work in other foundries but I have
raised the question with myself as to whether or not it will help these
men to go against the suggestion of the Wehr Steel Company, which so
far has stood 100 percent behind its Negro employees, but which I
believe also, will not continue to keep its doors closed through its
loyalty to Negro workers."[18]

The MUL and NAACP often joined forces in conducting these
activities. One of the most important of their efforts involved the
struggle for brewery jobs. The brewery industry became a major
target when a Volstead Act amendment permitted the manufacture of
light wines and beer in 1933. Although two of the largest breweries,
Schlitz and Pabst, were located in the Sixth Ward, neither hired
blacks. Kelley and attorney James Dorsey, president of the Milwaukee NAACP, contacted the local alderman and met with Mayor Hoan
and brewery heads on the matter, but both unions and employers
simply passed the buck and blamed each other for black exclusion.
Despite this failure to open brewery jobs to blacks, the struggle
cemented a tighter bond between the black middle class and Afro-
American workers, for decreasing industrial jobs not only hurt black
workers but also foreshadowed declining opportunities for Afro-
American business and professional people.[19]

Black unity across class lines heightened when the MUL, at the
urging of the national office, spearheaded the formation of Emergen-

cy Advisory Councils (EACs) in nearby Beloit and Racine as well as in Milwaukee. Organized in the summer of 1933, the councils aimed to eliminate abuses against blacks occasioned by the NRA minimum wages and hours codes. While the MUL suggested that some blacks lost jobs to whites on the heels of improved standards instituted by the NRA, actually blacks, with high unemployment at the outset of the codes, probably suffered more from failure of the codes to cover domestic and personal service workers and employer evasions of regulations. The EACs lost vitality and declined following the Supreme Court's decision declaring the NRA unconstitutional in 1935, but they were replaced in Milwaukee, as elsewhere, by vigorous Workers Councils, which embarked upon active programs of worker education.[20]

While the activities of the MUL and NAACP advanced with the concurrence and support of black workers, the Afro-American proletariat fashioned a distinctive and forceful thrust in its own behalf. Many Afro-Americans, like their white counterparts, initially avoided the relief rolls, but the institution of public works programs, giving priority to persons on direct relief, elevated the relief system to a central place among the coping strategies of black workers. The MUL report for March 1934 highlighted the painful shift for some: "We are, however, faced with a new problem. . . . Many men who have managed to shift for themselves through the past three or four years find themselves unable to obtain government jobs. A few of these have finally asked for relief in order to get work." Ernest Schirm, a black carpenter and veteran of World War I, who kept a rather extensive diary of his thoughts during the period, was one of those working-class blacks who held out as long as he could before taking a WPA job. Moreover, unlike most black workers, Schirm, a staunch Republican, remained intensely anti-FDR throughout the period. Just before capitulating to WPA work, Schirm bitterly wrote in his diary: "Cashed the rest of my world war one bonus and paid of(f) the mort(g)age. I should buy some clothes but at l(e)ast the mort(g)age on the house is paid off. I sure dident (sic) get any thing out of the dam war but a good gassing and bad health."[21] Acutely aware of the huge backlog of unemployed whites, Afro-Americans knew that any private employment which was offered them invariably constituted domestic service jobs or low paying, hazardous, and generally disagreeable work in industry. Conversely, public work, in addition to offering a skill for some, did guarantee a certain minimum wage, albeit inadequate, below which direct material relief was made available.

Black workers did not uniformly pursue the relief strategy. There was a decided difference, for example, between old residents and the newest arrivals from the South. Older workers, using their access to public relief, could afford to wait until somewhat better industrial positions became available. Newcomers, however, usually entered the low-wage private sector, especially in domestic service, because they were ineligible for work relief upon their arrival in the city. In its efforts to supply low-wage black labor to employers, the MUL expressed satisfaction with the slowly expanding pool of newcomers in the city: "The Urban League Employment Department is happy to have a fresh supply of efficient help to offer; for many of the people who could be recommended refuse to quit W.P.A. and P.W.A., while the recent migrants find themselves ineligible for W.P.A. and must accept other jobs."[22]

The relief strategy developed alongside other black responses to the Depression. One of the most telling examples of the black proletariat acting in its own behalf developed during the Wehr Steel strike. Trapped between the antagonistic demands of the union and the company's insistence on unflagging loyalty, Afro-Americans faced a delicate predicament. Such a situation required a cautious and even adroit response. Given their exclusion from union activities, the promise of protection from the company, and the strikers' demands for removal and replacement of blacks by white workers, Afro-Americans understandably crossed the picket line. When police joined white strikers in attacks on black strikebreakers, blacks defended themselves. "There was some shooting and cutting," the MUL reported, "with the Negroes being in on the active end of things." For their part in the struggle, blacks were carried to court and fined "$25 and cost."[23]

Many Afro-Americans who maintained their footing in the industrial workplace expressed themselves in formally organized labor unions. Several factors, including Section 7a of the NRA and the specific types of work performed, conditioned the labor response of these men, but most of their activities revolved around the cleavage between the AFL and CIO. Black workers, though most were initially cautious and even skeptical, perceived in the racial egalitarianism of the CIO and its mass-production orientation greater prospects for advancement. The CIO modified the traditionally strong anti-black attitudes and practices of white workers. As elsewhere, the CIO in Milwaukee enlisted black organizers and established a close association with the black community. LeRoy Johnson, a black butcher and packinghouse worker, described by associates as an "aggressive sort of a guy and quite articulate," became a major figure in the organization of Local 681 (later Local 50) of the United Packinghouse Union. Calvin Birts, another black packinghouse employee during the period, has noted that Johnson's leadership helped to make the CIO's packinghouse campaign in Milwaukee a success. Under Johnson's leadership, blacks entered the union in large numbers and played an active role in the successful CIO displacement of the AFL Amalgamated Meat Cutters local at the Plankinton Packing Company.

Blacks also joined the CIO's United Automobile Workers Local 248, at Allis Chalmers Corporation. As early as October 1940, through black committeeman Bill Wallace, Local 248 filed a grievance against the company's discriminatory layoff policies. Particularly gratifying to black workers, the Wisconsin edition of the *CIO News* consistently attacked racial discrimination by the railway brotherhoods and AFL unions like the boilermakers, plumbers, machinists, and a variety of others.[24] An even tighter bond between blacks and the CIO was cemented in 1937 when the United Automobile Workers Local 248 spearheaded the formation of the Milwaukee Scottsboro Boys Defense Committee. Part of a national Communist front (International Labor Defense) campaign to free nine black youths accused of raping two white women near Scottsboro, Alabama, the Milwaukee Scottsboro Defense Committee incorporated a cross section of black and white civic, labor, social, political, and religious institutions. Representatives of middle-class black institutions like St. Mark AME church and the Urban League joined the CIO and representatives of black workers in sponsoring a mass Scottsboro Defense rally. Shunning association with Communists, the Milwaukee NAACP conducted separate Scottsboro activities before joining broader efforts.[25]

The emergence of the CIO also affected the few blacks within AFL unions. The International Longshoremen's Association Local 815 was the only AFL union to incorporate black and white workers in significant numbers before the organizing thrust of the CIO, but Local 815, organized around 1934–35, deviated from the normal orientation of the AFL in nearly every respect. Blacks comprised more than one-third of the city's dock workers. The unstable, unskilled, and seasonal nature of the work helps to explain the high representation of blacks in this union. A declining volume of shipping at the Milwaukee harbor and neglect from the Milwaukee Federated Trades Council, the city-wide AFL organization, placed the longshoremen at a tremendous disadvantage with employers. The union's poor bargaining position forced it to emphasize the low wages for which it would work in efforts to attract shipping from other Great Lakes ports.[26] Although the long-shoremen's Local 815 reflected the range of weaknesses inherent in unions of seasonal and unstable workers, it nevertheless enhanced the worker consciousness and trade-union activities of Afro-Americans. Aaron Tolliver, a black man who became president of the local in 1938, and several others sought to move the union into closer alliance with the CIO. The union supported a CIO strike against the Canada Transport Company in August 1938. Such action culminated in the temporary suspension of Tolliver and six other men as tools of the Communists. While blacks and their white allies failed to transform Local 815 into a CIO body, their efforts reflected faith in the efficacy of achieving black proletarian goals through industrial unionism.[27]

While black workers and middle-class organizations strengthened their relationships and the black community increasingly allied with the CIO, the efficacy of these activities must not be exaggerated. The amicable connection that linked blacks, especially the middle class, to the CIO was tenuous. The MUL's support of black membership in labor unions, for example, was often highly generalized: "The impor-tant trend as far as Negro labor is concerned is that whether they belong to A.F.L., C.I.O., or an independent union, organized labor will be adequately cared for. . . . It, therefore, behooves every Negro, skilled or unskilled, to get into somebody's union and stay there." Moreover, although recognizing the few blacks who retained employ-ment in local plants, there is little evidence that the Milwaukee CIO made any special effort (before 1941–42) to promote the equal re-employment of blacks and whites. United Automobile Workers Local 248 at Allis Chalmers emerged as the strongest CIO union in the city, but Allis Chalmers hired no more than two blacks between 1937 and 1942, although thousands of whites returned to work.[28]

On the other hand, while the Depression lessened the cleavage be-tween black workers and the Afro-American middle class, internal class divisions persisted. The struggle for a black alderman in the Sixth Ward continued to highlight class divisions within Milwaukee's black community. Efforts to place an Afro-American on the city council split black professional and business people, who campaigned for racial solidarity, from advocates of working-class unity, irrespective of color lines. Carlos Del Ruy and Ernest Bland allied with the predominantly white Farmer-Labor Progressive party and opposed the election of black attorney James Dorsey as alderman from the Sixth Ward in 1936. The more egalitarian political climate of the 1930s encouraged Del Ruy and Bland to expand their emphasis on class unity between black and white workers, but the persistence of racial discrimination among white Progressives added a precarious quality to the efforts of Afro-Americans to create class solidarity across racial lines. Del Ruy, for example, often complained that white party members neglected the Sixth Ward "solely because so many Negroes are in it."[29]

Class and racial disunity within the black community and between blacks and whites, coupled with a long downturn in the economy, helped to prevent the industrial reemployment of blacks before the early 1940s. Not until the labor shortages of World War II and the vigorous activities of Afro-Americans produced the Fair Employment Practices Committee (FEPC) would blacks fully regain their industrial foothold. Some industries, especially the Chain Belt Company and International Harvester, began rehiring Afro-Americans before the supply of white labor was exhausted and before the labor shortage became acute. Most manufacturers, however, did not immediately drop barriers to black labor upon the "arsenal of Democracy" declaration. These employers, Kelley noted, "adhered to their customary policy until they were compelled to choose between employment" of blacks "and failure to meet contract deadlines." An MUL survey of fifty-six local defense industries in December 1940 revealed that only twenty-eight employed blacks. As late as January 1941, the Wisconsin Employment Service observed that Afro-Americans represented 3.0 percent of its active job applicants, but they comprised only 1.0 percent of placements despite their disproportionately high unemployment rate.[30]

Only when the manpower needs of war plants and the military draft depleted white supplies of labor by 1942–43 could the MUL enthusiastically announce: "For the first time in over a decade Negro labor was actually sought by heavy industry. Today there is hardly a Negro man in Milwaukee who is physically able and willing to work who is not employed." Even seniority rules would come to protect the jobs of some blacks who had managed to retain industrial positions through the Depression years. The majority, however, continued to occupy the precarious bottom rung of the industrial ladder, where they remained the "last hired and first fired" during alternating periods of economic retrenchment and expansion. This process largely excluded black women who, although entering industrial jobs in larger numbers, regained employment primarily in domestic and personal service; white women, by contrast, entered industrial jobs in greater numbers.[31]

Black employment in Milwaukee defense plants was not obtained without a vigorous campaign against both the racist hiring practices of employers and the discriminatory policies of labor unions. This struggle evolved within the context of the national, black, proletarian-oriented March on Washington Movement (MOWM). Seeking to end racial injustice in defense plants and the military, the organization threatened a massive demonstration of some 50,000 blacks at the nation's capital. In order to avert such action, President Franklin D. Roosevelt issued Executive Order 8802, which established a Fair Employment Practices Committee to work against job bias in government and defense industries. When the federal FEPC became operative in the summer of 1941, the MUL, NAACP, and black workers themselves intensified their struggle to secure an equitable share of defense jobs. Attorney James Dorsey, president of the NAACP, and William Kelley of the MUL assembled sworn affidavits of racial discrimination by several Milwaukee firms with millions of dollars of government contracts. In January 1942, the MUL and NAACP presented this evidence before the FEPC during two days of hearings in Chicago. Following the Chicago sessions, the FEPC cited five Milwaukee companies (Nordberg Manufacturing, A. O. Smith, the Heil Company, Allis Chalmers, and the Harnischfeger Corporation) for racial discrimination and directed them to "give written notice . . . advising that each plant will accept applicants for all classifications of employment without regard to race, color, creed or national origin." Failure to comply with the order, the companies were warned, "could result in government claims of contract violations and fines or, in severe cases not involving vital war materials, suspension of the contracts."[32]

Charges against the firms, all manufacturers of heavy metal products, included refusal to employ either Afro-Americans or Jews and the issuance of restrictive work orders to public and private employment agencies. The companies had sought "only white or only

Gentile" workers and placed similar advertisements in local news-papers. Some firms, such as Allis Chalmers, though employing several blacks, refused to hire Afro-Americans in capacities other than porters, janitors, and common laborers. James Price charged that the company denied him promotion from foundry to skilled work in the firm's chemical and research department "solely because of his race." Allis Chalmers officials defended their actions on the basis that Price lacked the prerequisite training and that he was unwilling to acquire the necessary practical experience, which entailed a great deal of unpleasant and difficult work. Indeed, the practical experience required of Price seemed calculated to discourage his request for promotion:

> After careful discussion of his formal training he was offered a chance to learn foundry practice by working on the cupola [a small furnace for melting metals], adding alloys to the metal. This job, although in-volving hard manual labor, is a first step in learning the practical side of cast iron metallurgy; and one which many of our skilled cupola men have gone through. — Mr. Price, after one half day on this job, refused to work on it any longer; thus indicating to the satisfaction of Company representatives in charge that he was not interested sufficiently to make the routine effort required.[33]

Affidavits filed by black workers with the FEPC detailed a series of humiliating responses from employment managers. The Harnisch-feger Corporation, manufacturer of cranes, simply informed blacks that the corporation did not "hire Negroes." The Nordberg Company asserted that "the company did not employ Negroes because it had no place for them, requiring only skilled white men." An employment manager at the A. O. Smith Company, producer of auto frames and tanks for the military, claimed that they "never did and didn't intend to employ Negroes." Another official, with a more correct historical view, informed blacks that it was "no use for them to apply for jobs, because A. O. Smith hadn't hired any Negroes in 20 years." With few exceptions, employment managers and company guards either stopped blacks at the gates or treated them so discourteously that "they felt it a waste of time to go back to the plant to look for employment."[34]

Despite evidence of gross inequality in their plants, each of the firms denied pursuing racially discriminatory policies. Testifying before the Chicago hearings, Arthur Coppin, secretary and counsel of the Harnischfeger Corporation, asserted that the company never issued racially restrictive work orders to employment agencies. Actually, the company's records with the United States Employment Service (USES) showed that twenty-five of the forty-two orders placed between 2 July and 9 December 1941 specified "white" only. Similarly, Clinton B. Stryker, vice-president of the Nordberg Company, claimed that the company did not issue discriminatory requests for labor, yet six of the company's nine orders placed with the USES between 14 August and 14 October 1941 called for "white" help.[35]

Most companies expressed surprise and some vitriolic indignation that they were named in the various affidavits. "We are somewhat surprised by the citation," Allis Chalmers officials replied. "To the best of our knowledge, we are the largest single employer of Negroes in Wisconsin. The ratio of our Negro employees is substantially the same as that of the Negro to the Milwaukee County population." While it is true that Allis Chalmers traditionally hired blacks and retained some through the Depression, during World War II the firm refused to upgrade Afro-Americans into skilled positions and pursued a discriminatory rehiring policy. Others with less grounds for surprise than Allis Chalmers were especially hostile in their reaction to the FEPC ruling. "The Heil Co. does not discriminate against applicants for employment because of race, religious, or national origin," replied Joseph F. Heil, executive vice-president of the company and governor of the state. Heil then offered a dubious rationale for the company's racial policies: "The fact that in arranging for the employment of an office boy the applicant may have been restricted to 'White' was not intended as such discrimination." Governor Heil, the NAACP's Dorsey argued, further responded by having Dorsey, as a major coordinator of the charges, arbitrarily removed from his post as government appeal agent for Milwaukee County Draft Board Number Six.[36]

Under increasingly acute labor shortages and accelerated pressure from blacks and their white allies (especially the CIO, as will be seen), Milwaukee industrialists gradually toned down their racially exclusionary hiring policies and employed blacks in larger numbers. As early as October 1941, the Milwaukee employment office reported that, unlike prior months, "there had not been any discrimination in the requests for help by employers. No company. . . notified the office" that blacks "would not be accepted." Although such companies as Nordberg and Harnischfeger continued to resist black employment, Afro-American movement into defense plants intensified after the FEPC orders. Allis Chalmers increased its black labor force from 110 at the time of the Chicago hearings to 434 by December 1943. Kelley reported that A. O. Smith Corporation, initially a staunch opponent of black employment, showed the "finest spirit of cooperation." With no blacks in its employ in January 1942, the company had 470 Afro-American employees by October 1942 and 802 by late 1943; blacks now constituted 5.4 percent of the firm's labor force, the highest percentage of any industry in the city. The Heil Company also significantly expanded its percentage of black employees from 0.1 percent of its labor force during the Chicago hearings to nearly 4 percent two years later. The Harnischfeger Corporation and the Nordberg Manufacturing Company remained adamant holdouts. Harnischfeger increased its black labor force from zero in 1942 to only eighteen or 0.5 percent of its total labor force in December 1943. The percentage of blacks employed at the Nordberg Company actually dropped between January 1942 and October 1942, even as the company's labor force significantly expanded from 2,290 to 3,250 employees. Thirty-five Afro-Americans worked at the plant at the time of the Chicago hearings and only forty were so employed by December 1943[37] (see Table 5.7).

Most jobs for blacks in defense industries opened in unskilled and semiskilled positions at the bottom of the work force. Of the first twenty new black employees at A. O. Smith, only three entered the production department. Others worked as janitors and common laborers. As late as 4 February 1943, A. O. Smith employed only three blacks on the production line. The company transferred one black employee from a production job after only one night of work: "The employment manager told me plainly that he was not going to put any more of us [black] fellows on that line."[38] By May 1943, 81.5 percent of black A. O. Smith employees worked in unskilled jobs. The majority of blacks at Allis Chalmers continued to occupy hot, difficult, and dirty tasks in the foundry. Nevertheless, unlike during World War I, blacks significantly expanded their numbers in skilled and semiskilled jobs. Several blacks gained employment in the Allis Chalmers machine shop and, by mid-1943, 34.8 percent of black employees at the plant worked in skilled and semiskilled jobs. Even a larger percentage (59.1) of blacks worked in skilled (16.9) and semiskilled (42.2) jobs at the Heil Company. While the firm's record was certainly atypical, it demonstrated how blacks in Milwaukee gradually broke the "job ceiling" at the level of skilled and semiskilled

Table 5.7. Nonwhite Workers in Selected Milwaukee Defense Industries, January 1942–March 1945

| | Jan. 1942 Date of Hearing— Chicago | July 1942 6 Months After Hearing | Oct. 1942 10 Months After Hearing | Dec. 1943 24 Months After Hearing | Mar. 1945 Near End of War |
|---|---|---|---|---|---|
| Allis Chalmers Company | | | | | |
| Total Employment | 17,022 | 20,632 | 22,597 | 24,862 | 17,686 |
| Nonwhite Employment | 110 | 129 | 196 | 434 | 693* |
| Nonwhite Percent of Total | 0.6 | 0.5 | 0.9 | 1.7 | 3.9 |
| Harnischfeger Company | | | | | |
| Total Employment | 3,200 | 3,495 | 3,490 | 3,309 | 3,124 |
| Nonwhite Employment | 0 | 5 | 10 | 18 | 27 |
| Nonwhite Percent of Total | 0.0 | 0.1 | 0.3 | 0.5 | 0.8 |
| Nordberg Manufacturing Company | | | | | |
| Total Employment | 2,290 | 3,225 | 3,250 | 3,759 | 3,212 |
| Nonwhite Employment | 35 | 8 | 15 | 40 | 37 |
| Nonwhite Percent of Total | 1.5 | 0.2 | 0.5 | 1.1 | 1.1 |
| Heil Company | | | | | |
| Total Employment | 2,400 | 2,485 | 2,130 | 2,958 | 3,070 |
| Nonwhite Employment | 2 | 140 | 135 | 115 | 92 |
| Nonwhite Percent of Total | 0.1 | 5.6 | 6.3 | 3.9 | 2.9 |
| A. O. Smith Corporation | | | | | |
| Total Employment | 6,484 | 8,594 | 10,372 | 14,790 | 14,526 |
| Nonwhite Employment | 0 | 237 | 470 | 802 | 872 |
| Nonwhite Percent of Total | 0.0 | 2.8 | 4.5 | 5.4 | 6.0 |

*387 of the nonwhites were Jamaicans.

Source: Regional Files, Region 6, Records of the Committee on Fair Employment Practices (National Archives, Washington).

jobs. Employers expressed general satisfaction with black employees and credited the MUL for providing "efficient" and "reliable help"[39] (see Table 5.8).

Afro-American women faced unique racial and gender difficulties in their efforts to gain defense industry jobs. The employment of black women in Milwaukee industries was clearly subordinated to efforts to get black men into positions. The most vigorous efforts to extend the benefits of the FEPC to black women focused upon traditionally white female-dominated industries, particularly garment manufacturers that had government contracts to make parachute jumpers and jackets. Lee Kimmons, chairman of Local 248's FEPC, noted the experience of black women seeking work at a new Allis Chalmers plant: "We also have cases of Negro women applying for work in a new Allis Chalmers plant who are chronically being put off, although hundreds of white women are being hired."[40] Black female complaints of racial discrimination in large heavy industries like Allis Chalmers, Nordberg, and Harnischfeger were frequently dismissed by the FEPC due to insufficient evidence, although some of their charges were as potently documented as those of black men. Consequently, some black women, apparently feeling that they could not receive a fair hearing from the FEPC, addressed their letters of complaint directly to Eleanor Roosevelt. Margaret Morgan, for example, wrote to the First Lady for assistance in receiving employment at the Allis Chalmers Company:

I am writing to you for help and advice. I went to Allis Chalmers Mfg. Co. and put in an application for work. I waited two weeks and I didn't get any reply. . . . I went back and they asked me was I willing to go to school and take up coremaking. I went to school. My instructor, Mr. Olson, told me that Allis Chalmers had called up for women coremakers. I went back to Allis Chalmers . . . they told me I would be called within two weeks. It seems as though they are using discrimination because several of [the] women who started [school] when I did are working there now. The only reason I can give is because they are white and I'm colored.[41]

At the end of World War II, Afro-American men retained their industrial foothold; black women, however, were again losing the few industrial positions that war emergency created for them. "There is not, at present, any whole sale unemployment among Negroes in Milwaukee," the Urban League's 1945 annual report observed. "On the contrary, plant managers, in a few instances, have expressed sur-

Table 5.8. Nonwhite Workers by Skill Levels in Selected Milwaukee Defense Industries, May 1942–May 1943

| | Skilled | | Semiskilled | | Unskilled | | Other | | Total | |
|---|---|---|---|---|---|---|---|---|---|---|
| | Number | Percent | Number | Percent | Number | Percent | Number | Percent | Number | Percent |
| Allis Chalmers | | | | | | | | | | |
| May 1942 | 0 | 0 | 0 | 0 | 110 | 100.0 | 0 | 0 | 110 | 100.0 |
| May 1943 | 7 | 1.8 | 124 | 33.0 | 242 | 64.5 | 2 | 0.5 | 375 | 100.0 |
| Harnischfeger Company | | | | | | | | | | |
| May 1942 | 0 | 0 | 0 | 0 | 0 | 0 | 0 | 0 | 0 | 0 |
| May 1943 | 1 | 5.5 | 3 | 16.6 | 14 | 77.7 | 0 | 0 | 18 | 100.0 |
| Nordberg Mfg. Co. | | | | | | | | | | |
| May 1942 | 0 | 0 | 0 | 0 | 3 | 100.0 | 0 | 0 | 3 | 100.0 |
| May 1943 | 0 | 0 | 20 | 32.2 | 42 | 67.7 | 0 | 0 | 62 | 100.0 |
| Heil Company | | | | | | | | | | |
| May 1942 | 0 | 0 | 0 | 0 | 35 | 100.0 | 0 | 0 | 35 | 100.0 |
| May 1943 | 24 | 16.9 | 60 | 42.2 | 56 | 39.4 | 2 | 1.6 | 142 | 100.0 |
| A. O. Smith Corp. | | | | | | | | | | |
| May 1942 | 0 | 0 | 0 | 0 | 90 | 100.0 | 0 | 0 | 90 | 100.0 |
| May 1943 | 40 | 6.0 | 82 | 12.3 | 542 | 81.5 | 1 | 0.1 | 665 | 100.0 |

Source: Regional Files, Region 6, Records of the Committee on Fair Employment Practices (National Archives, Washington).

prise, if not their impatience, because of our inability to find and refer
to them much needed manpower. Women have become the chief victims of unemployment." Under the pressures of returning service-
men, the number of unskilled black females in industry dropped from
620 in 1945 to 249 by 1947. The loss of war work among black women
caused a painful readjustment from industrial to domestic service
jobs. A mother of eight dependent children was laid off from her
defense industry job in mid-August 1945. Unable to find factory
work, she finally took a domestic service position at $0.50 per hour
compared to the $1.10 per hour she made as a war worker. Despite the
low wages of domestic work, the woman felt compelled to take the
position. "I don't see how I can keep my family on such a low income as
this domestic job offers. But if I don't take it they might deny my
unemployment benefits."[42] Through the USES, another black
woman applied for a job as a punch press operator, a position she had
held as a war worker. Upon arriving at the plant she was informed that
the job was filled. She then sent out a white female friend for the same
job; the white woman was hired.

The struggle for defense jobs not only attacked the racist policies of
employers but those of labor unions as well. While neither the AFL
nor the CIO was monolithic in its relations with Afro-Americans,
available evidence suggests that Milwaukee blacks aimed their criticisms of organized labor mainly at the insensitive practices of the
AFL. The AFL's continual rejection of black members, despite the
labor demands of World War II, was highlighted when the city sought
to establish a defense advisory commission in early 1941. In addition
to excluding blacks, the MUL noted, the AFL attempted to stifle the
newly organized CIO: "In the name of democracy and the cause of
patriotism, a local official of [the] machinists union belabored himself
most eloquently against the inclusion of a CIO representative on the
commission." By contrast, the CIO accelerated its interest in organizing blacks and developing rapport with the black community.[43]

Under the impetus of the FEPC and its own commitment to national unity in the war against the Axis powers, the Milwaukee CIO
dramatically expanded its activities on behalf of black workers and the
black community. UAW Local 248 established its own FEPC committee and vigorously worked for the employment and upgrading of black
workers at the Allis Chalmers Corporation. The union sent representatives to the Chicago hearings and endorsed written affidavits of
racial discrimination at the plant. It supported Stanley C. Dale's

claim that Allis Chalmers refused to hire blacks during a period of intensive rehiring of whites. The union also upheld the affidavit of James Price, charging that the company failed to upgrade or promote Afro-Americans into skilled and better-paying jobs. Local 248 criticized the firm's call for skilled labor, while passing over hundreds of skilled blacks with the "old, old alibi — 'what experience have you had in a shop.' " Calvin Birts, a black member of United Packinghouse Local No. 50, credited the CIO for his promotion from common laborer to meat grader at the Plankinton Company.[44]

After black men received employment in substantial numbers, the Milwaukee CIO promoted the hiring of black women. In its July 1942 issue, the *CIO News* highlighted Allis Chalmer's hostile reaction to Jessie Benjamin's application. The company first informed Benjamin, a black college graduate, that she needed a birth certificate, although such information was not a regular requirement for employment. Upon presenting a birth certificate, the applicant was told to produce marriage and divorce records. Local 248 filed the case with its own FEPC and pushed for her employment. Within a month, Benjamin and five other black women received production work with the company. For the remainder of the war, the Milwaukee Industrial Union Council emphasized the position of black women in industry and called for their equal employment.

In some cases, however, the call for black women workers resulted from the demands of white women, who wished to avoid long working hours in order to have more time for their families. The white women of United Steelworkers of America Local 1527, at the Chain Belt Company, resisted the firm's proposal for a ten-hour day and a six-day week by encouraging the employment of black women. These actions demonstrated how gender and class interests of white women could sometimes promote as well as retard industrial opportunities for black women. The Milwaukee IUC cemented a stronger alliance with local blacks in 1943, when it instituted the Milwaukee Interracial Labor Relations Committee. Through this mechanism, the CIO deepened its commitment to the hiring and promotion of black workers, while extending its relationship with blacks beyond the labor force into other areas, particularly housing.[45]

Despite its apparent interest in blacks, the CIO in Milwaukee, as elsewhere, often camouflaged existing racial discrimination within its own ranks. When Lester Granger, assistant secretary of the National Urban League, attacked discrimination by labor unions at a Milwaukee conference on black employment in 1940, Harold Christoffel, president of the IUC, told the meeting that "no CIO unions were discriminating against Negroes." While the CIO and the black community indeed forged a substantial alliance by the end of World War II, it was a tenuous association, for "competition in the labor market" remained "very much a fact." At the FEPC regional conference, held in Chicago in early 1944, William V. Kelley warned that it was not true that all racial discrimination in the Milwaukee labor movement emanated from the AFL. "There are some plants where labor unions and craft unions interfere, and that cannot be directed entirely against the A.F. of L. because in one plant a union of the A.F. of L. has been very cooperative. In another case the greatest difficulty has been found to be the CIO local."[46]

In the columns of the *CIO news,* Luther McBride, a black steward for Allis Chalmers Local 248, emphasized "the need to build understanding among the workers themselves and break down old prejudices which permit situations to occur where white workers are placed in competition with Negro workers and dangerous hostilities arise." Moreover, McBride went on to state, "I have actually seen situations where a member of management will play upon these prejudices to keep [black and white] workers in turmoil." Black leaders continually asked and the Afro-American proletariat wondered: "Will Negroes again as in 1921 and 1929 be the first to be fired?" Following the Detroit Riot of July 1943, the *Blade* noted heightened racial tensions in Milwaukee's labor market: "At the A. O. Smith Corp. a fight was reported between a white and Colored workers. In nearly all those plants where Colored never worked before the President forced them to be hired, tension is rising. In those plants where Colored have worked for years one can tell something is wrong." Perhaps the most poignant evidence of continuing racial discrimination within the ranks of organized labor, AFL and CIO alike, surfaced in the Milwaukee IUC's Labor Day parade in 1945. The parade contained entries from a wide range of industrial unions, steel, leather, auto, and others, yet black men and women from a variety of AFL and CIO unions joined black business and professional people and participated in the parade as a distinct community. "The 6th Ward Contingent represents a community on the march," the *CIO News* ironically reported.[47]

Paralleling the competition for industrial jobs during the Depression, residential segregation of blacks and whites intensified as housing competition accelerated between the two. The reemployment of blacks in the city's industries and renewed migration to Milwaukee during World War II aggravated these trends. Blacks became even more tightly circumscribed into a particular area of the city's space as the process of ghetto formation gained greater expression, yet the small size of Milwaukee's black community kept the ghetto, a nearly exclusively black, spatially restricted area of significant size, at bay. Contemporary observers noted that the Depression brought better housing for some blacks. Despite the hard economic impact of the Depression on Afro-Americans, Kelley stated: "It has provided better homes for many of them." The white journalist Robert Wells, writing at a later date, also claimed a beneficial impact of the Depression on Afro-American housing: "Landlords who slammed doors in black faces during the twenties had suddenly grown colorblind. Many of those on the periphery of the Negro district decided they weren't particular about a family's race after all, if it could pay the rent."[48]

Few blacks during the Depression could pay the higher rents necessary for significantly better housing; consequently, blacks expanded into the low-rent and decaying areas within and just north and west of the main pre-Depression black community. Afro-Americans increasingly filled the areas between Wright and Walnut streets on the north and 8th and 12th streets to the west, although State and Third streets, respectively, remained the southern and eastern boundaries. The expanding central business district gradually forced blacks north of State Street (see Map 5.1). Based on ward-level data, the index of dissimilarity between blacks and both American- and foreign-born whites increased over the decade, respectively, from indexes of 85.1 to 87.2 and from 78.7 to 81.7. Collectively, Afro-Americans in the Sixth (82.9) and Tenth (10.4) wards comprised 93.3 percent of Milwaukee's black population in 1940. The degree of residential segregation, however, is brought into sharper focus by an analysis of block-level data. Nearly 97 percent of the Afro-American population resided in blocks comprising the northern Near Downtown district, an area bounded by W. Wright, W. Kilbourn, N. 3rd, and N. 12th streets. Near the end of World War II, the Milwaukee Health Department conducted a special census of the forty-three blocks bounded by W. Galena, W. Juneau, N. 3rd, and N. 12th streets; the study revealed a population shift from just over half nonwhite in 1940 to two-thirds nonwhite by 1945. The total population in the area decreased by 16.2 percent as the black population increased by 43.2 percent (see Table

N

## Map 5.1. Milwaukee's Black District, 1940

Source: Wright Directory Company, *Wright's Map of Milwaukee* (Milwaukee: Wright Directory Company, 1918); Milwaukee City Engineers Department, *Map of Milwaukee Ward Boundaries, 1931* (City of Milwaukee, 1931); Paula Lynagh, "Milwaukee's Negro Community" (Milwaukee: Citizen's Government Research Bureau, 1946), p. 2.

Table 5.9. Milwaukee's Population by Race, 1945: Census Tracts 20 and 21
Area Bounded by W. Galena, W. Juneau, N. Third, and Twelfth Streets

| Year–Census Tract | Nonwhite | White | Total | Percent of Total | | |
|---|---|---|---|---|---|---|
| | | | | Nonwhite | White | Total |
| 1940 | | | | | | |
| #20 | 1,118 | 538 | 1,656 | 67.5 | 32.5 | 100.0 |
| #21 | 1,669 | 1,726 | 3,395 | 49.2 | 50.8 | 100.0 |
| Total | 2,787 | 2,264 | 5,051 | 55.2 | 44.8 | 100.0 |
| 1945 | | | | | | |
| #20 | 1,631 | 423 | 2,054 | 79.4 | 20.6 | 100.0 |
| #21 | 2,361 | 1,473 | 3,834 | 61.6 | 38.4 | 100.0 |
| Total | 3,992 | 1,896 | 5,888 | 67.8 | 32.2 | 100.0 |
| Change 1940–45 | | | | | | |
| #20 | + 513 | − 115 | + 398 | | | |
| #21 | + 692 | − 253 | + 439 | | | |
| Total | + 1,205 | − 368 | + 837 | | | |
| Total Percent Change | + 43.2 | − 16.2 | + 16.6 | | | |

Source: Paula Lynagh, "Milwaukee's Negro Community" (Milwaukee: Citizens' Government Research Bureau, 1946), p. 35.

5.9). While the index of dissimilarity and the Milwaukee Health Department survey show that blacks were becoming highly segregated, blocks of Afro-American residence were significantly dispersed among blocks of white residence. As late as 1940, 78.2 percent of the Afro-American population lived in the seventy-four blocks bounded by W. Brown, W. Juneau, N. 3rd, and N. 12th streets, but even within this core area, comprised mainly of census tracts 20, 21, 29, and 30, Afro-Americans made up only slightly more than half (52.8 percent) of the total population. In 1939, the Milwaukee WPA Real Property Inventory recorded only a single block of 100 percent black occupancy.[49] A high of 31.8 percent of all blacks in this geographical area resided in blocks of 0–25 percent black occupancy, and only 41.7 and 26.3 percent of blacks, respectively, lived in blocks of 26–75 and 76–100 percent black occupancy. Thus, Milwaukee blacks would remain more scattered among whites than their counterparts in other northern cities until the war's end. Indeed, Milwaukee's black ghetto would not fully emerge until the post–World War II era.

The increasing geographical segregation of Afro-Americans nevertheless reflected their continued relegation to the poorest housing stock. Nearly all housing in the northern Near Downtown area constituted the original seven square miles which became incorporated as the city of Milwaukee in 1846. Over two-thirds of the residences were built before 1900 compared to less than one-third for the entire city. The Real Property Inventory listed only 1.5 percent of the residential structures in the district as having been built after 1920; this sharply contrasted to 29.5 percent for the city.[50]

In an effort to secure federal funds for low-income housing, Mayor Hoan appointed a housing commission to survey housing in the black district in 1933. Utilizing a definition of "slum district" developed by the National Municipal League, the survey concluded that the black area was indeed a "slum district" where conditions were not "conducive to the physical and moral health of the inhabitants." A contemporary comparison of black and white housing in the area reported 67.7 percent of the black structures as in need of major repairs or "unfit for use," whereas only 6.5 percent of white houses were so reported. In a 1944 study of housing, the Milwaukee commissioner of health designated the entire black district, census tracts 20, 21, 29, and 30, as "blighted," meaning that the majority of buildings needed numerous major and minor repairs and that a large number of structures were "unfit" for human habitation. Although blacks and whites in the area shared similarly aged housing, they experienced drastically different conditions.[51]

Discrepancies between black and white neighborhood conditions were also evident in other characteristics of black housing, particularly home ownership and rents. According to the 1940 U.S. Census, blacks occupied 2,488 dwellings in Milwaukee; they owned only 41 or 5.7 percent of the occupied units compared to a 32.6 percent home ownership rate among whites. The average value of homes owned by blacks was about half ($2,762) that of whites ($4,485). Although rents decreased during the sharp rise in unemployment between 1929 and 1933, black tenants paid 10 to 30 percent higher rents from 1934 onward. "The tenants' wages don't matter," a 1937 MUL housing study noted. "Most often repairs are refused and rents raised apparently because repairs were asked for." Such practices accelerated with the initiation of war production. Blacks also paid higher rents than whites for housing of equivalent or less quality. Monthly rates paid by blacks averaged $19.00 in 1939 compared to $30.81 for the entire city. The low average for blacks was nevertheless disproportionately high. For example, in the area of the black district defined as a "slum," only one-third of black occupants paid less than $15 monthly rent in 1945 compared to two-thirds of white residents there.[52]

Despite the increasing concentration of blacks in the poorest housing, Afro-Americans did not uniformly experience the worst living conditions. Black business and professional people, joined by a few better-paid and skilled workers, occupied the better housing within and on the edges of the black district. Paying slightly higher rents, Afro-Americans on the periphery and in blocks of less than 25 percent black occupancy experienced better residential environments than their counterparts in blocks of high black concentrations. Blacks in these areas had fewer roomers, extra families, and other evidences of crowding than other black residents; they also resided in a smaller number of buildings in need of major repairs or "unfit for use." Of the structures in blocks with fewer than 25 percent blacks, 41.6 percent needed major repairs compared to 56.8 and 65.3 percent of such units in areas of 26–75 and 76–100 percent black residency, respectively (see tables 5.10 and 5.11).

Poor housing was closely aligned with poor health conditions and increased crime among Milwaukee blacks. Afro-Americans continued to have proportionately higher infant mortality, death, and disease rates than whites, although inequality between black and white health conditions decreased during the period. Afro-American death rates were 58 percent higher than rates for the city as a whole in 1930 (15.5, black; 10.6, city) and 38 percent higher than rates during the 1940s (13.6, blacks; 9.8, city). Blacks accounted for 10.8 percent of the city's deaths from tuberculosis between 1930 and 1939; by 1945, they registered 7.6 percent of such deaths. Afro-American infant mortality, syphilis, and other indicators of poor health dropped, but like the statistics for tuberculosis, the disparity between the races continued. An expanding incidence of certain crimes also accompanied the failure of Afro-Americans to gain equitable access to jobs, housing, health care, and other necessities. The most serious offenses revolved around prostitution and vice charges. Blacks ran the policy racket, a lottery game, which catered to blacks and some whites throughout the city. The policy game, despite several arrests growing out of it, apparently enjoyed a high degree of official sanction. "It is hard to get the district attorney to issue a warrant," one student of Milwaukee blacks noted, "and if a warrant is obtained it is hard for the police to get a conviction in the courts."[53]

The housing segregation of blacks resulted from several interre-

Table 5.10. Contract Monthly Rent of Tenant Occupied Dwellings: Milwaukee's Near Downtown, 1940 Census Tracts 20, 21, 29, and 30 — Area Bounded by W. Brown, W. Juneau, N. 3rd, N. 12th Streets

| Contract Monthly Rent | Number | | | Percent | | | Percent City | |
|---|---|---|---|---|---|---|---|---|
| | Total | Nonwhite | White | Total | Nonwhite | White | All | Black |
| Under $9 | 149 | 61 | 88 | 4.8 | 3.2 | 7.2 | 1.4 | 3.6 |
| $10–14 | 429 | 274 | 155 | 13.7 | 14.4 | 12.7 | 4.8 | 14.8 |
| $15–19 | 843 | 574 | 269 | 27.0 | 30.1 | 22.0 | 11.1 | 30.0 |
| $20–24 | 736 | 489 | 247 | 23.5 | 25.7 | 20.2 | 14.8 | 23.6 |
| $25–29 | 548 | 306 | 242 | 17.5 | 16.1 | 19.8 | 17.4 | 15.4 |
| $30–39 | 329 | 153 | 176 | 10.5 | 8.0 | 14.4 | 29.4 | 10.1 |
| $40–49 | 62 | 39 | 23 | 2.0 | 2.1 | 1.9 | 13.5 | 1.8 |
| $50 and Over | 30 | 8 | 22 | 1.0 | 0.4 | 1.8 | 7.6 | 0.7 |
| Total | 3,126 | 1,904 | 1,222 | 100.0 | 100.0 | 100.0 | 100.0 | 100.0 |

Source: Paula Lynagh, "Milwaukee's Negro Community" (Milwaukee: Citizens' Government Research Bureau, 1946), p. 68.

lated factors in addition to depressed economic status: municipal zoning ordinances, restrictive housing covenants, discriminatory federal housing policies, housing competition between blacks and working-class whites, and the internal social dynamics of the Afro-American community. Municipal zoning laws continued to exacerbate the poor housing conditions of Afro-Americans. The southern half of the black community, as noted in Chapter 2, was zoned exclusively for commercial and light manufacturing until a new law, passed in 1943, permitted residential construction. The new ordinance, however, did not sufficiently restimulate housing construction because factories could be erected on adjacent lots and laws requiring fireproof materials for new buildings heightened costs. Race restrictive covenants and "gentlemen's agreements" placed additional constraints on black housing. These agreements pledged white property owners not to rent or sell to blacks outside the area bounded by W. North, W. Juneau, N. 3rd, and N. 12th streets.[54]

Federal housing policy, particularly Section 203 of the National Housing Act of 1934, as enforced by the Federal Housing Administration (FHA), reinforced the pattern of de facto housing segregation within the city. FHA guidelines barred financing of black housing

Table 5.11. Selected Housing Characteristics by Percentage of Afro-American Occupancy: Near Downtown District, Census Tracts 19, 20, 21, 29, and 30

| Blocks: Percent Afro-American | 0–25 | 26–75 | 76–100 |
|---|---|---|---|
| Percent of total | 31.8 | 41.7 | 26.3 |
| Average monthly rent | $25.04 | $21.77 | $20.90 |
| Housing characteristics | Percent | Percent | Percent |
| Built 1919 or before | 98.7 | 97.8 | 99.5 |
| Needing major repairs — unfit for use | 41.6 | 56.8 | 65.3 |
| Owner occupied | 9.0 | 9.8 | 7.2 |
| With roomers | 13.9 | 15.4 | 18.7 |
| Extra families | 1.4 | 4.0 | 6.1 |
| With 1.5 persons per room | 3.3 | 3.9 | 4.2 |
| Children under 14 years of age — as percent of all residents | 20.4 | 20.6 | 23.5 |
| Occupied 5 years or fewer | | | |
|   Owner-occupied | 15.7 | 8.6 | 16.0 |
|   Tenant | 68.8 | 71.0 | 67.2 |

Source: Computed from City of Milwaukee, *WPA Real Property Inventory, 1939* (Milwaukee Public Library).

outside segregated areas until 1948, when the U.S. Supreme Court declared such policies unconstitutional. Milwaukee's FHA office, adhering to established procedures, excluded Afro-Americans from new housing, advancing loans to Afro-Americans for repairs on old buildings only. While discriminatory federal loan policies usually exacerbated the plight of the black middle class, who could more often afford housing in white areas, racial discrimination in public housing projects underscored the impact of the housing struggle between black and white workers.[55]

A singular illustration of the impact of the housing struggle between white and black workers was the controversy over Parklawn, the city's first federally subsidized housing project. Based upon a survey of housing conditions in the black district, Milwaukee applied for and received funds for Parklawn. When plans for the project gained federal approval, a rigid stance against black occupancy developed. The state senate debated the issue when Senator Charles H. Phillips, a Milwaukee Democrat representing the Sixth Senatorial District, introduced a bill to prohibit racial discrimination against blacks in real estate contracts. Phillips specified the value of Parklawn to black families because of their over-crowded and inadequate living quarters. While the Phillips measure received the support of Progressives like Senator Herman J. Severson of Iola, a Milwaukee Democrat, Senator Harold V. Schoenecker, of Milwaukee's Fifth Senatorial District, introduced a motion that eventually killed the bill. Schoenecker argued that "the housing administration had provided exclusive sections for Negroes." Some senators outside of Milwaukee County opposed the measure, as did Democratic Senator Morley G. Kelley of Fond du Lac, on the grounds that "this measure will destroy every lake resort, every real estate development in the state by letting down bars to negroes."[56]

The proposed Sixth Ward location of Parklawn provoked white resistance from several quarters. Arguing that the project would create a "race problem" and "lead to mixing of the races," white home owners in the area resisted the Sixth Ward site. One white family initiated a court case in order to prevent location of the project in the black district. Organized real estate interests opposed the project in general, sensing that the project might cut into their profits; the United Taxpayers Co-Operative Association and the Milwaukee Real Estate Board attacked Parklawn as "illogical, unsound, hastily conceived and nothing other than an unemployment relief experiment."

Such forceful opposition from different sources defeated the Sixth
Ward location of the project. In August 1937, the 418 low-income
housing units opened in the northwest portion of the city on W.
Capitol Drive, far beyond the northwestern limits of the black
community. The project, located within one mile of 15,000 almost exclusively white industrial employees, symbolized how blacks lost out
again, as in the 1920s, in the competitive housing struggle with
working-class whites. Officials justified the Capitol Drive site on the
basis that land in the area was cheaper than in the Near Downtown
location. Black leaders justly doubted the rationale; land in the northwest, a swampy area, required the added expense of rerouting Lincoln Creek before construction could begin. Only six black families
were admitted to the project.[57]

White resistance to black expansion into better housing intensified
under the exigencies of World War II production and renewed black
migration. When eighteen black families sought to purchase land for
the purpose of building new homes in 1944, no one would sell to them.
Only after a white man fronted for them did they obtain the property.
The group bought forty acres of land in the far northwest section of the
city, bounded by N. Sherman Boulevard, N. 47th Street, W. Fair-
mount Avenue, and W. Hampton Avenue. White residents, learning
that blacks owned the property and intended to build homes in the
area, held a mass meeting at the Hampton Avenue School and raised
$645 for use in a concerted campaign to block Afro-American occu-
pancy of the land. The group succeeded in having their alderman,
August Abe, maneuver a resolution through the city council that set
the land aside "ostensibly for a 'playground.' " The Abe Resolution,
though rescinded under a counter-campaign from blacks and their
white allies, symbolized the powerful resistance to better black
housing that characterized the entire era.[58]

Despite telling and even decisive evidence that the segregation of
Afro-Americans stemmed primarily from the complex interplay between their depressed economic status and white resistance, it would
be erroneous to assume that blacks played no part in the process of
ghettoization. Although less intense than elsewhere, the ideas and activities of Milwaukee blacks promoted a racially divided housing
market. Afro-Americans, especially middle-class blacks, often encouraged the territorial separation of blacks and whites for political,
economic, and institutional reasons. The idea that a spatially consolidated black population offered the best prospects for increased

political power and institutional growth was a constant refrain. As a contemporary student noted, when blacks began moving northwestward into the Tenth Ward, black politicians voiced concern that the demographic base for a black alderman would be undermined. By providing a variety of goods and services (housing, medical, legal, religious, and others), as will be seen in Chapter 7, black ministers, professionals, and business people perceived in a segregated Afro-American population opportunities for expanding the institutional framework of the black community and augmenting their own power, prestige, and wealth. Only a racially stratified housing market, for example, ensured the survival and development of the CBLA. Similarly, racial discrimination in the housing market and stiff competition with working-class whites led many black workers to perceive in segregation an opportunity for access to better housing. The housing needs of war workers accented the vested interest of black workers and business people in spatial segregation. Established in 1943, the Carver Memorial Homes Company capitalized upon the government's plans to build 402 war housing units in Milwaukee County. After strong pressure from local black residents, the National Housing Administration allotted a quota of 75 units for blacks and the corporation broke ground for its low-income project, the Sherman Hill Houses, in July 1944.[59]

While internal forces promoted the segregation of blacks and whites, the majority of Afro-Americans, workers and middle-class alike, were unwilling to forego better housing in order simply to sustain a separate black institutional, political, and cultural life. This was consistently reflected in their collective and often highly articulated efforts to destroy racial barriers in the housing market. When white resistance defeated the proposed Sixth Ward location of the low-income Parklawn project and excluded blacks from occupancy in the relocated project, Afro-Americans initiated a vigorous struggle to gain admittance. The black community and their white supporters organized protest demonstrations at both the construction site and downtown at city hall until blacks were admitted on a token basis.[60]

After the Parklawn disappointment, the MUL took a decisive and even militant role in the fight for a Milwaukee Housing Authority. The league actively participated in local housing conferences and printed a barrage of editorials proclaiming "LET THERE BE HOUSES" in efforts to pressure the common council into establishing a local municipal housing body. Formed in early 1942, the Joint Action Committee on Better Housing, a coalition of eighteen black and white civic, church, and social welfare organizations, gave attempts to ensure a local commitment to federally subsidized low-income housing greater articulation. By March 1943, blacks expanded their demands for better housing through the Sixth Ward Better Housing Community Club.

The Milwaukee Common Council defeated housing authority legislation until 1944. Only when the persistent campaign for a housing authority merged with the housing needs of war workers did the common council create a low-income housing agency. Under the active prodding of its black representative, Rev. Cecil A. Fisher, the new authority immediately approved the erection of a 144-unit war housing project for the Sixth Ward. The project had not gone beyond the stage of planning and land acquisition by the end of 1945. With the Parklawn experience fresh in mind, the black community remained alert, cautious, and even skeptical that housing for working-class blacks would materialize. Thus, the low-income housing struggle continued.[61]

As in their demands for access to public housing, Afro-Americans exhibited forceful unity in attempts to eliminate racial restrictions in the private housing market. These activities, as noted earlier, took sharp focus in the campaign to rescind the Abe Resolution. After passage of the discriminatory legislation, nearly 150 blacks and a few whites held a mass meeting at Association Hall and passed a resolution requesting the common council to repeal its action. Nearly 25 blacks and their white allies, mainly representatives of the CIO, confronted 150 militant white opponents at a subsequent common council meeting. Despite the violent temper displayed by white petitioners, Afro-Americans firmly and successfully insisted that councilmen repeal the nefarious ordinance. Attorney George Brawley, who spearheaded the action, declared: "We'll carry our fight to the courts if necessary. . . . No judge will order condemnation of our property on the flimsy grounds that a 40-acre playground is needed in an area where there are only 57 children within a radius of 14 blocks." Brawley called upon blacks and their white supporters to "attend every meeting of common council until the resolution in question is wiped from the records of our city government." When one property holder revealed that "white neighbors had attempted to intimidate him and to drive him out," black attorney George Hamilton responded: "I would have resorted to physical violence before I would have let them stop me from building my home. There are times when it would be better to be dead than to submit to such insults."[62]

Although racial competition in the housing market intensified during war production, the growing alliance between blacks and the CIO helped modify some housing conflicts. As early as September 1937, the *CIO News* denounced plans to build a new housing project on the South Side without providing similar housing in the Sixth and Tenth wards. Noting that only six black families had been permitted to enter the Parklawn project, the paper proclaimed: "This is discrimination in its worst form. All working class organizations should support the demand of the residents of the Sixth and Tenth Wards for establishing of a housing project in this area, open to residents of this area only." When two black U. S. Army enlistees died in a fire in a Sixth Ward lodging house, the *CIO News* used the incident to draw attention not only to unsafe and unsanitary conditions, but also to housing discrimination which caused blacks to double up in available units. In another instance, the paper reported the death of one child and the hospitalization of two others in a black steelworker's family. "You don't have to go down South to see the scourges and tragedies caused by segregation, 'restricted' property, and other forms of discrimination. —The largest city in Wisconsin—our own Milwaukee—prides itself on being 'debt free' while small children die in the 6th ward because of poor housing." In this case, the CIO met with the mayor to discuss remedies for poor housing among black war workers. The organization frequently attacked the racist sentiments of Milwaukee realtors, especially their claim that poor housing resulted from black "indifference and carelessness." Such thinking, the union insisted, reflected realtor excuses for the rent exploitation of Milwaukee blacks.[63]

When white residents of the Sixteenth Ward resisted black occupancy of homes in the area, the Milwaukee IUC urged the city council to reject such discrimination and "give assurance to all citizens irrespective of race, creed or color, or national origin that they will be fully protected in their right to live in the place they have chosen." George Bradow, the CIO's representative, accompanied blacks to city hall, defied the taunts of opposing whites, and vigorously defended the rights of blacks to build homes in the area. A *Milwaukee Journal* reporter documented Bradow's stand: " 'I wonder if these people know that the Negroes live in housing that is unfit for human beings.' . . . Bradow emphasized that he spoke for 100,000 CIO members in

the state.... The [white] petitioners, men and women alike, booed
him... Bradow continued, 'I'm speaking for democracy, in the name
of democracy.' A woman shouted, 'Throw him out.' — 'You can expect
such lynch atmosphere under the circumstances,' Bradow challenged."[64] Indeed, by the war's end the CIO had emerged as the
strongest ally of blacks in their push for a municipal housing authority
and low income housing.

The Depression accented the precarious nature of Milwaukee's
black industrial working-class and highlighted the weak economic
underpinning of the Afro-American community. Afro-Americans experienced prolonged unemployment because of the extended crisis in
the larger economy and the anti-black policies of labor unions and
employers. Only when the activities of blacks in their own behalf
intersected with the organizing drive of the CIO and the labor
demands of World War II did Afro-Americans regain their industrial
foothold. While racial tensions in Milwaukee's workplace and housing market heightened as black war workers reentered the industrial
economy in larger numbers, violent interracial conflict was allayed by
the growing black-CIO alliance and the significantly lower level of
black migration compared to that in cities with larger centers of black
population; nevertheless, racial bias within the CIO, but especially
within the AFL, and the uncertain duration of war-fueled employment undermined interracial and class unity. The development of
black politics, institutions, and race relations mirrored the socioeconomic and political processes that marked the proletarian experience
of blacks in Milwaukee during the Depression and World War II.
These issues are analyzed in Chapter 6.

NOTES

1. St. Clair Drake and Horace R. Cayton, *Black Metropolis: A Study of Negro
   Life in a Northern City,* vol. 1 (1945; rev. New York: Harcourt, Brace, and
   World, 1962), pp. 214–62, 287–311. Emphasis on the consolidation of an
   Afro-American industrial proletariat follows Richard Walter Thomas's
   argument for Detroit blacks: "From Peasant to Proletarian: The Forma-
   tion and Organization of the Black Industrial Working Class in Detroit,
   1915–1945" (Ph.D. diss., University of Michigan, 1976); Sterling D.
   Spero and Abram L. Harris, *The Black Worker: The Negro and the Labor*

*Movement* (1931; rept. New York: Atheneum, 1968), pp. 149–81. While Spero and Harris emphasize the agricultural pool of black workers, the term is used here to refer to unemployed blacks within the city as well.

2. This section on the urban context is drawn mainly from Bayrd Still, *Milwaukee: The History of a City* (1948; rept. Madison: State Historical Society of Wisconsin, 1965), pp. 476–514, and Thomas W. Gavett, *Development of the Labor Movement in Milwaukee* (Madison: University of Wisconsin Press, 1965), pp. 152–83.

3. Still, *Milwaukee,* p. 482; Federal Housing Administration, Milwaukee County, *Wisconsin: Housing Market Analysis* (Federal Housing Administration, 1939), p. 61.

4. Gavett, *Development of the Labor Movement in Milwaukee,* pp. 161–64, 174–75; Still, *Milwaukee,* pp. 528–31.

5. *Sixteenth Census of U.S.: 1940 Population, vol. 2, pts. 1–7* (Washington: Government Printing Office, 1943); Milwaukee Urban League Annual Report, 1942–43, Ser. 3, Box 16, National Urban League Papers.

6. MUL Monthly Report, Oct. 1937. *Sixteenth Census of U.S.: 1940 Population; State of Birth of the Native Population* (Washington: Government Printing Office, 1944), pp. 63–74.

7. MUL Monthly Report, Apr. 1941.

8. "Statement in Re: The Wehr Steel Foundry Strike, Milwaukee, Wisconsin," 15 Aug. 1934, Ser. 4, Box 8, NUL Papers.

9. Lloyd K. Garrison, chairman NLRB, to T. Arnold Hill, 18 Sept. 1934; William V. Kelley to T. Arnold Hill, 21 Sept. 1934, Ser. 4, Box 8, NUL Papers.

10. Interview with Calvin Birts, 18 Aug. 1979; Gavett, *Development of the Labor Movement in Milwaukee,* pp. 159–68; Still, *Milwaukee,* pp. 500–501; "A Tip to Negro Labor," MUL Monthly Report, Oct. 1937; interview with Calvin Birts, 8 Aug. 1979; MUL Monthly Report, Mar. 1933.

11. Katherine D. Wood, *Urban Workers on Relief: pt. II: The Occupational Characteristics of Workers on Relief in 79 Cities* (Washington: Government Printing Office, 1937); Paula Lynagh, "Milwaukee's Negro Community" (Milwaukee: Citizens' Government Research Bureau, 1946), pp. 21–22, 58. For a discussion of blacks on public works projects in other northern cities, see Richard Sterner, *The Negro's Share: A Study of Income, Consumption, Housing and Public Assistance* (New York: Harper and Brothers, 1943), pp. 239–53.

12. MUL Monthly Reports, May 1933, Mar. 1934, Oct. 1935, Oct. 1936, Aug.–Sept. 1937, Mar. 1939, Dec. 1939.

13. MUL Monthly Reports, Feb. 1934, Mar. 1936, Apr. 1939, Apr. 1940.

14. Josephine Prasser to William Pickens, 9 Jan. 1939, Box G-219, NAACP Papers.

15. Ibid.

16. MUL Monthly Reports, Nov. 1939, June–Aug. 1934, Nov. 1936, Nov. 1939; interview with Ruby Cook, 13 Aug. 1979.

17. "Resolutions from the Colored People of Milwaukee. . . . Concerning . . . the Position of Colored Probation Officer and Welfare Worker," Folders 1–3, Cecil A. Fisher Papers, 1921–66 (University of Wisconsin–Milwaukee, Area Research Center).

18. "Statement in Re: The Wehr Steel Foundry Strike, Milwaukee, Wisconsin," 15 Aug. 1934, Ser. 4, Box 8, NUL Papers; Kelley to Hill, 17 Aug. 1934, Ser. 4, Box 8, NUL Papers; MUL Monthly Report, Feb. 1937; James Dorsey to Walter White, national secretary NAACP, 24 Apr. 1933; Dorsey to White, 19 May 1933, Box G-219, NAACP Papers; William V. Kelley to T. Arnold Hill, 26 May 1933, Ser. 4, Box 31, NUL Papers; MUL Monthly Report, March 1933.

19. MUL Monthly Reports, June–Aug., Sept., Oct., 1933, and Jan. 1936.

20. Ibid. A discussion of EACs and workers' councils on the national level is found in Nancy Weiss, *The National Urban League, 1910–1940* (New York: Oxford University Press, 1974), pp. 276–80, 285–91.

20. Ibid.

21. MUL Monthly Report, Mar. 1934; Ernest Schirm, "Working Man's Diary of Hard Times," Box 1, Folders 3–5, Ernest Schirm Papers, 1918–69 (State Historical Society of Wisconsin). For a general perspective on antirelief attitudes, see Francis Fox Piven and Richard A. Cloward, *Regulating the Poor: The Functions of Public Welfare* (New York: Vintage Books, 1971), pp. 80–119.

22. MUL Monthly Reports, Feb. 1934, Apr. 1935, Oct. 1937, June–Aug. 1936.

23. "Statement in Re: The Wehr Steel Foundry Strike, Milwaukee, Wisconsin," 15 Aug. 1934, Ser. 4, Box 8, NUL Papers.

24. "Vote 248 for Your Bargaining Agency," *Allis Chalmers Workers Union News,* 10 Dec. 1937; "U.A.W.A. Convention Faces Big Auto Issue: Local 248 Hews to the Line of Unity and Progress," *Allis Chalmers Workers Union News,* 16 Aug. 1937; "Light is Green in Packingtown: CIO is Growing," *CIO News: Wisconsin Edition,* 8 Oct. 1938; "Meat Industry CIO: Plankinton Victory Winds Up Drive," *CIO News: Wisconsin Edition,* 26 Mar. 1938; "Plankinton Boys Busy on All Fronts," *CIO News: Wisconsin Edition,* 21 May 1938; "Allis Chalmers Denies Equality to Negro Workers," *CIO News: Wisconsin Edition,* 28 Oct. 1940; "Urban League Exposes AFL Negro Discrimination" and "The Negro and the AFL," both in *Allis Chalmers Workers Union News,* 16 Sept. 1937; interview with Calvin Birts, 18 Aug. 1979; Gavett, *Development of the Labor Movement in Milwaukee,* pp. 159–68; Still, *Milwaukee,* pp. 500–501. A general study of blacks and CIO unions is Horace R. Cayton and George S.

Mitchell, *Black Workers and the New Unions* (College Park, Md.: McGrath Publishing Company, 1939), especially chapters 11, 14, and 19.

25. Cora Meyer, secretary provisional Scottsboro Defense Committee, to Rose Shapiro, 28 Nov. 1937; Shapiro to Meyer, 29 Nov. 1937; Meyer to Shapiro, 4 Dec. 1937; Meyer to Scottsboro Defense Committee, 15 and 27 Dec. 1937, Box H-7, Addendum: Milwaukee Scottsboro Defense Committee, 1937-39, NAACP Papers. Also see Dan T. Carter, *Scottsboro: A Tragedy of the American South* (Baton Rouge: Louisiana State University Press, 1969).

26. H. T. Hoopes, president Great Lakes Transit Company, to Joseph D. Keenan, assistant to S. Hillman of War Production Board, 1 Apr. 1942; Dale Richards, secretary Local 815, to Hoopes, appended notes, 27 Apr. 1942, Correspondence, International Longshoremen's Association, Local No. 815 Papers, 1935-49 (University of Wisconsin-Milwaukee, Area Research Center); Harold Christoffel, president of Industrial Union Council, to Longshoremen's Association Local 815, 4 Aug. 1938, Correspondence, Box 1, Milwaukee County Industrial Union Council Papers, 1938-48 (University of Wisconsin-Milwaukee, Area Research Center); Frederick P. Mett, attorney NLRB 12th region, to A. Tolliver, president Local 815, 5 Aug. 1938, Box 1, Local 815 Papers; secretary, Local 815 to F. H. Ranney, general secretary FTC, 16 Oct. 1941; F. H. Ranney to Dale Richards, secretary Local 815, 13 Feb. 1942, Correspondence, Local 815 Papers.

27. Ibid.

28. "A Tip to Negro Labor," MUL Monthly Report, Oct. 1936.

29. Carlos Del Ruy to Hoan, 26 Apr. 1936; Daniel W. Hoan to Del Ruy, 29 Apr. 1936, Box 26, File 98, Daniel W. Hoan Papers (Milwaukee County Historical Society); interview with Ernest Bland, 8 Aug. 1979; Milwaukee County Board of Election Commissioners, *Biennial Report, 1940* (Milwaukee Legislative Reference Bureau).

30. MUL Annual Report, 1942-43, Ser. 3, Box 16, NUL Papers; Special Reports; MUL Monthly Reports, Dec. 1940, Jan. 1941; "Claims Unions Hurting Negro," *Milwaukee Journal*, 19 Dec. 1940 (Milwaukee Public Library, Newspaper Clippings File).

31. MUL Annual Report, 1942-43, NUL Papers.

32. Herbert Garfinkel, *When Negroes March: The March on Washington Movement in the Organizational Politics for FEPC* (Glencoe: Free Press, 1959), particularly pp. 37-61; John Hope Franklin, *From Slavery to Freedom: A History of Negro Americans* (New York: Alfred A. Knopf, 1967), pp. 578-80; "Negro Uplift Chance Seen," *Milwaukee Journal*, Dec. 1940; "Assert Jobs Here Barred Negroes," *Milwaukee Journal*, 31 Jan. 1941; James G. Fleming, FEPC field representative, to officials of Heil, A. O.

Smith, Allis Chalmers, and Harnischfeger Corporation, 12 Jan. 1942; Lawrence W. Cramer, FEPC executive secretary, to the five above-named companies, 9 Apr. 1942, all in Record Group 228, Records of the Committee on Fair Employment Practices (National Archives, Washington), hereafter cited as FEPC Records. "Accuse Firms of Color Line: Five Milwaukee Plants Named at Hearing, Charges are Denied," *Milwaukee Journal,* 31 Jan. 1942; "Stop Race Discrimination, Big Munitions Firms Told," *Milwaukee Journal,* ca. 13 Apr. 1942; "Study Negro Chances: Urban League Say Survey Shows Some Discrimination," *Milwaukee Journal,* 2 Oct. 1941.

33. Lee H. Hill, vice-president, Allis Chalmers, to FEPC, 27 Apr. 1942, FEPC Records.

34. Affidavits: Granville Natt and Stanley C. Dale vs. the Heil Company; James Morgan, William V. Kelley, Lester Reed, LeRoy Simmons, et al. vs. the Harnischfeger Corporation; Karney Henry, Carl Estrada, and Stanley Dale vs. Nordberg Manufacturing Company; James Means, James Sherrer, and Carl Estrada vs. A. O. Smith Corporation; Beauregard Gordon, Stanley Dale, and James Price vs. Allis Chalmers, all in FEPC Records.

35. Job Order Specifications and Spoken Testimony, Proceedings of the Chicago Public Hearings, FEPC, 19 and 20 Jan. 1942: Heil Company, Harnischfeger Corporation, and Nordberg Manufacturing Company; also see L. J. Parrish to Cramer, 25 Apr. 1942, and Lee H. Hill to FEPC, 27 Apr. 1942, all in FEPC Records; W. Harnischfeger, president, Harnischfeger Corporation, to Cramer, 11 Apr. 1942; A. H. Pfeiffer, personnel manager, Harnischfeger Corporation, to B. H. Thompson, manager, United States Employment Service, 20 May 1942; Cramer to William V. Kelley, 6 May 1942; C. T. Hibner, works manager, Heil Company, to Cramer, 18 June 1942 and 24 Apr. 1942; Cramer to Robert Washburn, executive secretary, Committee on Discrimination in Employment, 8 May 1942; "Compliance Report: Heil Company," 2 Aug. 1945; Cramer to Harnischfeger Corporation, 18 July 1942; Harnischfeger to Cramer, 9 and 28 Feb. 1942; Cramer to Harnischfeger, 26 Feb. 1942; George M. Johnson, assistant executive secretary, to Dan Travis, local black resident, 20 Oct. 1942; Travis to Franklin D. Roosevelt, 6 Oct. 1942; memorandum, Austin H. Scott, FEPC regional minority consultant, to Elmer Henderson, FEPC field representative, 24 Nov. 1942; Cramer to E. E. Stryker, vice-president, Nordberg Manufacturing Company, 4 Mar. 1942; Stryker to Cramer, 16 Feb. 1942, all in FEPC Records.

36. Joseph F. Heil, executive vice-president, Heil Company, to Cramer, 4 Mar. 1942; Cramer to L. J. Parrish, A. O. Smith Corporation, 29 Sept. 1942; W. H. Spencer, regional director, FEPC Region VI, to Theodore

Jones, administrative officer, FEPC, 24 Mar. 1943; Parrish to Cramer, 25 June 1942; Cramer to Parrish, 7 July 1942; Parrish to Cramer, 25 Apr. 1942; Kelley to Cramer, 23 Mar. 1942; Cramer to Kelley, 1 Apr. 1942; Lee H. Hill, vice-president, Allis Chalmers Corporation, to Cramer, 21 and 23 May 1942; Cramer to Hill, 8 May 1942; Hill to Cramer, 27 Apr. 1942; Fleming to Harold Christoffel, president CIO Local 248, 13 Jan. 1942; Fleming to Allis Chalmers, 14 Jan. 1942, all in FEPC Records; "Heil Accedes to Color Order," *Milwaukee Journal,* 4 May 1942; "Dorsey Asks Ouster Cause: Say Charges of Racial Discrimination at Heil Plant Might be Factor," *Milwaukee Journal,* 13 May 1942.

37. Compliance Documents and Employment Statistics, FEPC Records.
38. Walter Lee Kendrick to FBI (FEPC), 4 Feb. 1943, FEPC Records.
39. Ibid.; "Study Job Chances," *Milwaukee Journal,* 2 Oct. 1941; MUL Annual Report, 1942–43; Drake and Cayton, *Black Metropolis,* vol. 1, p. 288.
40. Lee Kimmons to Robert Weaver, director, Negro Manpower Service Division, War Production Board, 17 July 1942, FEPC Records.
41. Margaret Morgan to Eleanor Roosevelt, 19 Aug. 1942, FEPC Records.
42. MUL Annual Report, 1945, Ser. 6, Box 92, NUL Papers; Mel J. Humphrey, "Economic Status of Negro Workers: Milwaukee and Vicinity, 1949," Ser. 13, Box 17, NUL Papers.
43. "Government Levels Attack at Jim Crow in Industry," *CIO News: Wisconsin Edition,* 16 Nov. 1942; MUL Monthly Report, Feb. 1941, see n. 42; interview with Calvin Birts, 18 Aug. 1979; William V. Kelley to Meyer Adelman, secretary IUC, 28 Feb. 1943, Box 4, Milwaukee County Industrial Union Papers.
44. Beauregard Gordon, Stanley Dale, and James Price vs. Allis Chalmers, FEPC Records; "Firm Promises to Hire and Promote Negro Workers and Machinists," *CIO News: Wisconsin Edition,* 20 Apr. 1942; "We Feel Like Fighting Hitler Now: Say Negro Members of Local 248," *CIO News: Wisconsin Edition,* 18 May 1942; interview with Calvin Birts, 18 Aug. 1979; "Government Levels Attack at Jim Crow in Industry: Full Production Impossible Unless Bans Against Negro Are Ended," *CIO News: Wisconsin Edition,* 16 Nov. 1942.
45. "Negro Woman, College Grad, Can't Get Job," *CIO News: Wisconsin Edition,* 20 July 1942; "A-C Hires Six Negro Women," *CIO News: Wisconsin Edition,* 3 Aug. 1942; "Negro Girls Run Lathe, Weld: Everyone Treats Us Fine," *CIO News: Wisconsin Edition,* 17 Aug. 1942; "CIO Union Employs Negro Office Girl," *CIO News: Wisconsin Edition,* 16 Nov. 1942; "V Mass Meeting," 13 June 1943, Box 4, Milwaukee County Industrial Union Council Papers (University of Wisconsin–Milwaukee, Area Research Center); "Inter-Racial Committee Progresses," *CIO*

*News: Wisconsin Edition,* 3 May 1943; "Inter-Racial Labor Relations Body Meets," *CIO News: Wisconsin Edition,* 21 June 1943.

46. "FEPC Regional Conference, Morrison Hotel, March 25, 1944," FEPC Records; "CIO Continues Fight for Negro Rights," *CIO News: Wisconsin Edition,* 23 Dec. 1940.

47. "Union Opens Anti-Bias Drive," *CIO News: Wisconsin Edition,* 5 Feb. 1945; "Claims Unions Hurting Negro," *Milwaukee Journal,* 19 Dec. 1940; MUL Annual Report, 1942–43; "Race Hatred is Growing all Over the Country," *Blade,* 17 July 1943; "Jobs — Not Apples: Milwaukee Workers Demand," *CIO News: Wisconsin Edition,* 7 Sept. 1945.

48. Robert Wells, "Depression Opened Some Doors to Negro," *Milwaukee Journal,* 9 Nov. 1967; Kelley is quoted in Wells.

49. Karl E. and Alma F. Taeuber, *Negroes in Cities: Residential Segregation and Neighborhood Change* (Chicago: Aldine, 1965), p. 39; *WPA Real Property Inventory, 1939* (Milwaukee Public Library).

50. Lynagh, "Milwaukee's Negro Community," pp. 1–7, 16–17, 24–30, 33–35, 39.

51. Edith Elmer Wood, *Slums and Blighted Areas in the United States* (Washington: Government Printing Office, 1935); Lynagh, "Milwaukee's Negro Community," p. 24; Sterner, *The Negro's Share,* p. 190; E. R. Krumbiegel, "Observations on Housing Conditions in Milwaukee's Sixth Ward: A Report to the Mayor and Common Council" (City of Milwaukee, 1944); J. J. Brust, "Housing Survey in the Sixth and Tenth Wards" (Milwaukee Board of Public Land Commissioners, 1944).

52. Lynagh, "Milwaukee's Negro Community," p. 26; Thomas Imse, "The Negro Community in Milwaukee" (master's thesis, Marquette University, 1942), pp. 13–14; MUL Monthly Report, Nov. 1937.

53. Imse, "The Negro Community in Milwaukee," pp. 17–40; Lynagh, "Milwaukee's Negro Community," pp. 12–19, 47–56.

54. Still, *Milwaukee,* pp. 543–46; Lynagh, "Milwaukee's Negro Community," pp. 17–18, 28.

55. Robert Weaver, *The Negro Ghetto* (New York: Russell and Russell, 1948), pp. 69–76; "New Deal Practices Discrimination Against Negro Owners Here: Milwaukee Slant on F.H.A. Discrimination," *Blade,* 28 Sept. 1940.

56. "Negro Realty Bill Shelved: Measure Aimed to Open Parklawn to Tenants of African Blood," *Milwaukee Journal,* 6 Aug. 1934, Box G-219, NAACP Papers; The Wisconsin Legislative Reference Library, *The Wisconsin Blue Book, 1935* (State of Wisconsin), pp. 192–99.

57. Vivian Lenard, "From Progressivism to Procrastination: The Fight for the Creation of a Permanent Housing Authority for the City of Milwaukee, 1933–1945" (master's thesis, University of Wisconsin–Milwaukee, 1967), pp. 38–71; MUL Monthly Report, July 1937.

58. Interview with Bernice Copeland-Lindsay, 9 Aug. 1979; "Negro Homes Are Hit Again: Neighborhood Center is Voted in Area Where Lots Were Bought," *Milwaukee Journal*, 13 Sept. 1944; "Rally Attacks Racial Action: City Hall is Target," *Milwaukee Journal*, 11 Sept. 1944.

59. "Colored Home Owners in Milwaukee Increase as Property in Excess of $50,000 is Purchased," *Blade*, 16 Nov. 1940; "Carver Memorial Homes, Inc." (Milwaukee, 1944); interview with Bernice Copeland-Lindsay, 9 Aug. 1979; "Negro Housing Project on N. 4th St. Started," *Milwaukee Journal*, 24 July 1944; "2,000 See Negro Housing Project," *Milwaukee Journal*, 20 Nov. 1944; Imse, "The Negro Community in Milwaukee," p. 16.

60. Interview with Bernice Copeland-Lindsay, 9 Aug. 1979; MUL Monthly Report, Nov. 1937; "Proceedings: First Milwaukee Public Housing Conference, October 16, 1937" (Milwaukee: Legislative Reference Bureau); "Housing Board Created Here: Eighteen Civic, Church Groups Are Represented at Conference," Box 20, United Community Services of Greater Milwaukee Papers, 1903–66 (University of Wisconsin–Milwaukee, Area Research Center); Lenard, "From Progressivism to Procrastination," pp. 102–33; MUL Monthly Report, Nov. 1937; Cecil A. Fisher Papers, Folders 1–3, 1921–66 (University of Wisconsin–Milwaukee, Area Research Center).

61. "Petition Parley is Stormy One: Opposed Playground Plan in Areas in Which Negroes Have Bought Lots," *Milwaukee Journal*, 10 Oct. 1944; "Plan for Play Area Assailed: Negro Group Resolution," *Milwaukee Journal*, 18 Sept. 1944; "Rally Attacks 'Racial Action': City Hall is Target," *Milwaukee Journal*, 11 Sept. 1944.

62. Ibid.

63. "Residents of 6th and 10th Wards Protest Atrocious Housing," *Allis Chalmers Workers Union News*, 16 Sept. 1937; "Slum Conditions in 6th and 10th Wards: Serious Menace to Health," *Allis Chalmers Workers Union News*, 14 Oct. 1937; "Housing Conditions Blamed as Negroes Die on Army Leave," *CIO News: Wisconsin Edition*, 31 May 1943; "Negro Segregation Writes Tragic Story," *CIO News: Wisconsin Edition*, 14 Feb. 1944.

64. "CIO Demands End to Housing Discrimination Against Negroes," *CIO News: Wisconsin Edition*, 8 Mar. 1944; "The 16th Ward is Learning Something from this War," *CIO News: Wisconsin Edition*, 8 May 1944; "Petition Parley is Stormy One: Opposed Playground Plan in Areas in Which Negroes Have Bought Lots," *Milwaukee Journal*, 10 Oct. 1944.

# 6

## Race, Class, and Politics during the Depression and World War II

Economic, social, and political tensions during the early years of the Depression intensified racial hostilities toward blacks. As noted in Chapter 5, the Wehr Steel Foundry strike of 1934 dramatically revealed the competitive nature of race relations as violence erupted in Milwaukee's labor market. On the other hand, the organizing efforts of the CIO and the federal-government-directed movement of Afro-Americans into defense industry jobs modified racial cleavages in the industrial workplace and housing market. These forces also mitigated racial divisions in other areas of the city's life. Establishment of a Scottsboro Boys Defense Committee and greater support for diverse Milwaukee Urban League and NAACP civil rights activities reflected these developments.

Such interracial progress nevertheless fundamentally failed to arrest the deepening division between blacks and whites in the socio-economic and political life of the city. Racial separation gained greater institutional supports during the period. Concerted efforts to elect a black alderman, the persistence and expansion of parallel black institutions, and accelerated civil rights activities on several fronts accented the separation of blacks and whites in the urban social system. While intraracial class divisions lessened as the Depression plunged the majority of Afro-Americans into unemployment, the institution of New Deal measures sustained internal cleavages, and industrial employment during the war intensified them. These divisions, despite a great deal of intraracial solidarity, found expression in the institutional and political activities of the black community.

Although racial hostility against blacks erupted into violence in the Wehr Steel Foundry strike, the previous pattern of interracial cooperation persisted into the early 1930s. As in pre-Depression days, Mayor Daniel W. Hoan continued his cooperative relationship with Afro-Americans. Hoan put the prestige of his office behind the Columbia Building and Loan Association when the Depression threatened to close its doors. Lauding the CBLA as "one of the six best building and loan associations in Milwaukee," the mayor interceded for the organization with the Commonwealth Mutual Savings Bank: "May I recommend that you extend every possible courtesy and help to Dr. Turney and Mr. Halyard, who is the secretary of Columbia." Hoan also favorably responded to the efforts of local blacks to gain state-level civil service appointments. "I have been requested to call your attention to the fact that there is a large Negro population in Milwaukee and elsewhere in the state," Hoan wrote to the state treasurer, "and that they desire that someone of their group be recognized in your selections." In another instance, the mayor supported attempts of a black singing group, the Southern Harmonizers, to gain exposure on radio station WTMJ.[1]

The NAACP and MUL increased their importance as instruments of black-white interaction during the 1930s. Dr. E. LeRoy Dakin, pastor of the white First Baptist Church, was elected president of the local NAACP in the spring of 1934. Under Dakin's leadership, ca. 1934–37, the NAACP took steps toward a viable program of interracial alliance in attempts to eliminate racial injustice, particularly in national affairs. NAACP officials pressured Wisconsin senators to vote for the Costigan-Wagner Anti-Lynching Bill. The organization also drafted a letter to Senator Wagner on the Wagner Labor Disputes Act, urging endorsement of amendments, especially the clause prohibiting racial discrimination by unions, proposed by the National Urban League. Although the organization undertook a comprehensive local survey of social, political, and economic conditions among blacks and established a program of action, little effort was made to implement the program. Like their counterparts elsewhere, the white allies of Milwaukee blacks could readily attack the gross injustices heaped upon southern blacks, but they were less willing to antagonize local whites in efforts to eradicate racism in local affairs.[2]

The MUL continued its traditional week-by-week program of race

relations through public speaking engagements, pre-Thanksgiving
dinners, radio productions, and "tours of goodwill" through the black
community. Under the impact of World War II, new departures in
race relations developed. Following a series of riots throughout the
country in 1943, the league initiated the Interracial Federation of Milwaukee. Operating with several individuals and nearly thirty representatives from well-known organizations in the city, the Interracial
Federation vigorously articulated its interracial aims of promoting
"better understanding and good-will among the different cultural and
ethnic groups."[3]

Other organizations also reflected increasing interracial unity.
Spearheaded in 1931 by George E. Teter, a white professor at
Milwaukee State Teachers College, the Milwaukee Race Relations
Council became increasingly significant by the mid-1930s. Teter expressed his interest in blacks through assiduous attempts to build a
strong NAACP and promote black interaction with diverse ethnic
groups. Blacks not only belonged to the council but served in influential positions: Attorney George W. Hamilton served as vice-
president, and Wilbur Halyard and attorney George DeReef were
executive commitee members.[4]

By the mid-1930s, blacks and whites collaborated in seeking a more
inclusive state civil rights act than that of 1895 and subsequent revisions. Ben Rubin, a Milwaukee Farmer-Labor Progressive Federation legislator, introduced a new civil rights bill into the state
legislature in 1937. Rubin's bill, modeled on the New York Civil
Rights Act, sought to strengthen the law against discrimination in
places of public resort and amusement. Violators would be subject to
from $100 to $500 in fines. The bill also proposed a $1,000 fine against
utility companies that discriminated in employment and against insurance companies that issued discriminatory policies to blacks and
whites. The Wisconsin legislature eventually passed a tremendously
watered-down version of the bill, dropping fines for violations of the
law to a minimum of $25 and a maximum of $100 or a jail term of not
more than six months,[5] the same maximums established by the
original law. The amendment nevertheless confirmed the persistence
of interracial collaboration on civil rights issues.

Several developments reflected the expanding CIO influence on
race relations in the city. While Milwaukee and several other cities
held mass demonstrations to free the Scottsboro Boys in 1931, it was
not until 1937 that a strong local Scottsboro Defense Committee

developed. Initiated by the CIO United Automobile Workers Local 248, the committee held a massive Scottsboro Defense Rally in December 1937.[6] Sponsoring individuals and organizations included a broad cross section of black and white labor, religious, political, social welfare, and civic organizations. An overflow crowd of 600– 1,000 persons gathered at Liberty Hall. The meeting featured speeches by Roy Wright and Olen Montgomery, two of the Scottsboro defendants, and Richard Moore, a prominent black Communist and spokesman on the Scottsboro affair. Unlike former gatherings of this nature, blacks outnumbered whites, which caused some apprehension among white organizers. "The audience was mostly colored," wrote Cora Meyer, coordinator of the activities, "which of course had its good and bad sides. In the past it was mostly whites, this time mostly colored. So perhaps this will even out in the future." White radicals appeared, at least in this case, more concerned about a hostile white response to a vigorous interracial program dominated by blacks than about conservative reactions to radical ideas.[7]

As noted in Chapter 5, the CIO advanced its interracial program with the formation of the Milwaukee Interracial Labor Relations Committee in 1943. The committee held an interracial mass meeting at Calvary Baptist church in June. Black and white, local and national, labor leaders shared the platform in calls for racial justice in the socioeconomic life of the city. The meeting, entitled "V Mass Meeting," articulated support of the Fair Employment Practices Committee, as it campaigned for black endorsement of the war effort. During the same month, when race riots erupted in Detroit, the Wisconsin CIO condemned the attacks on blacks as a "disgrace to Our Country" and Local 248 joined the International UAW-CIO in asking for a federal grand jury investigation. The state body also called upon local affiliates to "join together in consultation with all responsible elements in various Wisconsin communities, both Negro and white, with the high resolve of seeing to it that no such disturbances are permitted to hinder the war effort or to work outrages against our Negro brothers who are making such a magnificent contribution to our country's labor and combat forces." Joe Ellis, a black tannery worker and chairman of the Interracial Labor Relations Committee, issued a strong statement requesting labor leaders and public officials to take firm steps to prevent racial violence in Milwaukee. Such preventive efforts partly explain the lower level of racial friction in Milwaukee than elsewhere.[8]

Despite evidence of remarkable interracial cooperation, continuing competition between blacks and whites blocked the integration of blacks into the larger socioeconomic structure of the city. The pattern of black leisure-time pursuits, racial restrictions on access to various public and private accommodations, and sharp criticisms of policy in the Sixth Ward accented racial cleavage within the city. Leisure-time activities represented one of the clearest indicators of continued racial separation. Widespread unemployment during the Depression raised recreational programs to a new level of importance. The MUL intensified its work as a separate social welfare agency as it struggled to meet the leisure time needs of Afro-Americans. This development took shape as early as 1932 when the Council of Social Agencies supported the MUL's transfer to larger quarters with enough space for a social center. Social activities at the league in 1931–32 served 36,000 people; by 1935 attendance had reached 47,000 and the MUL began to limit enrollments.[9]

The MUL's social center, albeit segregated, provided a variety of recreational and cultural programs, but black access to leisure-time facilities remained inadequate. Public playgrounds provided for Afro-Americans, the MUL reported, did not have "a sprig of grass" and were "exposed to the sun until late afternoon. No shade, no grass, no water for the younger children. Not a spot where a mother may carry the baby in arms for shade and fresh air." All surfaces for volleyball and softball, the chief outdoor sports, were hard top. The Haymarket Square recreation area (bounded by Vliet and McKinley to the north and south and Fourth and Fifth streets to the east and west) was used as a farmer's market and by city merchants for much of the day for six days a week in spring and summer. "This particular spot," the league noted, "has at times been left so littered with rubbish as to produce a health hazard. . . . Street play is almost necessary."[10]

Public and private recreation among blacks became even more segregated during World War II. The Municipal Recreation Department of the Milwaukee Public Schools, the chief public agency providing leisure-time services to blacks, operated two social centers in the black area: the Fourth Street School facility and the Lapham Park Social Center. Despite almost exclusive use by blacks, the Fourth Street School building, located in the east-central section of the district, had only five black group activities leaders out of twenty. There were no black coordinators at the Lapham Park center in the northwest section of the district. Whites still living in the black area and on the periphery sought to maintain control of Lapham Park. Blacks launched repeated charges of discrimination against the center. Bernice Copeland-Lindsay surveyed the center's programs during World War II and found that only 2 percent of the clubs admitted blacks. Although some blacks made use of the natatorium located at Seventh and Highland Avenue, the city's swimming pools also largely excluded Afro-Americans.[11]

While the city did not purport to have a department of black work, the Municipal Recreation Department nevertheless separated blacks and whites in leisure-time services. In 1941, following black demands for better recreation facilities, a large outdoor pool equipped with several locker rooms was installed at Tenth and Reservoir streets. Built by WPA at a cost of $250,000, the pool was perceived by some blacks as a sign to stay out of white areas and derisively referred to as the "ink well." Recreational provisions for Afro-Americans fell far below minimum standards. By 1945, only six acres of parks served an area requiring twenty-four acres, according to National Recreation Association standards. Such municipal policies reflected the low socioeconomic and demographic base of the city's black population. Afro-Americans in the Sixth Ward, with only 30.6 percent of the ward's population, found it difficult to compete with whites for full access to available recreational services.[12]

Private and commercial institutions, as earlier, segregated blacks in the community's leisure-time life. The Milwaukee YMCA, which had previously neglected black men, established a separate Booker T. Washington Branch in 1939. Black leaders endorsed the facility on the grounds that Afro-Americans "do not resent having a building just for Negroes as long as it is a voluntary proposition." Thomas Imse, a contemporary student of Milwaukee's black population, noted that most group work by nongovernmental agencies had a special "person in charge of activity within the district." Only dance halls operated in taverns, the Sixth Ward leisure-time study noted, admitted blacks. Three licensed dance halls in the district served only "white groups." Several pool halls and bowling alleys operated in the area, but only one of the latter welcomed Afro-Americans. By the late 1930s, blacks had gained access to the Regal Theater, when it shifted from a predominantly white to a predominately black clientele and received billing in the *Blade* as "our theater." Many Afro-Americans, especially middle-class blacks, refused to patronize the Regal "because of noise caused by children" and the lack of supervision.[13]

Coupled with limitations on black leisure-time opportunities, various places of public accommodations continued to bar Afro-Americans. In August 1935, the Plankinton House excluded a black man and his guest from a party at the establishment. The Milwaukee County Progressive party had invited one of its black members, Edward Woodley, to attend the affair with some friends. When Woodley and his wife arrived, the hotel's manager refused to honor his invitation because of his color. "Your reported conduct in action and words at a conference sought with you by an interested third party confirmed your discriminatory attitude," the Milwaukee NAACP concluded upon investigating the incident. Although the NAACP filed letters of protest against the hotel, such protests apparently had little impact upon the hotel's discriminatory policies. The presence of out-of-town guests continually highlighted racial restrictions in the city's hotels. Afro-Americans found welcome accommodations only in local black rooming houses and private homes. Young women arriving in the city could not stay at the main YWCA building; they were confined to rooming services provided by the Colored Work Department of the YWCA. Black men did not have the benefit of even segregated YMCA services until 1939.[14]

The strong reaction of some white social reformers to various forms of criminal activities also exhibited racial antipathy. Gambling, prostitution, and other forms of vice posed serious concerns for the Afro-American community, partly as a result of official sanction of such activities so long as confined to the Sixth Ward. Although various forms of vice did spread into other areas of the city, the Sixth Ward and blacks in particular received intense criticism. The 1940s opened with the Milwaukee Women's Club urging city officials to curb the Sixth Ward's "policy racket." These women believed that prostitution, gambling, and similar activities could be eliminated by strict municipal ordinances and law enforcement measures. The *Blade* excoriated the attack on policy in the black community while other modes of gambling—bingo, playing the horses, show homes, church raffles, and policy, too—proceeded unmolested among whites. Led by Josephine Prasser, the former Communist and activist among local blacks, and Inez B. Barr, president of the Scottsboro Defense Committee, the Women's Club campaign demonstrated how persons sympathetic toward blacks in some areas of the city's life could be insensitive and even hostile in another.[15]

As in earlier years, Milwaukee Afro-Americans sought simultaneously to maintain and extend their separate institutional life, while fighting forcibly for the inclusion of blacks in all aspects of the city's economic, social, and political existence. It is true that the black institutional structure that had emerged during the 1920s suffered decline when the black proletariat lost most of its industrial foothold. Yet, just as a core of black workers retained industrial work and others gained sustenance from various New Deal work relief programs, a nucleus of black businesses, professions, and institutions survived the Depression and vigorously revived during World War II.

As the Afro-American proletariat lost its footing in the industrial economy, both black businesses and professions suffered tremendous setbacks. High unemployment and underemployment intensified the other long-existing constraints against black businesses: lack of capital, prejudice by lending institutions, and lack of opportunities for technical training. The decline, sharper for black women than for men, removed Afro-Americans altogether from their minor positions in building contracting, trucking, and transfer enterprises. The number of blacks engaged as proprietors in Milwaukee decreased by 5.8 percent between 1930 and 1940. This reduction, registered mainly in enterprises conducted by black women, entailed a 50 percent decline of blacks employed as retail dealers. Black operators of boarding and lodging houses, an exclusively female preserve in 1930, dropped by an estimated 33 percent. While the number of black restaurant and cafe proprietors remained nearly stable, there was a reorientation of this business toward male rather than female ownership. In 1930, black women operated more than 65 percent of these establishments; by 1940 they accounted for only 23 percent of such businesses[16] (see tables 6.1 and 6.2).

The Depression modified but did not destroy the spirit of black enterprise. Throughout the period, blacks sustained previous businesses and embarked upon others. The CBLA, Community Drug Store, Raynor's Funeral Home, and the *Wisconsin Enterprise Blade* were among the most important black businesses to survive the Depression. Each establishment displayed its own genius for surviving hard times. When the CBLA could not deliver on savings to persons whose money had been used to make mortgages, Ardie Halyard utilized her influence with Goodwill Industries to hire some of the people who saved with the firm. In this manner, the CBLA maintained faith with key depositors. As noted earlier, the CBLA was also assisted by influential city officials and banking institutions. The

Table 6.1. Black Professional, Business, and Clerical Occupations by Sex, 1930–40

| | Male 1940 | | | | | |
| | Number | | Percent | | Percent Increase or Decrease 1930–40 | |
| | Black | All | Black | All | Black | All |
|---|---|---|---|---|---|---|
| Total Labor Force | 1,382 | 149,939 | 100.0 | 100.0 | − 50.5 | − 21.4 |
| Professional | 50 | 8,767 | 3.4 | 10.9 | − 48.4 | + 19.3 |
| Proprietary | 69 | 16,397 | 4.9 | 6.5 | + 2.9 | − 12.3 |
| Clerical | 33 | 26,046 | 2.3 | 38.6 | + 73.6 | − 17.7 |
| Total | 150 | 51,210 | 10.8 | 34.1 | + 18.0 | − 11.3 |
| | Female 1940 | | | | | |
| | Number | | Percent | | Percent Increase or Decrease 1930–40 | |
| | Black | All | Black | All | Black | All |
| Total Labor Force | 539 | 62,374 | 100.0 | 100.0 | − 35.9 | − 1.5 |
| Professional | 11 | 6,817 | 1.8 | 10.9 | − 62.0 | + 10.0 |
| Proprietary | 40 | 4,067 | 7.3 | 6.5 | − 35.4 | + 45.8 |
| Clerical | 28 | 24,087 | 5.1 | 38.6 | + 3.7 | − 3.8 |
| Total | 79 | 34,971 | 14.6 | 56.0 | − 33.0 | + 2.7 |

Source: See Appendix 6.

*Blade,* a regular weekly at the beginning of the Depression, published irregularly until World War II. Raynor's Funeral Home trimmed its services to fit the slim funeral allotments provided by the County Outdoor Relief department.[17] These entrepreneurial modes of adaptation could succeed because blacks, in various ways, maintained a degree of economic viability during the Depression.

The incomes of blacks who retained jobs through the Depression, meager wages on public emergency projects, and the earnings of women domestic service employees fundamentally sustained Afro-American enterprises. Upon this base, some blacks opened new businesses during the period. A major new enterprise to emerge was the Kinner Sausage Company, a packaged barbeque and sausage firm. Although H. B. Kinner, Sr. organized the company in 1929, its success lay in the 1930s, following the purchase of new property in 1934.

The most remarkable enterprise to emerge, however, was the People's Cooperative Store. In 1935, U. S. Johnson, inspector for the

Table 6.2. Selected Proprietary Occupations by Ethnicity and Sex, 1940

| Category | Blacks | | Whites | |
|---|---|---|---|---|
| | Number | Percent | Number | Percent |
| **Male** | | | | |
| Barbers, Beauticians, Manicurists | 10 | 14.4 | 961 | 5.8 |
| Manufacturers | 1 | 1.4 | 2,462 | 15.0 |
| Wholesalers | 16 | 23.1 | 1,185 | 7.2 |
| Restaurant and Cafe Operators | 13 | 18.8 | 1,570 | 9.6 |
| Retail Trade | 14 | 20.2 | 4,765 | 29.1 |
| Business and Repair Services | 2 | 2.8 | 371 | 2.2 |
| Personal Services | 5 | 7.2 | 246 | 1.5 |
| Miscellaneous Industries and Services | 5 | 7.2 | 365 | 2.2 |
| Boarding and Lodging House Keepers | 3 | 4.3 | 111 | 0.6 |
| Total* | 69 | 100.0 | 12,036 | 73.7 |
| **Female** | | | | |
| Boarding and Lodging House Keepers | 13 | 32.5 | 631 | 15.6 |
| Miscellaneous Industries and Services | 1 | 2.5 | 191 | 4.7 |
| Restaurant and Cafe Operators | 4 | 10.0 | 410 | 10.1 |
| Other Wholesale and Retail | 4 | 10.0 | 912 | 22.6 |
| Beauticians, Barbers, Manicurists | 18 | 45.0 | 1,215 | 30.1 |
| Total* | 40 | 100.0 | 3,359 | 83.4 |

*These figures are based upon an internal analysis of proprietary occupations alone.

Source: See Appendix 6.

U.S. Department of Agriculture, and the physician Dr. C. F. Turney, held meetings in the black community and persuaded scores of families to save their pennies for a cooperative grocery store. Johnson and Turney provided black families with tin cans and encouraged them to save three cents per day. For almost two years, as the MUL reported, "pennies were collected with clock like regularity from hundreds of persons who were willing to 'go along with the plan.' " Within a year, $1,800 was collected. The store opened by 1937 with "a line of stock," the league asserted, "the arrangement of which would be a credit to any chain store." Declaring a dividend each of its first three years of operation, the store provided full-time employment for four persons. Led by black business and professional people but dependent on the savings of working-class blacks, the People's Cooperative Store symbolized how the Depression helped to unify blacks of different classes. Although unsuccessful, efforts to develop new enterprises continued with the creation of the Afro-American Economical Society in 1940. Spearheaded by its president, Cleveland Colbert, an upholsterer, the organization aimed to "gain cooperation of the Negro people in starting and operating industrial plants in order to make the Negro economically strong enough to employ their own people."[18]

Although several established enterprises survived the Depression and new ones developed, Afro-American businesses would not regain the momentum that they seemed to enjoy during the 1920s until the return of full employment during World War II. The reentrance of blacks into the industrial work force and the renewed wartime migration laid the demographic and financial foundations for the expansion of businesses. The Carver Memorial Homes Company, formed in 1943, dramatically portrayed the restimulation of Afro-American enterprises accompanying war production. When the federal government announced its intention of building 402 housing units in Milwaukee, Bernice Copeland-Lindsay organized a group of citizens and petitioned the National Housing Agency to allot part of the quota for black occupants. Frank Kirkpatrick, Milwaukee War Housing director, supported the request and NHA set aside 75 dwellings specifically for blacks. Erected at a cost of $42,000 or $4,200 per unit, the Sherman Hill Houses compared favorably to the Ida B. Wells Homes of Chicago and the Harlem River Homes in New York.[19]

Not all black enterprises were legitimate businesses. During World War II, Clinton (Joe) Harris, a reputed "policy king," emerged to prominence in Milwaukee's black community. Reporting legal earnings of only $300 to $400 a month, Harris, owner of the 711 Club at 711 W. Walnut Street, was counted among Milwaukee's wealthiest blacks. He made generous contributions to various institutions and often received praise for his civic work. In a eulogy to Harris upon his death in the post-war era, Rev. C. A. Fisher asserted that nearly every black church in Milwaukee had "enjoyed the benefaction of his hand." Fisher also referred to Harris as a kindly and "gentle" man who daily "held court" in his tavern and resolved internal disputes between working-class blacks. Drake and Cayton's description of such illegal enterprises in Chicago aptly illuminates the activities (if less extensive) of Joe Harris: "This complex is composed of the 'policy' business, prostitution, and allied pursuits, and is intimately connected with the legal but none-the-less 'shady' liquor interests and cabarets."[20]

If the Depression was difficult for black business people, it was even more so for Afro-American professionals, whose number dropped by 51.5 percent from 126 in 1930 to 61 in 1940. Again black women, with a more restricted professional base than men from the outset, experienced the greater decline. Musicians, teachers of music, actors, and actresses registered the majority of losses. The number of blacks in law and medicine, all men with the exception of women nurses, remained stable, while the number of Afro-Americans in social work, teaching, and clerical occupations increased slightly. Black nurses, doctors, lawyers, social workers, secretaries, and teachers staffed the gradually expanding network of segregated social services directed toward Afro-Americans. Teachers, for example, served in the two predominantly black Fourth and Ninth Street schools (see tables 6.1 and 6.3). Subsequently, just as it gave new life to black enterprises, World War II further stimulated the expansion of Afro-Americans in the professions. New practitioners, exclusively men, augmented the ranks of medicine and law. Black women gained white-collar positions mainly as social workers, teachers, nurses, and clerical employees.[21]

Nevertheless, as in the pre-Depression era, though World War II stimulated improvements, Afro-Americans still remained confined on the whole to the least remunerative and prestigious business and professional pursuits. Of the professional occupations represented in the 1940 census, black men found entrance to only eleven and black women to only five; professional positions open to white men and women doubled those of Afro-Americans. A similar pattern prevailed for proprietary and clerical jobs. Moreover, Afro-Americans clustered in certain professional and proprietary occupations within their limited range. Black men had 31.2 percent of their numbers in the music field compared to only 4.9 percent among white males. Afro-American men and women continued to operate a restricted spectrum of barber and beauty shops, restaurants, and small retail businesses. Whites dominated building and construction, manufacturing, banking, and larger, more profitable retail establishments. This attenuated scope of businesses and professions sharply limited the expansion of blacks into clerical positions since most such employees found employment in black enterprises (see tables 6.2, 6.3, and 6.4). Although Milwaukee blacks held slightly more professional and proprietary positions compared to their counterparts in other northern cities, the larger demographic and economic foundations of such cities as Cleveland, New York, and Chicago sustained a broader array of

Table 6.3. Selected Professional Occupations by Ethnicity and Sex, 1940

| Category | Blacks | | Whites | |
|---|---|---|---|---|
| | Number | Percent | Number | Percent |
| Male | | | | |
| Authors, Editors, Reporters | 1 | 2.0 | 206 | 2.6 |
| Clergymen | 11 | 22.9 | 447 | 5.1 |
| College Presidents and Professors | 1 | 2.0 | 198 | 2.2 |
| Dentists | 3 | 6.2 | 436 | 4.9 |
| Lawyers and Judges | 3 | 6.2 | 885 | 10.1 |
| Musicians and Music Teachers | 15 | 31.2 | 430 | 4.9 |
| Pharmacists | 1 | 2.0 | 440 | 5.0 |
| Physicians and Surgeons | 6 | 12.5 | 739 | 8.4 |
| Social and Welfare Workers | 4 | 8.3 | 186 | 2.1 |
| Teachers (not classified elsewhere) | 2 | 4.1 | 944 | 10.8 |
| Dancers, Showmen, Athletes | 3 | 6.2 | 114 | 1.3 |
| Total* | 50 | 100.0 | 5,025 | 57.5 |
| Female | | | | |
| Dentists | 1 | 9.0 | 28 | 0.4 |
| Musicians and Music Teachers | 1 | 9.0 | 311 | 4.5 |
| Social and Welfare Workers | 3 | 27.2 | 227 | 3.3 |
| Teachers (not classified elsewhere) | 4 | 36.3 | 3,236 | 47.5 |
| Trained Nurses and Students | 2 | 18.1 | 2,417 | 35.5 |
| Total* | 11 | 100.0 | 6,219 | 91.3 |

*These figures are based upon internal analysis of professional occupations alone.

Source: See Appendix 6.

business, professional, and clerical pursuits than were available to blacks in Milwaukee.[22]

The Depression arrested but did not entirely freeze other institutional consequences of Afro-American participation in the industrial economy. While the number of Afro-American churches dropped from thirteen in 1930 to ten in 1936, institutions like these quickly revived and expanded under the impact of New Deal relief programs. One Church of God in Christ and two new Baptist churches opened during 1936–37. Under wartime conditions, black religious institutions expanded even more dramatically. By 1942, Imse estimated, about twenty-eight churches in the black district welcomed Afro-Americans. Most of these were all-black institutions.

Religious expansion took place primarily among poor storefront Holiness, Spiritualist, and small Baptist churches. While some of these bodies took roots and grew, there was an ephemeral quality

Table 6.4. Selected Clerical Occupations by Ethnicity and Sex, 1940

| Category | Blacks | | Whites | |
|---|---|---|---|---|
| | Number | Percent | Number | Percent |
| **Male** | | | | |
| Shipping and Receiving Clerks | 2 | 6.0 | 1,990 | 7.6 |
| Stenographers and Typists | 1 | 3.0 | 388 | 1.4 |
| Other Clerical | 17 | 51.5 | 8,495 | 32.6 |
| Canvassers and Solicitors | 1 | 3.0 | 542 | 2.0 |
| Hucksters and Peddlers | 1 | 3.0 | 233 | 0.8 |
| Insurance Agents and Brokers | 1 | 3.0 | 1,174 | 4.5 |
| Real Estate Agents and Brokers | 2 | 6.0 | 578 | 2.2 |
| Other Sales Agents and Brokers | 2 | 6.0 | 4,323 | 16.6 |
| Other Salesmen | 6 | 18.1 | 4,990 | 19.1 |
| Total* | 33 | 100.0 | 22,713 | 87.3 |
| **Female** | | | | |
| Bookkeepers, Accountants, Cashiers | 2 | 7.1 | 2,843 | 11.8 |
| Stenographers, Typists, Secretaries | 8 | 28.1 | 7,723 | 32.1 |
| Other Clerical | 11 | 39.2 | 4,878 | 20.2 |
| Canvassers, Peddlers, News Vendors | 1 | 3.5 | 120 | 0.4 |
| Other Saleswomen | 6 | 21.4 | 6,164 | 25.6 |
| Total* | 28 | 100.0 | 21,728 | 90.1 |

*These figures are based upon an internal analysis of clerical occupations alone.

Source: See Appendix 6.

about these institutions, as one student of the subject noted. "These store front churches, are in general sects that spring up and die off rapidly, although a few seem to last for some time." On the other hand, financial resources provided by World War II enabled established churches to purchase new structures or pay debts on old buildings. In July 1943, the *Blade* reported a successful $1,500 fund raising drive at Calvary and praised the church as the only black religious body "free of debt" on its edifice. Mt. Zion Baptist Church raised $1,300 during the same period. Even the Rehoboth Church of God in Christ entered new and "spacious quarters" at 1801 N. 11th Street. A similar dynamic marked the experience of black lodges, fraternal organizations, and social clubs.[23]

The Depression and World War II prompted a shift of blacks toward the Democratic party and further consolidated their political influence. The Afro-American population in the Sixth Ward increased from 4,421 in 1930 to 7,320 in 1940, an increase from 22.2 to 30.6 percent of the ward's total. Blacks further augmented their percentage in the ward during World War II. In presidential contests, the Democratic vote from predominantly black precincts of the Sixth Ward increased from 55 percent in 1932 to 87 percent in 1936. Although Roosevelt's margin declined during the economic downturn following the election of 1936, he nevertheless polled an estimated 78 percent of Milwaukee's black votes in 1940 and 1944.[24]

Afro-Americans did not blindly place their faith in the Democratic party; rather, they linked their growing allegiance to the Democrats to a concerted drive to elect blacks to local offices. Between 1933 and 1945, the number of Afro-American candidates for city, county, and state offices reached unprecedented levels. These office seekers reflected a variety of party affiliations: Democrats, Republicans, and Progressives, a coalition of dissident Republicans and Socialists; only after the Progressive party declined in the 1940s did political lines in Milwaukee become narrowly confined to the division between Democrats and Republicans.[25]

Following the dramatic defeat of efforts to elect a black alderman in 1932, Afro-Americans redoubled their struggle to elect a black to the city council. In the Sixth Ward aldermanic election of 1936, attorney James Dorsey posed a threat to white incumbent Samuel Soref. For the first time a black candidate advanced through the primary in an aldermanic contest. In the spring primary, Dorsey polled 39.7 percent of the votes to Soref's 39.9 percent. Despite his loss in the subsequent spring election, Dorsey made a forceful and competitive stand with 43.6 percent of the votes. He came even closer to winning the aldermanic seat in 1940 when Soref decided not to seek reelection. Dorsey received 9.7 percent more votes than his closest white competitor, Frank Meyer, in the spring primary, but he lost to Meyer by less than 2 percent of the votes in the spring election. Running again in 1944, Dorsey's margin was significantly reduced. His efforts nevertheless demonstrated the forceful thrust of Afro-Americans for elective office. Although unsuccessful, blacks sought to elect a county supervisor as well, and several Afro-Americans, Ernest Bland, Aaron Tolliver, and Hollis B. Kinner, Jr., gained positions as ward committeemen.[26]

In their greatest success during the period, Afro-Americans joined the push for local elective office with efforts to elect a state assemblyman. Their work appeared rewarded when Cleveland Colbert, a

Republican, won the Sixth District assembly election of 1942 by a margin of six votes over his white Progressive party opponent Phillip Markey. Colbert, initially certified as the winner, was unseated through a recount. Seeking to retain the seat, Colbert conducted an unsuccessful legal struggle before the State Election Commission, the Circuit Court, and the Wisconsin State Assembly. While racial discrimination was implied, Colbert fought his case on the basis of legal technicalities: that "ballots in the third and sixteenth precincts were not wired together, as required, and that the county election commission failed to inspect all ballots for initials."[27]

The campaign to elect a black assemblyman succeeded in the election of 1944. LeRoy Simmons, a realtor and earlier candidate for Sixth District supervisor, gained the endorsement of the Democratic party and outdistanced both Phillip Markey, the incumbent Republican, and the Progressive candidate, Joseph Valenti. Simmons polled 50.6 percent of the 7,923 votes cast. Markey and Valenti received 35.8 and 13.5 percent, respectively. With only about one-third of the district's population, Afro-Americans were able to elect a black assemblyman for the first time since 1906. Unlike the earlier period when Lucien Palmer gained office partly by camouflaging his identity, Simmons explicitly campaigned for both black and white votes. White Democrats supported Simmons not only because of increasing black demands for representation but also because of fear of Republican inroads on black votes, as reflected in Colbert's candidacy in 1942.[28]

In his assessment of black politics in northern cities between 1900 and 1940, Martin Kilson notes that, with the exception of Chicago, blacks in large northern cities — such as Philadelphia and New York — failed to have their "ethnic turfs" incorporated as an integral part of political machines. Chicago was unique in that neither Republicans nor Democrats had a "built-in majority" and each party relied on pivotal minorities for votes in city, state, and national elections.[29] As in most northern cities, Milwaukee blacks had little real influence on established political machinery, but unlike blacks in other cities, Afro-Americans in Milwaukee operated within a city strongly influenced by a third party for most of the period, the Socialist party to 1935 and the left-leaning Progressive party thereafter. Indeed, the competitive struggle for votes among Democrats, Republicans, and Progressives helps to explain the election of a black assemblyman in 1944. Nevertheless, World War II brought a resurgence of traditional Democratic and Republican politics, which set the stage for a gradual shift of Milwaukee blacks' voting habits toward the Chicago pattern.

The persistent efforts of blacks to gain elective office and their increasing margin of support reflected systematic attempts to exploit the political potential inherent in the expanding black working class. Although the earlier call for racial solidarity and self-help continued, issues confronting all blacks, but particularly the black proletariat, increasingly marked the appeal of politicians to black voters. The high rate of unemployment and poor housing among blacks in the Sixth Ward accented questions of jobs, adequate relief, and low-cost housing. Dorsey, in his bid for the aldermanic seat, consistently raised the issues of sufficient relief and the position of blacks in New Deal programs such as WPA. In a conference with Mayor Hoan in the spring of 1936, black leaders, bourgeois and proletarian, outlined the need for access to low-cost housing. Under the impact of production for war, better jobs and housing became even more intense political issues. Joe Ellis of the CIO Interracial Labor Relations Committee highlighted these demands in a statement to the black Ministerial Alliance during the aldermanic election of 1944: "Make the Sixth Ward a better place to live in: This means first of all more and better housing through both federal aid and private construction. . . . Continue and expand, now and after the war, the employment of Negro labor, both men and women, in industry at jobs for which they are trained, with expanded job training programs and upgrading."[30]

With the exception of Assemblyman Simmons and several ward committeemen, Afro-Americans failed to elect black officials, yet they tapped their expanding political strength in gaining various concessions from established political leaders. Following the NAACP's agitation for lights at Lapham Park, the city council passed a resolution authorizing the appropriation of nearly $800.00 for additional lighting. In the early 1940s, although some blacks disparaged the project, most Afro-Americans supported the fight for the WPA playground and pool project at N. 10th and Reservoir streets. Under the impact of World War II production, blacks achieved even more concessions. The most significant of these — involving a progressive alliance of several black and white civic, social welfare, religious, and labor organizations — was the creation of the Milwaukee Housing Authority in 1944. The new authority immediately turned to the erection of a 144-unit low-income housing project for war workers in the Sixth Ward.[31] Although inadequate and usually segregated, such concessions improved somewhat the access of Afro-Americans to city services, but only the labor demands of war production, coupled with growing Afro-American protests for equal access to industrial jobs, brought a significant shift in the socioeconomic status of Afro-Americans.

Afro-Americans were indeed active in their own interests between 1933 and 1945. The Depression heightened the need for intraracial unity as blacks sought to extend their separate institutional life and gain greater access to relief work and subsidies, low-cost housing, leisure-time facilities, political influence, and civil rights in general. While intraracial cleavages were less sharply drawn in Milwaukee than in larger northern cities, black unity continued to be undermined by several internal divisions: class, intraclass, and cultural. Although middle-class organizations adopted a stronger prolabor stance, the conflict between the proletariat and the bourgeoisie remained the most salient division within the black community. A variety of black protest activities, the struggle for an Afro-American alderman, institutional life, and a new wave of black migration mirrored intraracial friction within black Milwaukee.

Efforts to elect a black alderman divided advocates of racial solidarity, mainly Afro-American business and professional people, and proponents of working-class solidarity. Carlos Del Ruy and Ernest Bland allied with the Farmer-Labor Progressive Federation and opposed the election of Dorsey as alderman from the Sixth Ward. Blacks allied with the Progressive Federation nevertheless occupied a tenuous position because of racial discrimination within Progressive ranks. Del Ruy, as noted earlier, criticized white party members for neglecting Sixth Ward blacks. Such neglect, Del Ruy warned, would undermine the effectiveness of those blacks who supported Socialist and Farmer-Labor candidates: "All sorts of propaganda is afloat concerning prejudice among Socialists in the 6th Ward Branch and the total lack of Colored members in the 10th Ward is being broadcast daily as evidence of the Socialists' lack of interest in our welfare." Del Ruy informed party members that it was not easy for blacks to go against the sentiments for racial solidarity in the Sixth Ward: "Those of us who were loyal to Soref and a real program, sacrificed the good feeling that existed between ourselves and those of our racial group who supported the candidacy of Jim Dorsey. We still have to live here."[32]

Dorsey's attempts to gain an aldermanic seat also provoked vigorous dissension within the black middle class. J. Anthony Josey, editor

of the *Blade* and staunch supporter of Samuel Soref, hoped to discourage Dorsey's candidacy in 1936. According to Josey's assistant,
Bernice Copeland-Lindsay, Josey and Soref sought Dorsey's endorsement in 1936 in exchange for their endorsement of him in 1940.
Dorsey refused the offer and thus lost Josey's support. When incumbent alderman Soref decided not to run in 1940, Dorsey and three
other Afro-Americans sought the position: Hollis Kinner, the sausage
dealer, Clarence L. Johnson, the tailor and YMCA director, and attorney George W. Hamilton.[33] These intraracial divisions, coupled
with the small black proportion of the electorate, helped to defeat
Dorsey's aldermanic bid.

Although some conflicts gained articulation as controversies mainly within the middle class, such disputes invariably involved the interests of working-class blacks, who often supported the party they
deemed more nearly representative of their welfare. The struggle for
the WPA playground and pool, though a success, had its middle-class
detractors. The Young Peoples Lyceum, under the leadership of Bernice Lindsay, attacked the pool as a misdirection of funds. Working
with J. Anthony Josey on the *Blade,* Lindsay vacillated in supporting
separate black institutions. Speaking for the lyceum, Russell Bowers
declared that the money could have been used "to better advantage for
slum clearance." Lyceum opposition, however, was not enough to
assuage support of the project by such professionals as attorney James
Dorsey and working-class spokesman Carlos C. Del Ruy, both of
whom praised the project as a necessary addition to the leisure-time
needs of the black community.[34]

By the end of World War II, the cleavage had deepened within the
black middle class over the extension of social services to the expanding Afro-American population. When social welfare officials debated
the best mode of extending more leisure-time services to the black
community, the Milwaukee Urban League stood in strong competitive opposition to the newly emergent Booker T. Washington YMCA
and the continuing Colored Work Department of the YWCA, under
the leadership of Clarence L. Johnson and Bernice Lindsay, respectively. Each faction sought financial support from the Community Fund and Council of Social Agencies for a program of leisure-time
services to a largely segregated black population. The Community
Fund decided to finance the expansion of Y-work among blacks and
recommended that the league gradually terminate its group-work
programs and concentrate mainly on economic issues. While the

council's decision promoted diversification of services available to blacks, the agency also provided institutional support for continuing rivalry within the black middle class.[35]

More than any other incident, the fight for control of the Milwaukee NAACP represented a split within the black middle class. This dispute also mirrored the manner in which working-class blacks allied with the faction they perceived in closer tune with their interests. Competition within the black middle class reflected the persisting conflict between integrationist and separatist tendencies among bourgeois leaders. Above all, these intraclass controversies, under conditions of deepening Depression, reflected social tensions generated by efforts of black business and professional people to reap economic and political benefits from the small demographic and economic base of the Afro-American industrial working class.

As noted earlier, by the mid-1920s the new black business and professional elite, based mainly on services to the expanding black population, had consolidated its control over the NAACP. By 1929, Wilbur Halyard had become president, Dr. P. Jay Gilmer had become treasurer, and Rev. C. A. Fisher had become a leading board member. Even so, traditional integrationist ideas, though modified, persisted through Dr. L. T. Gilmer's activities as an influential member of the NAACP board. This roster of officers continued with few changes until early 1933 when attorney James Dorsey became president.

Dorsey and Fisher gradually emerged as the most important political figures in Milwaukee's black community, and the NAACP constituted an integral component of their influence. As head of relief and probation work among blacks, Fisher used his contacts with city and county officials to gain the loyalty of working-class blacks. Because of his ability to deliver relief benefits, Fisher became known as the black "patronage chief." Attorney Dorsey similarly consolidated his position as a lawyer by catering to the needs of an expanding black population. A substantial portion of his income came from positions with various city and county agencies, especially as public counsel for accused Afro-American adults and juveniles. Collectively, Fisher and Dorsey sought to consolidate the power of blacks in the Sixth Ward; they increasingly viewed the Milwaukee NAACP as an indispensable tool in this struggle.[36]

Fisher and Dorsey's strong local orientation during the early years of the Depression led them to neglect such national NAACP concerns

as the federal anti-lynching bill, the Crawford case, the Mississippi
flood control fight, and others. This opened the way for a faction, led
by Dr. L. T. Gilmer, to initiate moves to gain control of the local
branch. Gilmer consistently rejected organization of the black community primarily on the basis of race. Dorsey and Fisher's increasing
insistence that the NAACP serve as a vehicle for separate black
political, economic, and social development heightened Gilmer's opposition.[37]

In February 1934, the director of NAACP branches, William
Pickens, authorized Gilmer to hold new elections and replace old officers. Pickens was particularly concerned about the failure of the local
branch to forward membership dues to the national office. "The old
crowd," he asserted, "does not bank money, does not make financial
accountings to members, — have lost respect of honest people, white
and Colored."[38] Fisher and Dorsey strongly repudiated such interpretations of their work, emphasizing the poor economic position of local
blacks: "True, we have not been able to raise monies above the ex-
penses of our local program. . . .Our people are slowly returning to
work. The CWA has granted temporary aid in many cases, but piled
up debts have taken this money. We could not appeal to these classes.
In fact for them we exist."[39] The Fisher-Dorsey faction ignored the instructions to Gilmer and proceeded to carry out its own election. New
officers included Rev. C. A. Fisher, president; Emmett Reed, vice-
president; Dr. Edgar Thomas, treasurer; and Chestina Josey,
secretary. The national office countermanded this move by declaring
the offices of the Milwaukee NAACP vacant and inactive. In addition
to heightening local rivalry, this action touched off a bitter conflict between the new officers and the national office. In a strongly worded
letter to Walter White, C. A. Fisher affirmed local autonomy in the
work of the Milwaukee NAACP and refused to cooperate with a new
election.[40]

Strong local opposition prompted a personal visit by William
Pickens to oversee the election. Tensions between factions ran so high
that Pickens, upon arrival, stopped by the police station and persuaded the lieutenant to provide two uniformed officers and two
detectives for the meeting. Pickens's report of the affair described the
intraracial animosity and, although couched in extremely negative
terms, it revealed how Fisher and Dorsey garnered substantial support among working-class blacks:

I conferred with former officers and with the Rev. Mr. Fisher, who is now a politician.... I tried to get him and his crowd to "come on out," bring memberships and help us to organize. Instead of that they went all over town, got all the thugs and underworld characters and came to break up the meeting.... I opened up for election of officers and the fight was on: the gang got the floor and talked and "orated" and injected personalities and tried to stir up a physical fight. I gave them all their parliamentary rights and threatened to throw one or two of them out when they got awfully nasty. Some women got afraid; one started into a faint and had to be carried out. On the front bench near me the gang had brought out a dangerous murderous half-wit who kept interrupting and threatening and insulting.[41]

The meeting terminated favorably for Pickens and Gilmer when Fisher and his group were disqualified from voting after they refused to take out memberships at the meeting. A white minister, Dr. E. LeRoy Dakin, was elected president and whites also figured prominently among other officers and board members.

The NAACP controversy graphically illustrated how intraclass conflicts militated against racial unity. On the one hand, the dispute reflected the manner in which aspiring politicians like Fisher and Dorsey hoped to use the local branch as a tool for political power. On the other hand, the controversy revealed how different factions of the middle class developed contrasting relationships with the black working class. While such conflicts often entailed purely personal animosities between individuals, friction within the black middle class was fundamentally a consequence of increasing competition among black business and professional people for scarce opportunities within a city of extremely limited black socioeconomic and political means.

If there were divisions within the black middle class, there were also signs of fragmentation within the Afro-American proletariat. Divisions within the working class took the form of a familiar conflict between old and new residents, which indeed developed a different class slant by 1945. Before the Depression, the new-old resident cleavage mainly represented a split between the working class and bourgeoisie. During the Depression and World War II, the traditional division between old and new residents, while continuing, increasingly reflected a split within the black proletariat. Pre-Depression migrants increasingly adopted the attitudes of old residents toward the accelerated influx of southern blacks during the late 1930s and early 1940s. Complaints against the newcomers were particularly strong in defense plants; their behavior, old-timers argued, jeopardized the jobs of old residents. The MUL reported receiving "dozens of complaints" of "Negroes against Negroes." More importantly, however, the rift between new and old residents increasingly transcended the workplace and penetrated broader social and institutional relationships in the black community. Although in fundamental agreement with most criticisms leveled against newcomers, the MUL reacted to the growing abrasiveness of comments by reminding old workers of the hostile reaction to their initial entry into the city:

> Do you or don't you remember the days from 1916 to 1926 when we — you and I set out for a new world — the North? . . . How we then became frustrated . . . how the hometown Colored Brother was ashamed of us, apologized for us and left us very much alone? . . . Some of us seem to be afflicted with short memories. We are highly critical of the behavior of the newcomers. They embarrass us on the job with their "down home" jokes which keep the "white folks" laughing. They smoke on the cars and buses in violation of the law. They go to downtown show houses dressed in poor taste. They deport themselves ridiculously when shopping. They talk too loudly (incidentally, most of us are far from tops in this department) in public places, places of amusement and on the streets. They are making it hard for all of us. These criticisms are, in fact justifiable. But let us ask ourselves how much voluntary interest and guidance we have extended to the newcomers. . . . Don't forget when we came north we brought ourselves right along with us. So have our newcomers. People usually do.[42]

Internal divisions within the black bourgeoisie and proletariat notwithstanding, it was the divisions between them that marked the critical boundaries of intraracial class conflicts in Milwaukee. These divisions found expression in black religious institutions. While the Depression curtailed such cleavages, it did not eliminate them. The class orientation that separated the membership of St. Mark and Calvary Baptist from each other and both from the new storefront Holiness Church of God in Christ, though somewhat muted, persisted through the Depression and World War II. Ruby Cook, a member of St. Mark during the period, observed that the AME body retained its reputation as the "most prominent" black religious institution in the city. The people there, she noted, "dressed better" and "seemed to live better." St. Mark also maintained its stance against the shouting tradition that marked more decidedly working-class churches. While the distinction between St. Mark and the larger Baptist churches, Calvary and Greater Galilee, continued, a greater gulf increasingly divided all of these churches on the one hand from smaller Baptist and Holiness bodies on the other. By the end of World War II, the latter, with larger numbers of domestic service employees and factory workers and fewer professional and business people, maintained a strong shouting tradition and appealed to the religious and social needs of the expanding Afro-American proletariat.[43]

Milwaukee's inter- and intraracial relations underwent dramatic changes during the Depression and World War II. Unlike the experience of blacks in larger northern cities, the smaller demographic base of Milwaukee's black population, their lower percentage in the industrial work force, and cooperative efforts in race relations prevented the escalation of racial competition from developing into large-scale physical violence. The persistence of discriminatory industrial hiring policies and racial antagonism from working-class whites, however, simultaneously muted divisions within the black proletariat and fostered a continuing, though precarious, alliance between middle- and working-class blacks. On the other hand, proletarianization of Milwaukee's black population, the expansion and consolidation of the ghetto, and the increasing incidents of racial violence in the post-war era would culminate in large-scale racial conflicts. The city's Afro-American population would then lose much of its pre–World War II uniqueness and reflect the social, economic, and political processes characteristic of larger black populations throughout the urban North. Even so, in the years 1915–45, the experience of Milwaukee blacks was never entirely unique. The dynamics of industrial capitalism wrought similar changes in the lives of urban blacks in diverse settings. The comparative characteristics of these experiences are treated in Chapter 7.

## NOTES

1. Daniel W. Hoan to C. B. Whitnall, Commonwealth Mutual Bank, 14 June 1933; Hoan to Sol Levitan, 15 Jan. 1937; Hoan to William J. Benning, 9 Mar. 1934, Box 26, File 98, Daniel W. Hoan Papers (Milwaukee County Historical Society); interview with Ardie A. Halyard, 14 Aug. 1979.
2. William Pickens, "Summary of Milwaukee Visit," 3 Mar. 1934; G. D.

Daniel, secretary, Milwaukee NAACP, 12 Apr. 1934, 10 May 1934, Box G-219, National Association for the Advancement of Colored People Papers.

3. Milwaukee Urban League Monthly Reports, June–Aug. 1933, Nov. 1936, Feb. 1937, Mar. 1940; MUL Annual Report, 1942–43, Ser. 13, Box 16, National Urban League Papers; Circular Letter, Inter-Racial Federation of Milwaukee County, 30 Nov. 1943, Box 3, United Community Services of Greater Milwaukee Papers, 1903–66 (University of Wisconsin–Milwaukee, Area Research Center).

4. George E. Teter to Pickens, 21 May 1933; Wilbur Halyard to Pickens, 17 Apr. 1933; L. T. Gilmer to Pickens, 2 May 1933; Pickens to Gilmer, 8 May 1933; Gilmer to Pickens, 21 May 1933, Box G-219, NAACP Papers.

5. Ben Rubin to NAACP, national office, 18 Mar. 1937, 12 Apr. 1937, 21 Feb. 1939; E. Frederic Morrow, director of branches, to James W. Dorsey, president Milwaukee NAACP, 3 Mar. 1933; NAACP memo to the Beloit and Milwaukee branches, 21 Apr. 1937; text of Rubin Bill, Box C-227, NAACP Papers; *Wisconsin Session Laws: Including All of the Acts and Certain Joint Resolutions, 1939* (Madison: 1939), p. 599.

6. Dan T. Carter, *Scottsboro: A Tragedy of the American South* (Baton Rouge: Louisiana State University Press, 1969); Hugh T. Murray, Jr., "The NAACP Versus the Communist Party: The Scottsboro Rape Cases, 1931–32," in Bernard Sternsher, ed., *The Negro in Depression and War: Prelude to Revolution, 1930–1945* (Chicago: Quadrangle Books, 1969), pp. 268–81; Gunnar Mickelsen, secretary-treasurer of Wisconsin State Industrial Union Council to Anna Damon, secretary, Committee for Defense of Scottsboro Boys, 3 Nov. 1937; WIUC Resolution Re Scottsboro Boys, 30 Sept.–3 Oct. 1937, Box H-7, Addenda: Milwaukee Scottsboro Defense Committee, 1937–39, NAACP Papers.

7. Rose Shapiro, assistant secretary, Scottsboro Defense Committee, to Gunnar Mickelsen, 23 Nov. 1937; Cora Meyer, secretary, Provisional Scottsboro Defense Committee, to Shapiro, 28 Nov. 1937; Shapiro to Meyer, 29 Nov. 1937; Meyer to Shapiro, 4 Dec. 1937; Meyer to Scottsboro Defense Committee, 15 and 27 Dec. 1937, Box H-7, Addenda: NAACP Papers.

8. See Chapter 5, n. 45, "Condemn Detroit 'Race' Riots," *CIO News: Wisconsin Edition,* 28 June 1943; "248 Joins with UAW-CIO in Asking Grand Jury Investigation of 5th Column-Inspired Race Riots," *CIO News: Wisconsin Edition,* 28 June 1943; " 'No Strike Pledge,' 'Detroit Riots,' 'Farm Aid,' Text of State CIO Action," *CIO News: Wisconsin Edition,* 2 Aug. 1943; "Negro Unionists Make Vigorous Statement, Proposals, on 'Riots,' " *CIO News: Wisconsin Edition,* 9 Aug. 1943.

9. William V. Kelley, "The Story of the Milwaukee Urban League" (Newspaper Clippings File of the Milwaukee Urban League, ca. 1945).
10. Virginia W. Williams, "Negro History Makers in Milwaukee," *Echo* 9 (1967): 15–17; interview with Helen V. Kelley, 7 Aug. 1979; MUL Monthly Report, Aug.–Sept. 1937; interview with Audrey Davis, 14 Aug. 1979.
11. Community Fund and Council of Social Agencies, "Report of the Committee on Leisure Time in the Sixth Ward to the Social Planning Committee," Ser. 6, Box 92, NUL Papers.
12. Ibid.; "Approves WPA Playground and Pool Proposal," newspaper clipping, Box G-219, NAACP Papers; Thomas Imse, "The Negro Community in Milwaukee" (master's thesis, Marquette University, 1942), pp. 34–35; interview with Helen V. Kelley, 7 Aug. 1979.
13. Imse, "The Negro Community in Milwaukee," pp. 37–38; Community Fund, "Report of the Committee on Leisure Time in the Sixth Ward," NUL Papers; Virginia W. Williams, "Clarence L. Johnson: Echo's Father of the Year," *Echo* 22, no. 9 (1977): 31–37; "Y.M.C.A. Gives 2nd Annual Dinner: Booker T. Washington Branch is Big Success," *Blade,* 16 Nov. 1940; "Regal Theater," *Blade,* 2 Nov. 1940; "Vel R. Phillips Y.W.C.A. Rededication," personal papers, Bernice Lindsay; interviews with Clarence L. Johnson, 15 Aug. 1979; Audrey Davis, 14 Aug. 1979; Helen V. Kelley, 7 Aug. 1979; Lincoln Gaines, 23 Aug. 1979.
14. G. D. Daniel to Walter White, 10 Aug. 1935; Milwaukee NAACP to manager of the Plankington House, 22 July 1935; telegram, Juanita E. Jackson to B. Durner, Eagle's Club, 17 June 1937; secretary NAACP, national office, to William W. Hinckley, chairman American Youth Congress, 19 June 1937; telegram, Walter White to John S. Perry, secretary, Fraternal Order of Eagles, national headquarters, 19 June 1938; E. LeRoy Dakin to White, 18 June 1937; telegram, Roy Wilkins to Dakin, 21 June 1937; Charles H. Houston to T. G. Hendrick, secretary, Milwaukee NAACP, 26 June 1937; Conrad H. Mann, chief auditor, Eagles, to White, 21 June 1937, Box G-219, NAACP Papers; "Jews Breaking Down Color-Line," Box C-227, NAACP Papers.
15. "Third Degree for 5c Policy?: Women's Club Seek Investigation, Mrs. Barr Jabs at Sixth Ward Policy Again," *Blade,* 7 Dec. 1940; Imse, "The Negro Community in Milwaukee," pp. 39–40; interview with Felmers O. Chaney, 27 Aug. 1979; interview with Lawrence E. Miller, 30 Aug. 1979; *Milwaukee City Directory* (Milwaukee: Wright's City Directory, 1939).
16. "People's Cooperative a Going Concern," MUL Monthly Report, July 1937 (Milwaukee Public Library); Drake and Cayton, *Black Metropolis,* vol. 2, pp. 430–37; *Sixteenth Census of U.S.: 1940 Census of Business, vol. 1,*

*Retail Trade, 1939* (Washington: Government Printing Office, 1943); also see, *U.S. Census of Business, 1939, vol. 3* (Washington: Government Printing Office, 1939).

17. Interview with Ardie A. Halyard, 14 Aug. 1979; interview with Carl Watson, 5 Aug. 1979; *Blade,* 16 Nov. 1940, 4 Sept. 1943; Armstead Scott Pride, "A Register and History of Negro Newspapers in the United States" (Ph.D. diss., Northwestern University, 1950), pp. 166–67, 391–92; D. W. Whitnall, 14 June 1933, Box 26, File 98, Hoan Papers.

18. "People's Cooperative a Going Concern," MUL Monthly Report, July 1937; Mary Ellen Shadd, *Negro Business Directory of the State of Wisconsin, 1950–1951* (Milwaukee, 1950), p. 37; *Milwaukee City Directory* (Milwaukee: Wright's City Directory, 1939).

19. Interview with Bernice Lindsay, 9 Aug. 1979; "Carver Memorial Homes, Inc." (Milwaukee, 1944), personal files of Bernice Lindsay.

20. "Church Overflows for Joe Harris' Rite," "Wife Divorces 'King of Policy': Property is Divided," "Mrs. Lillian Mae Hall," Newspaper Clippings, Irene Goggins, personal files; interviews with Lawrence E. Miller, 30 Aug. 1979, and Felmers O. Chaney, 27 Aug. 1979; Drake and Cayton, *Black Metropolis,* vol. 2, p. 524.

21. "Early Negro Doctor Honored by Shriners," *Milwaukee Journal,* 21 Aug. 1968; Shadd, *Negro Business Directory,* pp. 27–33; "Rev. C. A. Fisher," *Echo* 21, no. 27 (1976): 24–26; "J. Howard Offutt," *Echo* 21, no. 27 (1976): 20–21; "A Tribute to James Weston Dorsey," Box 1, James W. Dorsey Papers, 1930–66 (Milwaukee County Historical Society); "This is Your Life: Rev. C. A. Fisher," Folders 1–3, Cecil A. Fisher Papers, 1921–66 (University of Wisconsin–Milwaukee, Area Research Center).

22. U.S. Census Bureau, *Sixteenth Census of U.S.: 1940, Population, vol. 3, pts. 2–5* (Washington: Government Printing Office, 1943); Drake and Cayton, *Black Metropolis,* vol. 2, pp. 450–51; Abram L. Harris, *The Negro as Capitalist: A Study of Banking and Business Among American Negroes* (Philadelphia: American Academy of Political and Social Sciences, 1936).

23. "Black Community Survey: Wilberforce University Questionnaire," William V. Kelley to Otto Hauser, 28 Jan. 1936, Box 26, File 98, Hoan Papers; Imse, "The Negro Community in Milwaukee," pp. 25–26; *Blade,* 17 July 1943, 26 June 1943, 26 Oct. 1940; interview with Clarence L. Miller, 30 Aug. 1979.

24. Milwaukee Board of Election Commissioners, *Biennial Reports, 1932–1944* (Milwaukee Legislative Reference Bureau); interview with Carl Watson, 5 Aug. 1979; Bayrd Still, *Milwaukee: The History of a City* (1948; rept. Madison: State Historical Society of Wisconsin, 1965), pp. 528–32; Thomas W. Gavett, *Development of the Labor Movement in Milwaukee* (Madison: University of Wisconsin Press, 1965), pp. 171–75; Keith Schmitz, "Milwaukee and its Black Community, 1930–1942" (master's thesis, University of Wisconsin–Milwaukee, 1979), pp. 57–60.

25. See n. 24.
26. Executive Committee of the Sixth Ward Branch of the Communist Party, "Our Position on the Election of 1936," Box 1, Dorsey Papers; "A Tribute to James Weston Dorsey," Dorsey Papers; interview with Ernest Bland, 8 Aug. 1979; Milwaukee Board of Election Commissioners, *Biennial Reports, 1932–1944* (Milwaukee Legislative Reference Bureau).
27. *Chicago Defender,* 3 Apr. 1943; interview with Carl Watson, 5 Aug. 1979; Milwaukee County Board of Election Commissioners, *Biennial Reports, 1936–1944* (Milwaukee Legislative Reference Bureau).
28. Ibid.; Shadd, *Negro Business Directory,* p. 35; Robert Wells, "War Broke up Segregation in Industrial Plants: Population Here Lagged Behind that of Other Major Cities," *Milwaukee Journal,* 12 Nov. 1967; Ben E. Johnson, "An Update of Wisconsin Black Legislators," *Echo* 22, no. 29 (1977): 46–47.
29. Martin Kilson, "Political Change in the Negro Ghetto, 1900–1940s," in Nathan I. Huggins, et al., eds., *Key Issues in the Afro-American Experience* (New York: Harcourt Brace Jovanovich, 1971), pp. 167–92.
30. Joe Ellis, "Statement: Presented to the Ministerial Alliance on the 6th Ward Aldermanic Elections," Box 5, Milwaukee County Industrial Union Council Papers; Thomas M. Johnson to Hoan, 19 Jan. 1936, Box 26, File 98, Hoan Papers; Josephine Prasser to William Pickens, 5 Sept. 1939, Box G-219, NAACP Papers; D. W. Hoan to Soref, Sixth Ward alderman, 27 May 1936, Box 26, File 98, Hoan Papers.
31. "Approves WPA Playground and Pool Proposal," newspaper clipping; Josephine Prasser to Pickens, 1 Feb. 1939, Box G-219, NAACP Papers; D. W. Hoan to William V. Kelley, 21 July 1936, Box 26, File 98, Hoan Papers; "Lights Asked for Lapham Park Grounds," 15 Aug. 1938, newspaper clipping, Box G-219, NAACP Papers; Vivian Lenard, "From Progressivism to Procrastination: The Fight for the Creation of a Permanent Housing Authority, 1933–1945" (master's thesis, University of Wisconsin–Milwaukee, 1967), pp. 102–33; Housing Authority of the City of Milwaukee, "Public Housing in Milwaukee" (Milwaukee, 1958); "Housing Board Created Here: Eighteen Civic, Church Groups Are Represented at Conference," Box 20, UCS Papers.
32. Carlos Del Ruy to Hoan, 26 Apr. 1936; Hoan to Del Ruy, 29 Apr. 1936, Box 26, File 98, Hoan Papers; interview with Ernest Bland, 8 Aug. 1979; Milwaukee County Board of Election Commissioners, *Biennial Report, 1940* (Milwaukee Legislative Reference Bureau).
33. Interview with Bernice Lindsay, 9 Aug. 1979; Milwaukee County Board of Election Commissioners, *Biennial Report, 1940* (Milwaukee Legislative Reference Bureau).
34. "Approves WPA Playground and Pool Proposal," Box G-219, NAACP Papers.
35. Community Fund, "Report of the Committee on Leisure Time in the

Sixth Ward," NUL Papers; "Statement of Purpose of Group Work Agencies in the Sixth Ward: Urban League, YMCA, YWCA, and Municipal Recreation Department," Box 3, UCS Papers; T. P. Pearman, general secretary, YMCA, to Fred D. Goldstone, vice-president, Community Fund and Council of Social Agencies, 17 July 1945; Milwaukee Urban League to Community Fund, 23 July 1945; interviews with Clarence L. Johnson, 15 Aug. 1979, and Bernice Lindsay, 9 Aug. 1979.

36. See Chapter 3; "This is Your Life: Rev. C. A. Fisher," Folders 1–3, Fisher Papers; interview with Helen V. Kelley, 7 Aug. 1979; "A Tribute to James Weston Dorsey," Box 1, Dorsey Papers; L. T. Gilmer to Pickens, 20 Feb. 1933, Box G-219, NAACP Papers.

37. Gilmer to White, 9 Feb. 1933; "Report of the Election of Officers," 23 Feb. 1934, Box G-219, NAACP Papers; Gilmer to NAACP, national office, 20 Feb. 1933; Pickens to Fisher, 15 Feb. 1934; White to Fisher, 20 Feb. 1934, Box G-219, NAACP Papers.

38. Ibid.; Pickens to White, 2 June 1933; Gilmer to Pickens, ca. Oct. 1933; memo, Pickens to Gilmer, 5 Feb. 1934; Gilmer to Pickens, 23 Feb. 1934, Box G-219, NAACP Papers.

39. Pickens to White, 2 June 1933; Fisher to Pickens, 13 Feb. 1934, Box G-219, NAACP Papers.

40. James W. Dorsey to White, 27 Feb. 1934; memo, Gilmer to Pickens, 21 Feb. 1934; Fisher to White, 26 Feb. 1934; Fisher to Pickens, 13 Feb. 1934, Box G-219, NAACP Papers.

41. William Pickens, "Summary of Milwaukee Visit," 3 Mar. 1934, Box G-219, NAACP Papers; G. D. Daniel to Pickens, 16 Apr. 1944; minutes, Milwaukee NAACP, 12 Apr. 1934; E. Frederic Morrow, coordinator of branches, to James W. Dorsey, 3 May 1938, Box G-219, NAACP Papers.

42. MUL Monthly Report, Oct. 1937; MUL Annual Report, 1942–43; "Short Memories," *MUL Observer,* Apr. 1945, Ser. 13, Box 17, MUL Papers.

43. Interview with Ruby Cook, 13 Aug. 1979; Bicentennial Project Committee, "Black Heritage–Wisconsin, 1776–1976: Religious Institutions," (Milwaukee, 1976), pp. 25–27; Shadd, *Negro Business Directory,* pp. 11–26; "St. Mark Burns Mortgage," Folders 1–3, Fisher Papers; "Church of the Anvil: St. Mark AME" (Milwaukee, 1969): "Church Pastor, votes to Sue No More," 10 Apr. 1945, newspaper clipping, Irene Goggins, personal files; Imse, "The Negro Community in Milwaukee," pp. 25–26; "Calvary Saga," *Echo* 21, no. 27 (1976): 13; "Dedicatory Program: Calvary Baptist Church History" (Milwaukee, n.d.): "Tabernacle Community Baptist Church: History" (Milwaukee, 1971); Rev. Ensworth Reisner, "Store Front Churches," *Echo* 9 (1967): 25; "A Brief History of St. Matthew Christian Methodist Episcopal Church" (Milwau-

kee: Personal Collection of Louise Bracey, Feb.–Mar. 1958); Joe Savage, "Good News, Chariots Coming: The Black Church in Milwaukee" (Milwaukee: Transcript WMVS Television Channel 10, ca. 1979).

# 7

## Proletarianization of Afro-Americans in Milwaukee, 1915–45: A Comparative Perspective

This chapter explores the larger meaning of the Afro-American experience in Milwaukee as an instance of proletariat formation. Briefly contrasting the experience of Milwaukee blacks with that of northern whites and Afro-Americans in northern and southern cities, the chapter suggests similarities and differences in the proletarianization process among blacks and between whites and blacks. The Afro-American urban experience may be divided into three distinct but interrelated chronological periods: the pre–World War I era (1870–1914), World War I and its aftermath (1915–32), and the Depression and World War II (1933–45). While each of these phases is important to an understanding of working-class dynamics, the analysis focuses on the interwar years, especially the period 1915–32, when the black industrial working class fully emerged; it was then that the formation of the black proletariat acquired its most characteristic expression.[1]

Available evidence suggests that the general dynamics of proletarianization in Milwaukee prevailed among other northern blacks. Curtailment of European immigration, the labor demands of World War I, and destructive conditions in southern agriculture promoted the transformation of northern blacks into an urban-industrial working class. As in Milwaukee, the movement of black agriculturists and urban domestic and personal service workers into northern factories was not a smooth process. Rooted in competitive socioeconomic conflict between blacks and whites, several factors impeded the transformation of blacks into industrial workers and relegated them to the lowest-paying, dirty, and difficult jobs: racist attitudes and hiring policies of industrialists, racial restrictions on black membership in labor unions, and the vagaries of the business cycle. Like Milwaukee blacks, however, Afro-Americans in other northern areas were not overwhelmed by these forces. Through the development of separate, all-black labor unions and through high turnover rates in certain low-paying and arduous jobs, black workers developed strategies that eased the impact of racial discrimination in the labor market. The dynamics of proletarianization also intensified the pattern of ghetto formation and the direction of several other facets of black urban life: emergence of a new black business and professional middle class, catering primarily to black customers; increasingly abrasive race relations; and accelerating social class stratification within the black community, reflected in its housing, institutional life, and politics.[2]

Though less sharply than in Milwaukee, the Depression and World War II dramatically highlighted the precarious nature of black working-class formation throughout the urban North. Afro-American unemployment rapidly exceeded that of whites and remained at disproportionately high levels for the entire era. Blacks remained confined primarily to public emergency work even as defense production accelerated by the late 1930s. Afro-Americans did not fully regain their industrial foothold in other northern cities, as in Milwaukee, until the depletion of white supplies of labor by 1942–43.

Despite the tenuous position of blacks in the industrial economy, a more consolidated Afro-American proletariat emerged in northern cities by the end of World War II. Afro-Americans employed in industry expanded their numbers, degree of seniority, and skills. On the other hand, the black working class itself gained greater internal differentiation. Established workers, some having achieved greater seniority as a result of positions held through the Depression years, increasingly refused to accept certain low-paying, dirty, and arduous jobs in the private sector that newcomers from the South had little choice but to fill. Other old workers used their access to relief and public emergency work to compete successfully with newcomers for better private sector occupations made available to blacks.

As in Milwaukee, a number of interrelated factors promoted the reentrance of blacks into industries of other northern cities during World War II: the organizing efforts of the Congress of Industrial Organizations, labor shortages arising from heightened war production and the military draft, numerous federal manpower agencies (mainly the Fair Employment Practices Committee), and the potent socioeconomic and political movement of blacks themselves for equal access to defense industry jobs. Conversely, the persistence of labor union discrimination among rank and file whites in the CIO, but especially in the American Federation of Labor, the racist employment policies of industrialists, and the sustained crisis in the urban economy blocked the equitable reemployment of Afro-Americans. As before the 1930s, such factors conditioned both inter- and intraracial relations. The protracted Depression, the Afro-American fight for equal access to New Deal relief programs, and the organizing thrust of the CIO created greater racial and class solidarity by 1945, although these developments were as yet still weakly expressed.

While available evidence indicates similarities in the proletarianization of northern blacks, the emergence of Milwaukee's black industrial working class had several unique features: small population size, a low level of ghetto formation, development within a strong Socialist context, and an exceptionally high percentage of workers in factory jobs. These characteristics in turn promoted other socioeconomic divergences in class structure, institutional life, race relations, and politics between Milwaukee blacks and their counterparts in larger northern cities. Increasing from 0.2 percent of the city's total population in 1910 to 1.6 percent in 1945, Milwaukee blacks exceeded only two other black populations in the twenty-five largest United States cities. Although exhibiting consistent signs of ghetto formation, as late as 1940 Milwaukee Afro-Americans comprised only a little more than half of the total population within their area of greatest concentration.

Unlike blacks in most northern cities, Afro-Americans in Milwaukee moved into industrial jobs in a city of strong Socialist influence. Between 1916 and 1940, blacks, like the majority of working-class whites, consistently supported Socialist Mayor Daniel W. Hoan. Mayor Hoan invariably backed labor unions in their efforts to prevent employers from importing black strikebreakers to take the jobs of striking whites. Local black opinion also reflected the strength of Socialists in city affairs. A cross section of black middle- and working-class organizations, for example, opposed the use of black strikebreakers in the 1922 Milwaukee Railroad strike. Even the nationalist Garvey Movement in Milwaukee, deviating from the central thrust of the UNIA elsewhere, supported this and other developments that highlighted the convergence of racial and class consciousness in the city. The complex interplay of these forces — the Socialist context, small size, and lower percentage of blacks in the total industrial labor force — prevented a major race riot or even smaller-scale physical confrontations in Milwaukee. Developing in the shadow of nearby Chicago and Detroit, Milwaukee never became a major target of migration from southern states; thus, the competition for industrial jobs and housing was less intense than elsewhere, and so was the racial violence that spread into other areas of race relations.[3]

Black industrial proletarianization had proceeded further in larger northern cities like Chicago, New York, and others than in Milwaukee during the pre–World War I era. The increasing proletarianization of blacks in such cities after 1915 largely intensified processes that were already well underway. Racial conflicts in the labor market, for example, had frequently erupted into violence and spread into the larger social structure. Largely as a result of its small size at the outset of the great migration, Milwaukee's Afro-American population (along with that of Detroit and a few other cities) had a greater proportion of its numbers in factory work by the mid-1920s than did blacks in most northern cities. Unfortunately, disproportionately higher unemployment among Milwaukee and Detroit blacks compared to other northern cities mirrored their heavier dependence on industrial employment and their vulnerability to falling demand for manufactured products ushered in by the Depression. In cities where blacks were more concentrated in domestic and personal service, in addition to transportation and trade occupations, they experienced the effects of high unemployment later and less intensely than blacks in manufacturing-intensive cities.

Larger northern cities had proportionately fewer blacks in industrial jobs than did Milwaukee during World War I and its aftermath. Even so, internal class divisions were more pronounced in larger urban centers. The tremendously broader demographic base of such cities provided more working-class blacks — factory, transportation and trade, domestic and personal service, and common laborers — upon which the Afro-American business and professional class could expand. The new black middle class emerged before World War I in these cities, whereas it did not fully emerge in Milwaukee until World War I and after. The experience of Milwaukee blacks would diverge even further from that of southern blacks.

Although Howard N. Rabinowitz's recent work on black life in five southern cities between 1865 and 1890 makes a significant contribution in closing the gap, little detailed research on black life in postbellum southern cities has been carried out. Still less has been done on the period 1890–1945, and the question of proletarianization in these cities as elsewhere is seldom raised. Nevertheless, sparse evidence suggests that proletarianization was an experience that blacks in Milwaukee and other northern cities shared with blacks in cities of the American South. Industrialization in both settings, in varying degrees of intensity, promoted the migration of blacks to industrial and away from agricultural areas; here they confronted the dynamic interplay of the economic and racial imperatives of both white industrialists and labor unions. The merging of these forces with fluctuations in the urban economy created a precarious position for black workers in the different contexts. Whites, employers and workers, sought to either bar blacks from the industrial workplace or to relegate them to the bottom.[4]

Divergent social, economic, and political contexts in the North and South, however, imply highly significant contrasts in otherwise similar experiences. Blacks in southern cities faced a lower level of industrialization and, after 1900, a set system of de jure segregation in the social, economic, and political life of the city. The demographic base of black populations in southern cities was also much larger than that of their northern counterparts. As late as 1930, blacks comprised 38 percent or more of Atlanta, Richmond, and Birmingham's populations, proportions with no pre–World War II parallels in the North. Moreover, black women in southern cities were more highly represented in the labor force than were northern black women, but, like their northern sisters, they worked mainly in domestic and personal service occupations. More than in Milwaukee and other northern cities, then, a combination of black male industrial workers, albeit in highly restricted occupations, and black female domestics provided the economic base of black life in the urban South. Although blacks in southern cities occupied a greater variety of industrial jobs than did northern blacks before World War I, southern blacks lost ground and gradually fell behind northern blacks during and following the war.[5]

Although tentative, data on the proletarian experience of southern blacks nonetheless suggest a great deal of variety within the region, between industries, and even within the same industry. Unlike blacks in the North, southern blacks traditionally functioned within a broad range of urban crafts, as masons, carpenters, blacksmiths, and others, which had developed during the slavery era. By the turn of the twentieth century, however, white workers had largely displaced blacks from their historic position in these skilled trades. This occupational pattern resembled the classical downward thrust of workers into unskilled jobs from positions of greater autonomy as skilled workers, and this pattern — a secondary theme in black proletarianization — was far more prevalent in the South than in the North. Whites monopolized jobs in textile manufacturing, the major growth industry in southern cities, which itself arose, in part, as a social welfare movement to create jobs for poor whites, especially those from agricultural areas and the mountains. Gradually expanding white labor unions and even the employment of white women strengthened the exclusion of blacks from southern textile mills. The bargaining power of white workers also intersected with the profit imperatives and anti-black attitudes of industrialists in creating a racially differentiated wage scale. By contrast, an economic differential between blacks and whites in Milwaukee and other northern cities became institutionalized through the types of jobs blacks entered, their weak seniority position, and their extreme vulnerability to up- and downturns in the economy. Despite southern white workers' failures to gain overt state power in the protection of their jobs against black competition, de jure segregation in other facets of southern life (e.g., the school system, social welfare agencies, and various public accommodations among others) undoubtedly bolstered racial discrimination against blacks in the urban labor market.[6]

The pattern of black exclusion from southern textile industries was by no means universal. Southern blacks did gain employment in certain designated industries such as tobacco, saw and planing mills, coal mining, and railroads. With the exception of railroad employment (and even here there were significant North-South differences), few northern blacks worked in these industries, partly because these were essentially southern-based enterprises. The percentage of blacks in the tobacco industry increased from 64.5 to 67.9 percent of the labor force between 1910 and 1930, and the cities of Winston-Salem, Durham, Louisville, and Richmond emerged as the major centers of tobacco production. The experience of blacks in tobacco firms shows how black employment varied within the same industry. Blacks were denied jobs in cigarette factories, where the introduction of machinery had begun to revolutionize the industry and create cleaner and less arduous work from the 1880s onward. Most blacks worked in the

processing aspects of the work, that is, in difficult, low-paying, unskilled, and semiskilled manual jobs. Moreover, when blacks operated machines, they did so in processing departments where dust
particles, stifling fumes, and a humid atmosphere made work extremely disagreeable.[7]

Blacks also figured prominently in the lumber and mining industries of the South. Although employment in southern sawmills
dropped from 466,624 in 1910 to 454,503 in 1930, the percentage of
blacks in the labor force increased from 23.8 to 25.1 percent during the
same period. Since both blacks and whites left the South in greater
numbers, sawmill operators turned increasingly to blacks. Likewise,
while the percentage of blacks in coal mining declined from 26.4 to
22.5 percent between 1910 and 1930, blacks continued to play a vital
role in the coal industry. The number of black coal miners in the bituminous coal industry of the southern Appalachian states increased
from 29,642 in 1910 to 44,266 in 1930. More significantly, however,
the percentage of black miners in the expanding coal fields of West
Virginia actually increased from 20.5 to 22.7 percent of the labor force
during the same period.[8]

The experience of blacks in the mining and lumber industries suggests critical variations in the proletarianization of blacks. Neither
lumber nor mining — extractive industries — were entirely rural. The
modes of production and settlement in both represented a distinct
shift from the farm, yet it is difficult to classify this work as urban-
industrial. These industries, it seems, operated at the interface between the black agricultural experience on the one hand and the black
transition to an urban-industrial foundation on the other. It is likely
that the economic as well as the cultural, political, and institutional
dynamics of proletarianization in these settings were quite different
from developments in most cities. Indeed, fragmentary evidence suggests that lumber and mining experiences often preceded the
migrants' arrival in the industrial city or mill town.[9] Here indeed lies a
fertile field for comparative research on black workers.

Black railroad workers also played a crucial role in the southern
economy. Unlike their northern counterparts, blacks were widely
represented in southern railroading, as brakemen, firemen, switchmen, and flagmen, but the majority of blacks on southern railroads
worked as maintenance-of-way track laborers. Between 1910 and
1930, blacks made up 73 percent of maintenance-of-way laborers on
southern roads. Unfortunately, Afro-Americans in more desirable

skilled positions — as brakemen, switchmen, firemen, and others — faced declining opportunities; the exclusively white railroad brotherhoods negotiated discriminatory contracts that dramatically reduced the number of skilled blacks. Before World War I, it was common for southern roads to employ black firemen on 50 to 60 percent of their runs; following the war, the number of black firemen dropped dramatically. An extreme case involved the Southern Railway Company. Afro-Americans made up 80 percent of the company's firemen during World War I, but only 10 percent by 1929. Like blacks in other skilled positions, the experience of black railway firemen, brakemen, and switchmen reflected a downward spiral in the proletarianization of black workers. By contrast, their northern counterparts entered the railroad industry almost exclusively as laborers and as pullman porters.[10]

Southern cities had varied residential patterns, yet, because of the historic proximity of black residences to those of white urban masters and employers during the slavery era, black and white homes in the South were generally more interspersed than those of Milwaukee and other northern cities. Some blacks lived on the periphery in small and geographically separate but heavily black clusters. Transportation innovations of the late nineteenth century, though to a far lesser degree than in northern cities, also enhanced the rearrangement of the spatial structure of some southern cities and encouraged the gradual emergence of central-city black ghettos. Although southern attempts near the turn of the century to legislate separate residential areas for blacks and whites were by 1917 pronounced unconstitutional by the United States Supreme Court, legislative segregation in a variety of other areas of southern life encouraged the residential separation of blacks and whites. With the exception of Indianapolis during the 1920s, whites in Milwaukee and other northern cities did not vigorously attempt the de jure segregation of black and white residences. The development of ghettos in Milwaukee and throughout the urban North was nevertheless intensified through economic competition attendant on increasing black proletarianization and such subtle and not so subtle racist processes as "gentlemen's agreements," restrictive convenants, and zoning ordinances.[11]

Evidence of the relationship between proletarianization and ghettoization in southern cities is contradictory, but ghettoization appears to have developed its most intense form in new South industrial cities like Durham and Birmingham. Blacks concentrated heavily in the tobacco and coal and iron industries, respectively, of these two cities. Conversely, the older pattern of dispersed residences apparently persisted for a longer period in Charleston, New Orleans, and perhaps in a few other old South commercial and capital cities. The pattern, however, was certainly not a simple one. An old South city like Richmond had developed an industrial base before the Civil War. Moreover, antebellum Richmond had employed slaves and free blacks in its iron, coal, and tobacco industries. Although the spatial segregation of blacks and whites intensified during the late nineteenth and early twentieth centuries, a high degree of residential intermixture evidently characterized Richmond's housing pattern well into the postbellum period. On the other hand, Atlanta developed primarily as a new South commercial and banking center rather than as an industrial center. Few blacks lived in Atlanta during the Civil War, but when Atlanta was rebuilt in the postwar era, black migration accelerated and ghetto formation proceeded apace. "Black settlement began in the center of the city," John Dittmer concludes in his fine study of black Georgia, "where there was less resistance. When [black] immigrants tried to expand first to the east and later to the west, their efforts met strong white opposition." Nevertheless, despite variation, perhaps even more than in northern cities ghetto formation was closely intertwined with the process of proletarianization. Here the southern context promises abundant opportunities for examining the complex relationship between ghetto and proletariat development.[12]

On the eve of World War I, a new black middle class of clergymen, teachers, doctors, lawyers, pharmacists, and small businessmen had developed on the base of industrial and domestic service occupations in the South. Following the war, unlike the northern new middle class which grew mainly because of expanding factory employment, supplemental domestic and personal service incomes, and increasing ghettoization, the new black bourgeoisie in the South depended more heavily upon domestic service wages. While receiving encouragement from the internal cultural, social, and economic dynamics of the black community, the new southern middle class was also greatly stimulated by legislation requiring racial segregation in a variety of public, educational, and private institutions and relationships. Clergymen and school teachers dominated the professional component of the new southern black middle class, while musicians and teachers of music predominated in Milwaukee and usually exceeded schoolteachers in other northern cities as well. Some professions found less favor in the

South than in the North, including lawyers, engineers, and even actors and actresses. A black lawyer, as historian Carter Woodson noted, could not appear in southern courts except in "a few large cities where the public" was "more liberal minded." Even then the black attorney's "life would be in danger if he tried to override public opinion" which proscribed black social, economic, and political life.[13]

The system of racial proscription helped to cement a stronger link between Afro-American workers and the black middle class in the South than in the less-hostile urban North. Racial solidarity between black workers and the bourgeoisie in southern cities was also enhanced by the broader demographic and economic base available for the expansion of black business and professional pursuits, which could employ increasing numbers of Afro-Americans. Black banking, insurance, and contracting firms, for example, were far more numerous in southern than in northern cities. In addition to creating jobs for blacks, the broader economic and demographic base of black professions and businesses provided potential for greater exploitation of blacks by blacks, namely the unequal use of resources generated by black workers chiefly for the advancement of middle-class interests. Black workers with few opportunities in the larger economy were forced to take even lower-paying, if not always equally dirty and difficult, jobs in the black economy. By 1890, Howard Rabinowitz has noted, the social, economic, and political experiences of the middle class were "far removed from those lowest in economic and social standing." But the role of these workers, often organized in separate workers' organizations, in southern black urban life is yet to be uncovered for the period from 1890.[14]

Tentative evidence suggests that the dynamics of racial discrimination in the economic, social, and political life of the South would foster a stronger and more persistent acceptance of Booker T. Washington's emphasis on self-help and racial solidarity by both workers and the middle class in the South than in the North. By the early 1920s, blacks in the South, like their northern counterparts, extended their separate institutional life (churches, secret societies, benevolent associations) and "pushed for greater participation in politics." Blacks in the South, faced with legal restrictions on their voting rights, pushed especially hard for paved, clean, and well-lighted streets; better water and sewer facilities; and equal protection under the law, especially protection from wanton racial violence.[15] While Milwaukee and other northern blacks sought similar things for their neighborhoods, their political objectives took focus in the struggle for patronage jobs through the election of black aldermen and other public officials.

Urban industrial working class formation was an experience which Milwaukee blacks shared not only with other blacks in diverse settings but one which had parallels among whites. Although much research remains to be done on the proletarian experience of both blacks and whites, some tentative conclusions are possible. The lives of both working-class blacks and whites were integrally linked to the dynamics of industrial capitalism, which promoted economic insecurity among all workers as mass production techniques and changes in the levels of supply and demand for manufactured goods forced many workers into alternating bouts of employment and unemployment. As Herbert Gutman has clearly noted, industrialists' characterization of blacks as unsteady workers had parallels among first-generation white industrial workers, both immigrants and American-born. Moreover, the opposite side of such behavior, irregular work habits as a form of resistance to the most exploitative aspects of the proletarian experience, developed among both blacks and whites.[16]

Nevertheless, if differences in socioeconomic contexts precipitated contrasting proletarian experiences among blacks, striking contrasts in the specific situations of black and white workers surely set their proletarian experiences even further apart. From the outset we must recognize that the white proletariat emerged earlier (by the turn of the twentieth century) than did the black proletariat and was not uniform in either its composition or industrial experience. A fundamental division within the proletariat in northern cities was that between the American- and foreign-born. This division, reflecting numerous divisions along ethnic lines, was closely linked to a second cleavage within their ranks: dividing skilled craftsmen on the one hand from unskilled and semiskilled operatives in mass production industries on the other. Although some newcomers (especially old immigrants from northern and western Europe) entered skilled positions, first-generation immigrants were disproportionately relegated to the lowest-paying, dirty, difficult, and unskilled jobs compared to their white, American-born counterparts.[17]

Such internal divisions notwithstanding, the urban-industrial experience of blacks in Milwaukee and other northern cities sharply contrasted with that of whites. While it is indeed true that blacks shared the cellar of the industrial economy with large numbers of whites (particularly unorganized and unskilled immigrant workers), white workers had significantly more of their numbers employed as skilled craftsmen. White skilled workers worried about the progressive erosion of old crafts with the increasing shift to simpler mass-production machinery and techniques. The loss of autonomy associated with traditional modes of manufacturing particularly chagrined these workers. New scientific methods of corporate management, as noted by David Montgomery, "fundamentally disrupted the craftsmen's styles of work, their union rules and standard rates, and their mutualistic ethic, as it transformed American industrial practice between 1900 and 1930."[18] Moreover, white workers from agricultural backgrounds often had lost prior access to family farms, either in Europe or in rural America.[19] Thus, for many white workers the proletarian experience represented a decided decline in status, autonomy, and probably income as well. By comparison, this pattern of proletarianization was only a minor theme among blacks.

While traditional treatments of white workers emphasize the forceful thrust of white labor unions for "better working conditions" and "higher wages," recent interpretations, like that of Montgomery's, argue that the white working class was moved by more than simply the imperatives of "collective bargaining" and "wage consciousness." White machinists (and increasingly less-skilled miners, railroad workers, and others) developed and to a large degree successfully practiced a theory of "workers' control," which sought proletarian autonomy over larger and more-detailed operations of the workplace during the late nineteenth and early twentieth centuries.[20] Through their unions and through informal collective interactions in the workplace, white workers certainly exerted influence over their working experience in ways that Afro-Americans could not, partly because of the anti-black attitudes and practices of both white workers and industrialists. Indeed, recent emphasis on white "workers' control" implies a greater role for white labor in black subordination within and exclusion from the industrial labor force than radical analyses, which emphasize employer manipulation of racial and ethnic divisions in the workplace, have heretofore admitted. Moreover, through urban machine politics, white workers exercised greater political influence in municipal affairs than did blacks, especially in a city like Milwaukee with its strong Socialist influence. The differential proletarian experience of blacks and whites also suggests additional contrasts between them. For example, although working-class whites would concentrate in clearly defined working-class and ethnic ghettos, more than their Afro-American counterparts, the greater economic security and political power of white workers undoubtedly enabled them to mitigate the process of ghettoization.[21] But again these are only tentative conclusions. Here is yet another area that promises rich prospects for scholars to investigate the comparative proletarian experience of American workers.

In conclusion, this study has sought to document the experience of Milwaukee blacks as a special case of proletarianization. Comparative analysis suggests both parallels and divergences between the proletarian experience of Milwaukee blacks and their counterparts in northern and southern cities. Similarities and contrasts between black workers involved the complex interplay of numerous factors: population size, level of ghettoization, nature of race relations, and especially racial competition in the urban-industrial economy. While Milwaukee's Afro-American proletariat shared several experiences with the white working class, contrasting economic and political potential, coupled with racial discrimination against blacks, accented differences as sharply as similarities between the two. Indeed, the persistence of racial discrimination within the socioeconomic life of the metropolis helped to sustain a bond, though fragile, between black workers and the Afro-American middle class. Yet, although modified by the vicissitudes of industrial capitalism and racism, the emergence of Milwaukee's black industrial proletariat thrust class, along with race and ghetto formation, to the center of the Afro-American urban experience.

## NOTES

1. Since nonblack minorities, Chinese, Japanese, Native Americans, and others, remained largely outside the urban-industrial workplace during most of the period covered by this study, they are not incorporated into the analysis. The general concept of proletarianization, though, has relevance to the experience of various nonblack minorities, especially Chicanos. See Albert Camarillo, *Chicanos in a Changing Society: From Mexican Pueblos to American Barrios in Santa Barbara and Southern California, 1848–1930* (Cambridge: Cambridge University Press, 1979); John Modell, *The Economics and Politics of Racial Accommodation: The Japanese of Los Angeles, 1900–1942* (Urbana: University of Illinois Press, 1977); Harry H. L. Kitano, *Race Relations* (Englewood Cliffs, N.J.: Prentice-Hall, 1974).

2. The comparative statements through n. 3 are drawn from relevant parts of preceding chapters.

3. Allan H. Spear, *Black Chicago: The Making of a Negro Ghetto, 1890–1920* (Chicago: University of Chicago Press, 1967), p. 206; Kenneth L. Kusmer, *A Ghetto Takes Shape: Black Cleveland, 1870–1930* (Urbana: University of Illinois Press, 1976), p. 185.

4. Harold Woodman, "Sequel to Slavery: The New History Views the Post-Bellum South," *Journal of Southern History* 43 (1977): 523–54 (Woodman stands out as an exception in suggesting that the period 1870 to 1900 in southern history be viewed "as a time marked by the making of a working class from former slaves [and formerly self-sufficient whites] and the making of a bourgeois employer class from former slaveowners"); Howard N. Rabinowitz, *Race Relations in the Urban South, 1865–1890* (New York: Oxford University Press, 1978); pp. 1–30, 61–96.

5. U. S. Bureau of the Census, *Negroes in the United States, 1920–1932* (1935; rept. New York: Arno Press, 1969); Herbert R. Northrup and Richard Rowan, eds. *Negro Employment in Southern Industry: A Study of Racial Policies in Five Industries,* vol. 4 (Philadelphia: Wharton School of Finance, University of Pennsylvania, 1970); Herbert Northrup, et al., eds. *Negro Employment in Land and Air Transport: A Study of Racial Policies in the Railroad, Trucking, and Urban Transit Industries,* vol. 5 (Philadelphia: Wharton School of Finance, University of Pennsylvania, 1971); Rabinowitz, *Race Relations in the Urban South,* pp. 61–96; Gunnar Myrdal, *An American Dilemma,* vol. 1 (1944; rept. New York: Pantheon Books, 1972), pp. 279–303; Lorenzo J. Greene and Carter G. Woodson, *The Negro Wage Earner* (Washington: Association for the Study of Negro Life and History, 1930), pp. 75–99, 224–46.

6. Rabinowitz, *Race Relations in the Urban South,* pp. 61–96; John Dittmer, *Black Georgia in the Progressive Era* (Urbana: University of Illinois Press, 1977), pp. 23–49; Sterling D. Spero and Abram L. Harris, *The Black Worker: The Negro and the Labor Movement* (1931; rept. New York: Atheneum, 1968), pp. 16–86; Philip S. Foner, *Organized Labor and the Black Worker, 1619–1973* (New York: International Publishers, 1974), pp. 120–34; William H. Harris, *The Harder We Run: Black Workers Since the Civil War* (New York: Oxford University Press, 1982), pp. 29–50; Richard L. Rowan, "The Negro in the Textile Industry," in Northrup and Rowan, eds., *Negro Employment in Southern Industry,* vol. 4, pt. 5, pp. 34–68; Greene and Woodson, *The Negro Wage Earner,* chapters 9, 10, and 16, and pp. 145–52, 295–307.

7. Northrup and Rowan, eds., *Negro Employment in Southern Industry,* vol. 4, pts. 2, 3, and 4; Northrup, et al. eds., *Negro Employment in Land and Air Transport,* vol. 5, pt. 1; Herbert R. Northrup, "The Negro in the Tobacco Industry," in Northrup and Rowan, eds., *Negro Employment in Southern*

*Industry,* pp. 18–39; Greene and Woodson, *The Negro Wage Earner,* pp. 152–54, 283–88.

8. John C. Howard, "The Negro in the Lumber Industry," in Northrup and Rowan, eds., *Negro Employment in Southern Industry,* vol. 4, pt. 2, pp. 25–39; Jerrell H. Shofner, "Forced Labor in the Florida Forests, 1880–1950," *Journal of Forest History* 25, no. 1 (Jan. 1981): 14–25; Darold T. Barnum, "The Negro in the Bituminous Coal Mining Industry," in Northrup and Rowan, eds., *Negro Employment in Southern Industry,* vol. 4, pt. 4, pp. 16–38; Spero and Harris, *The Black Worker,* pp. 206–45. Also see essays by Stephen Brier, Daniel P. Jordan, and David A. Corbin in George M. Fink and Merle E. Reed, eds., *Essays in Southern Labor History* (Westport, Conn.: Greenwood Press, 1977); Greene and Woodson, *The Negro Wage Earner,* pp. 124–33, 259–64; David A. Corbin, *Life, Work, and Rebellion in the Coal Fields* (Urbana: University of Illinois Press, 1981), especially Chapter 3.

9. Florette Henri, *Black Migration* (Garden City, N.Y.: Anchor Press/Doubleday, 1975), p. 21; Clyde V. Kiser, *Sea Island to City: A Study of St. Helena Islanders to Harlem and other Urban Centers* (1932; rept. New York: Atheneum, 1969); John Bodnar, et. al., *Lives of Their Own: Blacks, Italians, and Poles in Pittsburgh, 1900–1960* (Urbana: University of Illinois Press, 1982), pp. 29–54.

10. Howard W. Risher, Jr., "The Negro in the Railroad Industry," in Northrup et al., eds., *Negro Employment in Land and Air Transport,* pp. 35–58; Foner, *Organized Labor and the Black Worker,* pp. 103–7; Greene and Woodson, *The Negro Wage Earner,* pp. 100–110, 224–46, 265–71; Spero and Harris, *The Black Worker,* pp. 284–315. Spero and Harris noted two kinds of porters: trainmen and pullman. The latter exclusively served the passengers (carrying baggage, cleaning cars, and so on), while the former often performed brakemen's work under the conductor's instructions. These so-called porter-brakemen received porter's pay. Blacks dominated these positions until the pay for porter-brakemen was upgraded to the level of trainmen. White workers then pushed blacks out of the porter-brakemen jobs and relegated them nearly entirely to the pullman sector.

11. John H. Bracey, et al., eds., *The Rise of the Ghetto* (Belmont, California: Wadsworth Publishing Company, 1971), pp. 1–7; Robert C. Weaver, *The Negro Ghetto* (New York: Russell and Russell, 1948); Karl E. and Alma F. Taeuber, *Negroes in Cities: Residential Segregation and Neighborhood Change* (Chicago: Aldine, 1965), pp. 43–68; Roger L. Rice, "Residential Segregation by Law, 1910–1917," *Journal of Southern History* 34 (May 1968): 179–99.

12. Zane L. Miller, "Urban Blacks in the South, 1865–1920: An Analysis of Some Quantitative Data on Richmond, Savannah, New Orleans,

Louisville, and Birmingham," in Leo F. Schnore, ed., *The New Urban History: Quantitative Explorations by American Historians* (Princeton, N.J.: Princeton University Press, 1976), pp. 184–204; also see Blaine A. Brownell, "Birmingham, Alabama: New South City in the 1920's," *Journal of Southern History* 38 (1972): 21–48; T. J. Woofter, Jr., *Negro Problems in Cities* (1928; rept. New York: Harper and Row, 1969), pp. 37–77; Dittmer, *Black Georgia*, pp. 12–16; Ronald Lewis, *Iron, Coal, and Slaves: Industrial Slavery in Maryland and Virginia, 1715–1865* (Westport, Conn.: Greenwood Press, 1979); Charles B. Dew, *Ironworker to the Confederacy: John R. Anderson and the Tredegar Iron Works* (New Haven: Yale University Press, 1966); Charles S. Johnson, *Patterns of Negro Segregation* (New York: Harper and Brothers, 1943) pp. 3–12; also see Richard C. Wade, *Slavery in the Cities: The South 1820–1860* (London: Oxford University Press, 1964), Chapter 3.

13. Miller, "Urban Blacks in the South," pp. 193–99; Carter G. Woodson, *The Negro Professional Man and the Community* (1934; rept. New York: Johnson Reprint Corporation, 1970), pp. 34–35.

14. Rabinowitz, *Race Relations in the Urban South,* pp. 73–74; Walter B. Weare, *Black Business in the New South: A Social History of the North Carolina Mutual Insurance Company* (Urbana: University of Illinois Press, 1973), pp. 179–210.

15. Miller, "Urban Blacks in the South," p. 198; Paul Lewinson, *Race, Class and Party: A History of Negro Suffrage and White Politics in the South* (1932; rept. New York: Russell and Russell, 1963), especially chapters 6 and 7.

16. Herbert G. Gutman, *Work, Culture, and Society in Industrializing America* (1966; rept. New York: Vintage Books, 1976), pp. 3–78.

17. Ibid.; David Montgomery, *Workers' Control in America: Studies in the History of Work, Technology, and Labor Struggles* (Cambridge: Cambridge University Press, 1979).

18. Montgomery, *Workers' Control in America,* p. 26.

19. Bodnar, et al., *Lives of Their Own,* pp. 29–31, 153–54.

20. Montgomery, *Workers' Control in America,* p. 4.

21. Thomas Philpott, *The Slum and the Ghetto* (New York: Oxford University Press, 1978), especially chapters 1–8; Bodnar, et al., *Lives of Their Own,* chapters 3 and 8. Also see the collection of essays in Milton Cantor, ed., *American Working Class Culture: Explorations in American Labor and Social History* (Westport, Conn.: Greenwood Press, 1979), especially Alan Dawley and Paul Faler, "Working-Class Culture and Politics in the Industrial Revolution: Sources of Loyalism and Rebellion" and John T. Cumbler, "Labor, Capital, and Community: The Struggle for Power."

# Appendixes

# Appendix 1

## *Occupations of Milwaukee Blacks, 1880*

| | | | |
|---|---|---|---|
| Waiters | 32 | Bath Workers | 2 |
| Servants | 19 | Bartenders | 2 |
| Porters | 15 | Butchers | 2 |
| Laborers | 13 | Saloonkeeper | 1 |
| Laundry Workers or Operators | 13 | Nurse | 1 |
| Seamstresses or Dressmakers | 11 | Sailor | 1 |
| Cooks | 7 | Teamster | 1 |
| Barbers | 7 | Shampooer | 1 |
| Janitors | 3 | Telegraph Operator | 1 |
| Hostlers | 3 | Railroad Conductor | 1 |
| Bellboys | 3 | Minister | 1 |
| Whitewashers | 3 | Restaurant Operator | 1 |
| Messengers | 2 | Marble Polisher | 1 |
| Painters | 2 | Tailor | 1 |

Total: 151

Source: Thomas R. Buchanan, "Black Milwaukee, 1890–1915" (master's thesis, University of Wisconsin–Milwaukee, 1973), p. 142.

# Appendix 2

## *Black Occupations in Milwaukee, 1900*

| Male: Total Labor Force = 376 | Number | Percent |
|---|---|---|
| Professional | | |
|     Actors | 4 | |
|     Clergymen | 2 | |
|     Dentists | 2 | |
|     Journalists | 1 | |
|     Lawyers | 1 | |
|     Musicians and Teachers of Music | 21 | |
|     Officials (government) | 1 | |
|     Physicians and Surgeons | 1 | |
|     Teachers and Professors in College, etc. | 1 | |
|         Total | 35 | 9.3 |
| Proprietary | | |
|     Barbers | 8 | |

| Appendix 2 continued | | Number | Percent |
|---|---|---|---|
| Hotel Keepers | | — | |
| Restaurant and Saloonkeepers | | 8 | |
| Retail Dealers | | 3 | |
| | Total | 19 | 5.0 |
| Clerical | | | |
| Stenographers and Typewriters | | 1 | |
| Clerks and Copyists | | 5 | |
| | Total | 6 | 1.5 |
| Skilled | | | |
| Printers, Lithographers, and Pressmen | | 1 | |
| Blacksmiths | | 1 | |
| Carpenters and Joiners | | 1 | |
| Marble and Stone Cutters | | 2 | |
| Masons (brick and stone) | | 1 | |
| Plumbers and Gas and Steam Fitters | | 1 | |
| | Total | 7 | 1.8 |
| Semiskilled | | | |
| Soldiers, Sailors, and Marines (U.S.) | | 1 | |
| Watchmen, Policemen, Firemen, etc. | | 1 | |
| | Total | 2 | 0.5 |
| Unskilled | | | |
| Agricultural Laborers | | 1 | |
| Draymen, Hackmen, Teamsters, etc. | | 1 | |
| Hostlers | | 4 | |
| Livery Stable Keepers | | 1 | |
| Porters and Helpers (in stores, etc.) | | 22 | |
| Steam Railroad Employees | | 1 | |
| Iron and Steel Workers | | 1 | |
| Leather Curriers and Tanners | | 1 | |
| | Total | 32 | 8.5 |
| Domestic and Personal Service | | | |
| Bartenders | | 10 | |
| Janitors and Sextons | | 3 | |
| Laborers (not specified) | | 78 | |
| Servants and Waiters | | 164 | |
| | Total | 256 | 68.0 |

Female: Total Labor Force = 100

Professional
Musicians and Teachers of Music                     5

| Appendix 2 continued | | Number | Percent |
|---|---|---|---|
| Teachers and Professors in College, etc. | | 2 | |
| | Total | 7 | 7.0 |
| Proprietary | | | |
| Boarding and Lodging House Keepers | | 2 | |
| Barbers and Hairdressers | | 2 | |
| | Total | 4 | 4.0 |
| Clerical | | | |
| Stenographers and Typewriters | | 2 | |
| | Total | 2 | 2.0 |
| Skilled | | | |
| None | | 0 | |
| | Total | 0 | 0.0 |
| Semiskilled | | | |
| Dressmakers | | 7 | |
| Seamstresses | | 2 | |
| Housekeepers and Stewardesses | | 3 | |
| | Total | 12 | 12.0 |
| Domestic and Personal Service | | | |
| Laborers (not specified) | | 1 | |
| Laundresses | | 15 | |
| Nurses and Midwives | | 4 | |
| Servants and Waitresses | | 53 | |
| | Total | 73 | 73.0 |

Source: U.S. Census Office, *Twelfth Census, 1900: Special Reports, Occupations* (Washington: Government Printing Office, 1904), pp. 608-12.

# Appendix 3

*Selected Black Occupations in Milwaukee, 1910*

| Male: Total Labor Force = 438 | | Number | Percent |
|---|---|---|---|
| Professional | | | |
| Lawyers, Judges, and Justices | | 4 | |
| Musicians and Teachers of Music | | 14 | |
| Physicians and Surgeons | | 4 | |
| | Total | 22 | 5.0 |
| Proprietary | | | |
| Builders and Building Contractors | | 1 | |

| Appendix 3 continued | | Number | Percent |
|---|---|---|---|
| Managers and Superintendents | | | |
| (manufacturing) | | 2 | |
| Manufacturers and Officials | | 1 | |
| Saloonkeepers | | 4 | |
| Retail Dealers | | 5 | |
| Barbers, Hairdressers, and Manicurists | | 13 | |
| | Total | 26 | 5.9 |
| Clerical | | | |
| Commercial Travelers | | 3 | |
| Bookkeepers, Cashiers, and Accountants | | 3 | |
| Clerks (except clerks in stores) | | 2 | |
| Salesmen (stores) | | 2 | |
| | Total | 10 | 2.2 |
| Skilled | | | |
| Foremen and Overseers (manufacturing) | | 2 | |
| Blacksmiths | | 3 | |
| Brick and Stone Masons | | 4 | |
| Carpenters | | 2 | |
| Compositors, Linotypers, and Typesetters | | 4 | |
| Coopers | | 1 | |
| Electricians and Electrical Engineers | | 3 | |
| Engineers (stationary) | | 2 | |
| Machinists and Millwrights | | 4 | |
| Molders, Founders, and Casters (iron) | | 10 | |
| Painters, Glaziers, and Varnishers | | | |
| (building) | | 2 | |
| Locomotive Engineers | | 1 | |
| | Total | 35 | 8.0 |
| Semiskilled | | | |
| Painters, Glaziers, and Varnishers (factory) | | 2 | |
| Laborers (not otherwise specified) | | | |
| Breweries | | 1 | |
| Cigar and Tobacco Factories | | 9 | |
| Furniture, Piano, and Organ Factories | | 7 | |
| Tanneries | | 2 | |
| | Total | 22 | 5.0 |
| Unskilled | | | |
| Firemen (except locomotive and fire | | | |
| department) | | 3 | |
| Laborers (not otherwise specified) | | | |
| General and Not Specified Laborer | | 22 | |
| Helpers in Building and Hand Trades | | 2 | |

| Appendix 3 continued | | Number | Percent |
|---|---|---|---|
| Iron Foundries | | 1 | |
| Tanneries | | 1 | |
| Draymen, Teamsters, and Expressmen | | 5 | |
| Laborers (road and street building and repairing) | | 19 | |
| Laborers (steam railroad) | | 3 | |
| Deliverymen | | 5 | |
| Public Service Laborers | | 1 | |
| | Total | 71 | 16.2 |
| Domestic and Personal Service | | | |
| Servants | | 38 | |
| Bartenders | | 14 | |
| Janitors | | 7 | |
| Messenger, bundle, and office boys | | 2 | |
| | Total | 61 | 13.9 |

Female: Total Labor Force = 185

| Professional | | | |
|---|---|---|---|
| Musicians and Teachers of Music | | 2 | |
| Teachers (school) | | 1 | |
| Trained Nurses | | 1 | |
| | Total | 4 | 2.1 |
| Proprietary | | | |
| Retail Dealers | | 2 | |
| Boarding and Lodging House Keepers | | 11 | |
| Barbers, Hairdressers, and Manicurists | | 1 | |
| | Total | 14 | 7.5 |
| Clerical | | | |
| Bookkeepers, Cashiers, and Accountants | | 3 | |
| Clerks (except in stores) | | 1 | |
| | Total | 4 | 2.1 |
| Skilled | | | |
| None | | 0 | |
| | Total | 0 | 0.0 |
| Semiskilled | | | |
| Dressmakers and Seamstresses (not in factory) | | 18 | |
| Milliners | | 1 | |
| Candy Factories | | 1 | |
| Sewers and Sewing Machine Operators (factory) | | 4 | |

| Appendix 3 continued | | Number | Percent |
|---|---|---|---|
| Housekeepers and Stewardesses | | 4 | |
| | Total | 28 | 15.1 |
| **Unskilled** | | | |
| None | | 0 | |
| | Total | 0 | 0.0 |
| **Domestic and Personal Service** | | | |
| Laundresses (not in factory) | | 8 | |
| Servants | | 106 | |
| Waitresses | | 4 | |
| | Total | 118 | 63.7 |

Source: U.S. Bureau of the Census, *Thirteenth Census of the United States, vol. 4: Population 1910, Occupation Statistics* (Washington: Government Printing Office, 1913), pp. 565–66.

# Appendix 4

## *Black Occupations in Milwaukee, 1920*

| Male: Total Labor Force = 988 | | Number | Percent |
|---|---|---|---|
| **Professional** | | | |
| Authors, Editors, and Reporters | | 1 | |
| Clergymen | | 6 | |
| Dentists | | 2 | |
| Draftsmen | | 1 | |
| Lawyers, Judges, and Justices | | 2 | |
| Musicians and Teachers of Music | | 22 | |
| Photographers | | 1 | |
| Physicians and Surgeons | | 5 | |
| Teachers (school) | | 1 | |
| | Total | 41 | 4.1 |
| **Proprietary** | | | |
| Restaurant, Cafe, and Lunchroom Keepers | | 6 | |
| Retail Dealers | | 17 | |
| Barbers, Hairdressers, and Manicurists | | 13 | |
| | Total | 36 | 3.6 |
| **Clerical** | | | |
| Clerks in Stores | | 1 | |
| Commercial Travelers | | 1 | |
| Real Estate Agents and Officials | | 1 | |
| Salesmen (stores) | | 3 | |

| Appendix 4 continued | Number | Percent |
|---|---|---|
| Agents | 1 | |
| Bookkeepers and Cashiers | 2 | |
| Clerks (except stores) | 8 | |
| Total | 17 | 1.7 |

Skilled

| | Number | Percent |
|---|---|---|
| Apprentices to Building and Hand Trades | 1 | |
| Apprentices (other) | 2 | |
| Blacksmiths | 1 | |
| Cabinetmakers | 1 | |
| Carpenters | 4 | |
| Compositors, Linotypers, and Typesetters | 3 | |
| Cranemen | 2 | |
| Electricians | 1 | |
| Engineers (stationary) | 5 | |
| Foremen and Overseers (manufacturing) | 1 | |
| Forgemen, Hammermen, and Welders | 1 | |
| Ironmolders | 18 | |
| Machinists | 11 | |
| Mechanics (not otherwise specified) | 8 | |
| Painters, Glaziers, Varnishers (buildings) | 3 | |
| Plasterers and Cement Finishers | 2 | |
| Plumbers, Gas, and Steam Fitters | 1 | |
| Brakemen | 1 | |
| Locomotive Firemen | 3 | |
| Shoemakers and Cobblers (not in factory) | 3 | |
| Structural Iron Workers (building) | 2 | |
| Tailors | 7 | |
| Tinsmiths and Sheet Metal Workers | 1 | |
| Toolmakers and Die Setters and Sinkers | 1 | |
| All Other | 7 | |
| Total | 90 | 9.1 |

Semiskilled

| | Number | Percent |
|---|---|---|
| Chemical and Allied Industries | 3 | |
| Cigar and Tobacco Factories | 5 | |
| Clothing (suit, coat, cloak, and overall) | 4 | |
| Food (slaughter and packinghouses, et al.) | 35 | |
| Iron and Steel (auto, railroad shops, et. al.) | 18 | |
| Knitting Mills | 1 | |
| Lumber and Furniture Industries | 3 | |
| Painters, Glaziers, Varnishers (factory) | 1 | |
| Metal Industries (other than iron and steel) | 2 | |
| Printing, Publishing, and Engraving | 3 | |

| Appendix 4 continued | Number | Percent |
|---|---|---|
| Shoe Factories | 4 | |
| Tanneries | 16 | |
| Other Industries | 16 | |
| Other Trades | 2 | |
| Other Public Service | 2 | |
| Other Professional Service | 3 | |
| Other Transportation | 6 | |
| Other Guards | 1 | |
| Total | 125 | 12.6 |

Unskilled

| | Number | Percent |
|---|---|---|
| Building, General, and Not Specified Laborers | 37 | |
| Chemical and Allied Industries | 4 | |
| Food (slaughter and packinghouses) | 66 | |
| Helpers in Building and Hand Trades | 5 | |
| Iron and Steel (auto, blast furnaces, and rolling mills) | 155 | |
| Liquor and Beverage | 1 | |
| Lumber and Furniture | 4 | |
| Shoe Factories | 2 | |
| Tanneries | 68 | |
| Tinware Factories | 4 | |
| Other Industries | 49 | |
| Draymen, Teamsters, and Expressmen | 12 | |
| Laborers (road, street, and building repair) | 14 | |
| Laborers (steam railroad) | 18 | |
| Laborers (other transportation industries) | 12 | |
| Deliverymen | 1 | |
| Laborers (coal yard) | 8 | |
| Laborers (porters in stores) | 13 | |
| Firemen (except locomotive and fire department) | 11 | |
| Laborers (public service) | 4 | |
| Total | 488 | 49.3 |

Domestic and Personal Service

| | Number | Percent |
|---|---|---|
| Chauffeurs | 12 | |
| Bartenders | 3 | |
| Elevator Tenders | 4 | |
| Janitors and Sextons | 27 | |
| Servants | 19 | |
| Waiters | 12 | |

| Appendix 4 continued | | Number | Percent |
|---|---|---|---|
| Messengers | | 1 | |
| All Others | | 108 | |
| | Total | 186 | 18.8 |

Female: Total Labor Force = 289

| Professional | | | |
|---|---|---|---|
| Musicians and Teachers of Music | | 3 | |
| Religious, Charity, and Welfare Workers | | 1 | |
| | Total | 4 | 1.3 |
| **Proprietary** | | | |
| Boarding and Lodging House Keepers | | 15 | |
| Barbers, Hairdressers, and Manicurists | | 4 | |
| | Total | 19 | 6.4 |
| **Clerical** | | | |
| Clerks (stores) | | 2 | |
| Saleswomen | | 2 | |
| Bookkeepers | | 2 | |
| Clerks (except stores) | | 6 | |
| Stenographers and Typists | | 2 | |
| | Total | 14 | 4.8 |
| **Skilled** | | | |
| Forewomen (manufacturing) | | 2 | |
| Tailors | | 1 | |
| | Total | 3 | 1.1 |
| **Semiskilled** | | | |
| Dressmakers and Seamstresses (not in factory) | | 17 | |
| Chemical and Allied Industries | | 2 | |
| Cigar and Tobacco Factories | | 2 | |
| Clothing Industries (glove, hat, suit, et al.) | | 6 | |
| Iron and Steel Industries | | 5 | |
| Printing, Publishing, and Engraving | | 3 | |
| Shoe Factories | | 1 | |
| Tanneries | | 14 | |
| Textile Industries (knitting, et al.) | | 17 | |
| Other Industries | | 11 | |
| Other Transportation | | 2 | |
| Other Trades | | 2 | |
| Other Public Service | | 1 | |
| Other Professional Service | | 19 | |
| Housekeepers and Stewardesses | | 4 | |
| Laundresses (not in factory) | | 7 | |
| | Total | 113 | 39.1 |

| Appendix 4 continued | | Number | Percent |
|---|---|---|---|
| Unskilled | | | |
| Laborers (not otherwise specified) | | 11 | |
| All Other | | 1 | |
| | Total | 12 | 4.1 |
| Domestic and Personal Service | | | |
| Charwomen and Cleaners | | 8 | |
| Laundresses (not in factory) | | 10 | |
| Servants | | 90 | |
| Waitresses | | 5 | |
| All Other | | 1 | |
| | Total | 114 | 39.4 |

Source: U.S. Census Bureau, *Fourteenth Census of U.S., vol. 4: Population 1920, Occupations* (Washington: Government Printing Office, 1923), pp. 1141–44.

# Appendix 5

## *Black Occupations in Milwaukee, 1930*

| Male: Total Labor Force = 2,797 | | Number | Percent |
|---|---|---|---|
| Professional | | | |
| Actors and Showmen | | 5 | |
| Authors, Editors, and Reporters | | 1 | |
| Chemists, Assayers, and Metallurgists | | 2 | |
| Clergymen | | 15 | |
| Dentists | | 6 | |
| Lawyers, Judges, and Justices | | 3 | |
| Physicians and Surgeons | | 6 | |
| Musicians and Teachers of Music | | 58 | |
| Technical Engineers (civil and surveyors) | | 1 | |
| | Total | 97 | 3.4 |
| Proprietary | | | |
| Manufacturers | | 2 | |
| Builders and Building Contractors | | 2 | |
| Garage Owners, Managers, and Officials | | 2 | |
| Truck, Transfer, and Cab Company, Owners, Managers | | 3 | |
| Bankers, Brokers, and Moneylenders | | 1 | |
| Retail Dealers | | 25 | |
| Undertakers | | 3 | |

| Appendix 5 continued | Number | Percent |
|---|---|---|
| Restaurant, Cafe, and Lunchroom Keepers | 6 | |
| Officials and Inspectors (state and U.S. government) | 2 | |
| Barbers, Hairdressers, and Manicurists | 21 | |
| Total | 67 | 2.3 |
| **Clerical** | | |
| Commercial Travelers | 1 | |
| Real Estate Agents and Officials | 1 | |
| Salesmen | 7 | |
| Clerks (except stores) | 9 | |
| Stenographers and Typists | 1 | |
| Total | 19 | 0.6 |
| **Skilled** | | |
| Bakers | 1 | |
| Brick and Stone Masons and Tile Layers | 7 | |
| Carpenters | 12 | |
| Compositors, Linotypers, and Typesetters | 2 | |
| Cranemen | 7 | |
| Electricians | 1 | |
| Engineers (stationary) | 2 | |
| Foremen | 5 | |
| Ironmolders, Founders, and Casters | 28 | |
| Machinists (not otherwise specified) | 6 | |
| Mechanics (not otherwise specified) | 30 | |
| Millwrights | 2 | |
| Locomotive Firemen | 1 | |
| Painters, Glaziers, Varnishers (buildings) | 19 | |
| Plasterers and Cement Finishers | 10 | |
| Plumbers, Gas, and Steam Fitters | 1 | |
| Shoemakers and Cobblers (not in factory) | 1 | |
| Tailors | 25 | |
| Firemen (fire department) | 1 | |
| Total | 161 | 5.8 |
| **Semiskilled** | | |
| Filers, Grinders, Buffers, and Polishers (metal) | 10 | |
| Painters, Glaziers, Varnishers (factory) | 1 | |
| Chemical and Allied Industries | 7 | |
| Clothing Industries | 9 | |
| Electrical Machinery and Supply Factories | 3 | |
| Furniture Factories | 1 | |
| Other Lumber and Furniture Industries | 1 | |

| Appendix 5 continued | | Number | Percent |
|---|---|---|---|
| Iron and Steel (auto, blast furnaces, and rolling mills) | | 72 | |
| Metal Industries (except iron and steel) | | 5 | |
| Shoe Factories | | 2 | |
| Slaughter and Packinghouses | | 54 | |
| Other Food | | 1 | |
| Tanneries | | 15 | |
| Other Industries | | 98 | |
| Other Trades | | 9 | |
| Other Public Service | | 1 | |
| Other Transportation | | 213 | |
| Other Professional Service | | 22 | |
| Guards | | 5 | |
| Brakemen | | 1 | |
| | Total | 530 | 18.9 |
| Unskilled | | | |
| Firemen (except locomotive) | | 14 | |
| Chemical and Allied Industries | | 43 | |
| Food (slaughter and packinghouses) | | 87 | |
| General and Not Specified | | 74 | |
| Iron and Steel (auto, blast furnace) | | 123 | |
| Other Iron and Steel | | 465 | |
| Tanneries | | 167 | |
| Other Industries | | 39 | |
| All Other Occupations | | 112 | |
| Deliverymen | | 10 | |
| Draymen, Teamsters, et al. | | 3 | |
| Laborers (steam railroad) | | 67 | |
| Laborers (road and street) | | 72 | |
| Laborers (porters in stores) | | 109 | |
| Laborers (coal and lumber yards) | | 15 | |
| Laborers (public service) | | 32 | |
| Laborers (agriculture, mining, and forestry) | | 19 | |
| | Total | 1,557 | 55.6 |
| Domestic and Personal Service | | | |
| Chauffeurs | | 53 | |
| Janitors | | 49 | |
| Servants | | 49 | |
| Waiters | | 24 | |
| Messengers | | 188 | |
| All Others | | 3 | |
| | Total | 366 | 13.0 |

| Appendix 5 continued | | Number | Percent |
|---|---|---|---|
| **Female: Total Labor Force = 841** | | | |
| Professional | | | |
| Actresses and Showwomen | | 8 | |
| Musicians and Teachers of Music | | 9 | |
| Religious Workers | | 2 | |
| Social and Welfare Workers | | 5 | |
| Teachers and Laboratory Assistants | | 3 | |
| Nurses (trained) | | 2 | |
| | Total | 29 | 3.4 |
| Proprietary | | | |
| Boarding and Lodging House Keepers | | 24 | |
| Retail Dealers | | 4 | |
| Restaurant, Cafe, and Lunchroom Keepers | | 12 | |
| Barbers, Hairdressers, and Manicurists | | 22 | |
| | Total | 62 | 7.3 |
| Clerical | | | |
| Clerks (stores) | | 3 | |
| Saleswomen | | 8 | |
| Telephone Operators | | 1 | |
| Bookkeepers | | 4 | |
| Clerks (except stores) | | 8 | |
| Stenographers and Typists | | 3 | |
| | Total | 27 | 3.2 |
| Skilled | | | |
| Bakers | | 2 | |
| Forewomen | | 1 | |
| Tailors | | 3 | |
| | Total | 6 | 0.7 |
| Semiskilled | | | |
| Dressmakers | | 15 | |
| Clothing Industries | | 7 | |
| Electrical Machinery and Supply Factories | | 2 | |
| Knitting Mills | | 1 | |
| Other Industries | | 77 | |
| Other Professional Service | | 3 | |
| Other Transportation | | 1 | |
| Other Trades | | 19 | |
| Other Public Service | | 1 | |
| Housekeepers and Stewardesses | | 19 | |
| Laundry Operatives | | 22 | |
| | Total | 167 | 19.8 |

| Appendix 5 continued | | Number | Percent |
|---|---|---|---|
| Unskilled | | | |
| Laborers (not otherwise specified) | | 31 | |
| All Others | | 1 | |
| | Total | 32 | 3.8 |
| Domestic and Personal Service | | | |
| Janitors and Sextons | | 1 | |
| Laundresses (not in factory) | | 30 | |
| Charwomen and Cleaners | | 30 | |
| Nurses (not trained) | | 3 | |
| Servants | | 396 | |
| Waitresses | | 42 | |
| All Others | | 16 | |
| | Total | 518 | 61.5 |

Source: U.S. Census Bureau, *Fifteenth Census of the U.S.: 1930. Population, vol. 4: Occupations* (Washington: Government Printing Office, 1933), Table 12.

# Appendix 6

## *Black Occupations in Milwaukee, 1940*

| Male: Total Labor Force = 1,382 | | Number | Percent |
|---|---|---|---|
| Professional | | | |
| Authors, Editors, and Reporters | | 1 | |
| Clergymen | | 11 | |
| College Presidents, Professors, and | | | |
| Instructors | | 1 | |
| Dentists | | 3 | |
| Lawyers and Judges | | 3 | |
| Musicians and Music Teachers | | 15 | |
| Pharmacists | | 1 | |
| Physicians and Surgeons | | 6 | |
| Social and Welfare Workers | | 4 | |
| Teachers (not elsewhere classified) | | 2 | |
| Dancers, Showmen, and Athletes | | 3 | |
| | Total | 50 | 3.6 |
| Proprietary | | | |
| Barbers, Beauticians, and Manicurists | | 10 | |
| Manufacturers | | 1 | |
| Wholesalers | | 16 | |

| Appendix 6 continued | Number | Percent |
|---|---|---|
| Restaurant and Cafe Operators | 13 | |
| Retail Trade | 14 | |
| Business and Repair Services | 2 | |
| Personal Services | 5 | |
| Miscellaneous Industries and Services | 5 | |
| Boarding and Lodging House Keepers | 3 | |
| Total | 69 | 4.9 |
| **Clerical** | | |
| Shipping and Receiving Clerks | 2 | |
| Stenographers, Typists, and Secretaries | 1 | |
| Other Clerical and Kindred Workers | 17 | |
| Canvassers and Solicitors | 1 | |
| Hucksters and Peddlers | 1 | |
| Insurance Agents and Brokers | 1 | |
| Real Estate Agents and Brokers | 2 | |
| Other Sales Agents and Brokers | 2 | |
| Other Salesmen | 6 | |
| Total | 33 | 2.3 |
| **Skilled** | | |
| Bakers | 3 | |
| Compositors and Typesetters | 1 | |
| Electricians | 3 | |
| Foremen | 3 | |
| Locomotive Firemen | 1 | |
| Machinists, Millwrights, and Toolmakers | 3 | |
| Mechanics and Repairmen, and Loom Fixers | 35 | |
| Molders, Metal | 18 | |
| Painters (construction), Paperhangers, and Glaziers | 5 | |
| Plasterers and Cement Finishers | 6 | |
| Policemen, Sheriffs, and Marshals | 3 | |
| Plumbers and Gas and Steam Fitters | 1 | |
| Printing Craftsmen (except Compositors and Typesetters) | 1 | |
| Roofers and Sheet Metal Workers | 1 | |
| Shoemakers and Repairers (not in factory) | 2 | |
| Stationary Engineers, Cranemen, and Hoistmen | 10 | |
| Tailors and Furriers | 8 | |
| Other Craftsmen and Kindred Workers | 2 | |
| Total | 106 | 7.6 |

| Appendix 6 continued | Number | Percent |
|---|---|---|
| Semiskilled | | |
| Firemen (except locomotive and fire dept.) | 10 | |
| Laundry Operatives (except private family) | 5 | |
| Painters (except construction and maintenance) | 4 | |
| Welders and Flame Cutters | 1 | |
| Other Specified Operatives and Kindred Workers | 48 | |
| Food and Kindred Products | 89 | |
| Tobacco Manufacturers | 1 | |
| Woolen and Worsted Manufacturers | 2 | |
| Knit Goods | 1 | |
| Other Textile Mill Products | 4 | |
| Paper, Paper Products, and Printing | 8 | |
| Chemicals, and Petroleum and Coal Products | 13 | |
| Rubber Products | 2 | |
| Footwear Industries (except rubber) | 1 | |
| Leather and Leather Products (except footwear) | 29 | |
| Stone, Clay, and Glass Products | 2 | |
| Iron and Steel, and Not Specified Metal Industries | 53 | |
| Nonferrous Metals and their Products | 1 | |
| Machinery | 12 | |
| Automobiles and Automobile Equipment | 1 | |
| Other Manufacturing Industries | 2 | |
| Nonmanufacturing Industries and Services | 40 | |
| Other Semiprofessional Workers | 8 | |
| Guards and Watchmen | 5 | |
| Soldiers, Sailors, Marines, and Coast Guards | 1 | |
| Total | 343 | 24.8 |
| Unskilled | | |
| Longshoremen and Stevedores | 33 | |
| Other Specified Laborers | 81 | |
| Construction | 37 | |
| Food and Kindred Products | 14 | |
| Lumber, Furniture, and Lumber Products | 2 | |
| Paper, Paper Products, and Printing | 3 | |
| Chemicals, and Petroleum and Coal Products | 12 | |

| Appendix 6 continued | Number | Percent |
|---|---|---|
| Leather and Leather Products | 24 | |
| Iron and Steel and Not Specified Metals | 94 | |
| Nonferrous Metals and their Products | 1 | |
| Machinery | 10 | |
| Automobiles and Automobile Equipment | 1 | |
| Other Manufacturing Industries | 7 | |
| Railroads (including repair shops) | 32 | |
| Transportation (except railroads) | 3 | |
| Communication and Utilities | 19 | |
| Wholesale and Retail Trade | 35 | |
| Other Nonmanufacturing Industries | 3 | |
| Newsboys | 1 | |
| Chauffeurs, Truck Drivers, and Deliveryman | 47 | |
| Total | 459 | 33.2 |
| Domestic and Personal Service | | |
| Domestic Service Workers | 10 | |
| Personal Service Nonmanufacturing | 1 | |
| Messengers (except express) | 1 | |
| Attendants, Filling Station, Parking Lots | 7 | |
| Janitors and Porters | 228 | |
| Cooks (except private family) | 18 | |
| Elevator Operators | 2 | |
| Servants (except private family) | 11 | |
| Waiters and Bartenders | 32 | |
| Other Service (except domestic and protective) | 9 | |
| Total | 319 | 23.0 |

Female: Total Labor Force = 539

| Professional | | |
|---|---|---|
| Dentists | 1 | |
| Musicians and Music Teachers | 1 | |
| Social and Welfare Workers | 3 | |
| Teachers (not elsewhere classified) | 4 | |
| Trained Nurses and Student Nurses | 2 | |
| Total | 11 | 1.8 |
| Proprietary | | |
| Boarding and Lodging House Keepers | 13 | |
| Miscellaneous Industries and Services | 1 | |
| Restaurant and Cafe Operators | 4 | |

| Appendix 6 continued | Number | Percent |
|---|---|---|
| Other Wholesale and Retail Traders | 4 | |
| Beauticians, Barbers, and Manicurists | 18 | |
| Total | 40 | 7.3 |
| **Clerical** | | |
| Bookkeepers, Accountants, Cashiers | 2 | |
| Stenographers, Typists, and Secretaries | 8 | |
| Other Clerical and Kindred Workers | 11 | |
| Canvassers, Peddlers, and News Vendors | 1 | |
| Other Saleswomen | 6 | |
| Total | 28 | 5.1 |
| **Skilled** | | |
| Other Crafts and Kindred Workers | 1 | |
| Total | 1 | 0.2 |
| **Semiskilled** | | |
| Dressmakers and Seamstresses (not in factory) | 12 | |
| Laundry Operatives and Laundresses (except private family) | 16 | |
| Other Specified Operatives and Kindred Workers | 2 | |
| Food and Kindred Products | 2 | |
| Other Textile Mill Products | 18 | |
| Apparel and Other Fabricated Textile Products | 1 | |
| Paper, Paper Products, and Printing | 12 | |
| Leather and Leather Products (except footwear) | 4 | |
| Iron and Steel, Nonferrous Metal Products | 1 | |
| Transportation Equipment | 1 | |
| Other Manufacturing Industries | 11 | |
| Nonmanufacturing Industries and Services | 13 | |
| Protective Service Workers | 1 | |
| Housekeepers, Stewards, Hostesses (except private family) | 6 | |
| Other Professional and Semiprofessional Workers | 11 | |
| Total | 111 | 20.5 |
| **Unskilled** | | |
| Miscellaneous Specified Laborers | 1 | |
| Laborers Not Elsewhere Classified Mfg. | 6 | |
| Laborers Not Elsewhere Classified Nonmfg. | 13 | |
| Total | 20 | 3.7 |

| Appendix 6 continued | Number | Percent |
|---|---|---|
| Domestic and Personal Service | | |
| Domestic Service Workers | 235 | |
| Charwomen, Janitors | 9 | |
| Cooks (except private family) | 11 | |
| Elevator Operators | 6 | |
| Servants (except private family) | 45 | |
| Waitresses and Bartenders | 16 | |
| Other Service (except domestic and protective) | 4 | |
| Total | 326 | 60.4 |

Source: U.S. Census Bureau, *Sixteenth Census of the United States: 1940 Population, Labor Force, vol. 3, pt. 5* (Washington: U.S. Government Printing Office, 1943), pp. 991–96.

## *Afro-American Urban History: A Critique of the Literature*

Black life in northern cities received increasing scholarly attention from historians and sociologists by the 1960s and 1970s. The ghetto framework, documenting housing segregation as the basic indicator of hostile black-white interactions, came to dominate this literature. Ghettoization was indeed a significant development, but the ghetto-dwellers were also Afro-Americans from agricultural, urban domestic, personal service, and common laborer jobs moving into factory employment. This essay, a critical review of the historical and sociological literature on Afro-Americans in northern cities during the late nineteenth and early twentieth centuries, aims to explore these issues in some detail. Focusing roughly on studies covering the period 1890 to 1945, this analysis contains two basic objectives: to document the genesis of the "ghetto synthesis" or "ghetto formation" studies and to suggest proletarianization as an alternative theoretical departure in research on black urban life. The proletarian perspective is here offered as a complement and not a substitute for the valuable insights derived from the ghetto model. This critique is limited to research on blacks in northern cities, for, with few exceptions, scholars have only recently turned toward detailed studies of black life in the urban South.[1]

Initiated in 1899 with W. E. B. Du Bois's sociological study of blacks in Philadelphia, research on blacks in northern cities culminated in the 1960s and 1970s with what may be described as the "ghetto synthesis," historical monographs that incorporated the insights of earlier works and advanced a spatial interpretation of black urban life. Most of the research carried out before World War II, sociological in approach, focused primarily on questions of race contacts.[2] In effect, according to these scholars, the main explanatory factor in Afro-American life has been the nature of black-white interaction, usually in its most hostile, caste-like variety. Following the great migration of blacks to northern cities during World War I and its aftermath, however, sociologists increasingly believed that the Afro-American experience would lose its caste-like character and assume parallels with that of European immigrants.

While sociological works on blacks in contemporary northern cities continued to be written during the post-war period,[3] historical studies increasingly supplanted earlier sociological treatments, especially for the period 1890 to 1930. Post–World War II historical works have documented chiefly the process of "ghetto formation" or the spatial concentration of blacks in northern cities. This perspective has served several useful purposes: drawn attention to the presence of white racism in the socioeconomic and political life of the city; destroyed the erroneous notion that blacks were simply another immigrant group destined toward upward mobility; and, by adherence to the rigorous canons of historical scholarship, advanced our knowledge of black life in northern cities beyond the largely static sociological studies of previous decades. Yet, in documenting the emergence of black ghettos,[4] historians have adopted the sociological emphasis on the nature of race contacts. Neither the preceding "race contact" literature nor the ghetto synthesis has systematically traced the transition of blacks to an urban industrial working class. The link between the race relations focus of the sociological literature and the ghetto formation concern of historical studies was perhaps inevitable in view of how the ghetto synthesis emerged.

Du Bois pioneered in establishing the race contact emphasis in his classic study, *The Philadelphia Negro*. The Settlement House and Social Gospel movements in England and America influenced Du Bois's study. Charles Booth's 1880s study of London's poor inspired Jane Addams's *Hull House Maps and Papers*, published in 1895, and influenced Du Bois as well. Faith that the compilation and dissemination of empirical socioeconomic data would lead to the amelioration of poverty, disease, and crime undergirded these works.[5] Du Bois pursued his research in a similar spirit of using scientific investigation as an instrument of social reform. The study aimed to help resolve the many socioeconomic problems confronting urban blacks by shifting the focus away from black characteristics, which most scholars of the period defined as biologically and/or socially inferior, to the broader physical and social environment.[6] While emphasizing housing and neighborhood conditions, Du Bois placed greater emphasis on what he considered the "far mightier social environment — the surrounding world of custom, wish, whim, and thought" in explaining Afro-American economic, cultural, and political development. Thus, in the final analysis, his chief concern was "above all" race relations, or the relationship of blacks "to their million white fellow citizens."[7]

The attention given race contacts, or race relations, achieved more systematic theoretical formulation under the influence of the Chicago School of sociologists. Building upon the work of W. I. Thomas and Emory S. Borgardus, sociologist Robert E. Park established his theory of the race relations cycle following World War I. Park's cycle of race relations entailed four broad phases: contact, competition, accommodation, and assimilation. The contact phase involved initial encounters between Europeans and nonwhite people like blacks. Competition over scarce resources soon developed, with the stronger group (whites) forcing the subordinate group (blacks) into an accommodation with its superior power. A final stage, assimilation, evolved when the subordinate group had sufficiently internalized the demands of the superordinate group and was no longer viewed as a threat. Consequently, the dominant group permitted individual upward mobility into its ranks. Although the various stages of the process could be quite complicated, Park believed that the central thrust of the process was linear. Generalizing from empirical work among Hawaiian and West Coast Asians, Park argued: "In the relations of the races there is a cycle of events which tends everywhere to repeat itself. . . . The race relations cycle which takes the form, to state it abstractly, of contacts, competition, accommodation, and eventual assimilation is apparently progressive and irreversible."[8]

Before the 1930s, however, Park paid little attention to the movement of blacks into northern cities. He generally focused on the South and stressed the difficulties of black assimilation into the larger society because of salient physical differences. By 1939, Park added a new component to his theory by recognizing changes attendant on the increasing movement of blacks into northern cities following World War I. Park now believed that Afro-Americans were beginning to make the transition from a racial caste to a racial minority: "The Northern migration and dispersion have given him (the Negro) opportunities for education which he did not have in the South. . . . The consequence of this is . . . to diminish the distances between the races at the different class levels and . . . to transform the status of the Negro in the United States from that of a caste to that of a racial minority."[9] In short, Park believed, in their shift to the urban North, the experience of blacks increasingly resembled the pattern of European immigrants.

Ernest Burgess and others elaborated Park's race-relations theory into the human ecological approach to urban life. Human ecologists emphasized the competitive and selective spatial ordering of people in the urban environment, here described by Roderick McKenzie, a colleague of Park and Burgess: " 'Society is made up of individuals spatially separated, territorially distributed, and capable of independent locomotion.' These spatial relationships of human beings are the products of competition and selection, and are continuously in process of change as new factors enter to disturb the competitive relations or to facilitate mobility."[10] Human ecologists argued that the struggle for space underlay geographical segregation along numerous lines: ethnic, class, race, sex, and even age.

Drawing upon the theoretical insights of Park and Burgess, E. Franklin Frazier developed a complex class and spatial analysis of black life in northern cities (Chicago, 1931; Harlem, 1937). Frazier's research revealed, for example, that blacks in Chicago and Harlem sorted themselves out in spatial arrangements along socioeconomic lines. Frazier ultimately hoped to prove the validity of Park's racial relations cycle theory by noting how the most advanced blacks resembled white society on the periphery between black and white geographic lines: "It was old mulatto families of the third type who sometimes fled before the onrush of the uncouth Negroes from the South to . . . the periphery of the Negro community as shown in the case of the seventh zone in Chicago. . . . Their pattern of family life approaches that of the white middle class."[11] It was at this juncture that Frazier perceived the possibility of greater integration of blacks and whites. "Unless artificial barriers are raised to nullify the influence of efficiency in the competitive process," Frazier believed, "increased efficiency will mean greater participation [of blacks] in the [larger white] communal life."[12]

As Frazier sought to apply the theoretical insights of the Chicago School, other researchers on urban life, social anthropologists in particular, turned their attention to black life in northern cities. These scholars, led by W. Lloyd Warner, became dissatisfied with the ecological model's implicit and increasingly explicit assumption of blacks as a minority group. Warner and others noted the pervasiveness of color prejudice even in northern cities, especially when the Depression curtailed the industrial base from which blacks in northern cities had developed during the previous decade. They also noted the increasing disintegration of white immigrant ghettos, at the same time as black concentration became more pronounced. Finally, a new methodological departure, drawn from anthropology, informed this work. Warner and his associates shifted from the spatial orientation of the ecological school to status and power relations. The study of the New England (Newburyport) or "Yankee City," the first urban community study using the tools of social anthropology, revealed "a form of social stratification [according to the evaluation of community members] which placed the population at varying levels of prestige and power."[13] Although a class system which superordinated some individuals and subordinated others emerged in Yankee City, Warner documented significant social mobility between classes: "Members of a class tend to marry within their own order, but the values of the society permit marriage up and down. . . . A system of classes. . . provides by its own values for movement up and down the social ladder. In common parlance, this is social climbing, or in technical terms, social mobility." Moreover, Warner observed, individuals from a large number of white ethnic groups climbed up the class ladder in Yankee City.[14]

Since blacks confronted racially discriminatory legal and extralegal restrictions, Warner and others advanced the "caste and class" model to explain black life in both the South and, to a lesser degree, the North. This formulation elevated the concept of caste to center stage, while only using the term class to explain intraracial relationships within separate black and white communities. In research on blacks in *Deep South,* Warner and his associates produced the conclusion that Afro-Americans in the South, regulated by rules of endogamy, constituted a "caste" within a caste system of social relations. White and black castes, however, were internally stratified along class lines, which permitted movement within castes, while strictly limiting intercaste mobility.[15]

Chicago's black population was chosen to test the caste-class model of race relations in a northern setting. Although Drake and Cayton avoided use of the term "caste" in favor of "color line" in depicting divisions between blacks and whites in Chicago, they adopted the basic thrust of Warner's caste-class model. Following Warner, Drake and Cayton recognized internal class divisions on both sides of the color line. Examining Drake and Cayton's findings on informal bars to interracial marriage and other constraints on northern black urban life, Warner concluded that there was "still a status system of the caste type" operating in Chicago although he adjusted the model to fit the Northern context: blacks were not as severely restricted by de jure and de facto socioeconomic and political measures as in the South. Afro-Americans could vote and hold important elective and appointive offices in the North. They could also gain more equal access than southern blacks to public education, despite unofficial restrictions that prevented their full exercise of socioeconomic and political rights and privileges.[16]

The caste-class model gained its most elaborate statement when Gunnar Myrdal adopted Warner's ideas in his monumental study, *An American Dilemma* (1944). Myrdal avoided such concepts as race, class (emphasizing fluidity and upward mobility), and minority group in favor of caste, with internal class divisions, as the basic designation of blacks in the American social order. He rejected "race" because, for him, it carried negative connotations of innate inferiority. He by-passed "minority group" since it failed "to make a distinction between temporary social disabilities of recent white immigrants and the permanent disabilities of Negroes and other colored people."[17] Like Warner, Myrdal also rejected the notion of "class" in relation to blacks, as then popularly used, because the term implied a "non-rigid status group from which an individual member can rise or fall." Blacks, he argued, were locked into their low socioeconomic status by several social, economic, and political constraints including bans on inter-racial marriage. Myrdal also followed Warner in ascribing a modified form of caste to blacks in northern cities: "The caste line in the North exists, but has gaps."[18]

Both the race relations cycle theory of Park and Warner's caste-class model emphasized the character of race contacts in examinations of black urban life. Park and Frazier stressed the upward mobility of blacks as a consequence of World War I. While racial prejudice continued to mar the relations between blacks and whites, in their view, such limitations paralleled those experienced by numerous European immigrants in the urban North. Conversely, the caste-class approach of Warner, Drake and Cayton, and Myrdal highlighted continuing racial constraints on black economic, social, and political advance. Both the race relations cycle and caste-class perspectives placed the special mode of race contacts at the center of their interpretation of black life in northern cities. Du Bois's pioneering work on blacks in Philadelphia also stressed the character of black-white interaction; thus, there was a unity of emphasis in studies of Afro-Americans in cities from the late nineteenth century to the end of World War II. Emphasis on questions of race contacts provided the thread that linked the work of Du Bois, Park's race relations cycle theory, and Frazier's ecological approach, on the one hand, to the caste-class school of Warner, Drake and Cayton, and Myrdal on the other.

Myrdal's study extended the caste model and the image of its negative impact on black life to a broad spectrum of the post–World War II American public. Myrdal hoped to make white Americans aware that caste lines contradicted their fundamental ideals of social democracy and human equality: "The American Negro problem is a problem in the heart of the American. It is there that the decisive struggle goes on. . . . At bottom our problem is the moral dilemma of the American."[19] Myrdal's ideas, for example, underlay the Supreme Court's rationale for ending school segregation in *Brown v. Board of Education* (1954). Nevertheless, a postwar attack on the caste-class model emanated from both radical and liberal theorists. Oliver C. Cox delivered the most critical radical analysis of the caste model in his book *Caste, Class, and Race* (1948). Cox argued that the caste system existed only in India. Social inequality in India, he maintained, unlike that in the West, was an accepted fact of life for both upper- and lower-caste individuals and groups alike. Caste, Cox believed, did not characterize black life in the South much less the North; it was impossible, he argued, for "one caste to exist in an otherwise casteless society for castes are interdependent social phenomena." Racial exploitation, he concluded, was "merely one aspect of the problem of the proletarianization of labor, regardless of the color of the laborer."[20] Both the scholarly community and larger society rejected Cox's ideas in the postwar reaction against radical ideas. Cox however approached his work not as a political Marxist but as a social scientist in search of the most fruitful theoretical framework for interpreting his observations on black life.

The 1950s brought a strong reaffirmation of Park's race relations cycle in research on blacks in Northern cities. World War II and the 1950s migration of blacks to Northern cities, their slight shift upward into higher-skilled positions during World War II, and their increasing participation in labor unions seemed to confirm the process of socioeconomic integration into the larger society. Some writers viewed these changes as a denial that caste relations existed in northern cities and increasingly found validity in Park's idea of assimilation for Afro-Americans. The view that blacks were simply another immigrant group gained wide currency. In his study of Afro-Americans and Puerto Ricans in New York, for example, Oscar Handlin concluded: "The Negroes and Puerto Ricans have followed the general outline of the experience of earlier immigrants. These latest arrivals diverged from that earlier experience because color prejudice...impeded their freedom of movement, both in space and in social and economic status. That divergence in experience need not be more than temporary, however."[21]

Against the backdrop of an intensely racially segregated society (especially in the South) of the 1930s, the theory of assimilation could be described as progressive. It attacked the ideological assumption that blacks were inferior to whites and thus could not assimilate the socioeconomic and political values and customs of the larger society. In the changed socioeconomic and political climate of the 1950s, however, assimilation theory acquired increasingly conservative overtones: namely, that blacks no less than European immigrants could succeed in American society and any failures among them could be attributed to deficiencies within the group rather than to inequities within the society. Such views also served the U.S. foreign policy offensive against the Soviet Union and reinforced a growing Cold War mythology: American society lacked significant class divisions, which would entail fundamental inequalities of wealth, power, and prestige. It was negative scholarly reactions to the assimilation model, coupled with other social and intellectual forces, that laid the basis for the emergence of the ghetto synthesis by historians of the 1960s and 1970s.

Beginning with Gilbert Osofsky's *Harlem: The Making of a Ghetto, 1890–1930* (1963) and Allan Spear's *Black Chicago: The Making of a Negro Ghetto, 1890–1920* (1967) through David Katzman's *Before the Ghetto: Black Detroit in the Nineteenth Century* (1973), Kenneth Kusmer's *A Ghetto Takes Shape: Black Cleveland, 1870–1930* (1976), and more recently Thomas Philpott's *The Slum and the Ghetto* (1978) and James Borchert's *Alley Life in Washington: Family, Community, Religion, and Folklife in the City, 1850–1970* (1980), the ghetto synthesis fully emerged. It drew upon the preceding sociological studies and used the "ghetto" as the fundamental conceptual and theoretical framework for examining Afro-American urban life. While seeking to strengthen it in some particulars, adding a comparative dimension and giving more attention to the internal dynamics of black urban life, recent scholars have departed little from the prevailing ghetto model.[22] The pivotal nature of the "ghetto" in these studies is repeatedly emphasized. Osofsky revealed this focus in his study of blacks in nineteenth-and early twentieth-century Harlem: "As the major development of these years was the emergence of Harlem as a Negro ghetto, I have entitled this study *Harlem: The Making of a Ghetto*."[23] Allan Spear, in his well-documented *Black Chicago* (1967), set a similar task for himself: "This study documents the formation of a northern Negro ghetto. It examines the forces, both external and internal, that conditioned the development of separate Negro community life."[24] The chief aim of Kenneth Kusmer's model study of blacks in Cleveland "is to trace a number of aspects of black life — economic, political, social, and cultural — in a single city over a period of sixty to one hundred years, and to show how changes in each of these aspects were integrally related to the developing ghetto."[25] Even David Katzman, who, in his study of blacks in nineteenth-century Detroit, employs the caste model to explain Afro-American life, to a large extent frames his study in the vein of other works emphasizing black spatial and race relationships.[26]

One of the most recent accounts, Thomas Philpott's *The Slum and the Ghetto,* has elaborated the ghetto model to its most extreme limits. Philpott examines comparative residential arrangements of blacks and white immigrants in Chicago between 1890 and 1930 and concludes that, while white ethnics have experienced the slums (dilapidated housing), only blacks have experienced the "ghetto" (involuntary segregation along racial lines).[27] Finally, although focusing on alley dwellings in Washington, D.C., over a longer period of time and taking sharp issue with the ghetto literature's emphasis on social disorganization, particularly in family and kinship relations, Borchert nevertheless tends to place his study within the ghetto theoretical framework: "While this study is largely concerned with examining the patterns of order developed by folk migrants in Washington over a hundred-and-twenty-year period, the rise and zenith of alley housing took place between the 1860s and the development of massive northern ghettoes in the twentieth century. The alley experience represents part of that plantation-ghetto transition, both in scale and in chronology."[28]

Imagery for a ghetto synthesis had roots in the pattern of Jewish immigrant settlement, reaching back to the medieval period in the Western world, but the image of the ghetto as a theoretical construct crystallized when Lewis Wirth published *The Ghetto* (1928) with particular emphasis on Jews in Chicago. Wirth argued that the study of the Jewish ghetto would illuminate the history of other urban areas: "Little Sicilies, Little Polands, Chinatowns, and Black Belts."[29] Drake and Cayton adopted the term "ghetto" as the strongest visual evidence of a color line in their study of blacks in Chicago.[30] In *The Negro Ghetto* (1948), a comprehensive analysis of housing segregation in the North,

Robert Weaver built upon the works of Louis Wirth and Drake and Cayton in establishing a more systematic and historical perspective using the "ghetto" framework. He argued that the black ghetto was a relatively recent phenomenon with roots in the World War I migration to northern cities.[31] Almost without exception, ghetto formation studies have taken issue with Weaver and pushed the time frame back to at least the 1890s, and even earlier, emphasizing the long historical experience of small, relatively segregated, black urban communities in northern cities. Even so, they have accepted the basic thrust of Weaver's argument: that the black ghetto was not a remnant of race prejudice inherited from slavery but a product of the historical interaction of blacks and whites in the urban environment. Thus, in their view, a simple linear assimilation model could not adequately explain the sociohistorical experience of blacks in cities.

The ghetto synthesis has been a compelling force in the research on blacks in northern cities. Its power inheres in attempts to address deeply felt contemporary needs in American society. Uppermost among these has been the desire to explain the increasingly visible phenomenon of nearly all-black urban communities marked by decaying housing structures, delinquency, narcotics addiction, infant mortality, homicide, and abrasive race relations. Although partly relying on imagery drawn from the white immigrant experience, ghetto formation monographs have dispelled the notion of urban blacks as simply another immigrant group. These studies have also advanced our understanding by incorporating the valid findings of earlier sociological works and superseding these static synchronic analyses with dynamic historical perspectives. Probably more than anything else, the ghetto synthesis has reinforced and expanded the earlier sociological emphasis on the critical role of white racial hostility and prejudice in the development of Afro-American communities in northern cities.[32]

Despite its salient strengths, the ghetto synthesis alone is too narrow to organize a satisfactory history of blacks in northern cities. Focusing on the dynamics of racial hostility and spatial concentration, a tragic portrait of black urban life emerges from a large part of the ghetto literature. In a chapter titled "Harlem Tragedy: An Emerging Slum," Osofsky argued that the most profound change Harlem experienced during the 1920s was its emergence as a slum, described by such terms as "deplorable," "unspeakable," and "incredible." Osofsky later elaborated this perspective into the "tragic sameness" thesis of black urban life. Drawing upon the nineteenth- and twentieth-century experiences of blacks in New York and Philadelphia, he concluded that there "is an unending and tragic sameness about black life in the metropolis over the two centuries." Such a tragic view of black life, however, was not characteristic of Osofsky alone.[33] Allan Spear concluded his study of Chicago on a similarly tragic note: "From its inception, the Negro ghetto was unique among the city's ethnic enclaves. It grew in response to an implacable white hostility that has not changed. . . . Like Jewries of medieval Europe, Black Chicago has offered no escape. . . . Negroes — forever marked by their color — could only hope for success within a rigidly delineated and severely restricted ghetto society." With such emphasis on the tragic quality of black urban life at his disposal, it is no wonder that David Katzman explicitly adopted the caste model in his study of blacks in nineteenth-century Detroit and Thomas Philpott took the tragic connotation of the ghetto to a new level: "It was a place where segregation was practically total, essentially involuntary, and also perpetual."[34]

Treating blacks largely as victims of an increasingly hostile white population, the tragic theme implied a negative and often tragic view of black institutional life as well. Spear concluded that racial solidarity was essentially a negative "response rather than a positive force." Osofsky depreciated the importance of storefront churches which the newest black migrants to the city developed, and Philpott underplayed the positive role of black social welfare institutions.[35] While these studies argued for black activism in their own behalf, ways in which the increasing, though weak, economic, political, and institutional resources of blacks helped to deflect the impact of white racism, especially during World War I and its aftermath, were deemphasized.

If scholars like Osofsky, Spear, Katzman, and Philpott elevated pathos to the center of their description of black urban life, Kusmer and Borchert presented more paradoxical portraits of tragedy and triumph. Kusmer argued that the ghetto, although tragic, laid the basis for Afro-American solidarity in the struggle for equal rights. Spatial separation, he emphasized, provided a practical framework for the future assault on all vestiges of racism. In this sense, Kusmer sounded a triumphant note despite adversity for Afro-Americans in Cleveland. Partly by the decision to eliminate race relations from his analysis of alley life in Washington, Borchert convincingly refuted earlier emphases on social disorganization among black urbanites. He launched a frontal attack against the notion that forces in the urban environment destroyed the traditional cultural, familial, and institutional arrangements of Afro-American rural migrants to the city. Borchert, in effect, took the triumphant theme to the other extreme. A variety of factors, particularly the migrants' prior cultural experiences and the large numbers of absentee landlords, he argued, facilitated autonomous social interactions among alley dwellers. Accordingly, Borchert presented an almost uniformly triumphant picture of black alley residents: "In contrast to the 'conventional' social scientific and historical theory that folk migrants undergo a period of disorder as a result of their exposure to urban life, migrants actually . . . 'remade' their urban environment, both physically and cognitively, to fit their needs. While change did occur, it happened slowly and was a matter of degree, not a change in kind."[36]

Despite variation among them, with few exceptions, recent scholars of black urban life place spatial dynamics and some variant of race relations at the center of their work. Such emphasis on ghetto formation and the nature of race relations have misrepresented two essential features of black urban life: occupational status and class structure. Afro-American economic status is usually viewed as the consequence of a dual process involving the lack of training among blacks and the existence of racial discrimination by industrialists and labor unions.[37] This perspective, to be sure, contains key components, yet it systematically fails to highlight the process of black transition to an urban-industrial working class. "The ghetto" as a racial-spatial phenomenon is stretched beyond its limits — as in Osofsky's case — in efforts to employ it to describe the persistence of socioeconomic inequality between blacks and whites. Such inequality represents the complex interplay of changes in the larger economy and the state as well as the intensification of social, psychological, and institutional racism.

By its nearly singular focus on "blacks" and "whites," the ghetto synthesis has also camouflaged the dynamics of class divisions within the black population. True, these studies have documented the importance of cleavages between black elites,[38] but the division between the black bourgeois elite and the Afro-American urban-industrial proletariat has gained insufficient comment. While the ghetto synthesis has been useful, it has been over-worked; taken singularly, it now tends to distort more than it clarifies. Therefore, a fresh but complementary theoretical departure in research on black life in northern cities is needed.

The proletarianization framework — used in this study of Milwau-

kee blacks—suggests an alternative hypothesis for research on urban
blacks. Such a framework shifts the perspective from a primary focus
on hostile race contacts and their spatial embodiment to a central concern with questions of economic and class relations. The only detailed
historical works that focus on the process of Afro-American, urban-
industrial, working-class formation are Ph.D. dissertations by
Richard Walter Thomas on blacks in Detroit (1915–45) and Peter
Gottlieb on blacks in Pittsburgh (1916–30).[39] Thomas argues that the
most important influence on economic and social change in Detroit's
larger black community was the "formation and organization" of a
black proletariat. Although Gottlieb sets the documentation of black
migration to Pittsburgh as his central task, he also emphasizes "the
making of an industrial working class." The studies by Thomas and
Gottlieb constitute the immediate springboard from which proletarianization is here offered as an alternative perspective in research on
black life in the urban North. The making of Milwaukee's black industrial working class between 1915 and 1945 provides an additional
case study of these changes. Broader rationale for such an approach is
found in an emerging body of literature in social and labor history that
has as its basic objective the re-creation of working-class experience in
industrial countries. Although several American writers (particularly
Herbert Gutman and David Montgomery) have followed the pioneering lead of E. P. Thompson in documenting patterns of white
working-class experience in the United States, few of these insights
have been systematically applied to research on Afro-Americans in
cities. This literature, nevertheless, suggests theoretical perspectives
of value to research on urban blacks. Gutman has pinpointed the need
to uncover the history of working-class blacks in American cities, and
Thompson's emphasis on the "making" of a working class is relevant to
such a task. Thompson stresses "an active process" that owed as much
to the dynamic responses of workers as to the impact of industrialists
and machines.[40] Like the experience of the English proletariat, the
Milwaukee experience suggests that the black industrial working class
was no less active in its own making.

Scholars of black urban working-class history must be prepared,
however, to recognize sharp differences between the working-class experience of blacks and whites. The emergence of Milwaukee's Afro-
American industrial working class was of a different order from that of
whites as a result of racial discrimination against blacks by manufacturers, labor unions, and diverse ethnic groups. Moreover, unlike the

view held in conventional Marxist perspectives on proletarianization,[41] the emergence of the black proletariat did not entail a fundamental loss of autonomy over prior family farms or skilled crafts. The loss of craft skills and family farms was only a secondary theme in black proletarianization. Subjugated within an exploitative sharecropping system of virtual peonage and locked into domestic and personal service jobs in cities, the movement of blacks into northern industries represented an upward thrust in economic status. From the vantage point of northern industries, however, the proletarianization of Afro-Americans was a precarious process, relegating them to the cellar of the industrial economy. Undergirding this process was the complex interaction of changes in the economy and politics, and a shifting pattern of racial ideology and practice.

In short, the proletarianization of blacks entailed their movement into the industrial labor force as wage earners whose lives were shaped by racism as well as by the competitive interplay between labor and capital under industrialism.[42] Such powerful conditioning forces would foster a complex convergence of class and racial consciousness among black industrial workers. Moreover, patterns of inter- and intrarace relations, politics, institutional life, and housing would also reflect the dynamics of proletarianization.

While the proletarianization of Milwaukee blacks exhibited similarities with experiences of blacks in larger northern cities, there were important differences between the experience of Milwaukee blacks and Afro-Americans in other cities; therefore, it is necessary to conclude with a call for more research. We need more historical studies of black working-class formation in southern and western as well as northern cities. We need systematic analyses, in a variety of contexts, of the complex relationship between proletarianization, institutional life, politics, race relations, and particularly ghetto formation. Such vigorous research will help to sharpen our generalizations about the impact of industrialization on blacks. Indeed, only with additional research that links established insights with fresh perspectives can we properly transcend the limitations of the ghetto synthesis.

## NOTES

1. Howard N. Rabinowitz, *Race Relations in the Urban South, 1865–1890* (New York: Oxford University Press, 1978), pp. 1x–xvi; John W. Blass-

ingame, *Black New Orleans, 1865–1880* (Chicago: University of Chicago
Press, 1973); Zane L. Miller, "Urban Blacks in the South, 1865–1920:
The Richmond, Savannah, New Orleans, Louisville, and Birmingham
Experience," in Leo F. Schnore, ed., *The New Urban History: Quantitative
Explorations by American Historians* (Princeton: Princeton University
Press, 1975), pp. 184–227; Dwight W. Hoover, "The Diverging Paths of
American Urban History," in Alexander B. Callow, Jr., ed., *American
Urban History: An Interpretative Reader with Commentaries* (New York: Ox-
ford University Press, 1973), pp. 642–59.

2.  W. E. B. Du Bois, *The Philadelphia Negro: A Social Study* (1899; rept. New
    York: Schocken Books, 1967); John Daniels, *In Freedom's Birthplace: A
    Study of the Boston Negro* (1914; rept. New York: Arno Press and the *New
    York Times,* 1969); The Chicago Commission on Race Relations, *The
    Negro in Chicago: A Study of Race Relations and a Race Riot* (1922; rept. New
    York: Arno Press, 1968), a study written largely by Charles S. Johnson,
    then director of the Chicago Urban League's Research Department and
    later an eminent sociologist. Charles S. Johnson, *Patterns of Negro Segrega-
    tion* (New York: Harper and Brothers, 1943). E. Franklin Frazier,
    "Negro Harlem: An Ecological Study," *American Journal of Sociology* 43,
    no. 1 (July 1937): 72–88; E. Franklin Frazier, *The Negro Family in Chicago*
    (Chicago: University of Chicago Press, 1932); G. Franklin Edwards,
    ed., *E. Franklin Frazier on Race Relations: Selected Writings* (Chicago:
    University of Chicago Press, 1968); Robert A. Warner, *New Haven
    Negroes: A Social History* (1940; rept. New York: Arno Press, 1969); St.
    Clair Drake and Horace R. Cayton, *Black Metropolis: A Study of Negro Life
    in a Northern City,* vols. 1 and 2 (1945; rev. New York: Harcourt, Brace,
    and World, 1962).

3.  Charles Keil, *Urban Blues* (Chicago: The University of Chicago Press,
    1967); Elliott Liebow, *Talley's Corner: A Study of Negro Streetcorner Men*
    (Boston: Little, Brown, 1967).

4.  Robert C. Weaver, *The Negro Ghetto* (New York: Russell and Russell,
    1948); Gilbert Osofsky, *Harlem: The Making of a Ghetto, 1890–1930* (1963;
    rev. ed., New York: Harper Torchbooks, 1971); Gilbert Osofsky, "The
    Enduring Ghetto," *Journal of American History* 55, no. 2 (Sept. 1968):
    243–55; Allan H. Spear, *Black Chicago: The Making of a Negro Ghetto,
    1890–1920* (Chicago: University of Chicago Press, 1967); David M.
    Katzman, *Before the Ghetto: Black Detroit in the Nineteenth Century* (Urbana:
    University of Illinois Press, 1973); Kenneth L. Kusmer, *A Ghetto Takes
    Shape: Black Cleveland, 1870–1930* (Urbana: University of Illinois Press,
    1976); Thomas Philpott, *The Slum and the Ghetto* (New York: Oxford
    University Press, 1978). Three recent studies seek to modify the ghetto
    framework: James Borchert, *Alley Life in Washington, 1850–1970* (Ur-
    bana: University of Illinois Press, 1980); Douglas H. Daniels, *Pioneer

*Urbanites: A Social and Cultural History of Black San Francisco* (Philadelphia: Temple University Press, 1980); and Thomas C. Cox, *Blacks in Topeka, Kansas, 1865–1915: A Social History* (Baton Rouge: Louisiana State University Press, 1982). Several doctoral dissertations employing the ghetto model in research on blacks in northern and western cities include the following: David V. Taylor, "Pilgrim's Progress: Black St. Paul and the Making of an Urban Ghetto, 1870–1930" (University of Minnesota, 1977); Keith E. Collins, "Black Los Angeles: The Maturing Ghetto, 1940–1950" (University of California–San Diego, 1975); Lawrence B. de Graff, "Negro Migration to Los Angeles, 1930–1950" (University of California–Los Angeles, 1962); Albert S. Broussard, "The New Racial Frontier: San Francisco's Black Community, 1900–1940" (Duke University, 1977); Clement Alexander Price, "The Afro-American Community of Newark, 1917–1947: A Social History" (Rutgers University, 1975); Elizabeth Balanoff, "A History of the Black Community of Gary, Indiana, 1906–1940" (University of Chicago, 1974). The Afro-American experience in several western cities (Portland and Salem, Oregon; Seattle and Spokane, Washington; and others in Montana and Idaho) has received attention in a comprehensive dissertation by Quintard Taylor, "A History of Blacks in the Pacific Northwest, 1788–1970" (University of Minnesota, 1977). Studies that seek to depart from the ghetto theme are Ph.D. dissertations by Richard Walter Thomas, "From Peasant to Proletarian: The Formation and Organization of the Black Industrial Working Class in Detroit, 1915–1945" (University of Michigan, 1976), Peter Gottlieb, "Making Their Own Way: Southern Blacks' Migration to Pittsburgh, 1916–30" (University of Pittsburgh, 1977), and James R. Grossman, "A Dream Deferred: Black Migration to Chicago, 1916–1921" (University of California–Berkeley, 1982). Also see my Ph.D. dissertation, "The Making of an Industrial Proletariat: Black Milwaukee, 1915–1945" (University of Minnesota, 1980).

5. Du Bois, *Philadelphia Negro,* pp. xiv–xix, 1–5.
6. Elliott Rudwick, "W. E. B. Du Bois as Sociologist," in James E. Blackwell and Morris Janowitz, eds., *Black Sociologists: Historical and Contemporary Perspectives* (Chicago: University of Chicago Press, 1974), pp. 25–55; E. Franklin Frazier, "Race Contacts and the Social Structure," in G. Franklin Edwards, ed., *E. Franklin Frazier on Race Relations,* p. 45.
7. Du Bois, *Philadelphia Negro,* pp. 1, 322–55.
8. Robert Park, "Race Relations and Certain Frontiers," in E. B. Reuter, ed., *Race Relations and Culture Contacts* (New York: McGraw Hill, 1934), pp. 57–85; Robert Park, *Race and Culture* (Glencoe: Free Press, 1950), p. 150; James A. Geschwender, *Racial Stratification in America* (Dubuque, Iowa: Wm. C. Brown, 1978), pp. 19–38. Geschwender discusses the complexity of Park's ideas.

9. Park, "The Nature of Race Relations," in Edgar T. Thompson, ed., *Race Relations and the Race Problem* (Durham, N.C.: Duke University Press, 1939), pp. 3–45; Park, *Race and Culture,* pp. 81–116.

10. Robert E. Park, "The City: Suggestions for the Investigation of Human Behavior in the Urban Environment," in Robert E. Park, Ernest W. Burgess, and Roderick D. McKenzie, eds., *The City* (1925; rept. Chicago: University of Chicago Press, 1967), pp. 9–12; E. Franklin Frazier, in Edwards, ed., *E. Franklin Frazier on Race Relations,* pp. 121–22; R. D. McKenzie, "The Ecological Approach to the Study of the Human Community" in Park, et al., eds., *The City,* pp. 63–79.

11. E. Franklin Frazier, in Edwards, ed., *E. Franklin Frazier on Race Relations,* pp. 172–73. Also see, E. Franklin Frazier, "The Impact of Urban Civilization Upon Negro Family Life," *American Sociological Review* 2, no. 5 (Oct. 1937): 609–18.

12. E. Franklin Frazier, *The Negro Family in Chicago,* pp. 245–52; E. Franklin Frazier, *Negro Youth at the Crossways* (Washington: American Council on Education, 1940).

13. W. Lloyd Warner, "A Methodological Note," in Drake and Cayton, *Black Metropolis,* pp. 769–82.

14. Ibid., pp. 772–76.

15. Ibid., pp. 776–82; Allison Davis, et al., *Deep South: A Social Anthropological Study of Caste and Class* (Chicago: University of Chicago Press, 1941), pp. 15–58.

16. Drake and Cayton, *Black Metropolis,* pp. 778–82, and chapters 6 and 7.

17. Gunnar Myrdal, *An American Dilemma: The Negro Problem and Modern Democracy,* vol. 2 (1944; rept. New York: Pantheon Books, 1962), p. 667.

18. Ibid., p. 678.

19. Myrdal, *An American Dilemma,* p. lxix; Anthony Lewis, "The School Segregation Cases," in Melvin Drimmer, ed., *Black History: A Reappraisal* (Garden City, N.Y.: Anchor Books, 1969), p. 438.

20. Oliver C. Cox, *Caste, Class, and Race* (Garden City, N.Y.: Doubleday and Company, 1948), pp. 4, 21, 322–33, 569–70; Butler A. Jones, "The Tradition of Sociology Teaching in Black Colleges: The Unheralded Professionals," in Blackwell and Janowitz, eds., *Black Sociologists,* pp. 155–58.

21. Oscar Handlin, *The Newcomers* (Garden City, N.Y.: Doubleday and Company, 1959), pp. 1–3, 120–21.

22. Some scholars of Afro-American urban life like Kenneth Kusmer have begun to reassess the experience of blacks in cities, emphasizing non-race specific structural forces, particularly changes in the technological base of the city. See Kenneth Kusmer, "The Structure of Black Urban History: Retrospect and Prospect" (unpublished paper, presented at the 1980 Annual Meeting of the Southern Historical Association).

23. Osofsky, *Harlem,* p. ix.

24. Spear, *Black Chicago,* pp. viii–ix.

25. Kusmer, *A Ghetto Takes Shape,* p. xi.

26. Katzman, *Before the Ghetto,* pp. xi, 215–16.

27. Philpott, *The Slum and the Ghetto,* pp. xvi–xvii.

28. Borchert, *Alley Life in Washington,* pp. 218–41.

29. Lewis Wirth, *The Ghetto* (Chicago: University of Chicago Press, 1928), p. 6.

30. Drake and Cayton, *Black Metropolis,* pp. 77–91, 174–213, 383.

31. Weaver, *The Negro Ghetto,* preface to the 1967 edition, pages not numbered.

32. Osofsky, *Harlem,* pp. 35–52, 127–49, 150–58; Spear, *Black Chicago,* pp. 11–49, 201–29; Kusmer, *A Ghetto Takes Shape,* chapters 2, 3, 7, and 8; Philpott, *The Slum and the Ghetto,* chapters 5, 6, 7, 8, and 14; Borchert, *Alley Life In Washington,* chapters 1, 2, and 3; Katzman, *Before the Ghetto,* pp. 213–16.

33. Osofsky, *Harlem,* pp. 127–49; Osofsky, "Enduring Ghetto," pp. 189–201.

34. Katzman, *Before the Ghetto,* pp. 81–103; Philpott, *The Slum and the Ghetto,* pp. xv–xvii.

35. Spear, *Black Chicago,* pp. 226–27; Osofsky, *Harlem,* pp. 143–47; and Philpott, *The Slum and the Ghetto,* pp. 307–13.

36. Kusmer, *A Ghetto Takes Shape,* p. 274; Borchert, *Alley Life in Washington,* p. xii.

37. Kusmer, *A Ghetto Takes Shape,* chapters 4 and 9; Spear, *Black Chicago,* chapters 2 and 8; Osofsky, *Harlem,* pp. 4–7, 22–24, 62–66; Katzman, *Before the Ghetto,* pp. 104–34.

38. Spear, *Black Chicago,* chapters 3, 4, and 10; Kusmer, *A Ghetto Takes Shape,* chapters 5, 6, and 11; Osofsky, *Harlem,* Chapter 7. Katzman is an exception on this point; see *Before the Ghetto,* pp. 135–74.

39. Thomas, "From Peasant to Proletarian," p. iv; Gottlieb, "Making Their Own Way," pp. 9–10.

40. E. P. Thompson, *The Making of the English Working Class* (New York: Vintage Books, 1963) pp. 9–14; Herbert Gutman, *Work, Culture, and Society in Industrializing America: Essays in American Working Class and Social History* (New York: Vintage Books, 1977), pp. 3–19, 121–208; David Montgomery, *Workers' Control in America: Studies in the History of Work, Technology, and Labor Struggles* (Cambridge: Cambridge University Press, 1979), pp. 1–8.

41. For a recent discussion of proletarianization see Charles Tilly, *As Sociology Meets History* (New York: Academic Press, 1981), especially Chapter 7; also see T. B. Bottomore, trans. and ed., *Karl Marx: Selected Writings in Sociology and Social Philosophy* (New York: McGraw-Hill Book Company, 1964).

42. Historically oriented sociologists such as William J. Wilson and James A. Geschwender offer useful theoretical perspectives in handling the intricate convergence of racial and class issues in Afro-American history. These writers accept the Marxist notion that racism or racial problems are related to changes in the economy and class conflict, while rejecting the mechanistic contention that such problems are simply part of a superstructure. They recognize that once a racist belief system has been erected to justify socioeconomic inequality, it is capable of developing an independent life of its own, sustaining old and fostering new patterns of stratification. See William J. Wilson, *The Declining Significance of Race: Blacks and Changing American Institutions* (Chicago: University of Chicago Press, 1978) chapters 1, 3, and 5; Geschwender, *Racial Stratification in America,* pp. 2–17, 243–69; and Stanley Lieberson, *A Piece of the Pie: Blacks and White Immigrants Since 1880* (Berkeley: University of California Press, 1980), p. 383.

# Bibliographical Essay

A just and frequent lament of students of Afro-American history, indeed of the history of the working class and lower socioeconomic ethnic groups generally, has been the paucity of written source materials. The usual problem of sources was compounded in this study by two interrelated objectives: attempts to document the experience of a small black population on the one hand and efforts to trace the emergence of a black industrial working class, rather than simply the emergence of a ghetto, on the other. Even here, although the evidence is often scanty and one feels the frustration of not being able to tell a fuller story, the problem has not been insurmountable. A variety of U.S. governmental statistical reports, newspapers, manuscript collections, and oral interviews reveal valuable insights into the intricate cross currents of class and race. Despite different socioeconomic orientations, some of these data, particularly newspapers of both white and black middle-class leaders and U.S. census documents, offer crucial evidence on the intimate lives of black workers. More importantly, however, Afro-American workers have spoken for themselves through written correspondence, statements, and resolutions, through recent oral interviews, and through a range of overt and subtle behavior.

This study proceeded from a critical review of the historical and sociological literature on Afro-American life in late nineteenth- and early twentieth-century American cities. Interested readers are re-

ferred to Appendix 7 and subsequent documentation in the text itself
for a perspective on that literature. The following are major sources
for the substantive history of blacks in Milwaukee.

PRE-WORLD WAR I ERA, 1870–1914

Two master's theses provide the most useful secondary accounts of
black demographic, economic, social, and political life in Milwaukee
from the 1870s to World War I. Developments to 1870 are traced in
William J. Vollmar, "The Negro in a Midwest Frontier City, Milwaukee, 1835–1870" (master's thesis, Marquette University, 1968).
Especially valuable for this study has been Thomas Buchanan, "Black
Milwaukee, 1890–1915" (master's thesis, University of Wisconsin–
Milwaukee, 1973). Buchanan provides a detailed sketch of black employment, housing, institutional life, politics, race relations, and ideologies during the prewar era. His ideas on Afro-Americans in Milwaukee's labor force are also presented in the article, "Black Milwaukee's Labor Force," *Historical Messenger* 28, no. 2 (1972).

Both Vollmar and Buchanan used Milwaukee city directories and
United States and Wisconsin state decennial censuses in establishing
a strong statistical base for their works. I augmented their data by the
compilation of comparative ethnic, demographic, housing, and occu-
pational statistics from the decennial reports of the United States
Bureau of the Census. Also useful for the prewar era is the special
United States Bureau of the Census, *Negro Population in the United
States, 1790–1915* (1918; rept. New York, 1968).

Newspapers constitute an invaluable primary source of documentation of black life in Milwaukee before World War I. The richest
documentation is provided by extant copies of black weeklies. The
*Wisconsin Afro-American* (later changed to a monthly, *The Northwestern
Recorder)* was published between 1892 and 1893. Existing copies are
available on microfilm from the State Historical Society of Wisconsin.
A second black weekly, the most significant of the two, the *Wisconsin
Weekly Advocate,* was published between 1898 and 1916. Available
copies of the paper (for 1898–1907) are on microfilm from the State
Historical Society of Wisconsin.

There were no black weeklies in Milwaukee before the 1890s, but
the *Milwaukee Sentinel,* the city's first daily newspaper, proved surprisingly useful for the earlier period since a 1930s WPA project prepared
a comprehensive subject index of the *Sentinel* from its first issue in 1837
through 1879. A recent grant from the National Endowment for the

Humanities has brought the index up to 1890. The paper and index are located in the Local History Room of the Milwaukee Public Library.

Information on black politics during the prewar era is found in the *Wisconsin Blue Book* and the newspaper clippings files of the Milwaukee County Historical Society. The *Historical Messenger,* magazine of the Milwaukee County Historical Society, has edited and printed several primary documents on race relations, politics, and civil rights during the period (*The Negro in Milwaukee: A Historical Survey,* 1968).

The most important general histories of Milwaukee, Bayrd Still, *Milwaukee: The History of a City* (1948) and H. Russell Austin, *The Milwaukee Story* (1946) give little attention to black life between Reconstruction and World War I. An important exception is Thomas Gavett's brief reference to black labor activism during the 1870s in his *Development of the Labor Movement in Milwaukee* (Madison, 1967). Valuable data on the larger urban, demographic, economic, political, and social context of the black experience is provided in Still's *Milwaukee* and several other similar works: Ray Hughes Whitbeck, *The Geography and Economic Development of Southeastern Wisconsin* (Madison, 1921); Roger David Simon, "The Expansion of an Industrial City: Milwaukee, 1880–1910" (Ph.D. dissertation, University of Wisconsin, 1971); Gerd Korman, *Industrialization, Immigrants, Americanizers* (Madison, 1967); Justin B. Galford, "The Foreign Born and Urban Growth in the Great Lakes, 1850–1950: A Study of Chicago, Cleveland, Detroit, and Milwaukee" (Ph.D. dissertation, New York University, 1957); and John R. Ottensman, *The Changing Spatial Structure of American Cities* (Lexington, 1975). These sources also provide the larger urban context for analysis of Afro-American life in the interwar years.

INTER-WAR AND WAR YEARS, 1915–1945

*Statistical Data*

United States decennial reports comprise the pivotal statistical documentation for the interwar years. These include various population (migration, birth, death, and age) statistics as well as occupational and housing tabulations. In addition to the decennial accounts for the period 1910–40, several special volumes have proven useful. Of general value has been the United States Bureau of the Census, *Negroes in the United States, 1920–1932* (1935; rept. New York, 1966). The reports on unemployment, relief, housing, and families during the 1930s are particularly helpful: *Fifteenth Census of the U.S.: 1930:*

*Unemployment, vol. 1* (Washington, 1931); Katherine D. Wood, *Urban Workers on Relief: Part 2: The Occupational Characteristics of Workers on Relief in 79 Cities* (Washington, 1937); Edith Elmer Wood, *Slums and Blighted Areas in the United States* (Washington, 1935). Religious statistics are provided in the U.S. Bureau of the Census, *Religious Bodies, 1916, Part 1* (Washington, 1916).

Several contemporary sociological analyses and surveys provide additional statistical data on black demographic, economic, and social life. A surprisingly useful account of Afro-American migration to Milwaukee and the nature of black employment during World War I is Emmett J. Scott, *Negro Migration During the War* (1920; rept. New York, 1969); of the various northern cities covered by the study, Scott presented for Milwaukee the most detailed data on wages and specific firms in which blacks worked. Also see Chapter 2, n. 12 of this study.

Health, housing, employment, and a wealth of demographic statistics, particularly for the Depression and World War II, are analyzed in Paula Lynagh's statistical survey, "Milwaukee's Negro Community" (Milwaukee, 1946). Similar, though less detailed, is the study by Thomas Imse, "The Negro Community in Milwaukee" (master's thesis, Marquette University, 1942). Several Milwaukee studies offer valuable data on housing in the Sixth and Tenth wards: E. R. Krumbiegel, "Observations on Housing Conditions in Milwaukee's Sixth Ward: A Report to the Mayor and Common Council" (Milwaukee, 1944). Also see Vivian Lenard, "From Progressivism to Procrastination: The Fight for the Creation of a Permanent Housing Authority for the city of Milwaukee, 1933–1945" (master's thesis, University of Wisconsin–Milwaukee, 1967), an excellent study of the public housing controversy in Milwaukee. Lenard also presents much useful information on housing conditions and responses among blacks. One of the richest sources of statistical documentation on black housing conditions is found in the Milwaukee WPA Real Property Inventory of 1939, available through the City Archives of the Milwaukee Public Library; since the WPA study computed housing conditions by blocks and by race, it is possible to gauge the comparative housing conditions among blacks and between blacks and whites.

*Biennial Reports* of the Milwaukee County Board of Election Commissioners offer helpful statistical data on black office seekers during the entire period. Since most black candidates usually failed to advance beyond the primary election, primary contests reveal clearer insight into black political and community life than do regular elections.

For a useful analysis of Milwaukee ward-level election returns by race, see Keith Robert Schmitz, "Milwaukee and its Black Community, 1930–1942" (master's thesis, University of Wisconsin–Milwaukee, 1979).

*Newspapers*

The *Wisconsin Enterprise Blade* constitutes the most comprehensive written record generated by Milwaukee's black community. Although heavily biased toward the Republican party in national affairs, the *Blade* was quite independent on local issues. Established by J. Anthony Josey as a Madison-based weekly in 1916, the paper moved to Milwaukee by 1926 and published through World War II (see Chapter 3). There are extant copies of the *Blade* on microfilm for most of the period through 1932. Josey published the paper irregularly during the Depression. There are only a few extant issues from the mid-1930s through World War II. Microfilm issues of the *Blade* are available through the State Historical Society of Wisconsin in Madison.

Regional and national black newspapers frequently carried information on Milwaukee's black population: the *National Advocate* (Minneapolis-based), the *Chicago Defender,* the *Chicago Whip,* and others. Among citywide newspapers, the *Milwaukee Journal* and the *Milwaukee Sentinel* offer the most useful documentation on black life. With the exception of frequent racist comments on black crime, most treatments of black life (institutions, politics, employment, and race relations) in the white press develop from the late 1930s onward. These items are located in the newspaper clippings files of the Milwaukee Public Library. These clippings are particularly useful for race relations, housing, and the struggle for defense industry jobs. The Milwaukee Urban League also maintains a newspaper clippings file that is of some value for information on blacks during the interwar years.

The Wisconsin edition of the *CIO News* is a rich source of information on the relationship between black workers and the new unions between 1937 and 1945. It is also significant for evidence on the growing alliance between the CIO and the larger black community, particularly in housing and politics. Although items involving local blacks appear frequently between 1937 and 1941, the paper is most useful on the CIO's cooperation with the FEPC and the struggle for a local housing authority between 1941 and 1945. The *CIO News* is available on microfilm from the State Historical Society of Wisconsin. Bound issues are available for use at the Area Research Center, University of Wisconsin–Milwaukee. Although incomplete, several 1937–38 issues of the paper are deposited at the Walter P. Reuther Library of Labor and Urban Affairs, Wayne State University. An examination of the *AFL Auto Worker,* the official organ of the UAW-AFL and rival of the *CIO News,* produced little of value on the union's local relationship with black workers.

## Manuscript Collections

For a small black population, there are several significant manuscript collections by and about blacks in Milwaukee. The most important of these are the local files of the Milwaukee Urban League, the National Association for the Advancement of Colored People, and the Fair Employment Practices Committee. Both the Milwaukee Urban League and NAACP collections are located in the Manuscript Division of the Library of Congress. The Milwaukee Urban League papers contain various annual and monthly reports, special studies, and correspondence on employment, housing, race relations, and politics for the period 1926 through World War II. The reference section of the Milwaukee Public Library has most copies of MUL monthly and annual reports from 1925 to 1945.

Records of the Milwaukee NAACP cover the period from its inception in 1916 to 1945; special permission is necessary in order to consult records beyond 1940. The papers consist of extensive correspondence between local and national officers, membership lists, civil rights litigation, and a special file on the Milwaukee Scottsboro Defense Committee. These records provide a wealth of details on race relations, employment, politics, and intraracial relations among Milwaukee blacks and with the national office. The FEPC records, housed at the National Archives in Washington, D.C., illuminate a broad range of issues through an equally broad range of evidence: detailed affidavits of racial discrimination against various defense industries, compliance reports from industrialists, and numerous pieces of correspondence between the national office and local industrialists, labor unions, and black leaders. These records offer invaluable insight into the complex interplay of wartime class and racial relations: between blacks, employers, and labor unions on the one hand and between black workers and middle-class leaders on the other.

Additional unpublished manuscript materials are found in Milwaukee area archives. Chief among these are the papers of Rev. Cecil

A. Fisher, the black minister, probation officer, and social worker; black attorney James W. Dorsey; and Mayor Daniel W. Hoan. The Hoan papers are particularly rich with correspondence between the mayor's office and the local black community. This collection is especially revealing for black politics, race relations, and housing. Documents illuminating the relationship between blacks and Socialists are most useful. In addition to providing biographical information, the Fisher and Dorsey papers offer data on the activities of two of the most prominent black political figures during the period. The Dorsey and Hoan papers are located at the Milwaukee County Historical Society. Rev. Fisher's records are on file at the Area Research Center of the University of Wisconsin–Milwaukee.

The International Longshoremen's Association Local 815, AFL (University of Wisconsin–Milwaukee, Area Research Center) comprises the most useful manuscript material on blacks and organized labor unions in Milwaukee. The papers of Local 815 provide information on Aaron Tolliver, alternately its black president and vice-president, the precarious economic position of longshoremen, and the union's relationship to the emerging CIO. Ernest Schirm's unusual "Working Man's Diary of Hard Times" is available in the Ernest Schirm Papers at the State Historical Society of Wisconsin. Although mainly covering the post–World War II period, Schirm's diary and correspondence provide useful insight into the thinking of one black worker who remained loyal to the Republican party at the same time that most blacks shifted to FDR and the Democrats.

Although containing a few items of value, both the records of the Federated Trades Council of Milwaukee and the CIO's Milwaukee County Industrial Union Council are disappointing in their lack of materials on black workers. Likewise, there are no available papers of firms which hired large numbers of blacks. The papers of the International Harvester Corporation, a significant employer by the mid-1920s, are on file at the State Historical Society of Wisconsin. Unfortunately, large portions of those records are closed to researchers until the mid- and late-1980s. An examination of available indexes, however, reveals no direct references to blacks.

Important socioeconomic surveys and social welfare materials, chiefly of housing and leisure-time pursuits, are found in the records of the United Community Services of Greater Milwaukee, 1916–66 (University of Wisconsin–Milwaukee, Area Research Center). Some key manuscript documents have been misplaced or lost, including the

Wilbur and Ardie Halyard collection (University of Wisconsin–Milwaukee, Area Research Center), pertaining to the Columbia Building and Loan Association, and the Ku Klux Klan file in the Hoan papers.

*Personal Interviews and Other Data*

Nineteen personal interviews with Milwaukee residents who lived during the interwar years comprise key sources of documentation for this study. These interviews represent a cross section of persons engaged in business and the professions, the industrial labor force, and domestic service. Interviews with Calvin Birts, a packinghouse employee; Ernest Bland, a common laborer and leader of the Garvey forces in Milwaukee; Lawrence Miller, a tannery employee; and John Williams, a steel mill employee, were particularly useful in reconstructing the black industrial working class experience. James A. Field, whose father was a labor recruiter for the Illinois Steel Company, offered fascinating evidence on the rise and decline of the black labor force on Jones Island. An interview with Ruby Cook, a personal service employee during the period, helped to illuminate the role of female domestic service in black life during the Depression. Interviews with Ardie A. Halyard, a cofounder of the Columbia Building and Loan Association; Bernice C. Lindsay, an assistant to Josey on the *Blade* and director of YWCA work among blacks; Clarence L. Johnson, proprietor of a tailoring business, and Carl Watson, the funeral director, revealed several aspects of black business and professional pursuits, institutional life, and politics. Helen V. Kelley, daughter of MUL director William V. Kelley, and Audrey Davis, a resident of Milwaukee since the early 1930s, provided useful oral data on the leisure-time life of Milwaukee blacks, particularly of youth during the 1930s and 1940s. Other interviewees included Reverend Frank Morries; Lincoln Gaines, YMCA worker; Bill Mosby, longshoreman; Felmers Chaney, policeman; Frank Ziedler, former mayor of Milwaukee; Arbutus Westmoorland, of St. Benedict the Moor School; and Irene Goggans, homemaker. All interview data have been used critically in conjunction with newspaper accounts, manuscript data, and statistical documentation.

Additional sources for this study include several historical articles in *Echo* magazine, under the editorship of Virginia Williams. *Echo*'s 1976 bicentennial issue has proven particularly useful on black institutions, business, and professional life. Indispensable sources of biographical, institutional, and political data include Mary Ellen Shadd, ed. *Negro Business Directory to the State of Wisconsin* (Milwaukee, 1950) and Wright's *Milwaukee City Directory.* Finally, a variety of fugitive materials on institutions, politics, and employment has been gathered from various individuals, mainly from the nineteen oral interviewees. Special mention must be made of Irene Goggans's extensive private collection of newspaper clippings, articles, and special reports of black life in Milwaukee.

# Index

# BOOKS IN THE SERIES BLACKS IN THE NEW WORLD

Down from Equality: Black Chicagoans and the Public Schools, 1920-41 *Michael W. Homel*

Race and Kinship in a Midwestern Town: The Black Experience in Monroe, Michigan, 1900-1915 *James E. DeVries*

Down by the Riverside: A South Carolina Slave Community *Charles Joyner*

Black Milwaukee: The Making of an Industrial Proletariat, 1915-45 *Joe William Trotter, Jr.*

*Reprint Editions*

King: A Biography *David Levering Lewis* Second edition

The Death and Life of Malcolm X *Peter Goldman* Second edition

Race Relations in the Urban South, 1865-1890 *Howard N. Rabinowitz, with a Foreword by C. Vann Woodward*

Race Riot at East St. Louis, July 2, 1917 *Elliott Rudwick*

W. E. B. Du Bois: Voice of the Black Protest Movement *Elliott Rudwick*

The Negro's Civil War: How American Negroes Felt and Acted during the War for the Union *James M. McPherson*

ALVERNO COLLEGE LIBRARY
Black Milwaukee
977.595T858

2 5050 00193574 7

161653

977. 595
T858

REMOVED FROM THE
ALVERNO COLLEGE LIBRARY

Alverno College
Library Media Center
Milwaukee, Wisconsin

DEMCO